ALSO BY LORRIE MOORE

Bark
A Gate at the Stairs
Birds of America
Who Will Run the Frog Hospital?
Like Life
Anagrams
Self-Help

See What Can Be Done

See What Can Be Done

Essays, Criticism, and Commentary

LORRIE MOORE

BOND
STREET
BOOKS
DOUBLEDAY
CANADA

Bond Street Books and colophon are registered trademarks of
Penguin Random House Canada Limited

Library and Archives Canada Cataloguing in Publication
Moore, Lorrie
[Works. Selections]
See what can be done / Lorrie Moore.
Issued in print and electronic formats.
ISBN 978-0-385-69131-4 (hardcover).—ISBN 978-0-385-69132-1 (EPUB)
I. Title.
PS3563.O524A6 2018   813'.54   C2017-905913-0
C2017-905914-9

Jacket photograph © Adrian Lourie/Writer Pictures
Jacket design by Carol Devine Carson

Printed and bound in the USA

Published in Canada by Bond Street Books,
a division of Penguin Random House Canada Limited

www.penguinrandomhouse.ca

10 9 8 7 6 5 4 3 2 1

Anatole Broyard
(1920–1990)

Barbara Epstein
(1928–2006)

Robert Silvers
(1929–2017)

Contents

Publication Acknowledgments

Grateful acknowledgment is made to the following publications in which the pieces first appeared, sometimes under different titles and in slightly different form:

The Atlantic: "Leave Them and Love Them," December 2004.
Epoch: Review of Nora Ephron's *Heartburn,* Spring–Summer 1983.
The Guardian: "What We Were Reading," December 4, 2009.
Harper's Magazine: "Animal Instincts," August 2013.
Los Angeles Review of Books: "Thinking About Hillary, at This Late Hour," January 20, 2017.
Mademoiselle: "Love Lives of the Famous," February 1987.
The New Yorker: "Legal Aide," April 23 and 30, 2001; "Bioperversity," May 19, 2003; "Wizards," September 12, 2011; "Lena Dunham: Unwatchable in the Best Way," March 27, 2012; and "Canada Dry," May 21, 2012.
The New York Review of Books: "Made in the USA," August 12, 1999; "The Odd Women," April 13, 2000; "Patios & Poolsides," November 16, 2000; "Artship," January 17, 2002; "Burning at Both Ends," March 14, 2002; "The Long Voyage Home," October 10, 2002; "Home Truths," November 20, 2003; "Unanswered Prayer," November 4, 2004; "Love's Wreckage," August 11, 2005; "A Pondered Life," September 21, 2006; "The Awkward Age," September 27, 2007; "How He Wrote His Songs," March 26, 2009; "The Brazilian Sphinx," September 24, 2009; "In the Life of *The Wire,*" October 14, 2010; "What If?," May 12, 2011; "Very Deep in America," August 18, 2011; "Circus Elephants," September 15, 2011; "Werner Herzog on Death Row," November 10, 2011; "Sassy Angel," January 10,

2012; "Which Wisconsin?," July 12, 2012; "Double Agents in Love," February 21, 2013; "Gazing at Love," December 19, 2013; "Our Date with Miranda," March 5, 2015; "Sympathy for the Devil," September 24, 2015; "TV: The Shame of Wisconsin," February 25, 2016; "A Very Singular Girl," July 14, 2016; "The Case of O. J. Simpson," October 27, 2016; and "Ain't It Always Stephen Stills," August 17, 2017.

The New York Times: "The Modern Elizabethan," April 23, 2006.

The New York Times Book Review: "How Humans Got Flippers and Beaks," October 6, 1985; "Give Me Epic, Give Me Tragic, Give Me Cheap," October 18, 1987; "The Chekhov of Westchester," July 10, 1988; "What Li'l Abner Said," March 12, 1989; "Ordinary Life Always Went Too Far," October 22, 1989; "Bobbo Druff's Alcoholic Vaudeville," March 10, 1991; "Look for a Writer and Find a Terrorist," June 9, 1991; "Voters in Wonderland," November 3, 1992; "God Does Not Love Aunt Ellen," February 14, 1993; "Every Wife's Nightmare," October 31, 1993; "God Is in the Details," September 29, 1996; "A House Divided," June 28, 1998; "I'll Cut My Throat Another Day," November 7, 1999; and "The Wrath of Athena," May 7, 2000.

The New York Times Magazine: "Best Love Song; Two Girls and a Guy," April 18, 1999, and "A Man of Many Words," January 7, 2001.

Observer: "Unsolving JonBenét's Murder—Absent Narrative, Chaos Rules," April 5, 1999.

The Yale Review: "Theater in Review," January 9, 2007.

Grateful acknowledgment is made to the following for permission to reprint previously published material:

HarperCollins: *"Titanic,"* in *Writers at the Movies: Twenty-Six Contemporary Authors Celebrate Twenty-Six Memorable Movies,* November 14, 2000.

Penguin: "Better and Sicker," in *The Agony and the Ego,* January 4, 1994.

Penguin Canada: Introduction to *Modern Classics Moons of Jupiter,* April 4, 2006.

Picador: Introduction to "Ethan Canin, 'The Palace Thief,'" in *Object Lessons:* The Paris Review *Presents the Art of the Short Story,* October 2, 2012.

Introduction

The title of this book—*See What Can Be Done*—is not a boast but an instruction. I received it with almost every note I got from Robert Silvers, editor of *The New York Review of Books*. He would propose I consider writing about something—he usually just FedExed a book to my door—and then he would offer a polite inquiry as to my interest: perhaps I'd like to take a look at such and such. "See what can be done," he would invariably close. "My best, Bob." It was a magical request, and it suggested that one might like to surprise oneself. Perhaps a door would open and you would step through it, though he would be the one to have put it there in the first place.

Most of the pieces in this book are what could be done, at least by me, as I immersed myself in seeing what others could do; cultural responses to cultural responses. However personal and idiosyncratic they are, the pieces by and large fall into the category of "reviewing," although when a review gets long enough it may qualify as a "critical essay," and when it is succinct enough it can be a remark. (Remarks are not necessarily lesser: I believe Bette Davis should have won a Nobel Prize for "Old age is no place for sissies," a line Bob Dylan himself might covet.) Essays, reviews, occasional meditations are all included here. Whether there is really a reason to round them all up, even selectively, is a question I can't answer. But I can say that I did the gathering because, looking at my decades-long life as a fiction writer, I noticed another trail had formed—a shadow life of miscellaneous prose pieces—and I wondered about it as a trip, if not precisely a journey.

The pieces begin in 1983 in Cornell's literary magazine, *Epoch* (where I wrote reviews of books by Margaret Atwood and Nora Ephron), and they end, in time for the golden anniversary of the Summer

of Love, with a take on Stephen Stills—thirty-four years of, well, stuff. I
mercifully have not included every last thing, though it may seem as if I
have; in the late 1980s when I was once introduced to a particular guest
at a party, the guest said, "Oh, yes! I know you: you review books!" and
my heart sank. After my debut collection of stories was published, Anatole Broyard, then a *New York Times Book Review* editor, was the first
review-commissioner to phone me at my office in Wisconsin and offer
me work. Slightly terrified, I kept taking his assignments. "I think I've
become Anatole Broyard's slave girl," I said to my then beau. "I don't
know how to stop." And indeed I probably wrote too many reviews,
telling myself I needed the money.

But a fiction writer reviewing is performing—I still believe—an
essential task. Very few practicing artists review the work of their fellow
sculptors or painters or dancers or composers, and so the conversation is left to nonpractitioners. Although there are of course exceptions,
and although the film directors of the French New Wave began as critics, and the sculptor Donald Judd wrote reviews of his peers, as did
Schumann, Debussy (under a pseudonym), and Virgil Thomson, in
general the medium and the idiom of criticism do not belong to artists.
One cannot really dance a review of someone else's dance. One cannot
paint a review of someone else's exhibition. Criticism can be a rarefied
field, but that aspect is usually galling to the artist, especially when
the artist feels misunderstood and is reminded that critics have never
attempted let alone forged the creative work that they, the critics, nonetheless feel emboldened to evaluate. In the words of the jazz musician
Ben Sidran: "Critics! Can't even float. They just stand on the shore.
Wave at the boat." Or as Aristotle wrote in *Politics,* "Those who are
to be judges must also be performers." Conversely, perhaps those who
are performers must also be judges—once in a while. And so a contribution to the cultural conversation—by narrative artists themselves,
speaking in unmuddied, unacademic, unobfuscating critical voices—
I thought of as a difficult but obligatory citizenship: jury duty. (One of
the longest pieces here, coincidentally, is a defense of a jury.)

My own way of discussing the work of others, then, has been improvised and not grounded in any philosophy or theory other than lack of
philosophy or theory. It has been, de facto, I assume, a practitioner's
take. As for technique, I have always aimed for clarity of utterance and

organization but don't always succeed. I often move every which way in attempting to track my own thoughts about someone else's endeavor; sometimes I inappropriately include my own life in the conversation to show how narrative art intrudes, fits, or does not fit into the daily lives of those who are experiencing it. I have aimed for the human, but also for the eccentricities and particularities of the real encounter, and I do not always avoid stupidities. Sometimes I head for stupidities in order to discuss them, even if they are my own. Often a piece is constructed in a circular fashion, like a cat clearing a space before it naps. Other times I veer. I sometimes try to pull back as much as I can to look at something from a distance, without losing my balance. I then also try to move forward again and bear down.

When, in 1999, I began writing for *The New York Review of Books,* which published articles by people much better educated than I, but which also offered me more space than I was used to, my stance became that of the ingenuous Martian who had just landed on a gorgeous alien planet. With no agenda and only the usual amounts of research, I said, "What's this?" I tried to figure out what feelings the piece contained, what it made the reader feel, what that said about our world and our lives and the feelings we value. I aimed for simple (I aspired to "deceptively simple") and true. I aimed for bravery of opinion though I am not by temperament especially brave. But I admire iconoclasm if it is not too breezy or gratuitous. If what the Emperor was wearing was a mixed bag, I tried to indicate as much. I also tried to figure out what the Emperor had in mind, even if one is not supposed to guess at intention. I have tried to avoid petulance, Internet-ese, literary theory, the diction and dialect of the professionally educated critic, and never to use the word "relatable" instead of "sympathetic," or "impact" as a verb, or any form of the word "enjoy," which should be reserved for one's grandparents or other relatives. I tried not to drag readers by the scruff of the neck and march them from paragraph to paragraph, point by point, but did not always succeed. I allowed myself asides and tangents and personal anecdotes because circumnavigating a thing—the napping cat again, patrolling for snakes—is sometimes a useful approach. First-person assessments engage me—Dorothy Parker's reviews were full of them so she could employ her rapier with faux reluctance—and often the use of the first person is not arrogant but modest, hedged, and more accurate. One does not always have to write in the authoritative third-person voice of God: if you fail to sound like God (and you probably will), you may end up sounding like flap copy. The first-person pronoun can be a form of deference and is useful and precise when discussing the subjectivity and crowded detail of narrative art. It suggests one specific encounter paid close attention to. It appreciates the intersection of one individual reader's life with the thing that has been read. It breathes air into the conversation—or can. It reveals criticism to be a form of autobiography. When someone once said to me, "Your pieces in *The New York Review of Books* are the only ones I can actually understand," I knew it wasn't praise—the speaker's real subject was the difficult brilliance and impressive erudition of the other critics he admired there. Nonetheless, I decided to take it as a compliment. (One has to seize encouragement where one can.) Someone once also told me early on that there was a well-known list of six things a book review should always do. This caused me to break out into a cold sweat. I politely asked for the list but it was never given to me, nor did I ever find it anywhere, so I carried on, without knowledge of official requirements. And to this day I still don't know what those six things are.

I began writing about television by accident. I did not watch much television as an adult and had not watched much as a child, having grown up in a house where the watching of it was discouraged and highly supervised. We read the Bible every night at the dinner table, and in general television was considered a little wicked and lazy and for special occasions. Like eggnog. But in 2010, after *The Wire* was already out on DVD, I watched the series on a binge (also like eggnog)—living in David Simon's Baltimore for an entire summer—and afterward, intoxicated, and wanting to extend my experience there by reading what other people had to say (one terrific function of cultural criticism is a kind of afterlife of the original encounter), I could not find very much written about it. The London papers had some articles, but there was very little in the American press: nothing in *The New Yorker* and what seemed like minimal coverage in *The New York Times.* I asked Bob Silvers if he would like something for *The New York Review of Books,* and he quickly said yes. His sensibility was always spry, eager, open, a source of joy for everyone who worked for him. He was so hiply catholic in his tastes and interests that he was game for practically any kind of cultural commentary: meditations on regional politics, reports on every manner of book, television series, film, or event. Gameness is a beautiful quality in a person. My ignorance of a topic never deterred him from trying to assign it to me. He started offering more and more television for me to watch and see what could be done. I turned only a few things down. But I took on programs and films I was genuinely interested in watching and wrote about them in my Martian way. Montaigne's *que sais-je*. A little light, a little wonder, some skepticism, some awe, some squinting, some *je ne sais quoi*. Pick a thing up, study it, shake it, skip it across a still surface to see how much felt and lively life got baked into it. Does it sail? Observe. See what can be done.

LM

See What Can Be Done

Nora Ephron's *Heartburn*

Nora Ephron, whose name sounds like a neurotransmitter or a sinus medication, and who has made a reputation for herself with snappy, journalistic essays, is now, with the publication of *Heartburn,* a novelist with a vengeance. While much has already been made of the book's thinly veiled relationship to the real-life demise of Ephron's marriage to investigative reporter Carl Bernstein, *Heartburn* is interesting less for its roman à clef minutiae than as a text-as-test look at how and whether autobiographical art can function as therapy: What can art expurgate, what will art necessarily sentimentalize, from what can art never rescue anyone? Ephron's narrative itself seems unclear as to whether the literary telling of one's injuries is exorcism, revenge, or masochism. "It takes two people to hurt you," says Ephron's narrator and protagonist, Rachel Samstat. "The one that does it and the one who tells you." It is a remark that glimpses her own narrative dilemma. When the "teller" is both casualty and curator of her own bad news, might not the so-called cathartic narrative be, finally, an act of self-mutilation? A redundant pain? Do we, as Joan Didion says, "tell ourselves stories in order to live," or is there something decidedly else involved?

The artist in Ephron's novel is metaphorized into cookbook writer. Rachel Samstat, seven months pregnant and mother of one, retreats into Cuisinarts, linguine, and TV cooking shows, while her husband, Mark Feldman, a Washington, D.C., columnist, quietly falls in love with the wife of an ambassador—all within the townhouses of our nation's capital: "It's stuff like this that got us into Cambodia," says Rachel. The novel begins when Rachel first discovers Mark's affair and ends a few weeks later, when she finally lets go of her marriage, surrendering to her husband her beloved vinaigrette recipe, which she'd previously been withholding in a last-ditch effort at keeping him interested. Food in Rachel's world is power and downfall, hobby and social fabric; recipes can fend off unpleasantries. She recalls the sixties as being a time when people were always looking up and asking, "Whose mousse is this?" She deems the definitive pronouncement of the years following as "Pesto is the quiche of the seventies." Rachel's society is self-consciously bourgeois: "We would all say these things as if we had never said them before, and argue over them as if we had never argued over them before. Then we would all decide whether we wanted to be buried or cremated." Hers is a vaguely jet-settish world of talk-show therapists, celebrity dinner parties, large American Express bills, expensive country homes. Materialism battles uninvited poetry, unwelcome neurasthenia: "Show me a woman who cries when the trees lose their leaves in autumn," says Rachel, "and I'll show you a real asshole."

The success of Ephron's novel as art depends in some ways on its ineffectuality as revenge. Her generous inability to present a wholly unlikable portrait of Mark—he courts Rachel charmingly, sings her silly songs, lovingly talks her through two Caesareans—genuinely stirs the reader, although it betrays Ephron's continuing affection for the figure of the husband, permanently sentimentalizing a man who does not seem to have earned the bittersweet clemency much of the portrait grants him. Nonetheless, his character weathers even the novel's bitchiest moments because of it. Rachel exacts no satisfaction from this tale. At the end she seems her own victim: alone, unavenged, scarred by the untimely rips in her body and in her life.

As anyone who has ever eaten standing over a kitchen counter knows, cooking can be an act of excruciatingly delayed gratification. Things must be chopped, stewed, simmered, and the impulse that prompted it all can dissipate in the culinary shuffle. Ephron's *Heartburn,* like many acts of literary retaliation, has taken too much time and craft to be a potent swipe at anyone; artful preparation has mellowed and sweetened the ingredients. It is less revenge than revision, less actively asserted rancor than retroactively inserted wit. Though Rachel says to her therapist, "If I tell the story it doesn't hurt as much," and "if I tell the story I can get on with it," the story makes the reader feel too sorry for her to believe that telling it has done her any good at all. Ephron's nostalgia and revenge are simply different forms of one another. The sad deliciousness of concoction, even served with the best Ephron whine, seems more a miserable monument to sorrow than anything that could vanquish the muck of the real. Catharsis is nowhere to be glimpsed, which is how art should be.

(1983)

Kurt Vonnegut's *Galápagos*

Yes, American culture is more smart than wise. But Kurt Vonnegut, that clown-poet of homesickness and Armageddon, might be the rare American writer who is both. He dances the witty and informed dances of the literary smart, but while he does, he casts a wide eye about, and he sees. He is a postmodern Mark Twain: grumpy and sentimental, antic and religious. He is that paradoxical guy who goes to church both to pray fervently and to blow loud, snappy gum bubbles at the choir.

Galápagos, Vonnegut's new novel, boasts the energies and derring-do of his earlier works. It is the story, sort of, of a second Noah's ark, a 1986 nature cruise booked with celebrities (Mick Jagger, Paloma Picasso, Jacqueline Onassis, and others) that in the wake of planetary catastrophe—famine, financial crises, World War III, and a virus that eats the eggs in human ovaries—is fated to land on the Galápagos Islands and perpetuate the human race. Humanity "was about to be diminished to a tiny point, by luck, and then, again by luck, to be permitted to expand again."

All this may sound like a glittery and Darwinian *Gilligan's Island,* not really what *Galápagos* is at all. Although certainly the novel has something to do with the giant crush America has on celebrity, the famous people never really do make it into the story, and what we end up with is a madcap genealogical adventure—a blend of the Old Testament, the Latin American novel, and a lot of cut-up comic books—employing a cast of lesser-knowns that includes a schoolteacher named Mary Hepburn, an Ecuadorean sea captain named von Kleist, a former male prostitute named James Wait (whose skin color is "like the crust on a pie in a cheap cafeteria"), a dog named Kazakh (who, "thanks to surgery and training, had virtually no personality"), plus a narrator who turns out to be none other than the son of Kilgore Trout, that science-fiction hack from Vonnegut's earlier books.

Leon Trout, Vonnegut's doppelgänger, speaks to us, moreover, from a million years hence, from the afterlife, whence he can best pronounce on what was wrong with us twentieth-century folk—our brains were too big—and reveal what, through evolution and for purposes of survival, we became: creatures with smaller brains and flippers and beaks. Even if people of the future "found a grenade or a machine gun or a knife or whatever left over from olden times, how could they ever make use of it with just their flippers and their mouths?" Leon Trout asks. And: "It is hard to imagine anybody's torturing anybody nowadays. How could you even capture somebody you wanted to torture with just your flippers and your mouth?"

Vonnegut has probably always been a better teller than maker of stories. One continually marvels at the spare, unmuddied jazz of a Vonnegut sentence and too often despairs of his ramshackle plots. *Galápagos* is, typically and perhaps aptly, structured spatially, like an archipelago, tiny islands of prose detached from that apparently dangerous continent of time—childhood reminiscences, parables, interviews, real and invented history, nature writing, sapient literary quotations, a soldier's confession. (The literary novel, alas, has always lacked a natural form.) This is a narrative style engendered by emergency, the need to get directly to something. It is susceptible, however, to an unhelpful chaos and can defeat its own purpose by blithely wandering off and turning whole chapters into scrapbooks of blather and dead end.

But Vonnegut seems eventually to get where he wants, shining his multicolored lights and science-fiction what-ifs on the huge spiritual mistake that is the Western world. He wants to tell us things: It is not the fittest who survive; it is merely those who happen to survive who survive. The earth is a "fragile habitat" that our big brains have failed to take care of. We must hope for flippers and beaks or nothing at all. We are all, finally, being too mean to one another. "I'll tell you what the human soul is," a character in *Galápagos* says. "It's the part of you that knows when your brain isn't working right."

Although not as moving as, say, *Slaughterhouse-Five*, *Galápagos* does have moments (of father-son vis-à-vis) that bring a glug to the throat. And although more wobblingly cobbled and arrhythmic comically than *Breakfast of Champions*, *Galápagos* can be as darkly funny. Vonnegut asterisks the names of characters who are going to die and, after their inevitably gruesome deaths, kisses them off with the elegiac "Oh, well—he wasn't going to write Beethoven's Ninth Symphony anyway." Early in the novel, he even puts Captain von Kleist on *The Tonight Show*, and what follow are the best laughs in the book.

Vonnegut's work long ago broke ground for such writers as Richard Brautigan, Thomas Pynchon, Donald Barthelme, Tom Robbins—all curators of the rhetorical and cultural non sequitur. But Vonnegut's grumbly and idiomatic voice has always been his own, unfakable and childlike, and his humanity, persisting as it does through his pessimism, is astonishing, seeming at times more science fiction than his science fiction. As for his suspended concern for the well-made, big-brained novel, Vonnegut has opted to zoom in directly for the catch, the idea, the oracular bit. His books are not only like canaries in coal mines (his own analogy) but like the cormorants of the Galápagos Islands, who, in their idiosyncratic evolution, have sacrificed flight for the getting of fish.

(1985)

Malcolm Bradbury's *Cuts*

Henry Babbacombe, the writer-protagonist of Malcolm Bradbury's new novel, *Cuts,* has no need to search for Eldorado; it has come looking for him. Eldorado is a British television company aiming to ensure its solvency and future with a blockbuster "miniseries" (accented, perhaps, on the second syllable, to rhyme with *miseries*). In its previous effort, "Gladstone, Man of Empire," Eldorado lost its leading man, a famous and venerated old actor, when he was required to appear before the character of Queen Victoria in the nude and playing the ukulele. It was "fictionalised verity," explained the Eldorado Head of Drama Plays and Series. "You take real people and events but you're not slavishly bound to actual facts."

In such fiscally tight times, Eldorado Television can afford no more ukuleles. It wants a drama with "love and power and tenderness and glory, and a lot of mountains in the background." It wants "love and power. Past and present. Tears and laughter." It wants "love and feeling, ancient buildings and contemporary problems." It wants "contemporary reality, strong hero, elegant locations." It wants "something that's art, but is also life at its deepest and most telling." It wants "a lush foreign location where you can get malt whisky." It wants "epic." It wants "tragic." It wants "cheap."

In a quaint and decorous moment, Eldorado decides it also wants a writer—someone brilliant and postmodern, with a "decidedly bushel-hidden light." Someone with a rumbling stomach. That week, it so happens, Henry Babbacombe's agent is sleeping with an Eldorado executive, and it is suggested that Eldorado give Babbacombe a try.

As for Babbacombe, he desires no such thing. He lives contentedly and alone in a tiny northern hill village, where he teaches evening classes called "Sex and Maturity in the English Novel" and the somewhat more popular "Fiction and the Farm." During the day he writes obscure, Beckettian novels in the garden shed of his backyard. His workday includes the consumption of high-fiber cereal, the writing down of his dreams, and, at six o'clock, the preparation of "a simple salad." If he feels isolated and in need of cultural diversion, he whistles, usually something classical. When he is summoned to the glass highrise of Eldorado Television, he is baffled but he goes, bringing with him on the train a pile of student essays on *Middlemarch*.

After that, circumstances conspire to urge Babbacombe into accepting Eldorado's offer. He is more wined than dined at a long lunch where every course is served with kiwi fruit, including a scarlet rack of lamb and a "gorgonzola pâté . . . laid out so beautifully it was a pity to disturb it, as indeed it proved." When he returns to his provincial university to discuss with the head of his department the possibility of a leave of absence, Babbacombe is given a grim speech about university financial problems. Already the college has had to rely on private endowments in an unprecedented manner, as in "the Kingsley Amis Chair of Women's Studies." The chairman, whose problems before the cuts had always been either of fornication or of plagiarism, is now obliged to get rid of two staff members. He has already resorted to sending colleagues out on dangerous errands in the hope that they will be run over by buses. As dedicated a man as the French structuralist who named his daughters Langue and Parole has already left. A Shakespearean professor has retrained as an airline pilot.

Henry Babbacombe has given his chairman the perfect opportunity. The chairman must consider the impact of crass television work on the reputation of his faculty. The chairman himself "would never dream of hiring out [his] mind for vulgar profit." In fact, his department has generally refused even to publish books, "naturally preferring to transfer their thoughts by word of mouth to the two or three people who are fit to understand them." Envy and budget cuts team up, and

Babbacombe is fired from his academic Eden—his life of quiet eccentricity and bold indifference to reality, his world of sooty Gothic buildings papered with announcements of essay competitions on "whether
there should be a third sex." He is plunged instead into the dark farce
of a scriptwriting career.

What ensues is riotous if predictable misadventure. In the world
of script collaboration, Babbacombe is the prototypical literary naïf: a
country cousin, sans feck, sans hap, sans hope. Without his knowledge
or consent the setting of the series switches continents weekly. Eldorado personnel begin the rewrites before Babbacombe has finished the
"writes." Eldorado titles Babbacombe's script "Serious Damage," and
truly it is that. His literary ambitions in abeyance, Babbacombe, wooed
with kiwi fruit, becomes a kind of emissary of his own incapacitated
self, a venturer if not adventurer into the heartless illogic of commercial television. It is a world that believes all problems are problems of
"notional casting." It is a world in which an obscure Beckettian novelist
is asked to work up a totally spurious death scene, and does so, setting
a new "standard in rigor mortis."

To add injury to insult, the urban landscape Babbacombe encounters is one wrought by privation, privatization, moral calamity. Lovemaking is "staccato and short. . . . It was wise not to touch someone
who might have touched someone else who in turn had touched someone else. . . . Sex was being replaced by gender." And tenderness is
pruned to tender wedges and slivers of the diminishing national pie.
Says the omniscient narrator of *Cuts,* "The only pleasure left to make
life worth living, if it was at all, was money, poor little paper money,
which was trying to do all the work."

Malcolm Bradbury is the author of an impressive array of critical works
(including books on Evelyn Waugh and Saul Bellow) and of the novels *The History Man* and *Rates of Exchange.* What he has given us in
Cuts is once more a depiction of man as historical performer, this time
in a satirical romp through Thatcher England. "It was a time for getting rid of the old soft illusions, and replacing them with the new hard
illusions."

Bradbury has milked his title for all it is worth, and it is worth much. If he has left us feeling a bit severed at the end, it may have been one cut too many, but we get the authorial joke. There is so much fun, fury, and intelligence in this little novel, one can forgive its insistent cartoonishness or those rare moments when the wit is less rapier than spoon. If the insidious world of television as literary subject or sociological context manages by its very nature to preclude the writing of great literature, that would be this modest book's point. Bradbury has succeeded in doing what the social satirist must do: to amuse trenchantly, leaving in the throat "a strange taste rather like a rancid kiwi fruit."

(1987)

Anaïs Nin, Marilyn Monroe

In the love lives of the famous, romance is largely a public business: private affairs made public, public affairs made even more public. And at the bedroom doors of all those affairs lurk, inevitably, the writers—biographers, journalists, novelists, poets, diarists—intent on giving public shape to private muck, heedless of the wishes of the muckers or muckees. Occasionally this makes for daring and probing books, but more often it produces the literary equivalent of McDonald's: private passions, some long dead, are unearthed and reworked into public French fries.

Two recent books aid and abet, to varying degrees, this sort of literary cannibalism. Both fairly slim volumes, they describe two very different couples: Anaïs Nin and Henry Miller, and Joe DiMaggio and Marilyn Monroe. In the first we are given what is indeed a probing and daring book—a passionate diary account from the interior of the affair. In the latter we get fast food: a newspaperman's best guesses from Outer Mongolia.

When Anaïs Nin, at age sixty-three, published the first volume of her already notorious diary, in 1966, she excised an important chunk of the journal—and of her own personal history. In its edited form, the diary was a mesmerizing collage that included opinions on interior decorating, lyrical self-attacks, and compassionate psychosexual analyses of her friendships with some of the bohemians and bourgeoisie of thirties Paris. Nin had actually begun writing a diary as a young girl, conceiving it as a means of "talking to" her absent father, a celebrated violinist who had abandoned the family when Anaïs was nine. As one might expect, there is everywhere in her diary a search and hunger for father figures—attended by conflicting desires to seduce, retrieve, vanquish, and be loved by them.

The part of her journal that was originally deleted detailed some of the fruits of that search: Nin's discovery, at the age of twenty-eight, of two father figures, in the persons of writer Henry Miller, then forty, and his enigmatic wife, June. What resulted was something of a ménage à trois—a crush on June and a full-blown adulterous affair with Henry (Nin was also married at the time). For Nin, her relationship with the Millers was a "laboratory of the soul," a dangerous theater of self, and the diary served as a kind of dressing room to which she repaired. It is only now, nine years after Nin's death, that her publisher and her executor have seen fit to publish what she wrote. They have titled it *Henry and June: From the Unexpurgated Diary of Anaïs Nin.*

There is this to be said for expurgation and elision: it can be a writer's most effective tool. Put back in what the writer herself took out, and the work's edges may get lost, the essence clouded. Unexpurgated, Nin says of Henry Miller things like "He looks down and shows me his lanced desire again." Or, "Yesterday, in the very paroxysm of sensual joy, I could not bite Henry as he wanted me to." Whereas in the edited volume Nin is deftly attuned to the people around her, in *Henry and June* she is made to appear in a hormonal haze, erotically preoccupied, tortured by a question that seems to nag only women in their twenties: Is what I'm calling *love* really just *good sex*? And its heartbreaking corollary: Is what I'm calling *good sex* not even all that good? Nin wears black underwear. This is not the stuff of heavy philosophical inquiry. Nonetheless, Nin knew all about beauty and sexual game playing, and she wrote about it with a poetry and intelligence that can pass for profundity. Her sensitivity to the physical and emotional was such that virtually everything in her life—from meals to hand-holding—became an aesthetic moment.

"There are two ways to reach me," Nin wrote in December 1931, soon after meeting the Millers, "by way of kisses or by way of the imagination." June Miller reached her via the latter, and Henry via the former. Nin's relationship with June was, by and large, one of mutual infatuation, and it expressed itself in intense conversations, walks, gifts of perfume, stockings, jewelry. And although Nin had recurrent dreams in which June had a small, secret penis (surely somebody is rolling in a grave somewhere), their desire for each other seems to have remained delicate and unconsummated. "Our love would be death. The embrace of imaginings," Nin wrote. When, in early 1932, June left Paris for New York and a lesbian lover she claimed to have there, it was Henry, twelve years Nin's senior, with whom Nin became sexually involved, Henry with whom she experienced "the white-heat of living." "I'll teach you new things," he said. And a few weeks later Nin wrote in her diary, "It is easy to love and there are so many ways to do it."

Perhaps like no two other writers of their time, Nin and Miller were interested in erotic appetites. "For once," wrote Nin, "I stand before a nature more complicated than my own." Indeed, the pairing of Nin and Miller seems something like the Ali–Frazier match of literary sex. When they weren't checking in to hotels together at noon (and sometimes even when they were), they read each other's manuscripts, discussed their interests in Lawrence and Dostoevski, wrote at enormous, amorous length to and about each other. Miller's words were explosive, exhausting; Nin's were searching and metaphorical, attempting to grasp with poetry what she felt his "realism" could not capture. "My work is the wife of his work," she wrote.

Although Nin claimed to have grown enormously in this period, her fiery passion for Miller eventually subsided. She felt an increased tenderness toward her banker-husband, Hugo, a man who is shown in *Henry and June* to be Nin's real anchor, someone who provided her with a suburban home, a monthly allowance, and a famous psychoanalyst, with whom she also had an affair. True bohemianism gave her cold feet. Miller's worn lapels and jacket cuffs pained her, as did his terrible eyesight (made weak by his job as a newspaper proofreader). She grew discomfited by Miller's sponging of her money and by his spending it on prostitutes. Once when Nin brought Miller an elegant breakfast on a tray, "all he could say was that he longed for the bistro around the corner, the zinc counter, the dull greenish coffee and milk full of skin." By the end Nin had discovered the perverse boy at the core of the man, had exposed Miller's emotional and financial helplessness and his petty cruelty. She had conquered a father figure, but no longer quite believed in him. When the affair was over after less than a year, she wrote movingly, "Last night I wept. I wept because I was no longer a child with a blind girl's faith. . . . I wept because I could not believe anymore and I love to believe."

The very public and glamorous love shared by Marilyn Monroe and her second husband, retired Yankee star Joe DiMaggio, might have seemed, unlike the private adultery of Miller and Nin, fated to be happy. But it was patently *not* happy, and, since neither Monroe nor DiMaggio kept passionate diaries, few people have been privy to the intimate reasons for the failure of their marriage. The most recent in an endless stream of biographies, *Joe and Marilyn: A Memory of Love,* does little to remedy that state of affairs.

The biggest problem with this book is that it's simply not long on material. Monroe and DiMaggio's marriage lasted all of nine months, and DiMaggio, who is still alive, has refused to talk about Monroe with anyone, including author Roger Kahn. So Kahn has to do some rhetorical tap dancing. When, in *Joe and Marilyn,* Kahn runs out of things to say about the lives of "Mr. and Mrs. America" (as Monroe and DiMaggio were dubbed by the press), he shamelessly summarizes movie plots, lectures on sexual mores, extemporizes on batting streaks. Every once in a while, under the strain of improvisation, he simply throws up his hands and attempts one-sentence paragraphs like "What a hard, sad life."

Unlike Nin and Miller, DiMaggio and Monroe both enjoyed and paid heavily for quick rises to stardom from deprived backgrounds: he from poor Sicilian parents, she from a series of foster homes and a Los Angeles orphanage. When they met, each was aroused by the other's fame but also by some mistaken impression that they were kindred spirits. Each sought comfort in the homey fantasies they entertained about the other. For Monroe, DiMaggio was protective, courteous, fatherly. For DiMaggio, Monroe was the sexiest housewife in America. What Monroe got was an average Joe who liked to sit in front of the television watching sports all day. What DiMaggio got, among other things, was a woman who rarely ironed.

In his prime, DiMaggio was accomplished and revered, given to an old-fashioned reserve that may or may not have hidden a more turbulent nature, depending on to whom one listens. Monroe, by contrast, was an exhibitionistic and unfocused talent, denigrated by the very Hollywood that had made her a star. But Monroe wasn't stupid. As Kahn points out, she collected sophisticated books and displayed a sexy, impudent wit. Once, when asked what she had on during a photography session, Monroe replied, "The radio." About her husband she used to say, "Joe brings a great bat into the bedroom."

The latter example, writes Kahn, suggests why the couple broke up: their relationship was an overridingly physical one, with Monroe chafing under what she felt to be the marriage's intellectual constraints, and DiMaggio growing less comfortable with Monroe's hugely public sexuality, something that she called a "career." Kahn insists, however, that DiMaggio's love for Monroe continued long after their marriage, that it was "a lapping ceaseless flame," that he attempted to protect her from Hollywood "phonies" and overweening psychiatric wards. Nonetheless, Monroe's losing battle with mental illness has become Hollywood legend, and DiMaggio's something of an ineffectual knight-errant within that legend. JOE DIMAGGIO STRIKES OUT read newspaper headlines when he and Monroe announced the end of their brief marriage.

Kahn, speculating from the periphery, cannot hope to have put together a book that is much more than sympathetically rendered hearsay. And books such as his, unlike the rich personal document of *Henry and June,* are more evidence, if any were needed, of the cruel triviality and petty theft inherent in most celebrity biography. As a journalist, Kahn is only at the perimeter of his subject and must take up the role of voyeur. He writes, "We know that when she killed herself on August 4, 1962, Marilyn needed a pedicure." Is that what we want to know? Ghoulishly enough—as we watch Joe DiMaggio sell coffeemakers on TV and we wonder, still, about the men who married Marilyn Monroe—maybe the answer is yes?

(1987)

John Cheever

Literature, when it is occurring, is the correspondence of two agora-phobics. It is lonely and waited for, brilliant and pure and frightened, a marriage of birds, a conversation of the blind. When biography intrudes upon this act between reader and author, it may do so in the smallest of vehicles—photographs, book jacket copy, rumors—parked quietly outside. In its more researched and critical form—*the biography*—it may nose into the house proper.

Probably it is difficult for biography not to intrude at all, for the impulse toward it, in its insistence and irresistibility, resembles some-thing more physical than intellectual. The housebound correspondents wonder and invent and begin to make a being of the other behind the letters. So innocently insinuating is the biographical that even the pro-fessional biographer may begin a work entitled *John Cheever* with the words "This book is for Vivian," momentarily allowing his own biog-raphy to occlude his subject's in a pretty if irrelevant cameo. Such is the religious nature of the biographical that it believes all work must come from someplace, that one can give it, dedicate it like a prayer.

Whatever its seductive impingements, in literature biography is never the point. In biography's attempts to know the exact midwifery between life and art, it is always guessing. With its power to eclipse and compete, its attempts to own and undo mystery, it remains, as Twain once said, the mere clothes and buttons of the man. And it is an odd paradox that every such biographer must know this deeply and also deeply not know it. Real life—that collection of facts with an angle thrown in—has the importunate growl of stomach or wolf; it raps compellingly at all doors, including those behind which is conducted the preferential code of poetry and fiction. Literary biography has boasted some of the finest and bravest practitioners—from Boswell on Johnson to Gaskell on Brontë—yet there is always something a little guilty in it. Whatever its pleasures for the reader, for the subject biography is a kind of artistic tax, winging in during life like a complicated pamphlet, after death like a crow.

At least Scott Donaldson's new biography of John Cheever—the first to appear since Cheever's death in 1982—is not a lurid act of forensic medicine or necrophilia. Though it has none of the genius of its subject, it imitates honorably Cheever's politeness, intelligence, and reserve. Hobbled in its significance, perhaps, by the appearance in 1984 of Susan Cheever's memoir, *Home Before Dark,* and the forthcoming Cheever letters, Donaldson's biography manages, nonetheless, with sweat on its modest brow, to gather Cheever's life into a kind of mad English garden of data through which lovers of Cheever's fiction may not be able to resist a stroll. "Writing is very much like a kiss," said Cheever, thinking of those readers. "It's something you can't do alone." It is a remark that both denies and illustrates the solitude of a literary life, and it is a telling one. *John Cheever: A Biography,* though populated with the names of Cheever's colleagues, intimates, and admirers, seems primarily the story of a man who found himself alone in a way he could never quite accept, in a way that took him completely against his will.

Cheever grew up in Quincy, Massachusetts, the son of a failed shoe salesman and a stern Englishwoman whose entrepreneurial instincts were sounder than her spouse's (she came to own a successful gift shop). Like F. Scott Fitzgerald, whose life and work Cheever's most resemble, Cheever lived in the best neighborhood in town but with an impostor's sensitivity and insecurities, due, in part, to the failure of his father. Both Cheever and Fitzgerald had strong, autonomous mothers, and in their adult life each felt the desire to shore up the masculine side of himself, in fear of the strength of the feminine. They both lived very socially, forging new, more secure identities out of their abilities to charm and impress the rich, toeing the ragged line between court jester and town clown, Cheever with more grace, perhaps, but both with a powerful, liquored ambivalence.

Donaldson suggests that Cheever's talent came from his mother's side of the family, which was educated and artistic. But it was his father's side that Cheever himself tended to mythologize, with its somewhat spurious links to Ezekiel Cheever, the legendary seventeenth-century schoolmaster at the Boston Latin School. It was also Cheever's father who, while working full-time in a shoe factory, had once studied evenings to be a magician, one of his handbook tricks being "How to Cook an Omelet in Your Hat"—surely a significant bit in a writer's parentage.

Cheever, shy, plump, and only an average student, whose spelling, according to one teacher, was "unusual, to say the least," learned early the power of good storytelling (which he was encouraged to do in front of his classmates) and of excellent manners. As a mere kindergartener he was remembered as having been the only child who, upon leaving a party, spoke to the hostess. "Thank you for inviting me," he said. "I enjoyed it very much and I *mean* it!" At Thayer Academy, at the age of thirteen, he wrote astonishingly sophisticated poetry. He composed the winning slogan for Good Posture Week: "Make it Posture Week, not Weak Posture." And when, in 1930, at the age of seventeen, he was expelled for poor grades, he sat down and wrote a story titled "Expelled," sent it off to Malcolm Cowley at *The New Republic,* and had it accepted for publication. Out of rejection was launched his brilliant career.

It is a story such as "Expelled," the portrait of a prep school to which the young narrator has not been allowed to return, that no doubt causes Donaldson to use straightforward summaries of Cheever's fiction as mortar and sometimes as the bricks themselves in reconstructing Cheever's youth and young adulthood. Donaldson himself tells of Cheever's allergy to the unembroidered truth, so one can hardly believe that art and life serve each other well here. The trompe l'oeil of autobiography present in any fiction is difficult enough, but the presumption of it, foisted on Cheever's work, makes for a semblance of biographical desperation.

But it is not as if Donaldson hasn't done his research. He guides the reader through a detailed chronology—Cheever's move to New York in 1934, the trips to Yaddo, the marriage to Mary Winternitz, the military service at an Army camp that looked like "of all places, Harvard," the Guggenheim fellowships, the National Book Award for 1957, the journeys to Italy, the house in Ossining. Donaldson is fine, if careful, in his presentation of Cheever's long and finally turbulent relationship with *The New Yorker.* He is vivid, if short-winded, in his discussion of Cheever's deep attachment to his brother Fred, a relationship Cheever felt stirred the homosexual longings in him. He goes into great, anecdotal detail about servants the Cheevers had both in Italy and on the Vanderlip estate in Scarborough, New York, where they rented for some years. And he is strangely if respectfully tight-lipped regarding Cheever's wife, Mary, who never emerges very clearly and to whom the biography, at times, does seem beholden.

It is not until the book's last third that the picture of Cheever that Donaldson is after sharpens into something wrenching. By middle age, Cheever's heavy drinking had affected his work habits and made chaos of his family life. Bisexuality seemed at first to offer the connection and emotion that he felt had eluded him, despite all his gifts. Promiscuity ripped open a room in him. He had affairs with students, with men in gay baths, and, more notoriously, with Ned Rorem and with Hope Lange. At Boston University he was hired to teach the same year that Anne Sexton, also a faculty member, committed suicide; Cheever himself sank into a depression exacerbated by drinking. In the middle of the second semester he was sent home to his wife, and John Updike was brought in to take over the class.

By the end of his life Cheever had won his battle against alcoholism, but to some it seemed too late. "At your age," the poet Hayden Carruth told him, "I think I'd have gone out loaded." "Puking all over someone else's furniture?" Cheever replied. He had salvaged his life in time to write two more novels—*Falconer* and *Oh What a Paradise It Seems*—and to see his collected stories win the Pulitzer Prize in 1978. He felt a renewal of affection toward Ossining, took up bicycling, left parties early. And it was then, at the age of sixty-nine, that he fell victim to the perverse timing of disease and was diagnosed as having the cancer that would, a year later, kill him.

Fitzgerald was the only writer that Cheever ever chose to write about (in a short biography for *Atlantic Brief Lives* in 1971), and Donaldson, who has also written biographies of Fitzgerald and Hemingway, tells us "there is no disputing the fact that in composing his brief life of Fitzgerald, Cheever was writing about himself." Cheever's life, however, seems finally a more ordinary and more heartbreaking one than Fitzgerald's. As Wilfred Sheed once remarked, "Cheever . . . reminds one of the old story about the patient with the bed next to the window who invented a gaudy world outside to please the other patients, although his window overlooked a bank wall." One suspects, even feels, Cheever's intimacy with that wall. Trapped in the alcoholic purchase of oblivion and euphoria, residing within a marital carcass to which he claimed only formal loyalty, hoping somehow to allay the lovelessness he had felt from mother and wife (both women named Mary), Cheever constructed a life of beautiful speech: a voice blended with English and Yankee accents, a prose of ecclesiastical tones, of sadness and lyrical affirmation. So elegant were his spoken sentences that people not looking often thought he was reading. He was at once a "toothless Thurber," a wicked satirist, and the Chekhov of Westchester; in his work and spirit there was a struggle and division between "the celebratory and the deprecatory." When he was elected to the National Institute of Arts and Letters, he made light of it with the ditty "Root tee toot, ahh root tee toot, oh, we're the members of the institute." But he had great respect for ceremony and recognition, and in the years following he proposed nominations and citations for dozens of other writers whose work he admired.

Certainly it is in the work that one comes to know an author—his best and essential self—without being able to extricate or explain him. A short story is "the appeasement of pain," said Cheever, who felt the story form possessed an intensity the novel did not. "In a stuck ski lift, a sinking boat, a dentist's office, or a doctor's office . . . at the very point of death, one tells oneself a short story." Donaldson lingers in his discussion of Cheever's great stories—"Goodbye, My Brother," "The Country Husband," "The Geometry of Love"—like a gardener caring for them, though in his particular tasks they yield him beauty rather than fruit. Said son Fred Cheever of his father, "No one, absolutely no one, shared his life with him." Donaldson has this in common with his subject: the impulse to share a life that cannot be shared—though it can be written down a little with a gardener's care, the words planted like a kiss.

(1988)

Bobbie Ann Mason's *Love Life*

Bobbie Ann Mason writes the kind of fiction her own characters would never read. If they turn off the television long enough to look at a book at all, her characters are inclined toward the steamy, gothic romances they themselves refer to as "bodice busters." "I don't read," says one Mason character. "If I read, I just go crazy."

This puts the Kentucky-born Mason in that most lonesome and literary position of being neither wholly of the world about which she writes nor of the world to which she writes (most of her shorter work has appeared in *The New Yorker*). In this middle place, no axes to grind, no self is mythologized, no isms truly suit. She writes from a slight—and only slightly unsafe—distance, a place of friendly irony, and her pen neither condescends nor skewers. She is gentle with her good country people (whose idea of wickedness is to park at the mall in a handicapped parking spot) in a way that Flannery O'Connor (with whom Mason is sometimes, strangely, compared) could never have been. But she hesitates to prettify, to flash the ruby in the rube. Declining to dismantle them, to judge them, to be them, Mason seems to have simply collected her characters, collected the stuff of them, collected—in the insular spirit of the curator or the spy—what she knows, rather than what she thinks.

Which is why Mason's strongest form may be neither the novel nor the story but the story collection. It is there, picking up her pen every twenty pages to start anew, gathering layers through echo and overlap, that Mason depicts most richly a community of contemporary lives, which is her great skill. It could be argued that the quiet, cumulative beauty of Mason's *Shiloh and Other Stories* is rivaled in her oeuvre (which includes the novels *In Country* and *Spence + Lila*) only by her new collection, *Love Life*. There is depth here, in the way the word is used to describe armies and sports teams: an accumulation, a supply. When one story is finished, a similar one rushes in to fill its place. There is also profundity. Mason dips her pen in the same ink, over and over, because her knowledge of the landlocked Middle America she writes about—most of it centered in Kentucky and Tennessee—is endless and huge. Each small story adds to the reader's apprehension of that hugeness.

In Mason's new collection her themes of provincial entrapment and desire are present again, but here she has given them a new improvisatory sprawl. Though a few of the fifteen stories in *Love Life* (such as the title one) repeat the figure-eight structure found in *Shiloh*—a narrative that loops gracefully through several combinations of characters, then arches back to the original one—many of the stories in *Love Life* splay out unexpectedly, skate off, or in, at odd angles, displaying a directional looseness. "Midnight Magic" introduces the dramatic thread of a town terrorized by an unknown rapist, but then ends off to one side of it, with the moral dilemma over the reporting of a hit-and-run accident. "Piano Fingers" begins with a husband's sexual boredom and ends with a father buying his daughter an electric keyboard from the piano store. Certainly the beginnings and endings do illuminate each other, but only indirectly, diffusely. Along the way elements are seldom developed in a linear fashion and are often, once introduced, abandoned altogether.

But this unexpectedness keeps Mason's stories breathing and alive. Her writing is naked-voiced, without vanity. In "State Champions," a memory of small-town adolescence, the middle-aged narrator is made to understand belatedly and obliquely the significance of her high school basketball team's state championship. Twenty years after the fact someone not from her community recollects for her.

"Why, they were just a handful of country boys who could barely afford basketball shoes," the man told me in upstate New York.

"They were?" This was news to me.

Which leads, circuitously, to one of Mason's strongest stories about the emotional illiteracy of the provincial heart. The narrator recalls her teenage crush on a boy who gives her an "eight-page novel," a slightly off-color Li'l Abner comic strip. "It was disgusting, but I was thrilled that he showed me the booklet." When her best friend's sister dies, the narrator remembers avoiding her.

> I didn't know what to say. I couldn't say anything, for we weren't raised to say things that were heartfelt and gracious. . . . We didn't say we were sorry. We hid from view, in case we might be called on to make appropriate remarks, the way certain old folks in church were sometimes called on to pray. At Cuba School, there was one teacher who, for punishment, made her students write "I love you" five hundred times on the blackboard. "Love" was a dirty word, and I had seen it on the walls of the girls' rest room—blazing there in ugly red lipstick. In the eight-page novel Glenn had showed me, Li'l Abner said "I love you" to Daisy Mae.

What can and cannot be said is always at issue in Mason's small towns. "If you don't want to hear about it, why don't you say so?" begins the story "Private Lies." Psychological inarticulateness is everywhere. A conversation about death can quickly become a conversation about shoes. In "The Secret of the Pyramids," the fatal car accident of the protagonist's former lover is discussed this way:

> Then Glenda says, "Oh, wasn't that awful about Bob Morganfield?"
>
> "I know. I heard about it on the news last night." . . .
>
> "But he was so nice. Everybody liked him."
>
> "I got these shoes at his store this spring."
>
> "I just love those. I wish I could wear spike heels."

In "Big Bertha Stories," a man tells his wife about a young woman he knew in Vietnam. "What happened to her?" asks the wife.

"I don't know."

"Is that the end of the story?"

"I don't know."

Later, the wife, thinking of her husband, realizes that her own sympathies have gone mute from neglect and inexpression. "She hasn't thought of him as himself. She wasn't brought up that way, to examine someone's soul." Says a character in another story, "On *Moonlighting* they just talk-talk-talk. . . . It drives you up the wall."

For an edifying word on their troubles, Mason's characters watch the Phil Donahue show, where they find the various problems of their lives formulated for them. A woman in the story "Hunktown" says, "I can't stand watching stuff that's straight out of my own life." They seem to share a startling belief that their lives correspond to the television culture that has descended on them. But it is more hope than belief, a desire to refashion and locate themselves, to medicate their feelings of exile with cheap understanding.

For a good time they go to Paducah or Gatlinburg. "At a museum there, she saw a violin made from a ham can." They work in mattress factories, or plant tobacco, and when they brush up against glamour and wealth, it is in the form of people who own hot tubs or their "own bush-hog rental company." For spirituality there is the local Christianity—"He opens the Bible and reads from 'the Philippines'"—which may also include speaking in tongues. "He is speaking a singsong language made of hard, disturbing sounds. 'Shecky-beck-be-floyt-I-shecky-tibby-libby. Dabcree-la-croo-la-crow.' He seems to be trying hard not to say 'abracadabra' or any other familiar words." Only one Mason character ventures off to a therapist, whom she calls " 'The Rapist,' because the word *therapist* can be divided into two words, *the rapist.*" When he tells her that perhaps she is trying to escape reality, she says, "Reality, hell! . . . Reality's my whole problem."

Mason's women tend to be practical, disillusioned, self-preserving. They belong to cosmetics clubs, wear too much makeup, have names such as Beverly or Jolene. They are trapped mostly in their desire for Mason's men, who tend to be feckless, dreamy, drunk, between jobs. The sexes are a puzzle to each other here, and longing and distraction pervade their lives. Divorce seems the only remedy for a life where a couple "stayed married like two dogs locked together in passion, except it wasn't passion." Mason's use of the present tense in the majority of her stories serves as the expression of this trapped condition, but also as a kind of existential imperfect: the freeze in time suggests the flow; the moment stilled and isolated from the past and future is yet emblematic of them both, of the gray ongoingness of things.

Nevertheless, the characters in *Love Life* seem determined to amuse themselves. In "Private Lies": "He liked to clown around, singing 'The Star-Spangled Banner' in a mock-operatic style; he would pretend to forget the words and then shift abruptly into 'Carry Me Back to Old Virginny.' He was a riot at parties." In "The Secret of the Pyramids": "The last time he took her out to eat, they had to wait for their table, and Bob gave the name 'Beach' so the hostess would call out on the microphone, 'Beach Party.'" In "Memphis": "'I'm having a blast, too,' Beverly said, just as an enormous man with tattoos of outer-space monsters on his arms asked Jolene to dance." Their days are punctuated with attenuated joys and generosities. The large gestures of life are reduced by Mason to the smallest scale, inflaming them with meaning. "Steve's friend Pete squirts blue fluid on Steve's windshield—a personal service not usually provided at the self-serve island" ("Midnight Magic").

If such living is morally hemmed in, strewn with the junk of our culture, it is all that Mason's characters can avail themselves of. Buried in the very gut of America, feeling deeply the lock and cage of the land, they send up antennae and receive what they are able to, what there is. If they are mocked and demeaned by what they consume, they do not know it; to mock and demean are coastal pastimes, of which they haven't the spiritual or material means to partake. "Liz wished she could go to the ocean, just once in her life," one narrator says. "That was what she truly wanted." Despite the immodest imperative of its title, this wonderful collection is less about the optimist's advice to love life than about the struggle and necessity of some ordinary and valiant people to like it just a little.

(1989)

V. S. Pritchett's *A Careless Widow*

Sir Victor Sawdon Pritchett is eighty-nine years old this year, bringing to a close the seventh decade of a huge literary career: over three dozen books—biographies of Turgenev and Balzac, volumes of criticism, novels, travel writing, autobiography, and now yet another collection of short fiction, *A Careless Widow.* Such an event might be construed as literary miracle or professional reproof—instead of what it more likely is: the natural happening of a life of letters lived totally, without ever being faked.

The son of lower-middle-class parents, V. S. Pritchett grew up in a rough neighborhood of London, the setting of a somewhat Dickensian childhood: at times he and his brother lived as street urchins, the family home next to a loud mechanized bakery and a clattering roller-skating rink. As a young man wanting to write, he languished briefly in the leather trade before escaping first to France, then to Ireland and Spain. Almost an exact contemporary of Hemingway, Pritchett, too, was in Paris in the 1920s and Spain in the '30s, and he might have sought out and joined the other writers gathering in those places. But he didn't. Instead he went his own way (receiving, in 1975, a knighthood for distinguished services to literature), outliving, outproducing them all.

Although critics wrangle over whether he has written a major novel, debating in particular the merits of *Mr. Beluncle* (1951), there is no question as to the power and accomplishment of Pritchett's memoirs—

A Cab at the Door (1968) and *Midnight Oil* (1971)—nor of the greatness of his short stories. It was always the short-story form to which Pritchett returned most inspired. He has compared writing stories to ballad making, and one thinks of a Pritchett story not only as an orchestration of ironies but as a place where the author's sentences can do their humble, musical dazzle: "I have always liked the hard and sequined sheen of London streets at night," he wrote in the famous story "Handsome Is as Handsome Does." "The cars come down them like rats."

Pritchett has confessed to whittling many of his stories down from hundred-page novellas, and one can sometimes feel in his narratives the effect of that shrinkage: a strolling gait abruptly tensing, then relaxing again; a pulse in the prose. His stories have been called traditional, and he is often and aptly compared to Chekhov and Maupassant. Classically, a Pritchett story uses visitors or trips to disrupt the neatness or presumption of neatness in a character's life. His is a very English fiction of irony arrayed, hypocrisy exposed, eccentricity embraced. He captures the frustration and strain beneath the moral order of the average citizen, and he is nothing if not funny. Yet his humor never stiffens or distorts. His prose is always limpid—amused but not muddied by bemusement.

A Careless Widow is a collection of six stories, quiet and deceptively simple, like walks. In "A Trip to the Seaside," a widower makes a futile journey to court his former secretary, only to be confronted with portions of their past he has selectively set aside. In "Things," an older couple is paid a visit by the wife's witchlike and recalcitrant sister, whose improvised life rebukes their own (now congealing around the comforts and objects of bourgeois retirement). In "A Careless Widow," a solitary hairdresser takes a holiday to escape the dreary routine of his professional life: "Women came to him to be changed, to be perfected. They arrived tousled and complaining and they left transfigured, equipped for the hunt again. They were simply top-knots to him. When they got up he was always surprised to see they had legs and arms and could walk. He sometimes, though not often, admired the opposite end of them: their shoes." Such escape is possible for less than a day, before he discovers his London neighbor—the widow of the title—staying at the same hotel: "That was too much. She was ordinary life and ordinary life always went too far."

In all these stories, the past figures as a kind of character: a foil, a catalyst, a wise fool. Pritchett's people are well on their way out of middle age—but they do not feel old. Their relationship to the past is often unformed, unclear, yet to be negotiated. "It's a mistake to go back to the past. I mean at my age. Our age," says the careless widow. Appetites still abound—"She looked at him greedily, intently." The refrain "even now" is sighed like an old and bittersweet joke.

In "Cocky Olly," the narrator's thoughts journey irretrievably into her past, seemingly because she has refused—actually, bodily—to take the trip to the places of her childhood, places she passes on her way to and from London. "One of these days, when there is no one with me, I plan to go and look at these places, but I never do," she says. And so the story becomes enmeshed in a long childhood memory, never to return to the present time. "Then it was Cocky Olly again," she says, ending the story with a favorite childhood game, "and all of us racing around."

Situated—however sentimentally or awkwardly—in the rolling landscape of the past, a Pritchett character can turn a back to death. The author himself looks at death, if not squarely, at least wryly. It is his bleak jest that in the title story the local topography offers a place called "the Coffin" for ambitious climbers. In the bleakly comic "A Change of Policy," love and death attempt to outwit each other in bizarre plot shifts: a printer—his wife, Ethel, a comatose stroke victim—falls in love with Paula, an editor for whom Ethel was once a secretary. "I've the feeling that I've been standing up all night for years," he tells his new love. In her guilt, Paula pays the wife a visit in the hospital: "There was a sudden crash of oxygen cylinders that were being unloaded from a truck in the yard outside. The eyes did not move. Suddenly it occurred to Paula to speak in a peremptory office voice: 'Ethel!' she said. . . . There was no movement in the eyes." Just as the title suggests, circumstances change abruptly in this story, and nothing brings Ethel back from death's jaws faster than her husband's sudden death after a horseback riding accident. In yet another curious turn, the two women become close friends, taking a cottage together in another village. Death is turned a back on. The past, practically and resourcefully, is made usable in the present.

In the final story, "The Image Trade," Pearson—a famous older writer, perhaps not unlike Pritchett—must contend with a photographer intent on capturing his image for posterity: a kind of death mask. "You will miss all the et cetera of my life," the writer says. "I am all et cetera. . . . My face is nothing. At my age I don't need it. It is no more than a servant I push around before me. . . . It knows nothing. It just collects. I send it to smirk at parties, to give lectures. . . . It calls people by the wrong names. It is an indiscriminate little grinner. It kisses people I've never met. . . . I know I have a face like a cup of soup with handles sticking out. . . . What wouldn't I give for bone structure, a nose with bone in it!" The picture he finally sees is a quiet marbling of death and life: "No sparkling anemone there but the bald head of a melancholy frog, its feet clinging to a log, floating in literature. O Fame, cried Pearson, O Maupassant, O *Tales of Hoffmann*, O Edgar Allan Poe, O Grub Street."

One feels keenly in these stories a master's presence, sharp and even as that longed-for nose with bone in it. Pritchett's is a literature of deep humanity—a mature artist's extension of affection into unexpected corners, a lover's unflagging interest in life. "I looked at the heads of all the people in the room," one of his narrators says. "They seemed to be like people from another planet. I was in love with them all and did not want to leave."

(1989)

Stanley Elkin's *The MacGuffin*

Stanley Elkin's novels have sometimes been criticized for their disregard of form and organized plot, for what some might see as their overindulgence of the author's poetic gift—his besotted high style. In *The MacGuffin,* that mad, Joycean poetry is, pleasurably enough, still there. The sentences are long riffs of jazz; the words swarm and lather; the prose is exuberantly betroped, exhilaratingly de trop—one imitates it badly. But more self-consciously than in his previous novels—which include *The Living End* and *George Mills*—Elkin has placed at the thematic heart of his book a discussion of this "failure" of his at narrative construction.

The title may say it all. *The MacGuffin,* a term used by Alfred Hitchcock, refers to that element in a Hitchcock film—or in narrative generally—that is a mere pretext for a plot. The MacGuffin might be the papers the spies are after, the secret theft of a ring, any device or gimmick that gets the plot rolling. The plot, moreover, is simply a pretext for an exploration of character. The MacGuffin itself has little, if any, intrinsic meaning. The MacGuffin, said Hitchcock, is nothing.

In Elkin's novel, however, the MacGuffin appears to be a strangely metamorphosing idea. Or perhaps it is a fixed idea in an absurdly shifting world. One thinks of the joke from which the MacGuffin is presumed to have derived its name: Two men are on a train. "What is that package?" asks one. "That's a MacGuffin," answers the other. "What's a MacGuffin?" "It's for trapping lions in the Scottish Highlands." "But there are no lions in the Scottish Highlands!" "Well, then, that's no MacGuffin."

As personified in Elkin's novel, the MacGuffin is "the Muse of his plot line," the "odd displacements, the skewed idiosyncratic angle." It is an imagined voice, an inner imp, a guardian devil to the novel's protagonist, Bobbo Druff, Commissioner of Streets of a midsize American city. Druff, at fifty-eight, has lost his ease and wants it back, "the way some people wanted their youth." He is experiencing a kind of "aphasia, or Alzheimer's, or the beginnings of senility"; "something dark was going on in the old gray matter . . . some sluggish, white stupidity forming and hardening there like an impression formed in a mold." Druff's MacGuffin is the ordering force of paranoia, the seeing and making of plots, the reading of symbols in municipal routine, the straining after coincidence and story.

There are things that have set Druff up for this dementia, this "alcoholic vaudeville." There are the coca leaves in his pocket. There is his deteriorating health. And there is his guilty conscience: he has committed adultery; he has taken graft. He feels he will be found out. The "hair tars and breath shellacs," the "intimate cheeses and bitters," will give him away.

"If you've asked for the bribe they generally give you up to three weeks per thousand," Druff tells his worried son, Mikey, who is thirty and still lives at home. "If you've been bribed, they usually let you off with a fine. . . . It's your dad's policy only to accept bribes." "I know that," Mikey says, "it's what all those fines could do to your net worth."

What preoccupies Druff and his MacGuffin the most is the death of Mikey's girlfriend, a Shiite Muslim named Su'ad who has been killed in a hit-and-run accident. Druff himself once lusted after her, just a bit, while she held forth about the Shiite cause. "It all sounds to me like your typical power grab," he once told her. "We see it time and again down at the Hall." The local here stands for the universal. As Commissioner of Streets, Druff must find out why Su'ad has died in one of them. Could it have been a faulty traffic light? In Elkin's world there is nothing more complicated—or simpler—than municipal America.

The time span of this chapterless narrative is approximately two days, and in that period Druff spends many hours being driven around the city by his chauffeur, "Dick the spy," fantasizing himself the victim of sting operations, reminiscing about the days when he first met his wife (who had managed to turn her scoliosis into a "lewd suggestion"), and discussing with Dick the strange traffic in the middle of the night.

"It's the nurses," says his driver, the spy. "They come on at seven at night. It's experimental. It plays hell with their menses unless they have the middle shift, the eleven-to-seven one, but the thinking today is that PMS gives them an edge."

To which Druff can only ask, "Is this true?" Everything to him, a man "old enough to be from a generation that still marveled that there were car radios," has begun to seem plausible, equally convincing or unconvincing. This is particularly true of Su'ad's death. Did she smuggle rugs or legitimately import them? And what did she want with Mikey? She was "very devout . . . into that stuff like a terrorist," and his son planned on going back to Lebanon with her. "I was going to let them make me a hostage," he tells his father.

But Druff finally learns that minutes before her death Su'ad attended a lecture by "an Arab congressman from the state of Delaware with whose conciliatory views Su'ad was in strong disagreement." The congressman, referring to "our Israeli cousins," stressed the necessity for all sides to dedicate themselves to solutions in the troubled Mideast. Angry, Su'ad stood up and made a heated reference to a need for final solutions; an hour later she was dead.

There is no mystery solved here, no sacred story set like a table, not really. Elkin is brilliant, but in his own brilliant way. His vision is not, as the generals have referred to the Persian Gulf war, "scenario-dependent." It is less hollow, more nervous, than that. "Life is either mostly adventure or it's mostly psychology," says the voice of the Mac-Guffin, before it takes its leave of Druff. "If you have enough of the one then you don't need a lot of the other."

The MacGuffin, then, is not only an Elkinesque portrait of the sorrows of the body and the moral perils of work. It is a plea for the power of talk, for talk as its own resolution—even Druff's manic rapid-mouth-movement, all simile and parentheses and searching stammer, the deejay yak of the heart. Even this verbiage, the novel seems to say, perhaps especially this verbiage, this incoherence, is an intimacy, a negotiation—a prayer against death, a stay against war.

(1991)

Don DeLillo's *Mao II*

If terrorists have seized control of the world narrative, if they have captured the historical imagination, have they become, in effect, the world's new novelists? For sheer influence over the human mind, have they displaced a precariously placed literature? Are writers—lacking some greater if lethal faith—the new hostages? "Is history possible? Is anyone serious?" These are some of the questions posed by *Mao II*, the latest novel by Don DeLillo, who has already proved with such books as *Players, White Noise,* and *Libra* that no one can match his ability to let America, the bad dream of it, speak through his pen.

Mao II takes its title from one of Andy Warhol's famous portraits of Mao Zedong. For DeLillo, the Warhols are more than mock chinoiserie: they anticipate the televised image of the official state portrait of Mao, defaced with red paint in Tiananmen Square. In *Mao II,* the Warhol pictures marry the ideas of totalitarianism and image-making, prompting speculation about how fame is transformed into a death mask, how a portrait can freeze the mind behind the face. Fittingly enough, the novel begins and ends with a wedding, that most stereotypically photographed occasion. And yet, while this bookending creates a palindromic comedy, these are anticomedic, apocalyptic nuptials.

Not that *Mao II* doesn't now and then attempt a joke. As with so much of DeLillo's work, the novel has a discursive sweep, and its narrative movement from serious idea to serious idea is rigorously un-neat, like the gathering and associative movement of the brain itself. But as a story about a reclusive writer, written by a reclusive writer, it has a sense of humor. Early on in the novel, a mad street person, "great-maned and filthy, rimed saliva in his beard, old bruises across the forehead gone soft and crumbly," bursts into a bookstore; "I'm here to sign my books," he tells the security guard. Later, when the protagonist, a novelist named Bill Gray, falls into the company of a Maoist terrorist sympathizer, their tense conversation takes an unexpected turn: "There's something I wanted to ask the other evening at dinner," says the other man. "Do you use a word processor?"

But overall, as one might expect from DeLillo, this is a dark tale, one that is focused on the writer Bill Gray and the various characters circling his life at a time when Gray is particularly weary of his well-guarded seclusion. Indeed, that seclusion has become a kind of captivity; in a way, he is looking for a changing of the guard. Thus Gray escapes the confines of his country home to visit a friend at a New York publishing house, then finds himself agreeing to go to London to give a reading on behalf of a poet held captive in Beirut. When he arrives in London, however, the reading is postponed because of a bomb threat. But Gray moves ineluctably toward the Middle East (via Athens and Cyprus) and toward the fate of the poet-hostage, which, in an act of professional brotherhood but also of spiritual mystery, Gray insists on trying to prevent or share—or appropriate. In that contest between art and life, this is a scenario that both mirrors and *is* the "master collapse" that is Gray's final book.

The people in Gray's life at this critical time include Scott, a compulsive and maniacal fan who has tracked Gray down and volunteered himself as an assistant, enforcing Gray's solitude, managing Gray's career, commanding Gray's life. There is also Scott's lover, the waiflike Karen (who is sometimes Gray's lover as well), a former follower of the Reverend Sun Myung Moon, with a visionary streak that allows her to see what others can't and to speak, in eerie mimicry, what others speak. And there is Brita, the literary photographer whose portraits of Gray, she and he both briefly believe, will help usher him out into the world of the living, though it is not long before she gives up photographing writers and turns to those who make the real news—the terrorists.

DeLillo has written about terrorists before, in the 1977 novel *Play-*

ers, but *Mao II* has something else haunting it: the ordeal of Salman Rushdie. DeLillo shares a publisher with Rushdie, and in *Mao II* the New York publishing house that Gray visits is one at which there are visitor searches and guards. The idea of a writer held hostage is so understandably traumatizing to DeLillo that he has used his narrative to work variations on this theme: the blindfolded poet in a basement in Beirut; the hermitic and professionally hamstrung novelist in a study in upstate New York. And, lest the pairing seem merely a melodramatic metaphor, DeLillo, with a kind of insistence, makes these lives intersect. This can really happen, he seems to be saying. Look for a writer, and you will find a terrorist. And a hostage. This is the new literary dialectic. It is also the evening news.

No one's prose is better than DeLillo's. "I'm a sentence-maker, like a donut-maker only slower," says Bill Gray. DeLillo's description of a writer's face through the viewfinder of a camera becomes a poem complete unto itself: "She watched him surrender his crisp gaze to a softening, a bright-eyed fear that seemed to tunnel out of childhood. It had the starkness of a last prayer. She worked to get at it. His face was drained and slack, coming into flatness, into black and white, cracked lips and flaring brows, age lines that hinge the chin, old bafflements and regrets."

The novel is also filled with set pieces that show off the author's great skill with a scene and with multiple points of view. There is, for example, the Orwellian opening, a mass wedding of thirteen thousand at Yankee Stadium. "It's as though they designed this to the maximum degree of let the relatives squirm," says one of the "flesh parents," futilely scanning the bridal veils for her daughter. "How they hate our willingness to work and struggle," thinks Karen, the daughter she is looking for. "They want to snatch us back to the land of lawns."

When, toward the end of the novel, DeLillo has Bill Gray (who is suffering internal injuries from a hit-and-run accident in Athens) sit down in a Cyprus restaurant to make witty if coded chitchat with some British tourists, it is a portrait of the artist as the dying Mercutio, and it provides the book some of its best dialogue—speech that sounds like speech rather than writing. Often in the complex orchestration of his ideas, DeLillo makes his characters name and sing all his tunes for him, speaking in dazzling chunks of authorial essay that read as if they had been created by someone who no longer cared how people really spoke. Here, though, in this careful, bitter dinner scene, everything—the tension, the tone, the dialogue—is exactly right.

Among the myriad other things to admire in *Mao II* are DeLillo's way of capturing a representative slice of a city, his ability to reproduce ineffable urban rhythms, his startling evocations of sights and smells. He has a discerning and satirical eye, which notes unexpected details like Gray's "sepia toenails" or the "cancer coloring book" in the pocket of a car door.

Indeed, it is to the larger idea of the image—its use as a bridge between public and private, its doubtful integrity, its sanctimonious politics—that *Mao II* keeps returning. A mass wedding, a photo session with a writer, an international revolution—all attempt an elimination of the self through the imagistic replication of the self. Seen this way, imagery is a kind of cemetery, a repository for the proliferating residue of life. ("The room drained the longings out of him," DeLillo writes of the hostage poet in that basement cell. "He was left with images.") In DeLillo's metaphorical system, the self figured and multiplied is death: an army is the opposite of a person. Likeness is the canvas of farewell. Only anarchic Beirut seems to have "consumed all its own depictions"; Gray has trouble even finding a map of the place.

If one remains less moved by *Mao II* than engaged and impressed, that is the contract a reader must often make with a book by DeLillo; he is seldom an emotional writer. Nonetheless, one may find oneself hoping just a little for something approximating the feeling and power of, say, Marguerite Oswald's monologue in the closing chapter of *Libra*, or even the chill gallows humor of *White Noise*, which accomplished so much sustained and mournful queasiness.

Still, within its own defined parameters, within the boundaries of its own paradoxical discourse, DeLillo's new book succeeds as brilliantly as any of his others. One thinks of the novel's own refrains: Bill Gray's memory of a family joke, repeating the instructions in the hat section of a Sears catalogue, *"Measure your head before ordering,"* and the prayerful chant of an unheeded street beggar, "Still love you. Spare a little change . . . Still love you."

(1991)

Election Day 1992: Voters in Wonderland

Is it too late to note the left-handedness of all three candidates? It left, so to speak, an eerie impression. Not because of the various primitive biases against left-handedness—that it is sinister, like the Italian word (*sinistra*), or clumsy like the French (*gauche*), or that it suggests a brain organized in mystery and improvisation.

No, mostly it was eerie because in watching the candidates it seemed we were viewing a reflection in the mirror, as if this were all taking place through the looking glass, and that Lewis Carrollean quality was unnerving, particularly given the people involved.

I guess I mean the American people—a phrase I hoped never to hear again, but there it is, and without a southern drawl, a Texas twang, or a Camp David scoff. The American people: so fickle and unimpressed. What do they want? As I watched them being courted these many months, it occurred to me that the three candidates really were suitors, that they had courting styles—attitudes and tricks.

They were trying to get a date—November 3—with the American people. Bill Clinton was the etchings man, the guy with the soulful but collegiate gaze, the curly mouth, such heat in the face and itchy restlessness in a suit it seemed his clothes would fly off him. At his place there were jazz recordings and art. "It's time for a change," he said, looking around the joint.

Ross Perot came straight to the front door and rang the bell. "I'm crazy about ya. That's all there is to it." The American people noted the adjective but were charmed. When he skipped town, for the wedding of a relative, they blew their noses and began seeing other men. When two months later he showed up again at their office, the American people phoned 911. (Of course, they misdialed and got 411: information, infomercial.)

George Bush promised safety: "I won't drink and drive, not like you-know-who." But the trunk of his car was locked—Panamanian drugs? Deposit slips from Iraqi banks? Copies of *Hamlet*? Of *Richard II*?

It was painful to watch them in Richmond negotiate the stools. The informal seating of the second debate was daytime-talk-show theater—Oprah Winfrey, Phil Donahue—and this staging, somehow paradigmatic of the entire campaign, seemed particularly uncomfortable to President Bush, Bachelor No. 1.

Stealing that vulgar format for a debate was a kind of beheading—and Bush seemed to know that. He arrived anesthetized. He was too proud to flirt. He threw in the towel and waved to his wife in the audience. Hi, honey! He was still trying to figure out how Ronald Reagan had gotten away with sitting around doing nothing, but when he, Bush, had tried it, he got nailed. It's so unfair! Hi, honey!

Clinton remained hunched over on his own stool, but then rose like a torch singer when it was his turn, microphone in hand, giving himself in the style of Piaf or Garland to each questioner. A cross between a sweet cocktail and a legal pad, he bespoke desire and its difficult math.

Perot, meanwhile, used his stool as a kind of elevator shoe and seemed amused at his newly acquired stature. He worked up a running gag with the commander in chief. He had fun. Heck, look what he was doing: he was running for president!

But this was all taking place through the looking glass. In some other world. That Lewis Carroll world. Wasn't it?

Is this longest and dreariest of courtships—the televised flattery, the bad candy, the shifting hairstyles—the future of presidential campaigning? I'm reminded of a remark made once by a transvestite-turned-transsexual. "When I was a transvestite," she said, "dressing up like this was fun. But now that I'm a woman, it's such a chore."

In the world of Lewis Carroll, strangeness and vanity are laws of physics: Smiles linger in the air. Cakes are marked EAT ME, beautifully in currants. Turtles croon of their own soup. But after the election, whoever is our president is going to have to pass through the thick silver mist of the mirror, into our side, the American people's side, the real side, of the room.

(1992)

Charles Baxter's *Shadow Play*

Often when short-story writers go to write novels they get jaunty. They take deep breaths and become brazen—the way shy people do on wine. Donald Barthelme becomes mythic and parodic. Alice Munro boldly seamsterly (stitching novels from short stories). Andre Dubus asks us to reconsider the novella (as an equivalent form). Perhaps Grace Paley has shown the greatest bravado of all in simply not bothering.

Charles Baxter, whose three brilliant collections of short stories (*Harmony of the World, Through the Safety Net,* and *A Relative Stranger*) may place him in the same rank as the above writers, constructed his first novel in reverse chronology. *First Light* (1987), the hauntingly detailed story of a brother and sister from Five Oaks, Michigan, is an intricate unknotting, a narrative progression backward in time toward the moment when the boy, Hugh, first touches his infant sister's hand. It is a strategy intended, no doubt, to make the genre Baxter's own, as well as to show the inextricability of sibling ties. Now, in his second novel, *Shadow Play,* Baxter has returned to Five Oaks—a town of "prideful" lies, "sun-smelted" ponds, and "apples dry-rotting in the hot dust of the driveway"—as well as to the subject of siblings and inextricability.

Perhaps because he's been here before, Baxter is more confident this time. In *Shadow Play,* the novel is no longer a form to be seized and remade, but a capacious place in which to move around. Baxter is looser, less strict. The narrative has not been trained; Baxter indulges it, affectionately musses its hair, lets it go where it may. The result is, paradoxically, both a more conventionally constructed novel and a more surprising and suspenseful book.

Shadow Play is primarily the story of Wyatt Palmer, a fiercely bright and artistic boy who grows up to find himself stuck in the most pedestrian of existences: by day a bored government bureaucrat, by night a tired husband, father, and homeowner. When a chemical company called WaldChem sets itself up in town and pressures the city management (for the sake of the local economy, of course) to look the other way as health regulations are violated, Wyatt is suddenly and precariously placed at the center of a drama involving ethical behavior in "postethical" times.

In a contracting economy, too many citizens of Five Oaks appear willing to make a devil's pact: health for cash; lives for jobs. As assistant city manager, Wyatt would like to "notify the state that the on-site waste management guidelines and regulations and licensing restrictions are being violated."

But the head of WaldChem is a high school buddy; Wyatt plays golf with him; he has given Wyatt's wayward foster brother, Cyril, a job in the plant. And, as the city manager tells Wyatt, "the times are against you." By remaining quiet and polite and helpful to those around him, Wyatt strikes a most unholy bargain—with himself as well as with the world. He is no longer his troubled brother's troubled keeper; he is a member of the audience. As Baxter wrote in *First Light,* "No one knows how to do that in this country, how to be a brother."

Not unlike Shirley Jackson's story "The Lottery," Baxter's *Shadow Play* takes large themes of good and evil and primitive deal-making, and situates them in municipal terms and local ritual. He is interested in those shadowy corners of civilization in which barbarity manages to nestle and thrive. The America of this book has become a kind of hell. "The houses gave off a dingy little light, the light of I'm-not-sorry-for-anything, the light of Listen-to-me. . . . That way you didn't even need eternal fire."

Shadow Play is also an examination of how the midwestern values of niceness, passivity, helpfulness, and just-going-along can contribute to the rot and demise of a community. When Wyatt's foster brother develops lung cancer while holding down his custodial job at the plant, Wyatt is impassive. "They didn't have to make WaldChem so dangerous, those bastards," rages the dying Cyril. "They could have made it safer."

"You smoked, Cyril," Wyatt replies quietly. "You smoked cigarettes all your life." It is a response so wicked in its neutrality that later "he stood in his own living room, repressing the impulse to scream." "The verdict on him, he now knew, was that he was obliging and careless, an accessory." When Wyatt agrees to help Cyril commit suicide (one is reminded here of a fellow Michigander, Dr. Jack Kevorkian), he has not only enacted the central metaphor of the book but effectively set himself up for a nervous breakdown, one replete with tattoo, adultery, arson, and a move to Brooklyn.

This last is no amusing little fillip; in the geographical paradigm of Baxter's book, New York City is Eden as anti-Eden. Here the fruit of the tree of knowledge is not rotting in anyone's driveway. There are no driveways; the trees were cut down years ago. The good fight has long since been waged and lost, and here one can live in something akin to aftermath if not to peace. As a boy Wyatt had memorized a map of the New York subway system, and as a young man he was an artist, a painter of shadow portraits; now, in New York with his family, he can resume where he left off before the heart- and hinterland so rudely interrupted him. He can attempt something *un*-midwestern, something like a coda, a twilit sequel; in unecological times, an ecology of hope and loss.

One of Charles Baxter's great strengths as a writer has always been his ability to capture the stranded inner lives of the Midwest's repressed eccentrics. And here, in his second novel, he is at full throttle. The character of Wyatt's mother is a figure of alleged madness, but—whether it speaks to Baxter's talent or should be cause for this reader's concern— the passages that give voice to her insanity are lucid, lovely, sympathetic: "She knew that birds sometimes agreed or disagreed with their names but she kept that information to herself." "Angels," she thinks, "were so vain, so pretty. They wore coral earrings and distressfully unassembled hats." When Wyatt brings his mother to New York, and she finds the life of a bag lady a congenial one, Baxter treats this with a certain heartening dignity rather than a forlorn condescension.

He also gives much of the book over to the voice and point of view of Wyatt's bright, quirky Aunt Ellen, who functions as a sapient observer of the world of the novel. She believes not in a benevolent God but in a God of pure curiosity; moreover, she believes she is writing the Bible of that God. "There is absolutely no love coming to us from that realm," she says of the more traditional deity. "None at all. You might as well pray to a telephone pole."

Aunt Ellen, even more than Wyatt, is the moral center of the book—hers is the most trenchant of the solitudes fashioned and recorded here. That Baxter can traverse gender and offer such a deep and authentic rendition of a woman's voice and thoughts should not in itself be remarkable in contemporary fiction, yet still it is.

Because his work doesn't offer itself up in gaudy ways for popular consumption or intellectual play (theorists and critics have failed to descend en masse with their scissors and forks), Charles Baxter has acquired the reputation of being that rare and pleasurable thing: a writer's writer. He has steadily taken beautiful and precise language and gone into the ordinary and secret places of people—their moral and emotional quandaries, their typically American circumstances, their burning intelligence, their negotiations with what is trapped, stunted, violent, sustaining, decent, or miraculous in their lives. In writing about ordinary people he derives narrative authority from having imagined further and more profoundly than we have, making his literary presence a necessary and important one, and making *Shadow Play* a novel that is big, moving, rich with life and story—something so much more than a writer's anxious vacation from shorter forms.

(1993)

Margaret Atwood's *The Robber Bride*

Margaret Atwood has always possessed a tribal bent: in both her fiction and her nonfiction she has described and transcribed the ceremonies and experience of being a woman, or a Canadian, or a writer—or all three. And as with so many practitioners of identity politics, literary or otherwise, while one side of her banner defiantly exclaims "We Are!" the other side, equally defiant, admonishes "Don't Lump Us." In *The Robber Bride,* Atwood has gathered (not lumped) four very different women characters.

Probably it is the subject of women that has most completely dominated Atwood's novels (although for "women," one might as well read "a medium-size variety of people in general"). That women are individuals, difficult to corral, a motley and uneasy sisterhood; that feminism is often hard going and hard-won, sabotaged from within as well as without; that in the war between the sexes there are collaborators as well as enemies, spies, refugees, spectators, and conscientious objectors—all this has been brilliantly dramatized in Atwood's work.

The cruel Toronto girlhoods depicted in her novels *Lady Oracle* and *Cat's Eye,* replete with vague, insensitive mothers and sadistic girls, are in their way feminist dystopias akin to the totalitarian North America of her best-known work, the futurist novel *The Handmaid's Tale.* To restore the humanity of their cultural representation, Atwood's writing suggests, it is women who must look at women in discrete and unsentimental ways. Too often men are in power or love or the dark or the doghouse or the fog. So the attentive Atwood looks. And the women she sees are deformed by their own niceness, or given to mischief or dreaminess or carelessness. In a sexist society they meekly but inventively improvise a life. Or else they pounce and grab. Some work hard. Some yell. Some hide, some march, some drink, some fib. Some bite the dust, the bullet, the hand that feeds them. Some rule the roost. Some count their chickens before they're hatched. Goodness, what a richly hued tapestry of women the world has woven!

That this should in any way still be news tells us something of the condescension and categorical thinking of that world. In a recent introduction to the *Paris Review* anthology *Women Writers at Work*, Atwood remarked that the editors chose to bring together fifteen diverse writers, "over what in some cases would doubtless be their dead bodies." She went on to write, " 'Why not a gathering of women writers?' the editors were asked. Well, why not? Which is not quite the same as why."

In *The Robber Bride*, we meet three friends from college—Tony, Charis, and Roz—and their common nemesis and classmate, the beautiful, evil Zenia. Men in this novel are on the sidelines only. In this game they are the ante, the chips, but not the players themselves, not really even the cards. Men are marginal, symbolic. As texts they are hack, minor, obvious, predictable. It is the women Atwood is interested in. She wants a challenge. She wants to have fun. As with the fairy tales requested by Roz's daughters, she wants women in all the parts.

"Who do you want [the Robber Bride] to murder?" asks Tony, the storyteller of the title's revised Grimm tale. "Men victims, or women victims? Or maybe an assortment?"

The girls "remain true to their principles, they do not flinch. They opt for women, in every single role."

Tony is Antoinette Fremont, a war historian and a professor at a Toronto university. She teaches and researches the history of war, while Operation Desert Storm mobilizes abroad. In her cellar, using peppercorns, lentils, and Monopoly pieces for the various armies, she sets up dioramas of ancient French battles. She is happiest "in the company of people who had died a long time ago." Her friend Charis tells her such an interest in war is "negative" and "carcinogenic." One of her university colleagues tells her that in not focusing on social history Tony is "letting women down." The History Department, Tony thinks, is "like a Renaissance court: whisperings, gangings-up, petty treacheries, snits and umbrage."

Tony's "stronghold" is her house, where she lives and studies, childless except for her husband, West. For Tony, "war is there. It's not going away soon. . . . The personal is not political, thinks Tony: the personal is military. War is what happens when language fails." Besides, wars have their upside: while they're occurring, the suicide rate always drops.

Tony's point of view begins and ends the novel. By giving such strategic positioning to this character, Atwood announces and reinforces her metaphors and themes: that victimhood comes in all forms; that evil is a fact though not outwittable; that fighting fire with fire may have, for observers, its aesthetic and intellectual appeal.

Atwood braids two other characters' points of view into the narrative. One belongs to the half-zonked but psychic Charis—a New Age earth mother who in the 1960s "drifted through her university years as if through an airport." Charis believes in breathing exercises and teas and juices. She believes you can refuse to participate in certain emotions.

"I like hamburgers but I don't eat them," she says.

"Hamburgers are not an emotion," says Roz.

"Yes they are," says Charis.

The other point of view is Roz's. She is the founding editor of *WiseWomanWorld,* a successful women's magazine that has not entirely lost its social conscience. Roz sees to it that the magazine gives generously, if wearily, to charities: "Hearts, Lungs and Livers, Eyes, Ears and Kidneys."

Roz, Atwood tells us, "has her own list. She still does Battered Women, she still does Rape Victims, she still does Homeless Moms. How much compassion is enough? She's never known, and you have to draw the line somewhere, but she still does Abandoned Grannies. She no longer goes to the formal dinner-dances, though."

Raucous and irreverent, during her marriage Roz was also indulgent, vigilant, and wise. She checked her philandering husband "for rust spots, the way she would a car." She hoped that if he started to go

bald he wouldn't "get his armpit transplanted to the top of his head."
She sees the problems of her life mostly as narrative ones. Together, she
and her therapist try to "figure out what story she's in." If they succeed, "they can retrace her steps, they can change the ending." Though
perhaps the fairy tales are right, she thinks: "No matter what you do,
somebody always gets boiled."

Besides their alma mater, these three chums have one thing in
common: they've lost men, spirit, money, and time to their old college acquaintance, Zenia. At various times, and in various emotional
disguises, Zenia has insinuated her way into their lives and practically
demolished them. Charming and gorgeous, Zenia is a misogynist's
grotesque: relentlessly seductive, brutal, pathologically dishonest. Her
past is unclear and fictitious: she alternately passes herself off as the
orphaned daughter of White Russians, or Romanian Gypsies, or Berlin
Jews. Sometimes she is broke. Sometimes she is dying of cancer. Sometimes she is a journalist doing research, and sometimes she is a freelance
spy, part of some international espionage caper. To Tony, who almost
lost her husband and jeopardized her academic career, Zenia is "a lurk-
ing enemy commando." To Roz, who did lose her husband and almost
her magazine, Zenia is "a cold and treacherous bitch." To Charis, who
lost a boyfriend, quarts of vegetable juice, and some pet chickens, Zenia
is a kind of zombie, maybe "soulless": "There must be people like that
around, because there are more humans alive on the earth right now
than have ever lived, altogether, since humans began, and if souls are
recycled then there must be some people alive today who didn't get one,
sort of like musical chairs."

Yet oddly, for all her inscrutable evil, Zenia is what drives this
book: she is impossibly, fantastically bad. She is pure theater, pure plot.
She is Richard III with breast implants. She is Iago in a miniskirt. She
manipulates and exploits all the vanities and childhood scars of her
friends (wounds left by neglectful mothers, an abusive uncle, absent
dads); she grabs at intimacies and worms her way into their comfortable lives, then starts swinging a pickax. She mobilizes all the wily and
beguiling art of seduction and ingratiation, which she has been able
to use on men, and she directs it at women as well. She is an autoimmune disorder. She is viral, self-mutating, opportunistic (the narra-

tive discusses her in conjunction with AIDS, salmonella, and warts). She is a "man-eater" run amok. Roz thinks: "Women don't want all the men eaten up by man-eaters; they want a few left over so they can eat some themselves."

Yet almost everything that happens, happens because of Zenia, and so the reader gets interested and waits to see what Zenia will do. (When she seems to have died, the Rasputin-like Zenia comes back to life. What next?) That we never actually figure her out, or understand the mysterious, cartoonish extremity of her pathology, or even for a moment get her point of view is disappointing. For like Iago and Richard, she is no idiot. And, surrounded by boobs and chumps or even routine civility, she can feast like a shark. But she never gets her own aria or soliloquy, not really; she remains unsolved, unknown.

Perhaps Atwood intended Zenia, by the end, to be a symbol of all that is inexplicably evil: war, disease, global catastrophe. Zenia is meant to have no voice of her own: she is only a mad reworking of everyone else's. But an otherwise terrific story suffers for this particular suspense, one that only resolves itself in a kind of narrative hash. In its pacing and staging Atwood's conclusion is goofy, jerky, madcap—though certainly entertaining. The endings of her novels always seem to have perplexed and defeated Atwood, and in *The Robber Bride* she self-consciously throws up her hands: "Every ending is arbitrary," she writes, a little lamely, "because the end is where you write The end."

Still, *The Robber Bride* is as smart as anything Atwood has written, and she is always smart. (In the Grimms' story "The Robber Bridegroom," the clever heroine saves herself by telling a dream, a story, a fiction that contains the truth.) In *The Robber Bride*, Atwood has avoided the entomological listing of recollected detail that made up so much of her last novel, *Cat's Eye*, yet she retains her gift for observing, in poetry, the minutiae specific to the physical and emotional lives of her characters. A black leather suit makes Tony "look like an avant-garde Italian umbrella stand." The neon of Toronto "gives off a glow, like an amusement park or something safely on fire."

What's more, the novel opens with what may be the most eloquent and quintessential image of a woman in the late twentieth century (despite the great variety!): a working woman (Tony) in early morning, wearing only slippers and a dressing gown, frantically chases after a garbage truck, plastic bag in hand, because her husband (feckless though subsequently contrite) "is supposed to do the garbage, but he forgets."

(1993)

On Writing

Recently I received a letter from an acquaintance in which he said, "By the way, I've been following and enjoying your work. It's getting better: deeper and sicker."

Because the letter was handwritten, I convinced myself, for a portion of the day, that perhaps the last word was *richer.* But then I picked up the letter and looked at the word again: there was the *s,* there was the *k.* There was no denying it. Even though denial had been my tendency of late. I had recently convinced myself that a note I'd received from an ex-beau (in what was a response to my announcement that I'd gotten married) had read "Best Wishes for Oz." I considered this an expression of bitterness on my ex-beau's part, a snide lapse, a doomed man's view of marriage, and it gave me great satisfaction. *Best Wishes for Oz.* Eat your heart out, I thought. You had your chance. Cry me a river. Later, a friend, looking at the note, pointed out, Look: This isn't an *O.* This is a 9—see the tail? And this isn't a *Z.* This is a 2. This says 92. "Best wishes for 92." It hadn't been cryptic bitterness at all—only an indifferent little New Year's greeting. How unsatisfying!

So now when I looked at the *deeper and richer,* I knew I had to be careful not to misread wishfully. The phrase wasn't, finally, deeper and *richer;* it was deeper and *sicker.* My work was deeper and sicker.

What did that mean, *sicker,* and why or how might this adjective be applied in a friendly manner? I wasn't sure. But it brought me to thinking of the things that I had supposed fiction was supposed to be, what art was supposed to be, what writers and artists were supposed to do, and whether it could possibly include some aesthetics of sickness.

I think it's a common thing for working writers to go a little blank when asking themselves too many fundamental questions about what it is they're doing. Some of this has to do with the lost perspective that goes with being so immersed. And some of it has to do with just plain not having a clue. Of course, this is the curse of the grant application for instance, which includes that hilarious part called the project description (describe in detail the book you are going to write), wherein you are asked to know the unknowable, and if you don't, then just to say it anyway for cash. That a grant-giving agency would trust a specific and detailed description from a fiction writer seems sweetly naïve—though fiction writers are also allowed to file their own taxes, write their own parents, sign their own checks, raise their own children—so it is a tolerant and generous or at least innocent world here and there.

What writers do is workmanlike: tenacious, skilled labor. That we know. But it is also mysterious. And the mystery involved in the act of creating a narrative is attached to the mysteries of life itself, and the creation of life itself: that we are; that there is *something* rather than *nothing*. Though I wonder whether it sounds preposterous in this day and age to say such a thing. No one who has ever looked back upon a book she or he has written, only to find the thing foreign and alienating, unrecallable, would ever deny its mysteriousness. One can't help but think that in some way this surprise reflects the appalled senility of God herself, or himself, though maybe it's the weirdly paired egotism and humility of artists that leads them over and over again to this creational cliché: that we are God's dream, God's characters; that literary fiction is God's compulsion handed down to us, an echo, a diminishment, but something we are made to do in imitation, perhaps even in honor, of that original creation, and made to do in understanding of what flimsy vapors we all are—though also how heartbreaking and amusing. In more scientific terms, the compulsion to read and write—

and it seems to me it should be, even must be, a compulsion—is a bit of mental wiring the species has selected, over time, in order, as the life span increases, to keep us interested in ourselves.

For it's crucial to keep ourselves, as a species, interested in ourselves. When that goes, we tip into the void, we harden to rock, we blow away and disappear. Art has been given to us to keep us interested and engaged—rather than distracted by materialism or sated with boredom—so that we can attach to this life, a life which might, otherwise, be an unbearable one.

And so, perhaps, it is this compulsion to keep ourselves interested that can make the work seem, well, a little sick (I'm determined, you see, if not to read *sicker* as *richer* then at least to read *sicker* as *okay*). Certainly so much of art originates and locates itself within the margins—that is, the contours—of the human self, as a form of locating and defining that self. And certainly art, and the life of the artist, requires a goodly amount of shamelessness. The route to truth and beauty is a toll road— tricky and unpretty in and of itself.

But are the impulses toward that journey pathological ones?

I took inventory of my own life.

As a child, I had done things that now seem like clues indicating I was headed for a life that was not quite normal—one that was perhaps "artistic." I detached things: the charms from bracelets, the bows from dresses. This was a time—the early sixties, an outpost, really, of the fifties—when little girls' dresses had lots of decorations: badly stitched appliqué, or little plastic berries, lace flowers, satin bows. I liked to remove them and would often then reattach them—on a sleeve or a mitten. I liked to recontextualize even then—one of the symptoms. Other times, I would just collect these little detached things and play with them, keeping them in a wooden bowl in a dresser drawer in my room. If my dresses had been denuded, made homely, it didn't matter to me: I had a supply of lovely gewgaws in a bowl. I had begun a secret life. A secret harvest. I had begun perhaps a kind of literary life—one that would continue to wreak havoc on my wardrobe, but, alas, those are the dues. I had become a magpie, collecting shiny objects. I was a starling in reverse: harboring a nest of eggs gathered from here and there.

When I was a little older, say eleven or twelve, I used to sit on my bed with a sketch pad, listening to the songs on the radio. Each song would last three to four minutes, and during that time, I would draw the song: I would draw the character I imagined was singing the song, and the setting that character was in—usually there were a lot of waves and seagulls, docks and coastlines. I lived in the mountains, away from the ocean, but a babysitter I'd had when I was nine had taught me how to draw lighthouses, so I liked to stick in a lighthouse whenever possible. After one song was over, I'd turn the page and draw the next one, filling notebooks this way. I was obsessed with songs—songs and letters (I had a pen pal in Canada)—and I often think that that is what I tried to find later in literature: the feeling of a song; the friendly, confiding voice of a letter but the cadence and feeling of a song. When a piece of prose hit rhythms older, more familiar and enduring than itself, it seemed then briefly to belong to nature, or at least to the world of music, and that's when it seemed to me "artistic" and good.

I exhibited other signs of a sick life—a strange, elaborate crush on Bill Bixby, a belief in a fairy godmother, also a bit of journalism my brother and I embarked on called *Mad Man Magazine,* which consisted of our writing on notebook paper a lot of articles we'd make up about crazy people, especially crazy people in haunted houses, then tying the pages together with ribbon and selling them to family members for a nickel. But it was a life of the imagination.

When I was older, I suppose there were other signs of sickness. I preferred hearing about parties to actually going to them. I liked to phone the next day and get the news from a friend. I wanted gossip, third-handedness, narrative. My reading was scattered, random, unsystematic. I wasn't one of those nice teenage girls who spent their summers reading all of Jane Austen. My favorite books were *The Great Gatsby* by F. Scott Fitzgerald and *Such Good Friends* by Lois Gould. Later, like so many (of the "afflicted"), I discovered the Brontës. One enters these truly great, truly embarrassing books like a fever dream—in fact, fever dreams figure prominently in them. They are situated in sickness, and unafraid of that. And that's what made them wonderful to me. They were at the center of something messy. But they didn't seem foreign in the least. In fact, very little written by a woman seemed foreign to me. Books by women came as great friends, a relief. They showed up on the front lawn and waved. Books by men one had to walk a distance to get to, take a hike to arrive at, though as readers we girls were all well trained for the hike and we didn't learn to begrudge and resent it until later. A book by a woman, a book that began up close, on the heart's porch, was a treat, an exhilaration, and finally, I think, that is why women who became writers did so: to create more books in the world by women, to give themselves something more to read.

When I first started writing, I often felt sorry for men, especially white men, for it seemed the reasons for their becoming writers were not so readily apparent, or compelling, but had to be searched for, even made excuses for. Though their quote-unquote tradition was so much more celebrated and available, it was also more filled up. It was ablaze. What did a young male writer feel he was adding? As a woman, I never felt that. There seemed to be a few guiding lights (I, of course, liked the more demented ones—Sexton, Plath, McCullers), but that was enough. Admiration and enthusiasm and a sense of scarcity: inspiration without the anxiety of influence.

I feel a little less like that now, in part because I know the main struggle for every writer is with the dance and limitations of language—to honor the texture of it but also to make it unafraid. One must throw all that one is into language, like a Christmas tree hurled into a pool. One must listen and proceed, sentence to sentence, hearing what comes next in one's story—which can be a little maddening. It can be like trying to understand a whisper in a foreign accent: Did she say *Je t'adore* or *Shut the door*?

To make the language sing while it works is a task to one side of gender. How often I've tried to shake from my own storytelling the phrase *And then suddenly,* as if I could wake up a story with the false drama of those three words. It's usually how I know my writing's going badly; I begin every sentence that way: *And then suddenly he went to the store. And then suddenly the store was brick. And then suddenly he had been asleep for eight hours.* The writer marries the language, said Auden, and out of this marriage writing is born. But what if the language feels inadequate, timid, recalcitrant, afraid? I often think of the Albert Goldbarth poem "Alien Tongue," wherein the poet thinks wistfully, adulterously of an imagined language parsed to such a thinness that there is a tense that means "I would have, if I'd been my twin." What an exquisite, precision tool such a tense would be for a writer! Whole rooms could be added to scenes; whole paragraphs to pages; books to books; sequels where at first there were no sequels. . . . But then excessive literary production, George Eliot reminds us, is a social offense. As far as language goes we have to live contentedly, and discontentedly, with our own, making it do what it can and, also, a little of what it can't. And this contradiction brings one back, I suppose, to a makeshift aesthetics of sickness.

Writing is both the excursion into and the excursion out of one's life. That is the queasy paradox of the artistic life. It is the thing that, like love, removes one both painfully and deliciously from the ordinary shape of existence. It joins another queasy paradox: that life is an amazing, hilarious, blessed gift and that it is also intolerable. Even in the luckiest life, for example, one loves someone and then that someone dies. This is not *acceptable*. This is a major design flaw! To say nothing of the world's truly calamitous lives. The imagination is meant outwardly to console us with all that is interesting, not so much to subtract but to add to our lives. It reminds me of a progressive Italian elementary school I read of once in which the classrooms had two dress-up areas with trunks of costumes—just in case, while studying math or plants, a child wanted to be in disguise that day.

But the imagination also forces us inward. It constructs inwardly from what has entered our inwardness. The best art, especially literary art, embraces the very idea of paradox: it sees opposites, antitheses coexisting. It sees the blues and violets in a painting of an orange; it sees the scarlets and the yellows in a bunch of Concord grapes. In narrative, tones share space—often queasily, the ironies quivering. Consider these lines from the Alice Munro story "A Real Life": "Albert's heart had given out—he had only had time to pull to the side of the road and stop the truck. He died in a lovely spot, where black oaks grew in a bottomland, and a sweet, clear creek ran beside the road." Or these lines from a Garrison Keillor monologue: "And so he tasted it, and a look of pleasure came over him, and then he died. Ah, life is good. Life is good." What constitutes tragedy and what constitutes comedy may be a fuzzy matter. The comedienne Joan Rivers has said that there isn't any suffering that's one's own that isn't also potentially very funny. Delmore Schwartz claimed that the only way anyone could understand *Hamlet* was to assume right from the start that all the characters were roaring drunk. I often think of an acquaintance of mine who is also a writer and whom I ran into once in a bookstore. We exchanged hellos, and when I asked her what she was working on these days, she said, "Well, I *was* working on a long comic novel, but then in the middle of the summer my husband had a terrible accident with an electric saw and lost three of his fingers. It left us so sad and shaken that when I returned to writing, my comic novel kept getting droopier and sadder and depressing. So I scrapped it, and started writing a novel about a man who loses three fingers in an accident with a saw, and *that*," she said, "*that's* turning out to be really funny."

A lesson in comedy.

Which leads one also to that paradox, or at least that paradoxical term *autobiographical fiction*. Fiction writers are constantly asked, Is this autobiographical? Book reviewers aren't asked this; and neither are concert violinists, though, in my opinion, there is nothing more autobiographical than a book review or a violin solo. But because literature has always functioned as a means by which to figure out what is happening to us, as well as what we think about it, fiction writers do get asked: "What is the relationship of this story/novel/play to the events of your own life (whatever they may be)?"

I *do* think that the proper relationship of a writer to his or her own life is similar to a cook with a cupboard. What that cook makes from what's in the cupboard is not the same thing as what's in the cupboard—and, of course, everyone understands that. Even in the most autobiographical fiction there is a kind of *paraphrase* going on, which is Katherine Anne Porter's word, and which is a good one for use in connection with her, but also for general use. I personally have never written autobiographically in the sense of using and transcribing events from my life. None—or at least very few—of the things that have happened to my characters have ever happened to me. But one's life is there constantly collecting and providing, and it will creep into one's work regardless—in emotional ways. I often think of a writing student I had once who was blind. He never once wrote about a blind person—never wrote about blindness at all. But he wrote about characters who constantly bumped into things, who tripped, who got bruised; and that seemed to me a true and characteristic transformation of life into art. He wanted to imagine a person other than himself; but his journey toward that person was paradoxically and necessarily through his own life. Like a parent with children, he gave his characters a little of what he knew—but not everything. He nurtured rather than replicated or transcribed.

Autobiography can be a useful tool: it coaxes out the invention— actually, invention and autobiography coax out each other; the pen takes refuge from one in the other, looking for moral dignity and purpose in each, and then flying to the arms of the other. All the energy that goes into the work, the force of imagination and concentration, *is* a kind of autobiographical energy, no matter what one is actually writing about. One has to give to one's work like a lover. One must give of oneself and try not to pick fights. Perhaps it *is* something of a sickness—halfway between "quarantine and operetta" (to steal a phrase from Céline)—to write intensely, closely—not with one's pen at arm's length, but perhaps with one's arm out of the way entirely, one's hand up under one's arm, near the heart, thrashing out like a flipper, one's face hovering close above the page, listening with ear and cheek, lips forming the words. Martha Graham speaks of the Icelandic term *doom eager* to denote that ordeal of isolation, restlessness, caughtness an artist experiences when he or she is sick with an idea.

When a writer is doom eager, the writing won't be sludge on the page; it will give readers—and the writer, of course, is the very first reader—an experience they've never had before, or perhaps a little and at last the words for an experience they have. The writing will disclose a world; it will be that Heideggerian "setting-itself-into-work of the truth of what is." But it will not have lost the detail; detail, on its own, contains the universe. As Flannery O'Connor said, "It's always necessary to remember that the fiction writer is much less *immediately* concerned with grand ideas and bristling emotions than he is with putting list slippers on clerks." One must think of the craft—that impulse to make an object from the materials lying about, as much as of the spiritual longing, the philosophical sweep. "It is impossible to experience one's own death objectively," Woody Allen once said, "and still carry a tune."

Obviously one must keep a certain amount of literary faith, and not be afraid to travel with one's work into margins and jungles and danger zones, and one should also live with someone who can cook and who will both be with one and leave one alone. But there is no formula, to the life or to the work, and all any writer finally knows are the little decisions he or she has been forced to make, given the particular choices. There's no golden recipe. Most things literary are stubborn as colds; they resist all formulas—a chemist's, a wet nurse's, a magician's. There is no formula outside the sick devotion to the work. Perhaps one would be wise when young even to avoid thinking of oneself as a writer—for there's something a little stopped and satisfied, too healthy, in that. Better to think of *writing,* of what one does as an activity, rather than an identity—to write, I write, we write; to keep the calling a verb rather than a noun; to keep working at the thing, at all hours, in all places, so that your life does not become a pose, a pornography of wishing. William Carlos Williams said, "Catch an eyeful, catch an earful, and don't drop what you've caught." He was a doctor. So presumably he knew about *sicker* and *better* and how they are often quite close.

(1994)

Amos Oz

Amos Oz could not have chosen a more poetically suited name: Amos, the first literary Jewish prophet; Oz, land of the Wizard (and Hebrew for "determination"). In its mix of scold and humbug, its marriage of God and godlessness, Oz's name perfectly expresses the paradoxes of his native country. Born in Israel and the son of a Zionist, Oz has often been seen as one of the few strictly Israeli literary voices, rooted and homegrown, a Sabra, and as such he has often been read by his compatriots for whatever ideas of literary nationhood might emerge in his words. A prophet is not without honor even in his own country, if he plays his cards right. But a prophet will nonetheless overhear all those nagging questions around him: What is it that we have made? Who are we, really? What is this guy going to say about us next?

Oz's eleventh novel, *Don't Call It Night,* is full of people drinking iced tea; it turns up every few pages. Set in the desert town of Tel Kedar, the book is a modest one, simply revealing the lives of Theo, a sixty-year-old civil engineer, and his lover, No'a, a schoolteacher, both of them beset by the lassitude of their ordinary compromises and isolation. The desert—"no longer hills but like the notes of a muffled tune"—has parched them. The bloom is off their romance. But Oz's book is interested in the ways these two people fight back a little, mostly via their domestic rituals—the coffees, teas, baths, and suppers—and it reveals a resigned but romantic belief that such rituals not only are full of beauty but perhaps make up all there is of pleasure in life. Certainly in Oz's careful, lyrical prose they possess a loveliness and truthfulness, and may be the book's primary substance. "Anyone who has some good will can find good will everywhere," says an Irish traveler; it becomes one of the novel's refrains.

The plot consists mostly of a collection of circumstances, small standoffs and retreats. It is a story primarily of misorchestrated good intentions. A former student of No'a's has died of a drug overdose, and the boy's father, suspected of being an arms dealer, approaches No'a with the idea for a drug rehabilitation center dedicated to the memory of his son. The father will donate much of the money needed to establish it. No'a, flattered and amazed to be asked to head the center, runs some distance with the project. She organizes a small group of people to help her plan the clinic and its programs, and to raise money. The idea of the clinic becomes an opportunity for the novelist to look at the stresses and petty dramas of the community. Oz has a particular affection for the local eccentrics, and he writes from several points of view. He even eliminates quotation marks, as if to say: This is all one community; there is no important difference between one member and another, between inner life and outer, between voice and description, between people and land; it is all the same.

Nonetheless, the reader will be most interested in the many parts of the story that focus on No'a. She is a terrific character. When we first meet her, her voice is "young and bright, abandoning the ends of her sentences." She wafts "a trail of honeysuckle scent" through the apartment. She has recently been enlivened by the idea of the clinic, though the project has whisked her away from the older Theo, who watches her comings and goings and bursts of enthusiasm with a certain patient skepticism. After all their years together, Theo feels himself still filled with ardor for her, though his condition is perhaps, more accurately, a low-grade longing. She has wandered off from him a little bit (they sleep in separate bedrooms; her kiss has grown "cousinly"), and he spends his time waiting for her to return. When he attempts to help her out (as a city planner he is better connected to the municipal powers that be, especially the mayor of Tel Kadar, and runs interference for No'a, establishing some critical public relations groundwork for the clinic), No'a wanders off from the project, too, seeming to lose focus, as if the whole thing has been spoiled for her by Theo's own interest and participation.

The truth is that she is haunted by news she's received from a young woman named Tali that the dead student was slightly in love with No'a. Also, she is told by Tali, drug use in the community is not widespread or a serious problem. This causes No'a to lose concentration; she suddenly begins spending inordinate time shopping and going to movies with the young woman. Is Tali a daughter substitute, or is No'a's preoccupation with her simply a denial of her own middle age? Perhaps it doesn't matter. "No'a smoke without a fire," says someone of No'a's sudden attention deficit, and we are asked to see this as a vulnerability that she has always had, a dreaminess and restlessness she shares with Theo.

Theo himself is a character one may recognize from Oz's other novels. He perhaps most closely resembles Fima, from the 1993 novel of the same name. Both men share a certain kind of insomnia, drink much coffee and tea, do calisthenics, and love BBC news broadcasts. Both have complicated histories with women, which are filled with flight and impetuousness, yet which they see, in a somewhat blinded way, as essentially decent and generous. Both men are almost completely if gently self-absorbed. Their own gentleness hides them from themselves. They share as well, with their author and with each other, a love of the absurd and overstudied detail, such as this arithmetical bit from *Fima:* "They say that at the beginning of this passion Fima weighed 159 pounds and that in September, in the prison hospital, he weighed less than 132." Or this strange, sly anecdote in *Don't Call It Night:*

> Bozo's wife and baby son were killed in a tragic event here four years ago, when a young love-crossed soldier barricaded himself in the shoe shop, started shooting with a submachine gun and hit nine people. Bozo himself was saved only because he happened to go to the Social Security that morning to appeal against his assessment. To commemorate his wife and child he has donated an ark made of Scandinavian wood to the synagogue, and he is about to give an air conditioner in their memory to the changing room at the soccer field, so that the players can get some air at halftime.

Is God in the details? Certainly God—or God's heedless wit and painterly pen—is in Amos Oz's details. Like many of his novels, *Don't Call It Night*—published in Israel in 1994 and now translated by Nicholas de Lange—concerns itself with the tiny and extraordinary business of daily life in Israel. Such a narrative is invaluable, and in Oz's hands it is also vivid, convincing, and haunting. Yet one imagines that in a country as new and complicated as Israel, a more politically uncertain writer would not write such a tame and domestic book. (Consider the angry, brilliant novels of the South African writer J. M. Coetzee, whose recent narratives are so searching and searing, simultaneously antirevolutionary and antigovernment.) Despite the presence among its characters of a possible arms dealer, despite a reference to "a wide valley full of secret installations," and despite the casual discussion of various Israeli military victories and defeats, *Don't Call It Night* is really a novel about "neglected bougainvillea." It is about being old enough to glimpse at last one's own death, to see the set stage of one's own final years, and to accept it with only the shortest, politest bursts of argument. This novel is a piece of sweet but melancholy chamber music—light but not necessarily insubstantial. It belongs to a genre of restful novel that is ruled by an aesthetic of peace and a yearning for peace. If one is looking for politics, there is that—clearly, if quietly.

(1996)

Christmas for Everyone

Oy. The holidays with our two-year-old boy. Despite our anticeremonialist leanings, it is time to do something commemorative at home. There is, after all, a possibility that, at two, he will remember this as his first "holiday season." Performance anxiety pervades the household. We have to do all the holidays if we do any: Hanukkah for my husband, Kwanzaa for my son, and, of course, Christmas (I think in my Gentile-centric way) for everyone. Our family is an improvisation . . . "Do we have to do Kwanzaa? It's really just an invention," my husband says. "It's artificial."

"Unlike Santa Claus, who is so natural?" I own a book on Kwanzaa. I've opened it, spotted a lot of illustrations of craft items to make at home, then shut it in a sweat. I need more help with this. My husband's holiday indifference now seems like laziness. He hasn't a clue when Hanukkah begins this year. I find myself saying loudly, "Why does the shiksa have to get out the menorah every year? Why does the shiksa always have to light the candles? . . ."

All our two-year-old wants out of the holidays is gum. He spotted some once in the mouth of a babysitter, and since then he has staged his own toddler version of a radio pledge drive. Gum, gum, gum! He studies my mouth for telltale movements . . . If I bite my tongue, or if I have my marital tongue in my cheek, he says hopefully, "Mommy, what's in your mouth? You have gum?"

This year—it's 1996—we get a slightly dehydrated Christmas tree, park it close to the radiator, and decorate it in a crazed, slapdash way. Next morning, all the needles drop. The tree now resembles a giant TV antenna. On Christmas Eve, we build a fire, then snuff it out with an old wet towel, realizing, fearfully, that we haven't cleaned the flue in five years. Then the boiler breaks down. We plug in the space heaters. We order takeout Chinese.

Only then, when almost all is lost and I am feeling so unexpectedly sad, do I realize what a sucker I am for the beautiful fake Christmas that German-American commerce concocted for us years ago. I actually like the shopping, the gift wrap, the carols . . . I like the invented holiday miracles, the unexpected kindnesses and transformations—at least as they are portrayed on the TV specials. And, looking out the window and seeing only sleet, I realize that I even like the snow. Where, now, is that lovely perfect Christmas? On whose open fire are those goddamn chestnuts roasting? I have a fiction writer's weakness for fiction. It's an occupational hazard.

"Well," I say, serving sliced water chestnuts instead. Can I serve up some cheer as well? "Merry Christmas, you guys! Merry, merry Christmas!"

Our two-year-old is watching my lips and jaw. His eyebrows lift, and his eyes grow knowing and bright. "Mommy?" he says. "You have gum?"

(1997)

Starr–Clinton–Lewinsky

Oh, the autoimmune disorder that is the Starr–Clinton–Lewinsky matter. Inadequate foes—or somehow unimpressive ones—have our government geared up and attacking itself. We are paralyzed—and thrilled in that sickened sort of way. Terrorists can't bomb the scandal away; planes and stock markets can't crash it away; JonBenét Ramsey and Neil LaBute can't frighten it away. As was said in Chicago in 1968, "The whole world is watching"—while we collapse into our wheelchair (parked in front of CNN) and have our nervous breakdown.

Full disclosure: I find Linda Tripp's moral position intriguing and literary. I believe Paula Jones was degraded by her boss, probably illegally so. And I did not vote for Bill Clinton. (Though now I feel sorry for him, in the same way I felt sorry for Pee-wee Herman when he was arrested in that Florida movie theater.) I voted in various primaries and elections for Jesse Jackson, Jerry Brown, and Ralph Nader. Clinton, in office, has been dismaying in predictable ways: his centrist judiciary appointments, his botched national health plan, his gays-in-the-military debacle, his generally compromised or meretricious or dithering policy-making. I have mostly thought that he was a charming shark, a user, a yuppie, a bad actor, and a sexy, lying fool. This he has in common with many people (perhaps even poor Pee-wee Herman).

Still, at no point in his life did Bill Clinton ever say, "I am not a sex addict." Those who voted for him knew something of his unfortunate and compulsive personal life and decided they didn't care. Now, suddenly, voters care? (I don't think so.) Now, suddenly, Congress is shocked? Where are the true and the brave? Now, suddenly, congressional Democrats (and the First Lady herself) are feigning sad or angry surprise in order to effect a kind of independence from this guy and keep their pathetically unproductive jobs. Is the paycheck really *that* good?

Surely there are many reasons that the Lewinsky affair has taken over our national conversation.

(1) The political emptiness of the Clinton White House. Both nature and political theater abhor a vacuum: caught in a kind of Beckettian holding pattern, the Clinton presidency got overtaken by a sex comedy more popular with the summer-stock crowd.

(2) The fudged look of the Clinton marriage. We gaze upon the First Family the way children would—imagining we are part of it, always feeling on behalf of Chelsea and wondering what the heck Mom and Dad are up to. Yet Bill and Hillary's weird unhappiness repels us. Weird unhappiness is never as attractive as weird fun. And what is even more interesting is weird fun paid for with union support, cabinet trust, grand-jury testimony, public humiliation, and impeachment talk.

(3) Finally, there is the strange, not-to-be-thwarted character of Ken Starr, future *Time* Man of the Year. (And where is the stuff about the land deal, Mr. Starr?) That our ungentlemanly president's gentlemanly failure to kiss and tell should be subjected to the legalisms of judiciary procedure is, of course, total madness, a torture and a regicide, which could only have been brought about by Starr, the crazed zealot the right wing didn't even know it had. He is, of course, Victor Hugo's Javert. But he has not pursued Jean Valjean. In fact, in a bit of publicly funded intertextual surrealism (and downsized literary ambition), he has leaped completely out of the book and pursued Terry Southern's Candy.

For this we pay taxes. Dear God, bring back the NEA.

(1998)

Ann Beattie's *New and Selected Stories*

There is always something a little nervous-making about a book of "new and selected" work. There is a whiff of the memorial about it, a funereal taking of stock, maybe an anxious seeking of a new audience, which can signal a slowing of forward movement in the oeuvre. There is always some new work, but it is never the point: the new work has somehow wandered in, arrived unbidden. It is unselected, like neighbors crashing a family reunion.

Yet there is a kind of magnificence to Ann Beattie's *Park City: New and Selected Stories.* The collection comprises three dozen stories written over a twenty-five-year period, and in reading them, one after another, one feels amazed at the confidence, steadiness, and quality of the output. Certainly such a book will highlight its author's habits and predilections, and that is part of the fun and education of it for any reader. But *Park City* is also a book that should win the admiration of short-story writers and readers everywhere for its pointed reminder of Beattie's unshakably intelligent, deep-hearted, long, and unsurpassed devotion to the genre.

Ann Beattie's first collection, *Distortions,* was published in 1976, and she quickly came to seem an avatar of that particular time—its historical aftermath and drift, its growing affluence and friendly, generational narcissism. Now, of course, she is writing at a time that seems to have no avatars and, the end of the millennium notwithstanding, may not even be a particular time, so it is interesting to see the ways in which her work has both changed and not changed through the decades.

Distortions is represented here by four stories, all tales of marriage and divorce. In "Vermont," a couple play host to the wife's ex-husband, who brings with him not only some low-grade confusion but a very young new girlfriend. Everyone is nice. Everyone behaves. And the new girlfriend, appropriately enough, wonders aloud whether "every time we sleep we die; we come back another person, to another life." In "Dwarf House," Tammy Wynette sings "D-I-V-O-R-C-E" on a jukebox while a married man has a beer with his secretary. "Are you happy?" the story begins with him saying. "Because if you're happy I'll leave you alone." In "Wolf Dreams," a young woman on the eve of her third marriage becomes so agitated she writes an angry letter to the president. "She begins to think that it's Nixon's fault—all of it. Whatever that means." In "Snakes' Shoes," as in "Vermont," a remarried woman, here named Alice, is visited by her ex, with whom she has a daughter. The reason for the divorce, as stated by Alice at the time, reflects Beattie's own penchant for the uninflected event: "He acts like a madman with that boat. He's swamped her three times this year. I've been seeing someone else." At the end of the story, the former family takes an evening walk, just the three of them, and Alice, insisting on her turn in a game, says, "Don't forget me," and her ex-husband kisses her on the neck.

Here in "Distortions" we see the themes of almost all of Beattie's stories to come: sexual infidelity as plot point, divorce as cultural landscape, the comic desire for the personal somehow to be political, and the civilized management of the past by means of a creative mix of remembering and forgetting. From these very first stories straight through to the new ones in the book's "Park City" section, Beattie's recoupled couples are afflicted with a nagging fear of erasure. ("She thought for a moment about people who had disappeared: Judge Crater; Amelia Earhart; Mrs. Ramsay." Or: "He had wanted her to know that he had been there, a real person, someone she needed to factor into the landscape.") Because their world is white, educated, upper-middle-class, and pharmaceutically calm—no one ever struggles convincingly at a job; inheritances are referred to in many of the stories—the thing that jeopardizes their safety most, the precipitating event for any possible story, is the prospect and actuality of uncoupling. Alice's "Don't forget me," which in "Snakes' Shoes" is uttered as a simple, now-it's-my-turn request, is made, by Beattie's subtle art, into a pained and plaintive cry.

It is a cry that, along with the lyrics of Bob Dylan, echoes across the decades of Beattie's work. Everywhere her characters—parents and children—have been confronted with their own insignificance, not through any cosmic perspective but simply through the rude spiritual lens of broken marriage. For the reader, it must be added, these are highly literary breakups. Beattie isn't interested in any real anatomy of divorce. The usual stresses on relationships—issues of money, work, energy, and time—are not examined here. Divorce is effected swiftly—largely through mysterious, almost poetic acts of ego and infidelity. In Beattie's fictional world divorce is emotional crisis made narrative tool, the monster in the tale; the trick for her characters is somehow to defang it, live with it in a comic fashion, which they do, if bittersweetly. They have good, merry friends—Beattie's work is a tireless valentine to friendship—which helps.

It was in the 1970s, when Beattie began writing and publishing, that divorce first became epidemic, and, in insistently fashioning narratives around that social fact, Beattie, more than any other American writer, registered the event. She did so by assuming it—its newfound ordinariness, its sad but essentially untragic nature, its ability to redefine in curious ways the shape and composition of families. One can hear even in the titles of her subsequent collections—*Secrets and Surprises, The Burning House, Where You'll Find Me,* and *What Was Mine*—the songs and sighs of quiet and unavoidable domestic rupture.

One says unavoidable rather than inevitable, for the action of these stories does not build from or lead to a particular destination. A boulder—usually a treacherously held secret involving a supplementary lover—is rolled out onto the road, and the narrative, as Beattie constructs it, may either stay where it is or proceed and crash. As a result, there is much wheel spinning, or water treading, in an Ann Beattie story, and the present tense, especially in the early collections, is often relied upon to convey that sense of trapped and suspended animation. Such a strategy may be less effective in a novel, such as Beattie's own *Chilly Scenes of Winter,* where it can produce feelings of panic in a reader caught out on that glassy, shoreless narrative sea. But it is an effective device in Beattie's short stories, where it serves as a kind of flypaper. It catches the casual thoughts and material detail that define people, places, and times and does so without frustrating a reader's desire for completion, for aesthetic arrival of some sort.

Nowhere are Beattie's closings more beautiful than in the seven stories included from *The Burning House,* the collection most fully represented in *Park City.* "What will happen can't be stopped. Aim for grace," concludes "Learning to Fall." All of what Beattie does well is here on brilliant display: the theatrical ensemble act of her characters; the cultural paraphernalia as historical record; the not-quite-grown-up grown-ups, playing house; the charming, boyish men with their knife-like utterances. In "The Cinderella Waltz," a man who eventually leaves his wife and daughter for a gay relationship mocks his own domestic life by sifting through the Christmas presents for an oversize toaster, crooning, "Come out, my eight-slice beauty!" In "The Burning House," when a wife says to her unfaithful husband, "I want to know if you're staying or going," he gives her a speech:

> "Everything you've done is commendable. . . . But your whole life you've made one mistake—you've surrounded yourself with men. . . . Men think they're Spider-Man and Buck Rogers and Superman. You know what we all feel inside that you don't feel? That we're going to the stars. . . . I'm looking down on all of this from space," he whispers. "I'm already gone."

Beattie's gift for trenchant dialogue is surely the rival of some of our foremost living playwrights (one thinks especially of Terrence McNally and Wendy Wasserstein). Though much is usually made of Beattie's eye—she has written a monograph on the work of the painter Alex Katz, which adds to the public sense of her as a "visual" writer—it is Beattie's ear that gives her stories their sharp life, muscle, and surprise. The words and voices of her characters are the very fabric and organization of her work, and they give great pleasure, especially those of the antic, half-heartbroken boy-man she often puts center stage. Whether he is named Jake, Nick, Frank, Freddy, or Milo, he is invariably the spirit and force of a story that might otherwise remain inert. Beattie's boy-man is like Alex Katz's Ada (Katz's wife and frequent subject):

someone whose soulfulness cannot successfully be submerged into the flat illustration that would otherwise be his—and the canvas's—fate. Beattie's forgiving affection for her charming, neurotic men animates her work and suggests a largeness of authorial sympathy. Whether they are having their bee stings tended to, or dashing down the beach saying "Catch me," or having their MOM tattoos at long last removed, these exasperating love objects are the unexpected intelligence of every story they are in. They are the thinking woman's Punch to Beattie's Judys—women narrators and protagonists who, in some purgatorial condition, are apt to be custodians of the story rather than actual actors within it.

In the collections after *The Burning House* one can feel Beattie experimenting—in shape, pace, and subject—especially in *What Was Mine,* where she accomplishes a European setting, a metafiction, two narrations by men, and a moving novella, "Windy Day at the Reservoir." The wonderful title story of her newest collection, "Park City," shows off, too, not only old strengths but newer ones: a gift for the riotously comic set piece, plus a willingness to let central female characters struggle more against their own poses of vacancy and passivity (strengths evidenced also in Beattie's underrated recent novels, *Another You* and *My Life, Starring Dara Falcon*). In "Park City," a young woman, collecting other people's secrets and preparing to act on them, looks after her sister's boyfriend's fourteen-year-old daughter, Lyric, while the sister attends a screenwriting conference. Lounging at the hotel pool, Lyric is the voice of bored clear-sightedness, an adolescent-girl version of a Beattie man, given to such pronouncements about Utah as "It's against their religious beliefs to drink, but at the same time, they think stuff that people with the D.T.'s think."

This is what Beattie knows best: that when you put people in a room together they will always be funny. A typical Beattie story has as its controlling consciousness a muted, slightly shell-shocked young woman in company more lively than she; her sensibility, however, though one part bruised romantic, is three parts recording equipment. She is getting it all down.

In the hands of another writer this could make a story chilly and unnatural. A sparseness of prose style that in other writers can glibly falsify and flatten human nature Beattie has always used to complicated effect. No other writer manages such warmth and coolness simultaneously. In her work there are no loud noises or bright colors; there is little overt grief, rage, gloom, or giddiness. Hers is a palette of compassionately wielded pastels, and her stories are watercolors of the highest order. Do her characters sometimes seem similar from story to story? The same can be said of every short-story writer who ever lived. Does the imaginative range seem limited? It is the same limited range Americans are so fond of calling Chekhovian. Is every new story here one for the ages?

With a book this generous from a writer this gifted, we would be vulgar to ask.

(1998)

JonBenét Ramsey by Lawrence Schiller

There is something about the killing of a pretty little rich girl that disorganizes everybody. In the murder case of JonBenét Ramsey, first it was the Ramsey family, clumsily staging the ransom note and 911 call. Then it was the Boulder, Colorado, police, failing to secure the crime scene. Then there was the Boulder County District Attorney's office, inexplicably dithering and stalled. And now look: here comes the journalist Lawrence Schiller and his dizzyingly unnecessary *Perfect Murder, Perfect Town*. Typos, repetitions, contradictions, no intellectual gloss, no philosophical moment, no index, no pictures. What the heck kind of book is this?

Essentially, it is a hastily assembled scrapbook of textual material that millions of amateur JonBenét sleuths have already read in the tabloids (and discussed on the Internet). It is a review session and souvenir for forensic trivia buffs. In putting together six hundred pages of largely undigested material, Schiller has, in his own words, attempted to "create the most accurate record available for others." But all this serves as a reminder of what we have come to admire in other writing on various high-profile crimes: intelligent storytelling. Postmodern fiction aside, an exhaustive pasting together of notes, clippings, and recorded statements does not a narrative make, and it is only in narrative (with its elements of setting, theme, point of view, character; all the authorial work of stance and selection) that we feel close to the importance and truth of something. A complete and accurate record can obscure a subject's essence: a narrative, on the other hand, reveals, supports, and contains it. The rush to judgment that Schiller is so critical of in others (90 percent of the American public is familiar with the case) is simply a rush to narrative—narrative that the Ramseys, the prosecutors, and now Schiller himself have failed publicly or effectively to provide (though the Ramseys, it should be said, did try).

In *Mrs. Harris: The Death of the Scarsdale Diet Doctor,* Diana Trilling was able to see a story worthy of the Great American Novel, a story as rich as *The Great Gatsby* in passion and social implication. And she did not jealously guard her opinions; she criticized even the cruel amount of grapefruit in the doctor's famous diet. In *The Journalist and the Murderer,* Janet Malcolm made of the Jeffrey MacDonald case a brilliant and culturally provocative discussion of trust and deception. Even Jonathan Harr, whose raw materials were corporate crime and tedious legal maneuvers, created in *A Civil Action* a gripping human drama—something he would never have accomplished if he had set about merely to amass an accurate and nonjudgmental (read "indiscriminate") record.

But perhaps the Ramsey case is a particularly unworkable vortex. It is replete with the ingredients of a grotesque joke or a gothic mystery. (The former Little Miss Christmas was found, December 26, 1996, bludgeoned and garroted in the "grotto" of her own house, a red heart painted on her hand.) But though a joke and a mystery are both composed of incongruities, a joke's incongruities quickly release you; a mystery's do not. A mystery, unsolved, may not release you at all but pull you forever and maniacally into the black hole of its contradictions. This would explain the astonishing number of JonBenét websites and chat rooms, the amount of general conjecture. One falls into the grip of it.

Since Schiller refuses to participate in the barest hypothesizing, it is left to us—average readers, gentle citizens—to step into the breach. What can be said with some certainty is that at the mystery's heart is Patsy Ramsey, naïve, ambitious, and theatrically ungifted. When Meryl Streep says, "A dingo took my baby" (a dingo?), we believe her. But there is little that Patsy Ramsey has uttered or declaimed that convinces anyone of anything. Even at the beauty pageants in which she placed

JonBenét, her faulty aesthetic judgment was remarked. She "overdid it," noted an observer, once sexily dressing her daughter completely in feathers, causing even that audience to gasp in disapproval. Patsy's is a story of disoriented, miscalculating vanity. Her compulsion to display led not only to giant parties with Christmas trees in every room, the bedroom closets open for perusal, but to the cosmetic alteration and exhibition of her little girl before a surely unsafe pageant world. A beauty queen herself and journalism major, Patsy Ramsey stoked her interest in media and show business, even when mourning her child. With the help of a press representative, and an unwitting congregation, she choreographed an on-camera family departure from her own church. She phoned Larry King on the air. In response to the death of the People's Princess, Diana, she feverishly declared her own daughter America's People's Princess.

Did she kill her daughter in some petty rage? Did she kill her by accident? Did she catch her husband molesting the girl? Or—most spookily—did she kill her as a religious offering she felt was required of her, a bound sacrifice to God (pursuant to Psalm 118, to which the Ramsey Bible was perpetually opened), because she had been miraculously cured of Stage IV ovarian cancer? It all seems doubtful. She had never been someone given to parental anger or violence. Her grief, if not her words, seems authentic. Whatever her mistakes, her reckless endangerment of her own children, they are a far cry from murder.

Schiller points out (or, rather, repeats) that no one theory—intruder, father, mother, brother—accounts for all the evidence. But if one combines the theories, as in Agatha Christie's *Murder on the Orient Express,* where all the suspects are finally guilty, one can work out a fairly satisfying hypothesis. That is, a known intruder, working in friendly conjunction with the brother, killed the girl in some sort of sadistic fun, and the parents—fresh from Ron Howard's *Ransom* and remembering the play their neighbor had written in which a little girl was found murdered in her basement—were left to cover up. This explains the stun gun, the sexual staging, the parental alliance, the odd affect of the boy (with whom the little girl often slept), and other evidence, including the boy's red pocketknife, fingerprints, pineapple, duct tape, and an enhanced 911 call. It also explains the counterfeit ransom note, which is the centerpiece of the case against the Ramseys. The note is mystifyingly fake, with its diction and point-of-view problem ("we are a group of individuals that represent a small foreign faction"), its Ramsey family pride ("We respect your bussiness [*sic*] but not the country that it serves"), and its screenwriter's poetry ("if we catch you talking to a stray dog she dies"). The note rambles and searches for the kidnapping mot juste (there is a cross-out and a false start) and, with its length and inconsistent spellings, is such a compositional fraud and tactical blunder that it caused some detectives to believe it was the work of a professional trying to look like an amateur.

Sadly, it is more likely, more simply, the work of an amateur trying to look like a professional (the work of someone who would give her daughter her husband's name with a phony *accent aigu*). Rather tellingly, only the Ramseys seemed unalert to the note's goofiness. Patsy "overdid it" again. And yet, in this hypothesis, she emerges criminally heroic, if fantastically overconfident. She leads the nation on a two-year "low-speed White Bronco chase," in the words of Denver talk-show host Peter Boyles. She had—according to an acquaintance—no "sense of proportion." But she had phenomenal energy, arrogance, and nerve when it came to hanging on to her family.

This is a case rich with the story of catastrophic narcissism. It is about trying to be fabulous, Miss West Virginia style. It is about being community outsiders, if in our mobile society one can still speak of such a thing; but the Ramsey case does speak of it. The story is also about marital suffering and the neurotic cathecting of one's children. It is the story of that clubfooted masquerade that is the Happy Housewife— a masquerade enacted, sometimes, to the point of madness. It is also the story of carnivorous media coverage and the mutual manipulation of law enforcement, reporters, and suspects. It is a story, too, about the professional pride and frustrations of the Boulder police (who cannot afford to live in affluent Boulder), frustrations that were inflamed and complicated by the Ramsey case, culminating in the angry resignation of two police detectives. Finally, it is—quite possibly—the story of the sinister fantasy lives of alienated rich boys with golf clubs and computers.

We get almost none of these stories in this book, though probably it is too soon for such storytelling. (If one learns anything new from *Perfect Murder, Perfect Town,* it is how few people have alibis on

Christmas night, but how useful ATM machines are for this purpose.) Still, one wishes that Schiller's book weren't so exasperatingly like the Ramsey ransom note itself: brazenly put forward, chaotically improvised, and ventriloquized to an eerie kind of voicelessness—as if it were written by no one at all.

(1999)

Joyce Carol Oates's *Broke Heart Blues*

Our hungry manufacture and easy bestowal of fame (with its twin illusions of accessibility and inaccessibility) is a kind of communion: it brings the gods close and makes them edible. In the words of my four-year-old son, "Stars are farther than outer space. They are farther than South America. They are in Russia"—a remark that, despite the decrescendo and uncertainty of its geography, rather effectively expresses the idea that glamour and mystery are so elusive, quick, arbitrary, and surprising as to be found residing nearer by than one might think. (Although nearer by may also turn out to be far.)

No one knows this better than the American novelist. From Henry James to Scott Fitzgerald to Joyce Carol Oates, the dramatic effect of the (often newly) glamorous boy or girl next door upon the lives of ordinary citizens in proximity—and vice versa—is a story American writers have returned to repeatedly, pilgrims to a shrine-like trough. Such a story may be one of demise (*The Great Gatsby* or Oates's *Black Water*) or of semi-demise (*The Portrait of a Lady*), or it may have a menacing beam of satire relighting its events, as in Oates's astonishing new novel, *Broke Heart Blues*. In such a novel the extraordinary and the ordinary exchange fates, trade secrets, and—in Oates—locker combinations; the fevered, hierarchical world of adolescence (*Foxfire, You Must Remember This, Because It Is Bitter and Because It Is My Heart*, as well as her most famous short story, "Where Are You Going, Where Have You Been?") is Oates's great muse.

. . .

Broke Heart Blues is about the machinery of celebrity, local and otherwise, especially the local celebrity-making machine that is the American high school. (Every star needs a trapped and intoxicant-inclined audience.) Within that setting it is the story of a teenager named John Reddy Heart, who as a boy moves to the affluent Buffalo, New York, suburb of "Willowsville" with his sister, brother, grandfather, and mother, Dahlia, a Las Vegas blackjack worker, who has somehow—dare the neighbors ask?—inherited a mansion from a Colonel Edgihoffer, a local widower–turned–deceased gambler. It is the 1960s—in Willowsville, an outpost of the 1950s—and the Hearts arrive to this tartan plaid town of Pendleton and Jonathan Logan stores like characters from a David Lynch film, figures of demented glamour, misfittedness, and sex. A platinum blonde along the lines of Lana Turner, Dahlia Heart (dubbed "the White Dahlia") dresses only in white, wears sunglasses even at dusk, and is the object of salacious rumor and speculation. In less than three years she brings about a Lana Turner–type scandal as well: her son is arrested and tried for the shooting death of a prominent local businessman and brute named Melvin Riggs, who was also Dahlia's (married) lover. Her son's defense is that he was protecting his mother from Riggs's murderous fists.

At this point, if not before, the handsome John Reddy Heart becomes a high school pop hero and psychosexual mascot. He is both local and national news, and a rock band called Made in USA records a hit called "The Ballad of John Reddy Heart," which solidifies and commodifies his allure (Oates uses excerpts of this "song" for the epigraphs of her chapters). Briefly on the lam, John Reddy becomes a Christ figure, arrested in "Nazarene," New York. He is prayed for, written about, and otherwise mythologized and marketed. When acquitted by a jury not really of his peers (he is not only a village outsider but a minor tried as an adult), he finishes high school while living above a Chinese restaurant downtown. He is kind, and sexy; moreover, he can, it appears, make the lame walk (a classmate is cured of her multiple sclerosis sometime after a sweet encounter with him).

High school boys, in a condition of idol worship and study, admiringly remark his indifference to their company, his unique aroma, his idiosyncratic mystique, as well as his rust-flecked Mercury. Willowsville's high school girls, mooning over him, lose their virginity in his name. Fetching a Coke can from the trash, snatching it "from oblivion," they incant and hyperventilate: "His mouth. His actual mouth! . . . *John Reddy Heart's actual mouth touched this.*" Their erotic fantasies of group lovemaking with him, in the course of the novel, may or may not have come true; in Oates's surreal and wittily overheated narrative, fantasy for these high schoolers is reality. The narrative is too busy to split hairs.

Indeed, it is the narrative strategy of *Broke Heart Blues* that makes it such a stunning and unusual book. While its short middle section is, more or less, a conventionally constructed interlude from the point of view of the adult John Reddy Heart, now a "Mr. Fix-It" for rich or sexy widows with home repair needs, the main sections, which begin and end the book, are written in a kind of choral first person—multiple and overlapping soliloquies that periodically melt and give way to the more predominant first-person plural. It is a societal narrative, even if that society is only (only!) a high school. ("After high school in America, everything's posthumous," the novel winkingly insists.) The narrative is also deeply musical, rhythmic, and hallucinatory in its effects—what novel about high school could not be?

Yet it is difficult to think of any novel remotely like *Broke Heart Blues.* Oates's publisher claims that it is written in the "same tradition as" Oates's own *We Were the Mulvaneys,* but the narrative in the latter is more controlled, more reliably and conventionally written in the first person. Joan Chase's *During the Reign of the Queen of Persia* (1983) comes to mind, since it is told entirely in the first-person plural, but Oates's narrative is very different. In its circularity (its staggering and blending of voices that retell the same tale) it resembles a round. In its elaborately constructed community voice it resembles a chorus, though much more than a Greek chorus.

> Frankly, it's bullshit that John Reddy ever uttered the words *This will be the day I died.* Anyone who knew John knew he was an individual of few words, never anything fancy. Where the rest of us chattered and goofed off continuously like monkeys in a monkey house, John Reddy had dignity.

Here the chorus does not come in and comment on the action or advise the protagonist. It *is* the action, it is the only voice that counts, and it pours forth like liquid (absent are the tidy, well-muscled paragraphs of Oates's essays and more conventional fiction) even as it mutates, reexamines, and repeats the same information, with a kind of ecstatic, combing effect. In its suspense and tone, it is as urgent and pulsing as the dramatic choral finale from *Carmina Burana* but with some doo-wop thrown in for street wisdom and bounce.

It is a technique that conjures, then consumes, surrounding and exalting its subject, its hero—John Reddy Heart—at the same time that any real portrait of him is made impossible. That is its point. Certain kinds of adoration obscure. A high school's local fame-making apparatus (the invented celebrity fueled by both religious and erotic energies, as Oates depicts it, not a completely benign hysteria) is ultimately fearful and repulsed. It devours the human in favor of a ghostly god; Oates's community choir prefers a creation of its own great choral mind to anything actual. John Reddy Heart is seized and embraced by both town and media—but seized and embraced as a dark idea, a magical object, a powerful toy, and so he is also eventually set aside. Oates's narrative purposefully imitates the photograph a classmate tries to take of John Reddy Heart driving through town—a "blurred movement along a familiar roadway . . . like background in a picture in which the foreground, the actual subject, is missing."

The "subject" is missing, too, because for all its raucous amusements—myriad miniature set pieces involving people who cannot outgrow or get over John Reddy Heart—*Broke Heart Blues* is a story about economic segregation and social class in America. This becomes most explicit in the book's final, chapterless section, entitled "Thirtieth Reunion," which brings us forward to the nineties: John Reddy Heart's Willowsville High School class has reassembled to take inventory of one another's accomplishments and get back in touch with their inner teenagers.

It was a delirious time. It was a profound time. A time to celebrate, and to cast one's thoughts within: "It's, like, in my deepest heart, you're all *me*." A time for hilarity and a time for gratitude. A fun time—but also a tragic time. A time none of us is likely to forget.

And, historically, once-in-a-lifetime: our thirtieth WHS class reunion.

"Who'll be missing this time, d'you think?"

"Missing, or dead?"

"Dead *is* missing."

So Oates archly begins, in mock-Dickensian fashion, the account of "a record *eighty-seven* of us out of a graduating class of *one hundred thirty-four*" converging on "the first weekend in July upon the Village of Willowsville. By plane, by car, practically by foot we came." Perhaps the prose style urged her on, kept her mindful of Dickens's purposes as a class portraitist, but Oates's satirical impulses here no longer cast about gently. *Class* is a kind of pun, even if *reunion* is not. And what Oates gives us is an appalling collection of affluent children grown up to take their place in the established American order. The birds that have winged their way back to the pampering nest are Willowsville's "high-profile achievers"—a computer software magnate, a renowned criminologist and adviser to the attorney general, a movie star, a college president, a famous writer, an accomplished poet, a political cartoonist for *The Washington Post*, et cetera.

The girls by and large have returned as "brave-smiling streaked-blond women with sinewy golfers' legs and flaccid upper arms, necks that would require artful arrangements of scarves in another few years." The boys return, perhaps, with an "earnest smooth flushed bulb of a head, oyster-pouchy eyes, maroon sport coat and white fishnet pull-over." They are *"faces like lost souls that're your own soul—y'know?"* Oates has fun with them all, especially with the poet Richard Eickhorn, author of "Happiness: An Elegy" ("We clapped for Ritchie, we were proud of Ritchie—America needs poets!"), and the novelist Evangeline Fesnacht, author of *Death Chronicles* and winner of a National Book Award, every one of her books *"in trade paperback for Christ's sake."*

Even at the party, distinction is sought and awards are given (for best-preserved hair, best-preserved figure), the most controversial award being for "the individual who'd made shrewdest use of the bankruptcy law since the last reunion." Only one person complains of noninclusion and faulty directions to the pig roast: "It's exactly as outsiders used to say of Willowsville—it's a closed, private community! A community of privilege!" The rest involve themselves in an incessant cataloging of accomplishment, heartlessly vague about the difficult lives of the less fortunate. Says the reunion's cochair, still speaking in the voice of her girlhood, "I'm a co-chair of this weekend and damned if I'm going to let anything spoil it. *This is our thirtieth, guys!*"

Their revels collapse a redwood deck, shortly after midnight, and there is, briefly, hope for some true injury. Probably there will only be divorce.

Mack Pifer had long considered himself a "tough player" in the competitive world of high-stakes medical insurance, and he and Millie had endured the protracted adolescences of three typically American children, but his nerves were close to shattered by this party. "Even if the deck hadn't collapsed, it's likely the Pifers were going to separate soon. The way Millie was dancing with some of the guys—she'd never have behaved that way back in high school. It wasn't just she'd been drinking, our Millie was *hot*."

At four in the morning a half-dozen pizzas are delivered "by a wide-eyed black kid in a Cornell T-shirt who ventured with comical caution into our midst like Odysseus descending into the Land of the Dead." Does John Reddy Heart make it to the reunion? The novel refuses to say exactly. What the reader does know is that he is there in invocated spirit: all of Willowsville has dined out on his memory, made a kind of pornography of him, even its distinguished writers—perhaps especially its distinguished writers. His classmates have made pilgrimages to his old house and haunts—even to his old parking spaces. They have indulged in group shudders and mournful sighs. But if he has in fact returned—*look out, old Mackie is back*—no one succeeds in recognizing him (ah, allegory), and he goes away. Later, there is the sound of an unanswered knock, a motorcycle roaring off, and only then some despairing female cries. More prosaically, there is a middle-aged man in a red bathing suit, sitting at pool's edge, whom no one can identify and whom no one likes.

Broke Heart Blues, in its cataloging of the cultural paraphernalia of an era, has a touch of John Updike (the Updike of the Rabbit novels), and in fact Oates has dedicated her book to him. With its infernal dreaminess and contradictory tones there is also a touch of Bertolt Brecht. Certainly there is more than a bit of Brecht in the novel's final call to the people who did not come to the reunion—inconsequential kids, invisible kids, rougher kids with rougher lives—and the ending's theatrical cry of "we miss you, we're thinking of you, we want to see you again, *we love you*" breaks one's heart with its boisterous, American-style insincerity. The close is Oates at her blazing best, and one may finish this richly witty and despairing book and recall the loveliest of the Maxwell Anderson–Kurt Weill lyrics that ponder God's abandonment of man: "And we're lost out here in the stars . . ." Joyce Carol Oates has set the cosmos in Buffalo and written its school song.

(1999)

Dawn Powell

Letters, the writing writers are writing when they should be writing, have a few, but only a few, of the satisfactions of art. Salvos, rescue flares, confections, or curtsies, primarily they are greetings from a kind of literary R & R—art's sweet hooky. Though not exactly conversation, they hold the amusements and consolations of talk. Typically they announce a writer's relations with the world beyond her work and her desire to organize, nurture, and be (if only verbally) in that world. Invariably they are a function of friendship. Prompted and flavored by the specifics of an occasion or of its chosen audience of one, a letter brings to its writer what a novel (or journal or diary) cannot: the idea of an immediate, intimate reader other than oneself. Ah, a social life. Letters may be masks, shields, pieces of ventriloquism, or theatrical assemblages of some other sort, but they are in service to a real-life relationship rather than an imaginary one. The writer assumes a voice and point of view for the consumption of a specific (though passive) person: a project now largely taken over by email and psychotherapy. In these soliloquies a life is both revealed and concealed.

The American novelist Dawn Powell, in her day dubbed a "lady wit" by those on red alert for the freakish, lived her entire adult life in the heart of Greenwich Village. She wrote hundreds, maybe thousands, of letters. ("There is this about letter-writing," she says in an early one.

"One can gas on ad infinitum about the eternal ego without receiving any personal violence in return or any interruption. Thus is it superior to conversation.") According to Tim Page, a former music critic for *The Washington Post,* now an undeterrable Powellian and editor of *Selected Letters of Dawn Powell,* much of Powell's correspondence has been lost or destroyed, and many letters probably tossed out. "One cannot escape the horrific vision of a line of plastic garbage bags, with some precious and incongruous literary cargo buried amid the debris, waiting to be taken to the dump," he writes in his introduction. "It is the stuff of nightmares."

Page's devotion is a moving thing. Though he never met Dawn Powell, he is, without academic affiliation or other sponsorship, her ultimate scholar, biographer, fan: many of her letters are from Page's personal collection, just as many of the photographs in his 1998 biography of her are his own property as well, and he has written warm and perceptive introductions to new editions of her books. Tim Page is the kind of reader Powell never knew she could or would have. Even during her own lifetime, her struggling though productive career seems to have been in constant semirevival. Novels fell quickly out of print; reviews of her new ones often wondered why no one read her more. Perhaps it was because of her name, one British reviewer suggested, which made one think of a romance writer instead of the brilliant satirist she was. (Powell herself thought her name sounded like that of an "unsuccessful stripper.") Although Edmund Wilson and Gore Vidal eventually wrote long appreciations of her work, it is Page's diligent resuscitation and guardianship that have been by far the most successful, and tireless. When they meet in literary heaven, surely Powell will buy all his drinks—and not let go of his hand.

She will also introduce him to everyone, for Powell, born in 1896, the same year as Scott Fitzgerald, seems to have known everyone: Ernest Hemingway, John Dos Passos, Edmund Wilson, Sara and Gerald Murphy, E. E. Cummings, Maxwell Perkins, Malcolm Cowley, J. B. Priestley, Dorothy Parker, Libby Holman, Jean Stafford, A. J. Liebling, Franz Kline. To name some. On her only trip to Europe, which was to Paris in 1950, she met Jean-Paul Sartre, Simone de Beauvoir, and Samuel Beckett ("one of Peggy Guggenheim's lovers"). Powell had a social gift—

a combination of skill, appetite, and habit—and it makes her surviving letters mesmerizing reading. The vices of a small-town gossip, she felt, quite rightly, were virtues in a writer.

The letters start in 1913, shortly before she began attending Lake Erie College, a women's college in Painesville, Ohio. Powell wrote home often to her aunt Orpha May Steinbrueck, who had raised her (her mother died when Powell was only seven, and at fourteen she ran away to her aunt's boardinghouse in order to escape a wicked step-mother). With these letters to her Auntie May she begins her lifelong habit of sounding like the fun, amusing, clever girl she often was. (Later in life people who knew her tended to describe her simply as "nice.") Of her drama club tryout, she wrote to her aunt: "I was thwarted in my design to be the Angry Mob. I am a foundling instead and also a chorus." (Powell's ardent love of theater—much more than any deep involvement with books—is everywhere in her correspondence.) Gre-garious and petite, she was cast as Puck in *A Midsummer Night's Dream.* It seems a lifelong role, for the Puckish, pluckish voice of her letters rarely abates. Here she is writing from her Connecticut suffragist work in 1918: "I met a man the other day who was some remote connection of General Sherman. I confessed modestly that I was too—am I?—that the General was in fact own mother to my granddad, if not closer." Once Powell moves to Manhattan she writes to a friend:

There are three stages you go through in regard to the Village. First and foremost "Oh-so-this-is-Bohemia!! My dear! Don't you just love it all? Everything is so—well, so absolutely spon-taneous." . . . Stage No. 2 . . . you begin to see it with jaded eyes. Everyone . . . wants to be noticed—does everything for effect and down in his heart is worse than ordinary—is in fact a 10-cent rube like yourself. . . . Stage No. 3—you combine and condense and admire and sift.

So current and alive is Powell's epistolary voice, even in the earliest letters, that one is tempted to suggest that what we now think of as the contemporary American voice—in journalism and the arts—is none other than hers: ironic, triumphant, mocking, and game; the voice of a smart, chipper, small-town Ohio girl newly settled in New York just after the First World War. Its roots are oral, in an intelligent vernacular, for Powell despised writing that had people speaking in ways that no one actually spoke. She loved the salty and the anecdotal and in letter after letter is indefatigably given over to entertaining her friends. Her lightheartedness seems the utmost generosity. From her only trip abroad: "I have figured out the way Paris is laid out, now—and 'laid out' is right." Of some diet pills, she wrote, "A woman I knew got very thin on them and has stayed so for years but advises everybody against them as she's had liver, onions, kidneys and other disorders ever since." "I am really fascinated by the aging process," Powell later wrote to her sister, "even if the victim is me." Only at the very end, when Powell is tired, ill, and prey to bitterness and block, do self-pity and ugliness creep into the letters. One can only guess at the exhaustion that caused her in 1965 to write this stupidity to John Dos Passos: "I am sick of Civil Rights and well-heeled 'underprivileged' types screaming for justice when writers are the worst-privileged and . . . underpaid and oppressed of any race."

Although her writer friends may not have always served her well— Dos Passos probably encouraged a politically conservative streak in her; Edmund Wilson, at a time when she most needed championing, refused to blurb her books and actually wrote a negative review of her novel *My Home Is Far Away*—still she had fun with them. Especially in letters to others. Sartre is "the Hopalong Cassidy of France . . . a commercial enterprise like cornflakes or Shirley Temple." Of Jean Stafford, she wrote: "I never do get these lady writers who are Foremost of All Writers, Ladies, and go to bed in their laurels the way I go to bed in my roller skates. . . . Oh well, I suppose we can't all be riffraff." She added, "I would cut my throat but the house is such a mess." To Edmund Wilson, she wrote of the biographer Andrew Turnbull, who interviewed her about Hemingway's coarse letters and Fitzgerald's gentlemanly ones. Powell claims to have responded that "perhaps Ernest was not writing to him (Turnbull) but to his friend Scott, and that perhaps Scott was not writing to Hemingway but to him (Turnbull—i.e., posterity)."

What is clear from Powell's letters is that she was indeed writing to those named—not to posterity, not really. By turns dutiful, cheerful, and irreverent, they are not the great, meditative letters of Gustave

Flaubert or Flannery O'Connor. What they offer is something equally if differently satisfying, and that is a portrait of a hardworking, resilient female artist and professional.

In fact, Powell's life is deeply interesting both for its ordinariness (she is middle-class wife, mother, sister, and drinking buddy) and for the weird specificity of its troubles. When he was twenty, her mentally ill son—otherwise gentle and eccentrically brilliant—beat her so severely she was hospitalized for two weeks. Her own ill health included colon cancer, alcoholism, anemia, and a tumor with teeth and hair (a teratoma) attached to her heart. ("I was very glad," she wrote of the tumor, "that he hadn't popped out of my chest during a formal dinner party, me in my strapless and him grabbing my martini.") Her rocky marriage (to an ad executive), not much discussed in these letters, persisted mysteriously. Financial problems stalked her—she was briefly homeless—yet like many writers she could not maintain a taste for good business decisions. Among the Hollywood offers she rejected were projects that eventually became *The Wizard of Oz* and *Funny Girl.* "I turned down an offer from MGM for $2,000 a week for 18 weeks," she wrote to her sister in 1938. "I think if they'd offered me 50 cents or something I could have understood I would have snapped it up. As it was it just annoyed me to think of having to lug all that money around." Her forays into her beloved New York theater world were dispiriting flops. And she was published badly, even by—especially by—the esteemed Maxwell Perkins. There is a gently if icily weeping letter to him about it.

Powell wrote fifteen novels and is primarily known for *The Wicked Pavilion* and *My Home Is Far Away,* her best titles if not her best books. She was skilled at the quick, acidic portrait, the rhythmically set forth and psychologically astute observation. If one had to criticize Powell's novels for anything, it might be that in both narrative strategy and satirical content they sometimes lack a sustained point of view. They are "dart-throwing fiestas," to borrow one critic's words. *The Wicked Pavilion,* for instance, is on the brittle brink of being mere mood— mean and elegant, but whose?

There are, however, no point-of-view problems in Powell's endlessly engaging letters. A reader comes to the last of them already missing their company (her diaries contain a less composed version of their voice). One cannot help believing that if she'd been male and Ivy League–educated her career would never have fallen into disarray—not with fifteen novels—and we would have had these letters years ago. In the final line of this amazing collection, Powell says to her cousin Jack Sherman, "I admire your guts in the midst of strangers." It is the writing life, sitting back and speaking eloquently—in a letter—of itself.

(1999)

Best Love Song of the Millennium

Opinions on music can be stubborn and lonely things. I believe, for instance, that the twentieth century's most intoxicating waltz is "Let's Go Fly a Kite" from *Mary Poppins*. But don't ask me, with any strenuousness, to justify it, or I will gnaw my fist and stare forlornly out the window. Nonetheless, a calm certitude can descend when considering the finest love song of the millennium. Such a song is really a matter less of opinion than of clear fact, the determination of which can be helped along by the following scientific method.

A millennium is a long time. Very few love songs written in the first three-quarters of it have we even heard of. These, therefore, we automatically eliminate. The few we do know are dubious confections, peppered with *Hey nonnies* or *Ho nonnies* or else strange, violent deaths befalling the lovers—briars and vine roses sprouting from the corpses. The slaying and planting of people is poison to the love message of a song. It is a corruption, too much antithesis for the thesis. If death is imminent and about, it will always steal focus from love. And then we have a death song, more than a love one. A love song with no death in it, love that is not a fatal bargain or an addiction: that is a love song for the ages.

And so if we continue in this vein and eliminate from consideration all the songs of the nineteenth and twentieth centuries in which death quickly befalls the singing lover, we can really make some progress. All the Liebestods and would-be Liebestods gone: most of Puccini, all of Wagner, even "As Long as He Needs Me" from *Oliver!* (Did I fail to mention we are doing only Western music, and despite the marvelous "You're a Hard Dog to Keep Under the Porch," no country-western music at all? In fact, we are scarcely venturing outside the category of show tunes. Science has its demands.)

This brings us closer to the lighter popular song of the twentieth century, and even here there is much pruning to do. "You Belong to Me" is too possessive, even materialistic; "You Were Meant for Me" is sweet but fraught with the hopeless yearning of bachelors secretly in love with solitude. "On the Street Where You Live" is the theme song of a stalker. "They Can't Take That Away from Me" is a gorgeous laundry list of what to pack in the heart's knapsack when fate forecloses on love; its genius is to rhyme the emotional souvenirs "the way you hold your knife" and "the way you changed my life." But it can be sung terribly, and too often is. Then there are the blues, which, although full of the language of failed negotiations, can be friendly and delicious. But they are really about the long, slow dying of the singer, and not purely love songs at all.

Which brings us, finally, to the only logical choice for the greatest love song of the millennium: the final trio from Richard Strauss's *Der Rosenkavalier,* of course. Here we have one of the most beautiful things ever written; if it can be sung at all, it will not be sung badly. It occurs at the opera's penultimate moment, when the older woman (the Marschallin) elegantly gives up her young lover (Octavian) upon glimpsing him newly in love with someone his own age (Sophie). Love, in the story by Hugo von Hofmannsthal, is simultaneously embraced and selflessly surrendered—what are trios for? Light and wise, the song has the melodic depths and passion of Wagner but the libretto and spirit of Mozart. It is, as superlative musical things often are, a building upon, a historical summation, the borrowing by genius from genius. And in its breathtaking high notes it surely contains the music of the spheres; if the angels have teakettles they whistle like this. "I chose to love him in the right way," sings the Marschallin, "so that I would love even his love for another! . . . Most things in this world are unbelievable when you hear about them. But when they happen to you, you believe them and don't know why. . . . So be it." The clock has run out on the

Marschallin's romantic life. She has had her chance, her time, and now she must bow out—how suited to the close of this last thousand years. It is a knowing, queenly love song, in its exquisite sweetness and generosity, not unlike Dolly Parton's sublime valedictory "I Will Always Love You."

And so here I must stop: I have landed on country-western music again, surely the opposite of science.

(1999)

Titanic

I sometimes think of female adolescence as the most powerful life force human nature has to offer, and male adolescence as its most powerful death force, albeit a romantic one. For those of you who thought rationality and women's studies courses had gotten rid of such broad and narratively grotesque ways of thinking, welcome. Coffee is available at the back of the room.

I will admit up front that I have often had a hard time getting people to go to the movies with me. My taste in movies is not a completely inexplicable thing, though perhaps I should insist preemptively that it is, so as not to tempt someone's brutally analytical eye. I am interested in the cinematic grapplings of Eros and Thanatos as performed, attractively, by young people. Such dramas comprise a kind of middle-aged pornography, which is usually made by middle-aged American men such as John Hughes (that "Chekhov of high school," to quote one critic). But I have been afflicted with a taste for this sort of film for decades, and for several years dated someone who refused to go with me to those "stupid teenage girl movies you like so much." So I grew accustomed to going alone, which made my experience of each one all that much more intense, overwhelming, and perhaps even sick. Passion in isolation is passion indeed.

So, without further ado, let me say this. By the third time one sees James Cameron's *Titanic*, believe me, its terrible writing is hardly even noticeable. The appalling dialogue no longer appalls. The irritating and obtrusive framework that surrounds the central narrative and that gives the viewer long, lingering gazes at a minor actress with whom the director is having an affair tumbles away. By this time, too, one clearly no longer cares that not one adult one knows and respects doesn't despise the film; nor does one care what any of these respectable adults might think about anything. Love misunderstood—the heart societally, perhaps cosmically, rebuked—is one's theme.

What is to be most appreciated about *Titanic* has little to do with its poster boy, Leonardo DiCaprio, though he is a brilliant actor for someone carrying on with Mariel Hemingway's face and such a thin, awkwardly pitched voice. What is to be appreciated about this film is that supported—and not overpowered—by a stunningly executed visual spectacle (surely unsurpassed in moviemaking) is an ephemeral little love story—part *Wild Kingdom,* part *Lady Chatterley's Lover*—in which we are allowed to see something very compelling that in real life can be awful and dispiriting to see: what young women in love are willing to do.

Certainly, at the end, DiCaprio as Jack gives Kate Winslet as Rose the best seat on their bit of flotsam, and upon his apparent death she does pluck him too precipitously from his post; still, it is Rose who surprises not just her mother but surely love itself and leaps from the safety of a lifeboat, through water, through air, to save her man, madly swimming upstream, through the corridors of a sinking ship (oh, girls, don't we know it) like a salmon to spawn. The hormonal conviction of it is exhilarating to watch, and much more reminiscent of walruses than of Edwardians.

Such ardor is an athletic enactment of grace (unanticipated, unearned, as grace always is). It is love that exceeds the deserts of the beloved. (The Germans got this down wonderfully, too, in *Run Lola Run.*) Writers from Shakespeare on have adored this idea of a young woman's macho cupidity, and why wouldn't they? Who wouldn't? It flatters everyone. It is, shall we say, fantastic. Juliet, dagger plunged to chest, was pure machismo compared to Romeo and his delicate, mishandled poison. A young woman in love is a titanic force—at least it is time-honored theater to think so.

And so we—or I—go to the movies.

The successful communication of feeling is dependent on timing. Timing is dependent on editorial instinct. The dramatic last hour of *Titanic* entails glorious editing. Has there been a movie that so rhythmically and succinctly joins the smashing up of a great groaning ship with the astonishing range of brutish panic and altruistic courtesy with which our species greets catastrophe? The frenzied rush to the ropes and lifeboats, the demented elegance of Mr. Guggenheim, the small moments of fellowship and concern among the ship's musicians, the helplessness of the terrified crew; the gentle words between mother and child are not imagined in any original fashion, yet, perfectly spliced, their heartbreaking accuracy cannot be doubted.

This is, after all, a movie with more than just a mechanical interest in maritime disaster on its movie mind. It is interested (even if ham-handedly) in the human animal, social class and injustice, grief, death, and shipboard romance as existential truth. As in every steerage-meets-first-class love story, the movie traffics in clichés, but it does so fluently; the clichés here are sturdy to the point of eloquence. From the sexually explicit names of the lovers, to the wicked fiancé (Billy Zane's mustache-twirling performance is something that improves on additional viewing; one can see he understood exactly the movie he was in), to Jack's dying, Gipperesque quip ("I don't know about you, but I intend to write a strongly worded letter to the White Star Line about all this"), to the blithe repudiation of financial thinking (cutting corners to save money is what weakened the ship to begin with!).

Cameron loves all the familiar stuff. It is amusing to watch the number of times characters simply throw money away into the air—in a film that, while shooting, went extravagantly over budget. It is hypocrisy, of course, that wealthy people make films saluting the poor, but let them benignly pretend. Even *Lady Chatterley's Lover,* a novel that sympathetically portrays a noblewoman's renunciation of her wealth for love, concludes with an afterword by Lawrence that is a multipaged fury about not having made a dime from foreign sales and pirated copies. One can toss it into the air, but money doesn't really go away that sweetly. One can, nonetheless, dream.

One can also admire *Titanic's* Victor Garber, the Sondheim tenor, who, although he has no songs, plays the ship's architect almost musically, his spoken voice (here in a Belfastian lilt) as lovely and precise as his sung one. The intrepid can even admire the movie's pseudohymn "My Heart Will Go On," sung by Céline Dion, accompanied by a baleful Irish fiddle. Part folk song, part cola anthem, the song struggles valiantly to do operatic work. Its harmonic progression ascends the scale not unlike Wagner—though not really like it either. A cheesy Liebestod may not be more beautiful than a great one, but it can, given its subject and context, be truer.

One can also admire Cameron's curtain call of the dead, who, arranged along the ship's mezzanine and sweeping staircase at the end, make a moving tableau when the aged heroine finally revisits them; the camera races, searches, swims like an eager mermaid through the ship until light bursts forth, doors swing open, and it finds them. DiCaprio, a physical actor, turns, in a subtle blend of surprise and expectation, but he does not rush forward. He is now pure spirit. He smiles soulfully, extends a hand, and is mercifully quiet. At the end, life has provided and preserved only one golden memory, one great emotional adventure, as random as a lottery ticket: it is both too meager and too rich. Possession and loss at life's close are irrevocably knotted. The ghosts bearing witness applaud. The audience weeps.

Only hopeless romantics need to be told yet again that love is an illusion, that it dies, that it is for lunatics, addicts, and fools. The rest of us may occasionally like—even love—a little respite from what we know. This is what Hollywood movies, so humanely, have always been for.

(2000)

Claudia Roth Pierpont's *Passionate Minds*

Weekly, the coffee shop near my house has what the owner calls Trivia Tuesday: anyone who can answer the trivia question posted on the cake case wins a free cup of coffee. One Tuesday not so long ago I ventured in at around four in the afternoon. The question, written in black marker on a white card, was "What American playwright/actress was arrested and jailed for her work?" No one that day had answered the question correctly. No one had not said "Lillian Hellman." I summoned the cashier, pointed at the sign, and said, a little triumphantly, "Mae West."

I knew the answer because I had recently read a piece about West written for *The New Yorker* by Claudia Roth Pierpont. I knew that West was arrested on charges of obscenity for her theatrical hit, *Sex,* which she had written under a pen name. She did a week in the lockup on Welfare Island (now Roosevelt Island) and complained only about the underwear. As I drank my free coffee and privately toasted both West and Pierpont, whoever and wherever she was, I began to wonder why it is, in an age when readers know the hobbies of Vladimir Nabokov, the wives of John Updike, the girlfriends of Philip Roth—all fairly private men—we know so little about our women writers. Why did a hundred intelligent coffee drinkers imagine that Lillian Hellman had somehow done jail time, or that she was also an actress? Why do hardly any of us think of Mae West as a writer at all? And why was the question about Mae West's jail time even considered "trivial"? It was not remotely on the same level as the queries regarding batting averages and running yardage that usually graced the cake case. Soon, my happy, free coffee had become a problem. It is sometimes, as a feminist in the world, difficult to stay pleased.

Somewhat to the rescue comes Claudia Roth Pierpont's new collection, *Passionate Minds: Women Rewriting the World,* which despite its soporific title is one of the most ceaselessly interesting books I've read in some time. Within its pages one will find Pierpont's Mae West piece (which inspired not just Trivia Tuesday but James Lapine's current stage production, *Dirty Blonde*) as well as biographical essays on eleven other women writers: Olive Schreiner, Gertrude Stein, Anaïs Nin, Margaret Mitchell, Zora Neale Hurston, Eudora Welty, Marina Tsvetaeva, Ayn Rand, Doris Lessing, Hannah Arendt, and Mary McCarthy. "There is hardly a woman here who would not be scandalized to find herself in company with most of the others," Pierpont says in her introduction. But she chose these literary women for their "influence" (different from their "literary influence") and for the unorthodox ways they "worked out their destinies in an age of momentous transition for their sex." She has organized her book in three sections that deal "broadly speaking" (a pun that occurs several times in the book) with issues of sexual freedom, race, and politics. She needn't have. There is so much inevitable overlap in theme, and Pierpont's portraits, written independently of one another, are so far-reaching (despite their brevity) and so thesis-resistant that not one of them stays put within her diaphanous divisions. It affects the book's quality not at all.

Pierpont begins with Olive Schreiner, the only clearly nineteenth-century writer in the group, though Schreiner stood in opposition to almost everything that typified that century. She grew up in the dry South African wilderness and made her reputation with her very first novel, *The Story of an African Farm,* which became an international sensation even as it questioned all that conventional Victorian spiritual life had typically held dear. As to sex, God, and race, Schreiner was a freethinker: a suffragette, an agnostic, an anti-apartheidist. These were intellectual commitments, and did not arise out of any particularly bold or rebellious temperament, for physically and emotionally she was delicate, shy, ill for much of her life. Within the English libertine circles with which she came to associate, she was by comparison restrained, with a pesky predilection for falling in love.

Schreiner was born in 1855, the same year Charlotte Brontë died, and she seems in many ways a continuation of Brontë. They had much in common: a minister father, a bleak childhood in a stark landscape, the early deaths of beloved siblings, fragile health, unusually short stature, work as a governess, an early and determined desire to write, a concern for the predicament of women, an admiration for *Wuthering Heights*. Although surely Pierpont must have noticed this tie with Brontë, such is the exquisite distillation of her portraiture that the comparison goes unmentioned. She has no room for an observation that may be, well, a little idle. As in all her portraits, she wields a poet's economy: she hasn't the space to wander. Shrewdly she is after the knottiest, thorniest things she can find, which are, invariably, the relationship of the writer to her society's impediments, to her love life, and to her mother; Pierpont sees them all as inextricably bound to the story of the writer's work.

Schreiner saw her own well-educated English mother as "a grand piano closed up and locked, and tragically mistaken for a common dining table." She was one of the many mothers described here who had "vital, unused energies" of which their literary daughters were keenly aware. Schreiner's mother spoke French and Italian, was something of a painter and musician, then married a German missionary and was consigned on the edge of Basutoland to "a devastating range of household tasks." Owing to a variety of infractions, Gottlob Schreiner had difficulty hanging on to his posts (the feckless colonial father is an element of Doris Lessing's life as well), and the family had to move constantly, from mission to mission, often living in wagons. Olive eventually escaped to England, but not without the crucial help of her brother Fred, whom she called "Dada." (Curiously, among Pierpont's portraits, this is one of only two instances of a brother playing a prominent role in a woman writer's life—the other being Gertrude Stein's brother, Leo.)

Schreiner hoped for a career in medicine. Instead she became a lifelong patient (asthma, anxiety, emphysema, heart failure) and a writer; her manuscript of *African Farm* was accepted in 1882 by the novelist

George Meredith, then a reader for the publishing firm of Chapman and Hill, who swiftly made the novel an international success. The book's penultimate lines give sympathetic voice to Schreiner's modern, science-fed thoughts: "The soul's fierce cry for immortality is this,—only this:—Return to me after death the thing as it was before. . . . Your immortality is annihilation, your Hereafter is a lie. . . . All dies, all dies!" The blasphemous drama of faith understandably shaken, of doubt sympathetically saluted, was one the world was ready to read.

After *African Farm*, Schreiner's writing came more slowly. She had a love affair with Havelock Ellis, the sex "scientist." She fell unrequitedly in love with the mathematician Karl Pearson. She eventually returned to South Africa and married a young farmer who had written her a fan letter. He took her name, gave up his farming, and followed her to England, awaiting the big book she promised to write. She wrote a tract called *Woman and Labour,* which in 1911 reestablished her as a "social prophet," and in which she claimed to have lost twelve chapters of another, larger book to a fire set by British soldiers during the Boer War. Her husband insisted, after her death, that the story was a lie.

Their life was not easy, and they separated for six years, living on different continents. When she returned to him in Africa, essentially to die, he did not recognize the old woman she'd become. In her loneliness and peripatetic exile, she wrote over six thousand letters (a fraction of which were later published by her husband), and her political work on behalf of women, blacks, and even Afrikaners (she found the Afrikaner commitment to the land preferable to the rapaciousness of the British colonials) was vigorous and unyielding to the end. Her husband, ever awaiting the big book that would save them financially, was not wholly forgiving. Even after her death he continued to accuse her of having confused thinking with working. Such an accusation, full of bitter incomprehension, leaves one in a wince of sadness and recognition.

The downward turn of the Schreiner narrative typifies that of most of these women of *Passionate Minds*. There is no lovely deathbed, its perimeter studded angelically with grandchildren. Tsvetaeva commits suicide; Nin becomes a bigamist then ill with an excruciating gynecological cancer; West remains a show-business joke but one she is no longer in on; Mitchell is struck and killed by a New York cab before she writes a second book; Hurston, deemed a traitor to her race, lives her last days in obscurity and poverty, working as a maid in Miami. There is no elegant endgame: the end is absurd; at best a quiet, ordinary mockery.

Relatively speaking, Gertrude Stein, Pierpont's second subject, did all right, though this "mother of confusion," this author of "suspiciously significant nonsense," this literary love child of William James and Tweedledee, died in 1946 just after completing her libretto about Susan B. Anthony (*The Mother of Us All*), without ever seeing it staged. A collaboration with Virgil Thomson, it is arguably her most movingly political work. In fact, for the author of *The Autobiography of Alice B. Toklas, collaboration* is a rich word indeed, especially in the last years of Stein's life, years that may have goaded and transformed her. Pierpont here characteristically seeks the problem spots—the weird, the unreconcilable, the troubling—as a missile seeks heat. How *did* Stein and Alice Toklas, two Jews living in occupied France, survive the Nazis? Apparently through the requests of a high-ranking Occupation librarian, a friend of theirs, who asked that they not be disturbed. But they were disturbed, though not in the expected manner: German soldiers, it seems, were billeted for a time at their house. Stein and Toklas, ever the hostesses, served dinner. In Stein's now out-of-print *Wars I Have Seen*, Pierpont says, "one feels her struggling with the effort not to look away: the very term 'collabo'—which is all she manages to spit out of it—causes her to stumble on the page, falling into a repetitive stutter that seems not a mannerism but a kind of seizure."

Surely the most terrifying and heartbreaking life recounted in these pages is Marina Tsvetaeva's. Born at the same time as Anna Akhmatova, Boris Pasternak, and Osip Mandelstam, she was famous in her day yet is still the least known of this dazzling Russian quartet whose poetry spans the Revolution. Her subject was "the torment of passionate, sexual love," and her virtually untranslatable poems were often emotional dares "addressed to men she briefly worshipped or desired." Tsvetaeva, the daughter of an aging professor whom her mother, an accomplished pianist, had married on the romantic rebound, "had no ideology save romance and provocation." Her own mother's rebellion and longing, she claimed, had grown in her children "to the level of a scream."

Mandelstam fell in love with Tsvetaeva, as later did Pasternak, but they married others; Tsvetaeva married a tubercular teenager she met at the beach. She wrote poems against the Revolution and against the czar, and when she was stranded in chaos-stricken Moscow, her husband at war, her family house dismantled for firewood, she wrote plays. She barely managed, dependent on small fees for reciting her work and on friends and handouts for food. The squalor she and her small children lived in became well known. One daughter died of starvation. Tsvetaeva did get out, and for three years she lived in Prague with her husband, who had now been drawn into the Soviet secret service and was implicated in several murders, including that of Trotsky's son. When her husband fled to Moscow, Tsvetaeva packed her bags and followed him, in Pierpont's words, "into Hell." Once there, she was no longer a renowned poet but a pariah: a former supporter of the White Guard and the wife of a by then disgraced Soviet agent. Both her husband and her daughter were informers and worked to implicate each other as well as Tsvetaeva herself. Her daughter was arrested and spent seventeen years in prison camps. Her husband was shot in 1941. She herself was taken in by sympathetic strangers and that same year hanged herself in one of their outbuildings. Even Mandelstam's widow, who knew well the tragedies under Stalin, was eventually to claim to know no more terrible a fate than Tsvetaeva's.

Tsvetaeva's tale alone, for those unfamiliar with it, is worth the price of Pierpont's book, illustrating as it does the fascination and worth of a writer's life story—in "our insatiable age of biography"—even when the writer's work has not been much read or made readable. Resourcefulness, artful organization, a keen interest in history, perceptive reading of the available texts, and an intelligent way with gossip are the keys to Pierpont's mesmerizing telling. Moreover, she reminds us to consider the curious detail. The economist Alan Greenspan was once a member of Ayn Rand's inner circle. Eighteen-year-old Hannah Arendt's clandestine meetings with the married Martin Heidegger involved an "elaborate signal system of lights switched on and off." The *Gone With the Wind* film premiere in Atlanta included a costume ball, celebrating "the days at Tara Hall, when every man was a master and every man had a slave"; it included entertainment by the Ebenezer Baptist Church choir, and among the onstage "pickaninnies" was the minister's ten-year-old son, Martin Luther King, Jr. Such finds—which Pierpont sometimes confines within parentheses—eloquently reveal the complicated, often surreal landscapes from which cultural figures are both made and freed.

Which is not to say that readers will not quarrel with Pierpont. They will. That is part of the pleasure of such a book. Independent-minded, perhaps to a fault, Pierpont herself is an equal-opportunity quibbler, though one sometimes suspects that her allergy to groupthink causes her to go out of her way to dispute a feminist or a Communist. She occasionally ridicules Lessing: "You can take the woman out of the galaxy but you can't take the galaxy out of the woman." She turns Ayn Rand into a harmless if grotesque figure of fun. Margaret Mitchell, relegated to a shallow social type, eludes her almost entirely. And she is dismissive of Nin, devoid even of reluctant praise for Nin's intermittently astute writing; the powdered mask and sexual theater that Pierpont so approves of in West and the promiscuity she disregards in Mary McCarthy are suddenly completely repellent to her in Nin. As if beauty, availability, and desire weren't sufficient to explain Nin's long list of lovers, she exclaims that Nin must have been "simply astonishing in bed," then sets about to prove Nin frigid. Which sends a reader to the dictionary to look up the word *astonishing*. Also the word *bed*.

Pierpont has, too, the biographer's predictable habit of looking to the work for the life, but she sometimes takes it a bit further, into what might be called the therapeutic fallacy, suggesting that writers are cathartically working out their problems in their writing. "She had discovered that the only way to relieve her suffering was by writing," she says of Stein. Saying that writers write from what is on their minds is different from saying they are relieving their suffering—"getting better"—by writing. The distinction is an important one. To venture slightly into Steinese, the only suffering of the writer a writer might relieve by writing is the suffering of not writing. Art is hardly therapy.

. . .

Pierpont will be most controversial in her take on the deeply gentle, much-loved, and still-living Eudora Welty, whose profile she titles, with some irony, "A Perfect Lady," and whom she correctly notes has entered the national pantheon as a kind of favorite literary aunt, "the Pallas Athena of Jackson." One has to applaud Pierpont's sense of justice here, with regard to the little things—"It is appalling that just about everyone willing to speak about Welty in her youth refers to her physical unattractiveness"—as well as to the harder, larger ones.

In Pierpont's view it is Welty's interrupted, and eventually unlocatable, moral and social discernment that is most disturbing to a reader of her oeuvre. Despite a brilliant interlude as a photographer in the 1930s, when her subject was Mississippi blacks, Welty seems to have kept from the center of her work the racial story everywhere around her. In Pierpont's mind Welty has been polite, perhaps blinkered, rarely writing anything that would inconvenience or offend her Jackson, Mississippi, neighbors and her residence among them. (Welty, now ninety, still lives in the house of her childhood.) "The uncertainly educated denizens of Welty's ingrown, post-historic, Coca-Cola-sodden South" are to Pierpont "truly akin to monsters—albeit, at Welty's dismaying best, entirely guileless and extremely funny ones."

The "dismaying best" says it all. That Welty's work doesn't just record but too often imitates the social refusal and denial all about it, Pierpont believes, should not to be overlooked because of Welty's literary gifts. Pierpont does not address aesthetic ideas of naturalism or that more antique word, *regionalism;* it does not matter to her that the glancing way in which race is mentioned by Welty might be accurate to the segregated, white world she portrays. Pierpont sees Welty as having struck an unholy bargain with the charming South: she would keep its hatred and ugliness out of her work, in exchange for acceptance.

Such a flat-footed assertion is of course both thrilling and naïve: it is impossible that a writer of Welty's stature would be capable, even unconsciously, of such a coarse and poisoned contract. One wonders here whether Pierpont has perhaps encountered a generosity of spirit and called it ingratiation. She is also likely flunking Welty in political homework unassigned to Welty's northern peers; one detects in Pierpont's account a geographical bias. Pierpont also declines to emphasize the complicated ironies and portraits of internal exile that abound in Welty's work.

But, Pierpont writes well—and so not unpersuasively. Since she is interested less in literary criticism than in the wrong turns of a writer's life, she claims that Welty's alleged spiritual failing and artistic turnaround are attributable to two people Welty loved and desired to please: John Robinson, the attentive, handsome, and homosexual step-grandson of a racist Mississippi governor; and Welty's own overbearing mother. If, upon her father's death, Welty had not had to return from New York, where she was then living, and taken up residence with her mother, her work, Pierpont suggests, might have continued on a very different path. (In one of Pierpont's searing parentheticals, she notes that Katherine Anne Porter in 1952 visited Jackson and was incensed when Welty, then forty-two, had to ask her mother if Porter might come for dinner. To make matters worse, Welty's mother said no.) The jazz improvisations and grim social complexities that were included early on in Welty's stories gave way, Pierpont insists, to "something akin to the folksy humbug of Will Rogers."

Of course, all writers are vulnerable to accusations of having left things out—wittingly or unwittingly—of having avoided or transformed certain things because of the difficulty of addressing them head-on. Often it is a kind of modesty, a writer's underestimation of his or her abilities, that keeps the work—and perhaps the life—so constricted. Welty, by virtue of birthplace and temperament, may be particularly vulnerable to such complaints. When she was growing up, "the only black people she appears to have seen were contented servants. According to her own report, quite unremarkably she questioned nothing." Works such as *Delta Wedding* appear to Pierpont—and others—to traffic in the flattering, local white myths. Quite tellingly, in her twenties, Welty apologized publicly, if a bit sarcastically, for not having been in jail or trodden grapes like other young people. But then Welty was always famously "nice." When her *Collected Stories* appeared in 1980, her publisher removed the word *nigger* from a significant portion: Welty gave her consent.

.   .   .

Passionate Minds, with its unintimidated questions and explorations, is provocative and bracing, a wizard's mix of innocence and fire. One can only guess how that playwright-actress Lillian Hellman might have fared within its pages.

(2000)

Philip Roth's *The Human Stain*

For admirers of the shrieking, lyrical work of Philip Roth, the 1990s were a feast. First came *Patrimony* (1991), Roth's magnificent memoir of his father, one of his few books to stir tears not simply of laughter. Then came the intellectually exquisite *Operation Shylock* (1993), followed by *Sabbath's Theater* (1995), Roth's masterpiece of erotic and tragicomic mourning. Three stunning books in quick succession: it seemed an outpouring of unstoppable, idiosyncratic genius.

In terms of sheer productivity, brilliance, distinctly American diction, philosophical rage, comic irritability, dramatic representations of solitude, uniqueness of voice, and unwavering repugnance toward heterosexual convention, it is difficult to think of a contemporary artist with whom Roth might even be compared. If one strains and reaches into another medium entirely, Stephen Sondheim comes to mind. Both have committed their lives to a single (if commercially ailing) art form, provocatively pushing at its margins with piercing wit and multitonal notes, for the avid consumption of the more literate members of an essentially middlebrow audience—their loyal fans.

The condition of the fan over time, however, is a complicated one. The fan's admiration may grow proprietary, neurotic, and fussy—conducted no longer in the language of love but in the unattractive tones of disappointed connoisseurship. Such a condition, with time, resembles something vaguely if unilaterally marital, replete with dashed hopes, eccentric pronouncements, insincere forgiveness, nagging, muttering, and some occasional really extremely minor drinking.

So. . . . Now vee may perhaps to begin. Yes?

Roth's Pulitzer Prize–winning *American Pastoral* (1997), despite its many lively and sharply observed passages, was, to this reader, a falling-off from the three books before it. The novel's disdainful depiction of sixties radicals (who are given little of intelligence to do or say) and the portrait of its sweet, hollow hero appeared fatally under-imagined. *American Pastoral* was followed by *I Married a Communist* (1998), which sometimes seemed cripplingly awash in unwarranted— and therefore sentimental—emotion.

Rage is often Roth's highly effective muse, but it may have failed *I Married a Communist* because it was made too talky, rendered tonal before it was rendered dramatic. The leading male characters all join forces to heap their disgust upon the female characters just a tad too soon. The novel's events are insufficient up front to subject the narration so quickly to such bile. Of course, T. S. Eliot once made something of the same criticism of *Hamlet.*

Roth's new novel, *The Human Stain,* loosely belongs to a trio that includes these last two novels. They have many things in common: a nostalgia for old Newark; a handsome hero-fool; the handsome hero-fool's tell-it-like-it-is brother; and the presence of Nathan Zuckerman, Roth's literary doppelgänger, who is observer, bit player, and imaginary channeler of all three novels. Moreover, although none of these novels is a political one per se, each is set in a politicized landscape, positioning a messy family drama within the politically charged setting of the presidential years of Nixon, Eisenhower, and Clinton, respectively. Of the three, *The Human Stain* is, to this reader, the most interesting book; its particular hero-fool is arguably the most socially intriguing character to whom Roth has ever devoted himself.

Jewish identity crises are, of course, Roth's signature subject: his fictional portraits tend to be of Jewish men fashioning for themselves independent ways of being Jewish; authenticity and existential freedom are his themes, and his narratives generally proceed by argument, often in the form of dialogue. In *The Human Stain,* Roth gives us Coleman Silk, classics professor at fictional Athena College in western Massachusetts. Silk is a neighbor of Nathan Zuckerman, as Gatsby was of Nick

Carraway, and "was also the first and only Jew ever to serve at Athena as dean of faculty." But Silk's Jewishness contains a secret. As it turns out, he is not actually Jewish at all. Roth has given us a man struggling with a truly independent way of being Jewish: pretending to be Jewish. Being Jewish, for Coleman Silk, means being white. Silk is actually a light-skinned black man, the son of a New Jersey optician, who, in his early twenties, seeing he could pass for white, decided to go ahead, disown his family, and pass. "To become a new being," thinks Zuckerman. "To bifurcate. The drama that underlies America's story, the high drama that is upping and leaving—and the energy and cruelty that rapturous drive demands."

When Silk tells his mother his decision, her stoicism is heartbreaking. To see her future grandchildren, she says, she'll just sit quietly on a park bench if Coleman will walk them by. "You tell me the only way I can ever touch my grandchildren is for you to hire me to come over as Mrs. Brown to babysit and put them to bed, I'll do it. Tell me to come over as Mrs. Brown to clean your house, I'll do that." It is a valedictory between mother and son on a par with Hector and his weeping mother (just before Hector is slaughtered by Athena). Not for nothing is Coleman Silk a classics scholar. His favorite book, in fact, is the *Iliad.*

The cost and purposefulness of Silk's reinvention is extraordinary, even within the fictional world of an author who has written valentine after valentine to the idea of trespass.

> Did he get, from his decision, the adventure he was after, or was the decision in itself the adventure? . . . Was it the social obstruction that he wished to sidestep? Was he merely being another American and, in the great frontier tradition, accepting the democratic invitation to throw your origins overboard if to do so contributes to the pursuit of happiness? Or was it more than that? Or was it less?

It is a decision that Silk's fate comes to mock profoundly. Roth gives Silk a Jew's life but also a Jew's death—that is, he is singled out as a Jew by an anti-Semite and marked for death. The message of the kaddish, Zuckerman notes, is "a Jew is dead. Another Jew is dead. As though death were not a consequence of life but a consequence of having been a Jew."

In a novel abounding with harsh ironies, one of the most peculiar is the one the novel begins with, the one that has Silk summoning Zuckerman before him. Professor Silk, we come to learn, has been forced into retirement. Two years before, he used the word *spooks* in class, meaning ghosts or phantoms, but it was mistaken for a racial slur and a complaint was brought against him. When he refused to apologize in any way whatsoever, and instead grew more and more furious, his resignation became inevitable. This incident, he feels, is his tragedy (slaughtered by Athena!), for he devoted his life's work to the college, as both teacher and esteemed dean. He blames the scandal for the death of his wife, Iris (in the midst of the controversy she died of a stroke), and in his sorrow and fury continues to alienate not just his colleagues but his children and friends. He begins writing a book called "Spooks" and asks Zuckerman to help him with it.

Although Zuckerman does not directly help Silk, he begins tentative investigations on behalf of his own book, *The Human Stain,* a title that clearly refers not just to the taint left upon this earth by our species but also to the pigmentation that so arbitrarily colors human skin. Zuckerman's imagining of Silk's story leads him to other ones, especially that of Silk's new girlfriend, Faunia Farley, who is a janitor at Athena College and is a woman so unformed by societal expectations, so unimaginably assaulted by life, that she is accepting of everything Silk could possibly reveal about himself. "It was the closest Coleman ever felt to anyone! He loved her. Because that is when you love somebody—when you see them being game in the face of the worst. Not courageous. Not heroic. Just game."

The novel's weakest parts involve hatefully rendered interior monologues of two characters, the first being Lester Farley, Faunia's psychotic ex-husband and Vietnam veteran, whom Roth seems to construct from every available cliché of the Vietnam vet. The second is Delphine Roux, a lonely young classics professor who dresses like a schoolgirl and becomes the target of Roth's fierce but unconvincing satirical commentary. (In what can only be described as a kind of pedophobia, the villains of Roth's last two novels were schoolgirls—spoiled and oddly dangerous to middle-aged men.) The book indulges in the sort of tirade against political correctness that is far drearier and more intellectually constricted than political correctness itself. Roth, usually fond of both sides of an argument, fails to extend understanding toward—and only makes fun of—the possible discomfort of minorities or women in settings like Athena, where prejudice may be trickily institutional and atmospheric, causing events like the *spooks* utterance to be seized hold of and overinterpreted. Such seizing is like nabbing Al Capone for tax evasion—neither accurate nor wrong. And despite the protests against Black History Month, brazenly placed in the mouth of Silk's African-American sister, the novel shows that Zuckerman's education would indeed have benefited from such a month.

The novel is strongest and is even magical when Zuckerman is actually present on the page—and, in this case, in the room with Coleman Silk, observing him with articulate infatuation. Silk is quick, lithe, charismatic, in ways indomitable, "an outgoing, sharp-witted, forcefully smooth big-city charmer, something of a warrior, something of an operator, hardly the prototypical pedantic professor of Latin and Greek." At one point they fox-trot together on Silk's porch. "Come, let's dance," says Silk, bare-chested and in shorts, hearing a Sinatra song on the radio.

"But you mustn't sing into my ear," says Zuckerman, who, once he is dancing, adds, "I hope nobody from the volunteer fire department drives by." The homoerotic moments in *The Human Stain* are not "overtly carnal" but playful and warmhearted. At one point the book even contemplates the sexual allure of Milan Kundera—from the point of view of Delphine Roux, but still: as a writer, Roth knows how to have fun.

In addition to the hypnotic creation of Coleman Silk—whom many readers will feel, correctly or not, to be partly inspired by the late Anatole Broyard—Roth has brought Nathan Zuckerman into old age, continuing what he began in *American Pastoral*. Alone, prostateless, now outside the sexual fray, Zuckerman has become a melancholic poet of twilight and chagrin; the combination of perspicacity and weary tranquillity becomes him as a narrator. He is like that beloved American character, the retired private eye, brought back in for one more case. When he accidentally befriends an African-American, the national story of race opens up for him in all its particularities—or, rather, one fascinating set of them. He says of Silk:

> The dance that sealed our friendship was also what made his disaster my subject. And made his disguise my subject. And made the proper presentation of his secret my problem to solve. That was how I ceased being able to live apart from the turbulence and intensity that I had fled. I did no more than find a friend, and all the world's malice came rushing in.

The Human Stain is an astonishing, uneven, and often very beautiful book.

(2000)

Matthew Klam's *Sam the Cat*

Before Robert Gottlieb became editor of *The New Yorker* for a brief five-year term (from 1987 to 1992), the fiction printed in the magazine was famous (among those associated with smaller literary magazines) for its squeamish gentility. No body fluids, sounds, or smells were permitted in its pages. Other banished and corrupting vulgarities included the word *wig* (instead of *hairpiece*) as well as the barbarism "yellow light" (one was required to say "amber light" when writing of a traffic signal).

Of the several young fiction writers who came speeding headlong through the amber light of Gottlieb's interregnum, no one seemed more provocatively expressive of current American vernacular (in its white male form) than the then twenty-seven-year-old Matthew Klam. The narrative voice of "Sam the Cat," his first of seven stories to be published in *The New Yorker,* was so alarmingly, vitally full of forbidden utterance that it seemed to set the pages of the magazine on fire. "The downstairs smelled like cat piss," that first story read, worrying the line between candor and scatology. "Skippy's litter box was like an overflowing minefield." If its youthful antiheroics and attention to style and myth made it seem quite a legitimate descendant of John Updike's renowned "A&P," the helpless prurience and bumbling belligerence of its voice owed something to the theatrical monologues of Lenny Bruce and Spalding Gray. "You walk into a supermarket or a restaurant, your girlfriend goes in first and you're looking at her ass. And you say to yourself, 'Isn't that the most beautiful ass? That's mine. It's beautiful.' Like it's going to save you. An ass isn't going to save you. What's it going to do? Hide you from the police?" The story was greeted at the time with dismay, shock, and delight—sometimes simultaneously in a single reader.

How interesting to reread it now, these nine years later, as the title story of Klam's long-awaited first collection: its lunacies no longer shock. Of course, one should hardly need reminding that timing and context are everything where provocative art is concerned: Philip Roth's *Portnoy's Complaint* was shocking when it first appeared, in 1969, no longer shocking in the 1970s, then shocking again in 1990 (I taught it that year to students, many raised on women's studies curricula, who were taken aback in a manner few students in the 1970s would have been). Meanwhile, in the year 2000, what opens up before the reader of Matthew Klam, once the transgressive effects of his fiction soften or are no longer experienced at all, is the enduring comedy and essential sweetness of his work. He is mostly too interested in confusion to be brutal. "I try to laugh as much as possible," says one narrator. Klam does not traffic much in sustained fury or hate—a difficult accomplishment for comic writers—and is, oddly, frequently interested in justice. "If I were a girl I'd fuck ten guys a day," declares Sam the Cat, the boilerplate Klam protagonist. "I swear. I'd never want to be a girl, though, for they have the worst deal in history." Sam more confesses than narrates, and his confession has to do with a sudden crush he develops on a man in a rock band. "I went home and shut my eyes and tried to sleep, except there was this guy, the guy who looked like a chick, walking around the party in my mind. I watched him walk up to the bartender, I saw him reach into his front pocket to get money, and I saw how his round butt stuck out a little—somebody stop me."

No one does—not even his current girlfriend, who holds the receiver near the grinding Cuisinart when he phones. He gets a makeover at the mall. He shows up at the musician's door bearing flowers. (The musician turns out to be straight. "Girls—I mean women—it's a crazy thing," Sam says wildly to the musician.) However undomesticated, Klam's narrators seldom put anything forward unapologetically—they apologize compulsively, in virtually every story. "I'm sorry. Why did I say that? Is it too late to take it back?" is practically a refrain. They beg—

and amuse—for mercy. They speak like recovering altar boys. "Mother of God, listen to the way I'm talking," says Sam. Says another narrator, "When I hate Lynn, or when I can't stand to look at her or be near her, when I feel putrid, when I wish God would just erase me, I look at the garden." Their assaultive imaginations—lunging at love, then puzzling over its elusiveness—seldom spare themselves. "Am I a good person or a bad person?" asks one narrator. "I'm not a great person—I know that." Says another, "I'll tell you who I should marry: myself." Their bravado is laughingly gossamer: "I'm a fantastic lover. I've got to give me that."

Sam's fantasies, of course, are the stuff of childhood. "We could sail around the world together. . . . The ship would be my kingdom. I'd have a sword and an eye patch, some movies on video below-decks, for when the wind dies. I'd love the seagoing life." He remains the eternal boy, his desire incited mostly by thoughts of itself. Note the classic crescendo of neurosis: "I almost want her back. It's not a joke. I'd do anything to get her back." Passion is inflated by words; gesture brings momentary conviction. "I've had a girlfriend since I was in second grade," he says, all he knows of love deriving from that time, "and I'll probably have one until I croak."

Girlfriends, in Matthew Klam's world, are the sanctuary from the pursuit of other girlfriends, and erotic farce is his primary focus in the early stories. But what soon emerges to eclipse this as the stories proceed and grow through the collection is Klam's skillful social satire. His stories, from the second one on, begin to become studies of the toxicity of American affluence. Klam guiltily reviles the rich—they are absurd and repellent and also the only people he knows—and one after another he positions his protagonists as feckless young spies among them. "A lot of people go to Harvard," he has one narrator say. "I didn't." His world bursts preposterously with plutocrats. There is this from a fellow guest at the Caribbean resort of "The Royal Palms":

He told me there were guys out there living forty feet up in the trees, pot growers with machine guns who almost shot him but then took him in and befriended him. He said they were the most amiable guys, and he talked with them and smoked pot and sang reggae. They gave him a tour of their jungle hideout. They'd made crude musical instruments out of tin boxes and wire, and they had their feet propped up on crates of ammo. He said, "One of them went to Oxford."

His characters know the kings of tiny islands off Sri Lanka or call Al Gore "Al." Says the just barely straight-faced narrator of "Linda's Daddy's Loaded," "We met an interesting group of people when we moved in, all our neighbors who'd built elegant houses out here like ours—the men worked in the city and the women were all psychologists." By the end of the book we are, for long stretches, in the grip of strategically piercing and culturally observant work. (The one exception, "There Should Be a Name for It," a story about an abortion, is the weakest in the collection. The subject is not the right match for Klam's untethered nuttiness and is a difficult one anyway for the swiftness and antic melancholy of the story form: perhaps only "Hills Like White Elephants" [1927] by Ernest Hemingway and "Day-Old Baby Rats" [1972] by the underknown and now-deceased *New Yorker* writer Julie Hayden have done it well.) In "Not This," Klam's narrator discovers with alarm that his brother's newly acquired wealth is from public relations work he does solely for the Mafia. "He wiped his eyes with the palm of his hand and said, 'But look—they're gonna make us a pool,' pointing with the telephone."

In "The Royal Palms," the protagonist's professional life thrives while his marriage falls flat: "We had more money now . . . , but what were we going to do next? Something was missing. We needed the next phase, and we needed what was missing to get to the next phase." In "Linda's Daddy's Loaded," the husband says, in perfect Klam rhythm, "We had a glorious yard, a beautiful pool, sliding glass doors leading out to a patio, lawn chairs with pillows, a dog, a special electric fence to keep the dog from running away, a thing on his collar to shock him if he tried, track lighting in the kitchen, a marble pastry block." It is the dog, glancingly brutalized and tucked between pillows and track lighting, that best typifies not just the skilled comic sequencing of Klam's writing but its strugglingly moral and socially stunned heart.

All of Klam's gifts and themes are in symphonic play in the last two stories of the collection, "Issues I Dealt with in Therapy" and "European Wedding." These are Klam's longest and most artistically accomplished narratives—if it were not such a spiritual misdescription one might here use the word *mature*—though they emerge naturally from a voice and style established at the book's start. The breath and skin quality of every girlfriend or wife continues to be noted, clinically, for abnormalities, but his real scrutiny is saved for larger game (social class, ethical identity, the Faustian bargains of the young), and the stories' erotic matters are wrapped up with ribbons of idiosyncratic uxoriousness. The bitterly but cleverly titled "Issues I Dealt with in Therapy" (there is no therapy session in the story, or even a mention of one) is set on a "preppy East Coast resort island" at the wedding of the narrator's "incredible friend Bob."

Bob is an old, formerly progressive pal who studied civil rights law and worked to desegregate a school district in Mississippi. Klam's nameless narrator, who works "at a nonprofit that attacked the military-industrial complex, but I'll tell you right now it did nothing," worships his incredible friend Bob. But then Bob wins a big case. "Soon he was having chats with Janet Reno, riding with her over to Congress. . . . They had some sticky problems in Immigration and Naturalization: They were trying to figure out how to throw Haitians back in the water. When I phoned him at work he could only whisper." Bob "had whole families, Rwandans who were here seeking asylum, removed from the homes where relief agencies had put them, shipped back to Africa for sure death." Afterward Bob became a " 'media catastrophe consultant.' . . . He 'befriended politicians under fire.' "

When asked to toast the groom, Klam's now-unbeguiled narrator begins, "You've had a lot of jobs, Bob. . . . Unfortunately I'm blanking on some of your successes." The testimonial builds angrily, for several pages, including advice for the bride ("Stand up and start running and never look back") and may be the funniest wedding toast since the one Robert Cohen wrote in his 1996 novel *The Here and Now.* "That," says Klam's narrator's girlfriend when he finally sits down, "was a disaster."

Lest we forget that Klam desperately desires a comedic world, he closes his collection with not one but two weddings. "European Wedding," the book's ultimate story, is also the first and only one Klam has written in the third person. This point of view—allowing him the perspectives of three separate characters—serves him well, and he it.

Up until this story the book that *Sam the Cat* may most resemble is Julie Hecht's amusing *Do the Windows Open?* (1997), whose stories also appeared in *The New Yorker* and registered the gender-related vanities and anxieties of East Coast metropolitan society, drawing repeatedly from a single, ongoing personality for its narratives. Hecht created a book-length vocal solo, even though it was a collection, and Klam comes close to doing the same. The third person of his concluding story, however, allows him both more density and more room. It gives him just enough tools to show us the kind of authoritative, vocally limber, and devastating writer he can be.

The aptly, inevitably named Rich is marrying the well-to-do Gynnie at a Loire valley château straight out of a Three Musketeers movie, but first, back home, in his prenuptial ambivalence he contemplates an affair with Nora. "Nora was his only client. Nora's happiness was his full-time job. . . . She wasn't Gynnie. . . . She was someone else. She could die tomorrow, he didn't care." This loveless union is consummated—briefly for Rich, at length for the reader—and the five pages documenting the coupling are among the few deeply merciless passages in Klam's book. "Some of her lipstick had come off. She grabbed the back of his head and jacked it toward her. Her own head moved forward steadily—like a shark's head, like a prosthetic limb, some football wrapped in bologna. She threw her tongue down his throat like a waterlogged sneaker." The scene continues somewhat pathologically and at length from there. This is not really misogyny (at least I don't *think* it is) but panic and loss of appetite served up as sick hilarity: "During the last few moments Rich had begun hoping that a crazy person would break in and beat them to death with the spade beside Nora's writhing head." Its gruesomeness casts a deliberate shadow across the entire subsequent story—much like the mammoth hurricane that keeps most of the guests from being able to attend the wedding—and the marriage of Rich and Gynnie that proceeds regardless, in another country entirely, must gather together what few genuine consolations can be fashioned or found.

The story's other two perspectives belong to Gynnie and to an ominous, dissipated old German friend of her mother's, Emile Marcus, who comes to the wedding because he has "a real affinity for repulsive American overkill" and, unbeknownst to Gynnie, believes himself to be her biological father. Gynnie herself is one of Klam's typical young women: too intent on doing good in the world and on losing weight at the same time to screw up the energy to leave Klam's difficult males. Besides, Klam has made largely sympathetic company of his childish men by making them smart, in both meanings: he inflicts pain on them and makes them bright. And so the night Rich arrives in France and asks, "Why are we doing this?" (meaning unpacking the contents of the suitcases into the dresser), both misunderstanding and understanding all too well, Gynnie sums it up for him:

> "Because we're desperate and we're lonely and nothing better came along. . . . You're all I've got now, and you'd better get used to it. We're on the grownup train, and we don't get off until the graveyard." Rich held up his folded shirts. He said he was talking about the clothes.

For the rest of the story Gynnie attends to a pedicure, throws up her meal, worries about Somalia, and wonders why her mother's European family had to leave France *after* the Nazi occupation was over.

Klam's radar—or perhaps one should say nose—is for all that is unclean, especially money. In the end, his book is a reminder that the wealth of the American upper middle class, and the suburban materialism of its lifestyle, is not old news, already sufficiently taken up by literary writers of previous decades. In the excessive ways it is experienced now, American affluence is unprecedented, socially and globally isolating in a manner that is new, overwhelming, and sinister to those looking on. Klam speaks from within this affluent milieu but in his stories is dividedly looking on, and askance, in the manner of a houseguest or an in-law (sometimes his characters are quite literally that), wrestling with his own scathing criticism, his own generation-specific nausea, his own particular patios and poolsides, until politeness can no longer be managed nor righteous rudeness subdued. Throughout his work he steadily reveals his complicated interest in all that revolts—in both senses of the word.

One could argue that the bursts of indignation are too intermittent, their effect somehow decorative, and therefore not finally the strongest current in any of the narratives; the strongest current may simply be a kind of animal desire for peace and sleep (all the characters move in that direction at story's end, which gussied up can look like forgiveness or benevolence instead of the exhaustion that it is). After all, Klam has brilliantly reminded us all along—from the book's title forward—that even tucked between pillows and track lights we are nothing but animals. Repeatedly electrocuted by a fence, we will tire and stay in the yard. But only then.

(2000)

Legal Aide: My First Job

In the 1970s a new para-profession was getting a foothold in urban law firms—that of the legal assistant, or paralegal—and some college graduates, uncertain how to pay the rent or fund their art, were venturing into this day job. In New York, these jobs paid slightly better than entry-level publishing positions but involved a level of exploitation that had actually caused the paralegals at one prominent Manhattan firm to strike. Upon graduation from college, fresh from editing the school literary magazine, perplexed at the number of people I knew going in an automatic fashion to law school (when I asked them what it was a lawyer did exactly, none of them could say), I entered this strange professional racket. I would find out what a lawyer did exactly. Others I knew at the time who also embarked on this pursuit included a woman with a just completed master's thesis on Carlyle's *Sartor Resartus* (who promptly used her employer's legal services to change her last name from Schmunk) and a high school teacher with a deep case of burnout.

Paralegals did not type! This was a kind of rallying cry. Nonetheless, I often coveted the jobs of the secretaries who did, for if they stayed after five they were paid overtime, and the kind of mindless typing they did looked restful to me. I, meanwhile, had to organize documents—which fell under the category of "exhibit preparation"—and, murmuring into a Dictaphone, to digest depositions into a kind of telegraphic code ("W can't recall Palm Too din. w/ Stutz"), reducing the testimony of deposed witnesses to what was optimistically called its "essence." I also had to make the occasional and terrifying court appearance to get an adjournment on a motion. This is now almost always done by attorneys, but in the seventies Manhattan paralegals were a cheap substitute. "In this city you would make more money as a paraplegic than as a paralegal," I was continually told by one of the associates.

I was twenty-one and mute with shyness. Up until this point in my life I had lived only in tiny towns in northern New York. The midsized, midtown firm I worked for comprised a dozen lawyers, all Jewish, all men, with names like Ira and Julian, which to a provincial ear did not even properly sound like boys' names. The staff was not Jewish: the goyim served, grumblingly and winkingly; everyone smoked and drank too much coffee. My boss, the senior partner, had apparently made his name with a big case for Sears, Roebuck in the 1940s, and he had coasted on this reputation for years. With his money he bought antiquarian books, boxes of which he ripped open hungrily when they arrived, as well as some Calder prints, which he displayed in the firm's lobby and which made a big impression on me. His clients still tended to be department stores, and the case he had me working on involved the firing of the chairman of Bonwit Teller, whose makeup counters I dreamily visited during lunch hours. My boss was alternately tetchy and expansive; he spoke loudly and crazily, as all bosses, in my experience from summer jobs, did. By the time I came on board, he was also a little hard of hearing. When after two years I told him I was leaving for graduate school in writing, he thought I'd said "riding" and made a crack about horses.

But this is what my first real job brought me: what I thought of as my first grown-up friend (a lawyer fifteen years my senior who remains my friend to this day). And though I envied the chicly dressed young women who worked in the Pace Gallery and at Cambridge University Press, housed in the same building and sharing the elevators, my own exquisitely wrong job did bring me, for a brief period, a life in Manhattan—improvised, lonely, exhilarating. I lived on Eighteenth Street and First Avenue, above a restaurant, and was always broke, though it was middle-class poverty—temporary, part of youth and art, more a game to be played than a deep condition. It produced in me an eccentric economy. Tired from work and fearful of the subways at night, I would get into a cab and say, "Give me a dollar-fifty's worth, please," then hop out at Murray Hill. I had one suit, which I wore all week: the jacket on Monday with slacks, the skirt on Tuesday with a blouse, the jacket and skirt together—at last!—on Wednesday, and so on. I ate hamburgers but not cheeseburgers, which cost ten cents more. Still, I spent twenty-five dollars to see Bette Midler on Broadway, and another twenty-five dollars to see Liza Minnelli at Carnegie Hall. I was like a fourteen-year-old gay boy escaped to the bright, big city from the farm—which is perhaps what, in my heart, given even the slimmest of paychecks, I continue to be.

(2001)

Frederic Cassidy

Although Fred Cassidy—linguistic historian, detective, and bard—was a colleague of mine, I didn't really know him. When I first arrived at the University of Wisconsin sixteen years ago as an assistant professor, soon dividing my year between the futon on a friend's Madison sunporch and a sparsely furnished Hell's Kitchen rat shop nine hundred miles east, Professor Cassidy had long been a distinguished figure in the English Department. Already officially emeritus, an eminence, a spritely and regal widower who lived atop a hill in a stately brick home coveted by a perennially house-hunting friend of mine, he presided over what the department called DARE, well before the acronym took on its current drug-awareness meaning. *DARE*—the *Dictionary of American Regional English*—was a gargantuan, decades-long project then housed several offices down from mine and was always spoken of in astonished and reverential tones. My first week of teaching, I was shown the closed door of the busy *DARE* office and told solemnly, "They are still only on *C*."

To capture in a single reference book all of American local idiom seems a brilliant folly (like, say, maniacal lepidopterology or the corking of breezes in bottles) as well as a practical, useful item it's amazing someone didn't think of before. The pages of the actual dictionary (which in its published form is now three volumes long and up to the letter *O*) are full of whimsy and science, maps and pronunciation guides, and a neutral fascination with words for their own sake, whether they be offensive, improper, gorgeous, or odd—from *bladderpod* to *cattywampus* to *olykoek*. The vanishing names for our vanishing natural world abound in *DARE*'s pages—all manner of flora and fauna are richly retrieved; it is sometimes like taking a walk in the woods just paging though the book. The everyday words for our everyday lives are the target of the research, but with its penetrating fieldwork, the project's historical and geographical reach illumines the story of a country forged under the most disparate (and occasionally half-forgotten) of influences.

In comprehending his tireless devotion to this linguistic enterprise, it is tempting to psychologize, or metaphorize, Cassidy's own background. What Kingston-born son of a Jamaican mother and a Canadian father who then grew up to marry a Frenchwoman in Michigan would not have been constantly sorting out and deciphering the vernacular of various places, interrogating the idiomatic phrases that must have flown around him incessantly, enticingly, bewilderingly? Language surely was a daily family matter for young Fred Cassidy, and in trying to capture and locate it regionally, to make a hunting and gathering of it, perhaps he most resembles his fellow islander John James Audubon, who also set out to capture in its natural habitat a colorful, winged thing and bring it to the pages of a book for study.

At university gatherings, when I happened to spy Professor Cassidy, he seemed always to be excitedly hazarding a guess about the origins of someone's name, usually the name of the person to whom he was talking, who would listen, rapt and flattered. He came to my office only once, wearing one of his pale suits, not a staple of midwestern academic attire but a staple of his. "Who is your literary agent?" he asked. I was taken aback by the sheer business of it but told him her name, and he wrote it down. Then he looked up. "I have a book I am writing about my life," he said, smiling boyishly and dreamily. "And I'm going to go to New York, take her out to lunch, and tell her about it!"

I don't know precisely what happened to that memoir, although I'm told it was never completed. The book that of course remains the story of his life is *DARE*, with its rousing, perfect title for a life story. "On to *Z*!" was Fred's characteristically buoyant cry—one with which he liked to close letters, exit a conversation, depart a room.

"Don't feel constricted by the life," I was advised by *The New York*

Times Magazine upon agreeing to write this appreciation of Professor Cassidy. (Perhaps it forgot that I, too, am a Wisconsin academic; or perhaps it was remembering.) But when one contemplates Fred Cassidy's life, constricted is not what one feels. Nor is crimpled. Nor is hendered.

Not (as is said chiefly in scattered regions of the South) hardly.

(2001)

Alice Munro's *Hateship, Friendship, Courtship, Loveship, Marriage*

"Love never dies," says a character from Alice Munro's 1994 collection, *Open Secrets.* And the woman listening to him feels "impatient to the point of taking offense. This is what all the speechmaking turns you into," she thinks, "a person who can say things like that. Love dies all the time."

The birth and death of erotic love, and the strange places people are led to because of it, "on the lookout for an insanity that could contain them," as it is put in "Vandals," another story in that same collection, is Munro's timeless subject. In her new collection, *Hateship, Friendship, Courtship, Loveship, Marriage,* showing that the impulse toward love, if not love itself, dies hard, she follows her characters' erotic lives straight through the chemotherapy ward, into the nursing home, on into the funeral parlor. In "The Bear Came over the Mountain," a faithless husband puts his wife into a nursing home only to watch her acquire there a new, wheelchaired beau. In "Family Furnishings," a woman in a nursing home incessantly chants "fit as a fiddle and ready for love." In "Floating Bridge," a terminally ill woman is led out into the woods for a kiss by a strange young boy who is both god of love and angel of death—Munro would naturally see these figures entwined. In "Comfort," the protagonist has a romantic encounter with an undertaker, whose activities of bloodletting and body cavity drainage (like those of the taxidermist-lover in "Vandals") suggest perhaps one darkly funny opinion of Munro's regarding the drama of love. The narrator of "Queenie," surrounded by couples, "each . . . with its own heat and disturbance," notes her own desire for solitude, "for there was nothing I could see in their lives to instruct me or encourage me."

Like Henry James, Alice Munro knows that love's "floating bridge" between worlds—and over swamps—can bring a ruinous fate as easily and indifferently as can its absence. But Munro also knows that the arranging of love, improvised or institutional, and the seismic upheavals of its creation and dismantling—the boards rising and falling precariously beneath the feet—is both a kind of pornography of life and the very truth of it: it is often the most persuasive and defining force in the shape of individual existence and individual fate. Not that this is to be valued, or judged—in Munro's world there is a powerlessness before the whole matter—only that such a thing is to be maturely understood and perceptively watched. "Their marriages were the real content of their lives," she writes in "Comfort," "the sometimes harsh and bewildering, indispensable content of her life." Unlike James, a permanent tourist in the land of marriage and romantic union—a subject endlessly suited to the short-story genre—Munro is intimately informed about what actually goes on there, and it is but one of the many reasons she is (to speak historically, and to speak even, say, in a Russian or French or Irish saloon, loudly and unarmed) one of the world's greatest short-story writers. As the writer Ethan Canin once said, "The stories of Alice Munro make everyone else's look like the work of babies."

She is also interested in social class. And there is not one of her stories in this new book that does not put together characters with real if subtle class divisions between them. This Munro does with a neutral, unsentimental eye and limber sympathies. In the stories she tells, a character's passage across these divisions may be thwarted or assisted by love, or by ambition or by art, or by the tiniest, imperceptible sorts of revolutions, enacted in loneliness, or conspiracy, or both. She has a vision of the world that is like a novelist's, and a typical Alice Munro story contains a novel's breadth and satisfactions, in miniature, fitted in like a ship in a bottle, or a beautiful bonsai tree. Because she tends toward the long story, and writes with a long view of life as well, time is both her subject and her medium, its mysteries and flukes both pondered and employed. Her narratives leap and U-turn through time, and the actual subject and emotion of a story may be deferred in such gymnastic travel, or may be multiple or latent. The particular and careful ways Munro's themes are laid into her narrative trajectories cause them to sneak up upon the reader. They surprise—like the rogue but graceful syntax of a complex wine.

Possibly there will be some consensus among her readers on the new collection's weak link as well as its crown jewel. As to the former, the title story may come under the most fire, but it is here that Munro lays out one of her signature themes—the random, permanent fate brought about by an illusion of love. The story proceeds at first like a *ronde*, passing its point of view from a peripheral train station agent to a Scottish housekeeper buying a ticket, on through the various characters (the housekeeper's former employer, the employer's shoemaker, the shoemaker's daughter, the daughter's friend, who is the housekeeper's former charge), who all have some bearing on the outcome of the story.

A fictitious epistolary courtship is staged by the two girls, who have only random mischief on their minds, but it sets in motion a real marriage between the Scottish housekeeper and her employer's former son-in-law, replete with a baby named Omar. "For where," thinks the young, undiscovered author of the love letters, "on the list of things she planned to achieve in her life, was there any mention of her being responsible for the existence on earth of a person named Omar?" The remark contains Munro's sly amusement at how things turn out between men and women ("her heart had been dry, and she had considered it might always be so. And now such a warm commotion, such busy love"), as does the awkward title, which is the girls' game of writing down the letters of a boy's name then ticking off "the counted number on your fingers, saying, *Hateship, friendship, courtship, love-ship, marriage,* till you got the verdict on what could happen between you and that boy." The title, by the end, loses its ungainliness, acquires much rightness for explicitly announcing the collection's themes, one of which is the power of writing itself, and in the end seems oddly perfect, as does the story's focus on the doings of young girls, for it is the first story in a book whose final one completes the picture with a stark, wicked, and moving tale of old age.

In this last story, "The Bear Came over the Mountain," Fiona, the beloved but mentally ailing wife of a retired literature professor named Grant, is condemned to the hell of a nursing home—"its dribblers, head wagglers, mad chatterers"—and like Rilke's Eurydice, she there grows indifferent to her earthly husband, a little forgetful of him even, falling in love with a fellow resident instead. She is vague but courteous when her husband comes to visit, always turning her attention back to her new companion, Aubrey. This new love involves a retrieval of a lost thread from her past—a predilection of Munro's stories; the past rises up and breathes out ghost after ghost—since Fiona knew Aubrey when she was young, had even gone out with him once, before some arbitrariness on the part of her father interrupted their courtship. Now she has him again, at last, albeit in a wheelchair, and they have in a sweetly demented and embarrassing way become smitten. That Grant, during their marriage, had routinely been unfaithful to Fiona is both ironic and fortunate. "Nowhere was there any acknowledgment that the life of a philanderer (if that was what Grant had to call himself . . .) involved acts of kindness and generosity and even sacrifice," Munro writes both hilariously and seriously. For when Fiona's well-being is threatened by Aubrey's removal from Meadowlake by his buxom wife, Marian, Grant has the largeness of heart, and the convenient old sexual habits, to ensure something better for his wife, whom he does, in fact, deeply love, and so proves.

The past resurfaces challengingly in other stories here, such as "Nettles," where the newly divorced narrator, while visiting her friend Sunny, encounters her old girlhood sweetheart, the son of the local well driller, sitting in Sunny's kitchen (making his characteristic ketchup sandwich, one of Munro's many clues of childhood deprivation survived). He is a fellow guest there, as the narrator observes, and the coincidence which their hosts "might think remarkable was to us a comically dazzling flare-up of good fortune." Their attraction knows its bounds, however, and nothing romantic comes of it. The story concludes that it was

> love that was not usable, that knew its place. (Some would say not real, because it would never risk getting its neck wrung, or turning into a bad joke, or sadly wearing out.) Not risk-

ing a thing yet staying alive as a sweet trickle, an underground resource. With the weight of this new stillness on it, this seal.

I never asked Sunny for news of him, or got any, during all the years of our dwindling friendship.

The swift and economical use of the word *dwindling,* thriftily closing two stories at once, is Munro at her crafty best.

Arguably the finest story in *Hateship, Friendship, Courtship, Love-ship, Marriage,* and surely one of several here that are among the most powerful stories she has written, "Family Furnishings" is less about love as fate and more an ambivalent, even bitter exploration of the spiritual escape and emotional cost of becoming a writer. (Writing is often construed more generally in Munro, too, and plots that turn on notes and letters abound in her work, this collection containing three such stories.) About this subject there is not a more moving piece by anyone that I can think of. "Family Furnishings" is written in the first person, and in it the narrator focuses her recollections on Alfrida, one of the "career girl"–slash-aunt figures that have made their appearance from the beginning of Munro's work (from Fern in *Lives of Girls and Women,* 1971, to Polly in "Post and Beam" or, also in this new book, Queenie in the story of the same name). They are women who lose their significance to the heroine as they get older and clearer in their sadnesses, but who hold a glamour for her when she is young and in need of emissaries from the world outside her immediate family.

Alfrida is only in the most general sense a writer; she is a small-town journalist, "one of the people who wrote under the name of Flora Simpson, on the Flora Simpson Housewives' Page":

> Women from all over the countryside believed that they were writing their letters to the plump woman with the crimped gray hair and the forgiving smile who was pictured at the top of the page. But the truth—which I was not to tell—was that the notes that appeared at the bottom of each of their letters were produced by Alfrida and a man she called Horse Henry, who otherwise did the obituaries.

She also writes under her own name "Round and About the Town with Alfrida." She is the narrator's father's cousin, and more like a close sister to him, since her own mother was killed in a kerosene lamp accident.

This accident, and its effect on Alfrida, which Munro describes briefly, as if in passing, is in some ways the emotional heart of the story. "You're just better off not to see her. You would not want to see her, if you knew what she looked like now," a grandmother tells the young, wailing Alfrida, while her mother is dying in the next room. And Alfrida cries, "But she would want to see me." Alfrida herself does not understand her own story and says, "I must've thought I was a pretty big cheese, mustn't I? *She would want to see me.*" But the narrator does understand—and a writer is born: she says, "And the minute that I heard it, something happened. It was as if a trap had snapped shut to hold these words in my head. . . . *She would want to see me.* The story I wrote, with this in it, would not be written till years later, not until it had become quite unimportant to think about who had put the idea into my head in the first place."

When the narrator goes off to college in the city where Alfrida lives, she only visits her once, mostly not returning her phone calls. The narrator's new fiancé shows little interest in her cousin Alfrida: "He admired opera and Laurence Olivier's *Hamlet,* but he had no time for tragedy—for the squalor of tragedy—in ordinary life. . . . His resolute approval of me did not extend to my ramshackle background." And so Alfrida drifts away, her affair with a married man amounting to little; at the time of the narrator's father's death, she sits half-cracked in a nursing home. It is years earlier, from her father and then later from Alfrida's daughter (put up for adoption at birth), that the narrator learns of Alfrida's distress at seeing her life used in her young cousin's published writing. The narrator gives the writer's standard defense:

"It wasn't Alfrida at all. . . . I changed it, I wasn't even thinking about her. It was a character. Anybody could see that."

But as a matter of fact there was still the exploding lamp, the mother in her charnel wrappings, the staunch, bereft child.

To escape the claustrophobic anti-intellectualism of Alfrida and her world, who see real literature as pretentious "hot-shot reading," the narrator cuts short her one lone visit with her cousin and, walking back to her student apartment, stops to spend an hour in a drugstore drinking coffee instead. It is an act of both betrayal and survival, and it expresses at its core the literary impulse. Here, Munro's writing ascends like Isolde:

> The coffee was reheated, black and bitter—its taste was medicinal, exactly what I needed. I was already feeling relieved, and now I began to feel happy. Such happiness, to be alone. To see the hot late-afternoon light on the sidewalk outside, the branches of a tree just out in leaf, throwing their skimpy shadows. To hear from the back of the shop the sounds of the ball game that the man who had served me was listening to on the radio. I did not think of the story I would make about Alfrida—not of that in particular—but of the work I wanted to do, which seemed more like grabbing something out of the air than constructing stories. The cries of the crowd came to me like big heartbeats, full of sorrows. Lovely formal-sounding waves, with their distant, almost inhuman assent and lamentation.
>
> This was what I wanted, this was what I thought I had to pay attention to, this was how I wanted my life to be.

This gorgeous Liebestod should not be mistaken for a resounding affirmation of the literary life, but understood, instead, as an acknowledgment of its emotional distances and thefts and its willing trade of the human for art. It is a song of relief alloyed with shame. Munro has beautifully registered the ambivalent conscience of the writer—not judgmentally but helplessly, as before love and the life story love brings before dying.

(2002)

Edna St. Vincent Millay

The photograph of the mutable Edna St. Vincent Millay that peers out from the cover of Nancy Milford's new biography recalls the face of a Vermeer. But not a Vermeer painted in the likely way—upside down, via camera obscura, so the features and creamy surfaces come together abstractly, with the sweet extraterrestrial look of sainthood or Down syndrome. The portrait on the cover of Milford's book, despite the tortured Flemish-flapper coif, beneath which sits the elegant bone structure and porcelain finish of a teapot, is mesmerizingly human: Millay's unaverted gaze is seen right side up, captured not as a collection of abstract qualities but as part of the living, breathing features of a complex and elusive woman.

And so it is with Milford's biography. Neither empirical nor worshipful, *Savage Beauty: The Life of Edna St. Vincent Millay* bears up under its twenty-odd years of research and deluge of detail to manage a rich, moving picture of a rich, moving target. Milford, the author of a celebrated biography of Zelda Fitzgerald, has assembled her portrait of Millay largely from bundles of documents kept for decades by Millay's literary executor and less-than-industrious sister Norma (who died in 1986 at the age of ninety-three). And sensitive to the literary significance of her subject and the impact of this biography in revisiting if not securing Millay's historical importance, Milford's decades of excavation and narrative piecework have paid off in something slightly—perhaps inevitably—disorganized as well as original and spellbinding.

Millay was the second renowned American poet to spend years in a city called Camden, though hers was in Maine. She was petite, intense, bright, witty, romantic, freckled, auburn-haired, self-dramatizing, and beautiful. (As a poet friend recently remarked to me, "Why has Judy Davis not yet played her in the movie?") At one time arguably the most famous living poet in the world, her work lauded by Thomas Hardy, Elinor Wylie, Edmund Wilson, Sarah Teasdale, and Louise Bogan, Millay lived stormily and wrote unevenly, so that her place in American letters was in descent even in her lifetime. In her day she was hailed as a feminist, lyric voice of the Jazz Age, yet she went largely unclaimed by the feminism of subsequent decades. She owned, perhaps, too many evening gowns. And her poems may have had an excess of voiceless golden birds (she did not strain for her metaphors; on her mantelpiece at home were two gold bird figurines, souvenirs from a trip to Asia). Her work could be occasionally modernist, but only occasionally, and so was not taken up by the champions of modernism, with their passion for Pound and for Eliot, of whom Millay once wrote a "murderous" satire. (Of E. E. Cummings she once wrote, "powerful writing [as well as some of the most pompous nonsense I ever let slip to the floor with a wide yawn].")

Her reputation, despite her sharp critical mind, enormous popularity, and a Pulitzer Prize (she was the first woman to win one), suffered for these exclusions. A gifted formalist and prolific sonneteer, a literary heir to Donne, Wordsworth, Byron, and, well, Christina Rossetti, Millay today has been admired only slightly or reluctantly, if at all, her poetry viewed, sometimes by its detractors as well as its devotees, as anachronistic, unreconstructedly Victorian, sentimental, recycled. Even the critic Colin Falck, who writes in his impassioned introduction to her *Selected Poems* that the "occulting of Millay's reputation has been one of the literary scandals of the twentieth century," nonetheless finds only a quarter of her poems worthy enough "to entitle her to consideration as one of the major poets of the century." (Such lilting lyrics as "And better friends I'll not be knowing! / Still there's no train I'd not get on no matter where it's going" or "We were very tired, we were very merry— / We had gone back and forth all night on the ferry," which would have burnished the lyrical reputation of such ironists as Bob Dylan and Philip Larkin, did not seem especially to add to hers.)

A quarter, however, is probably not bad, probably usual for a major poet, and in Millay's case, probably high. One can see scattered throughout her poems—some weak and famous, some stronger and lesser known—enough elegant and beautiful lines, so that one wonders what she was thinking in the rest of the, too often, soggy poem. Her sonnets are especially susceptible to this: she wrote them as a short-story writer constructs a story—with the end strongly in mind. Between the Petrarchan and Shakespearean sonnet, the latter, with its dramatic closing couplet, is sometimes considered the more vulgar of the two, and it was at these that Millay excelled. The pseudofeminist "I shall forget you presently, my dear" closes cleverly:

> *But so it is, and nature has contrived*
> *To struggle on without a break thus far,*
> *Whether or not we find what we are seeking*
> *Is idle, biologically speaking.*

"I think I should have loved you presently" ends with this rhythmic, mock mournfulness: "A ghost in marble of a girl you knew / Who would have loved you in a day or two." Other of Millay's endings involve such epigrammatic wisdom as "Let us go forth together to the spring; / Love must be this, if it be anything" ("I pray you if you love me, bear my joy"). And "Pity me that the heart is slow to learn / What the swift mind beholds at every turn" ("Pity me not because the light of day").

If she had gone into commercial songwriting, she might have been praised more enduringly as a poet. Among her more ad lib verse, "Wild Swans" and "Elegy" (from *Memorial to D.C.*) have particular strength. The former, one of her simplest, shortest, and best compositions, is straightforward and affecting in its swell of feeling and cry of exile:

> *I looked in my heart while the wild swans went over.*
> *And what did I see I had not seen before?*
> *Only a question less or a question more;*
> *Nothing to match the flight of wild birds flying.*

> *Tiresome heart, forever living and dying,*
> *House without air, I leave you and lock your door.*
> *Wild swans, come over the town, come over*
> *The town again, trailing your legs and crying!*

Contemporary critics often praise "Bluebeard," a first-rate sonnet written sympathetically from the point of view of the merely private though disobeyed husband. ("I must never more behold your face. / This now is yours. I seek another place.") Long before Anne Sexton's *Transformations,* Millay was boldly looking twice at literature's alleged villains and staking out radical positions for herself.

But Milford is mistaken that the mawkish and folksy "Ballad of the Harp-Weaver," also a kind of fairy tale, and inspired by and dedicated to Millay's mother, "is a terrific poem." Its wearying twenty-nine stanzas begin:

> *"SON," said my mother,*
> *When I was knee-high,*
> *"You've need of clothes to cover you,*
> *And not a rag have I."*

And so on. Milford is understandably moved that last June in New York City she overheard two girls on MacDougal Street reciting it by heart. (Surely in that context one would be moved even to hear "There was a young lady of Niger.") But that cannot change the quality of Millay's too-mortal poem, the sentimental doggerel of which makes it probably indeed best suited to children. The poem's attachment to themes of maternal self-sacrifice in the Millay family give it power for Milford, for whom, naturally, biographical readings are the interesting ones. (That Millay's mother might have written it herself is never mentioned, though such a thought did occur to me.)

As a result, we have, with Milford's biography, the story of the life that eclipsed the work. It is a life that began in bookish poverty. Millay's mother, an itinerant nurse and hair weaver (one is reminded slightly here of a Victorian update of the medieval barber-surgeon), also kept a roomful of books open as a kind of public reading space for the neighborhood schoolchildren; it was a larger and finer collection than that possessed by the local library.

Mrs. Millay herself, however, was rarely home. Her three beautiful daughters—a phrase already out of a fairy tale—largely looked after themselves. Constructing a childhood of work and magic, fusing chores with skits, they memorized and performed poetry and songs, enchanting all who heard, or almost all. Edna, the eldest, known as Vincent (after St. Vincent's hospital, where a relative was convalescing at the time of her birth), or Sefius or Sefe to her mother, short for Josephus, for her role as alto and "son" and perhaps caretaker of the younger girls (the faux aliases the family concocted for themselves were a stewpot of loopy nicknames), was also the most beautiful, the most enchanting, and the most gifted. She was the leader of the sisters' imaginative play as well as primary housekeeper. When the river in Camden overflowed and the weather turned cold, Milford tells us, "the kitchen floor flooded and froze and the girls gleefully ice skated across it." (There is a melancholy echo of this game, in the last year of Millay's life, when a caretaker at her upstate New York home of Steepletop recalls of the ill and recently widowed Millay, "I remember that I had to wax the floor and I asked her where the heavy polisher was to buff it. And she sort of smiled at me and, putting on her socks, she skated and danced across my freshly waxed floor, and did it shine!")

Even as a girl, she calculated her effect and cut a magical figure. One childhood friend recalls her opening the door one evening dressed in

> a blouse of white muslin with cuffs and boned collar made of rows of insertion edged with lace. A full gored skirt came to the tops of her buttoned boots; a patent leather belt circumscribed a wide equator around her tiny middle; and a big blue bow spread its wings behind her head where her hair was fastened in a "bun." Books were piled on the floor from a table Vincent had cleared for games and in the center was a plate of still warm fudge.

When it came time to leave, she showed her guests to the door, lamp in hand, and taking up the refrain of the last song she'd sung for them, sang out, "Adieu, adieu, kind friends, adieu." "She has built up so enormous an image of herself as the Enchanted Little Faery Princess," recalled another friend much later in life. "She is the oddest mixture of genius and childish vanity, open mindedness and blind self-worship, that I have ever known."

In American mythological terms, Millay's is an actress's childhood: drunken, absent father; divorced, ambitious stage mother; a dreamy desire for the theater manifest everywhere from her reinvented speech and musical numbers with her sisters to her passion for sewing and costumes (she was a lifelong clotheshorse; not for her the fate of the redhead resigned to only kelly green). All the while, she wrote—poems, stories, even two novels, one written when she was eight, the other at fifteen. (Eventually, she would also write an opera, *The King's Henchman,* which would have its premiere at the Metropolitan Opera House in 1927.) She read all of Tennyson, Milton, Wordsworth, Longfellow, Shakespeare, Keats, Shelley, and Coleridge and practiced and composed piano pieces. She was given early to dramatic recitations of the many poems she memorized, and she memorized her own poems first, composing them in her head, before she wrote them down, a habit she kept throughout her lifetime.

This habit of public recitation was responsible for an early turning point in her life when, at twenty, she presented her own poetry at a summer hotel where her sister Norma worked, and a potential benefactress, Caroline Dow, became smitten and promised to send her to Vassar (Vincent was also offered, by another benefactress, free tuition to Smith, which she turned down). Such was her magical effect on people. There was no protracted, lonely obscurity for her: almost from the beginning she was noticed and sponsored. Even when her first famous poem, "Renascence," did not win a prize in the then widely read journal *The Lyric Year,* it became a kind of cause célèbre because it hadn't, various readers and poets registering their dissent, and the actual first-place winner refusing his prize money. Millay's failure to win the contest had been preceded by a long, coquettish, perhaps scandalous correspondence with one of the editors and judges, Ferdinand Earle, which, her brazen flirtation in the end leading nowhere useful, concluded with her writing to him in bitter disappointment:

> Let me congratulate you on your convincing impersonation
> of a genuine man. . . . How can I be expected to understand a
> person who got his education in France, his business-methods
> in Siberia, his behaviour in vaudeville, and his brains in a raffle?

It is a loss to the occasion of this minirevival of Millay that her correspondence, first published in part in the fifties by her sister Norma, has not also been issued, for Millay's prose is sparkling and fierce—on a par with Dorothy Parker's, to whom she was occasionally, in her time, compared.

Although she was already twenty when she started college, and therefore older than the others, among the young Vassar girls, too, Millay became a kind of pet. Girls fell in love with her and it was with them she first began—necessarily or gratuitously (Millay's cruelties are hard to categorize)—breaking the hearts of people infatuated with her. She was a master of the sudden distance, as well as the sudden intimacy, but she was also a discreet and loyal friend, which, if her lovers could forgivingly manage such a friendship—and Edmund Wilson, later on, was one of these—proved a lifelong reward. Strong-willed and ambivalent about student life that did not involve her poetry, Millay bore up under the strictures of Vassar and the sternness of the hypermanagerial Miss Dow, her benefactress, though not without bumpiness. Millay was already famous and feeling hemmed in by the regulations of the college. For skipping classes she was both rescued and reprimanded by Vassar's president—"I don't want any dead Shelleys on my doorstep," he said to her. "On those terms," she replied cockily, "I think I can continue to live in this hellhole." "I hate this pink-and-gray college," she wrote in a letter to a friend:

> If there had been a college in *Alice in Wonderland* it would be
> this college. . . . They treat us like an orphan asylum. . . . I am
> thinking seriously of going to the University of Moscow, and
> taking a course in Polite Anarchy & Murder as a Fine Art.

Her brief suspension shortly before graduation was met with much protest from admiring students and professors. She had been the star of all the class plays, and written two herself. She was a kind of beloved student queen and had trouble deferring to anyone, doing pretty much as she pleased. "I want you different from the usual type of poet who claims a freedom bordering on license," Miss Dow wrote her scoldingly, when Millay missed a meeting with one of Dow's distinguished friends. Throughout her life people initially saw in Millay what they wanted to see, then later were disabused. When her first book was published, Millay sent one to Miss Dow, only to receive this stinging note:

> Of course I am happy to have an "author's copy," and hope it is only the beginning of better things. . . . If I had not heard from several sources how bored you have been in the atmosphere of our home, I would have been glad to have you bring Norma up to dinner some time—but I hesitate to suggest a return to a place which seems to have been dull.

She added, paradoxically, that Millay would always be as welcome as when "we were all you had."

After Vassar, Millay headed for Greenwich Village, where she wrote and, along with her sisters and mother, performed with the Provincetown Players. Her play *Aria da Capo*, which she directed, was a resounding success. She traveled to France, England, and Albania, and helped keep things afloat financially by writing pseudonymously for *Vanity Fair* under the name of Nancy Boyd, reporting and advising on the social scene around her. Her many lovers included the most attractive of her political and artistic crowd: Floyd Dell, Edmund Wilson, John Peale Bishop, probably Jack Reed, probably Malcolm Cowley. (She also had an affair with Thelma Wood, Djuna Barnes's lover, earning Barnes's lifelong jealousy, and once made a pass at Georgia O'Keeffe, which was rebuffed.) Wilson strangely attributed Millay's promiscuity to her having had a delayed start on sex: this despite her many lovers at Vassar (he didn't count girls) and despite that he was a virgin himself before he met Millay (who was his age) and so had gotten a much later start than she—inconsequentially, one imagines.

. . .

But maybe too much generally has been made of Millay's love affairs—Daniel Mark Epstein, in a strange arithmetical moment in *his* biography of Millay, puts the official count at one hundred, with the implication that the unofficial tally would be much higher. The most important person in her life was not really any of them. Nor was it exactly her mother—though this is occasionally asserted by her biographers, and certainly there was an intensity and love between Millay and her mother, who, however, often seems more like yet another admirer, steeped in yearning, her letters to her daughter full of a lover's phrases and begging. The hardworking and literate Cora Millay had been for Vincent less a mother than a sister, coach, and friend. She kept close tabs on Vincent's work and publications and even competed with Vincent in poetry contests, being something of a poet herself. (This close mother-daughter literary bond is perhaps rivaled in American letters only by Carson McCullers and her mother, who was sometimes suspected of writing her young daughter's work. Neither Epstein nor Milford reports any such suspicion here, though it is interesting to note that in both McCullers's and Millay's cases the writer's work went into conspicuous decline after the mother's death.)

Cora shared with everyone else an undying infatuation with Vincent—she was at times less stage mother than president of the fan club—wondering, it seemed, how she, a mere mortal, could have given birth to such a goddess. But she was not without her own ego vis-à-vis her daughter, once writing,

> *We all know the poet who shot into fame*
> *As Edna St. Vincent Millay,*
> *But who was the poet who gave her the name*
> *Of Edna St. Vincent Millay?*

Vincent perhaps did as much to care for Cora later on in life—bringing her to Paris, buying her a house—as Cora had ever done for her. Edmund Wilson's recollection of Vincent's mother included her once saying that she "had been a slut herself so why shouldn't her girls be?" Wilson found Mrs. Millay shocking but felt that, even more than with Edna, Cora had "passed beyond good and evil . . . and that she had attained there a certain gaiety."

Perhaps it would not have been possible for her daughters to love Cora in any conventional way. Their adult protectiveness toward her was more likely a forgiving cover for her prior maternal negligence. She was at times hectoring and emotionally demanding. She had sent their father away, divorcing him, after developing a crush on a local minister. She consigned to her eldest astonishing quantities of housework. She gave her daughters a book on witchcraft, which in the absence of parental care became a kind of bible to them. She was a self-invented herbalist who made Vincent quite ill with a potion designed for homemade abortions. The daughters vied for her attention, courting her and looking after her, but when, as an older woman, she became more available to them, they plotted their little escapes from her. When Vincent writes to her, "We all love you better than anything, just as we did when we were little kids," one hears more obligation and desperation and hollowly constructed reassurance than truth.

No, surely the great love of Millay's life—and the great mother—was her husband, the Dutch aristocrat Eugen Boissevain, whose former wife was the suffragist Inez Milholland (also a Vassar graduate, who died tragically at twenty-eight). Boissevain was, according to Millay's brother-in-law, "the solution to a lot of problems" for Millay. He was "the mother type" and in terms of continuous devotion and care a more effective parent to Millay than her own parents ever were. As literary husbands go, even Leonard Woolf may pale by comparison. Boissevain loved caring for Millay and boasted of it—he called her Vince—just as Millay boasted, "I have nothing to do with my household. Eugen does all that kind of thing. . . . I have no time for it. I want to go into my dining room as if it were a restaurant, and say, 'What a charming dinner!' It's this unconcern with my household that protects me from the things that eat up a woman's time and interest."

Millay and Boissevain married when she was scheduled for intestinal surgery and his official spousal status was required for visitation. They gathered together with a few witnesses at his house in Croton-on-Hudson, she threw mosquito netting over her head for a veil, and immediately afterward they drove to New York Hospital. It was an open marriage (each had affairs known to the other; hers with the poet George Dillon seems even to have been actively encouraged by Boissevain), but theirs remained nonetheless a close and rancorless union. As he had squired his first famous wife on her speaking tours, Boissevain accompanied and nursed Millay on her grand, whistle-stop readings (she read to nothing but packed houses), and generally saw her through illness, spiritual crises, and family dramas, especially with her youngest sister, Kathleen, who was by then severely alcoholic. When they hit financial difficulties, Boissevain remained characteristically buoyant. He wrote to his brother that he was down to his last dollar but needed it for magic tricks. (Millay's wit, too, remained undeterred by money issues: she wrote of her publishers, from whom she borrowed large sums, "Although I reject their proposals, I welcome their advances.")

When her husband died, during surgery for lung cancer, Millay was, of course, devastated. Her own actual death—a fall down the stairs—seems a drunken suicide (she was not without such tendencies), a leap that perhaps echoes her having been "thrown" from a car in a Florida accident years before, after she lost a manuscript in a hotel fire. ("O Florida. O, cold Florida! Could any state be horrida?" she joked afterward.) When her back injury from the car accident led subsequently to morphine addiction, Eugen kept close and helped record her alarming dosages (these notebooks Milford calls "among the most troubling and pitiful documents in American literary history"); he even tried the drug himself to attempt to understand her dependence on it.

A contemporary reader of the lives of Millay and her peers will be struck by how much alcohol and drug intake was required of these sensitive Victorians–turned–Jazz Agers in negotiating their own pain, psychic and otherwise, in a fast-changing age of loosened mores. (Millay was considered successfully detoxed when the nurses got her breakfast down to tea, toast, and claret.) It was ultimately husbandly love that was Millay's ballast, and, on her own after her husband's death, she died within a year, found in a bloody heap at the foot of her stairs with three lines circled in a poem she'd been writing. "I will control myself, or go inside. I will not flaw perfection with my grief. Handsome, this day: no matter who has died."

·   ·   ·

In the end, Millay's life seems a love story of a different kind than indicated really by her poetry ("I shall forget you presently, my dear" or "My candle burns at both ends"). This is quite forcefully arrived at by Milford at the conclusion of her biography, and acknowledged to a lesser degree by Epstein, whose book, finally, is of a different sort. Epstein does many things quite well—he is more organized than Milford and more intent than she on recording what Edmund Wilson called Millay's "dedicated and noble presence." Milford's sources seem more often to recall Millay's vanities, and so in this way Epstein's book is less catty, more adoring, more literary and generous—more what Wilson himself might have written. Epstein attends better to the poetry than Milford does, and has a good ear for Millay's best work, even if he occasionally overstates ("Renascence," written when Millay was only twenty, may be precocious, but is it really a "marvel of twentieth-century poetry"? Did neither Eliot, Moore, Frost, nor Stevens produce three love poems comparable to Millay's?)

Epstein hasn't missed Millay's love of the racetrack (she was an enthusiastic gambler) the way Milford has, and he is better at certain background information, such as Boissevain's life before Millay. But his book is also stranger, as when he seems to turn the young Vincent into the precious heroine of a young adult novel, presuming her interior thoughts and motives, assembling his prose as narrative ("Her hands were small, but she stretched them strenuously each day over the piano keys, praying that they might grow"), even referring to her as "our heroine."

To be fair, there are parts even of Leon Edel's brilliant biography of Henry James that verge on something similar; such intimate but fictional fashioning is a hazard of biographical obsession. Epstein, however, may not always have put obsession to good use. He is a little startling, for example, on the subject of Millay's naked breasts, about which he exults—photographs of which he apparently pored over in the files of the Library of Congress (which could not authorize their release and reproduction at that time). When he gives us his own feverish descriptions, readers may become a little frightened, but eventually he moves on, and I do believe everyone recovers. Such an instance does not, how-

ever, prevent him from other periodic overheatings ("Her coloring, the
contrast between her white skin and the red integuments, lips, tongue,
and more secret circles and folds her lovers would cherish, had become
spectacular after the girl turned twenty"), which if they do not actually singe and bubble the page, at least prompt a reviewer's exclama-
tion marks in the margins. Epstein's index includes multiple entries
for Millay's physical appearance: "physical appearance: body"; "physical
appearance: hair"; "physical appearance: mouth"; "physical beauty and
charisma." Plus, quite pointedly, "power to drive men mad."

Milford's biography, on the other hand, remains poised and employs an unusual bicameral structure, which has been criticized by some
reviewers, but which in fact is part of the book's great strength and
originality. Once per chapter or so she interrupts the main biographical
account with ongoing conversations she as biographer had with Millay's sister Norma (and Norma's husband) in the 1970s and '80s, during
the book's research at Steepletop. In these metatextual moments Norma
Millay emerges as a brilliant character herself—eccentric, witchy, funny,
balky—not a coauthor of the biography, but a kind of cospirit behind
it. She and the stunning Eugen Boissevain almost threaten, as characters, to upstage the portrait of Edna Millay the book is trying to bring
into light. As when the vivid minor characters of a Dickens novel begin
to engage the reader more than the protagonist does, it is a delightful,
accidental, and never wholly fatal problem for an author to have.

(2002)

Darryl Pinckney and Caryl Phillips

In singling out three "mavericks of black literature" for his book *Out There,* Darryl Pinckney, who has written much on black literature, perceptively and with the animated brilliance of a passionate reader (he is also the gifted author of the novel *High Cotton*), has employed a working definition of *maverick* that includes the phrase "a striking eccentricity of purpose." They are words that are as good as any and more apt than most to describe the work of the Jamaican journalist J. A. Rogers, the expatriate American memoirist Vincent O. Carter, and, perhaps to a lesser degree, the contemporary British novelist Caryl Phillips. These are, at any rate, the three writers whose literary lives inform the pages of Pinckney's collection, and though their work and biographies are treated with Pinckney's own eccentricity of approach (the essays were originally lectures given at Harvard and will seem, perhaps, brief for those readers seeking comprehensive details of a writer's childhood or formative romances), they are full of great personal feeling, intellectual curiosity, and original, groundbreaking research.

J. A. Rogers was, according to Pinckney, a kind of through-the-looking-glass Kipling, documenting those spots around the world "where the white and the nonwhite are not in their ordained places." Born in Jamaica in 1883, and emigrating as a young man to the United States, Rogers became a kind of popular historian of black achievement and was thought of as the first black war correspondent (though one wonders why George Washington Williams, who was born almost thirty-five years before and by 1890 was reporting on the Belgian Congo, has not been given that title). Rogers's purpose was black pride and moral restitution for the Negro, and in his three volumes of *Sex and Race* he became obsessed with compiling a kind of historical *Believe It or Not* of people of color, even going out on a limb and including the swarthy, brooding Beethoven—and if not Beethoven, well then Beethoven's accompanist—to prove that race mixing is the reality of history. Rogers desired to serve the black community, as was the wish of many subsequent literary radicals, but he worked within white-defined categories of history and culture.

As Pinckney writes, "We don't need to claim Beethoven." Rogers was considered half-nuts by some, including his fellow countryman Claude McKay, who came to doubt very much Rogers's stubborn accumulation of "Amazing Facts." Rogers was especially interested in such things as Warren Harding's reputed African-American blood (Bill Clinton may imagine he was the first African-American president, but he may be simply the first to boast of it). The part-disparaging, part-prideful parlor game of ethnic naming (the Polish genius—Conrad, Chopin; or the Jewish sex symbol—Paul Newman, Kirk Douglas) engages in any minority some group feeling of unjustified insecurity and a suspicion of cover-up in the mainstream culture. But in such a game of self-esteem, which is the project Rogers was interested in, one must walk through the room of bias and prejudice, noting the insulting stereotypes, before attempting to demolish them. The well-intentioned racial archaeology that seeks (for purposes of celebration and accuracy) any hidden drop of African blood sometimes seems a weird inversion of the racist's similar preoccupation. "Africa is everywhere, both the nightmare and the dream proclaim," writes Pinckney.

Rogers's restless cataloging led to overstepping and guessing and digressive blind alleys. Pinckney says, "The experience of reading *Sex and Race* is one of embrace and recoil as Rogers indiscriminately loads us down with the provable and the forever dodgy, the serious and the frivolous."

Rogers even fudged slightly his own entry in *Who's Who in Negro America?*, apparently dissatisfied with his own many achievements and listing a book he never actually completed. Perhaps the only writer who made his living entirely within what was then known as the Negro press, Rogers remained virtually unknown in the white world, but his sheer energy (he toured and lectured tirelessly, selling his books as he went) seems an amazement now. He died leaving many of his own questions (most hinging on Europe's proximity to Africa) unanswered: "What images were removed from churches and museums in Italy following the declaration of the purification laws of 1938? Are all the images of the Black Madonna in Eastern Europe the result of centuries of smoke?"

Rogers claimed that a painting by the Belgian artist Charles Verlat "depicts the blackest, most Negroid Christ he'd ever seen." That Rogers felt he needed not just Cleopatra but Jesus and Mary as well for his encyclopedia shows the persistent allure of these questions. It also shows the odd fierceness of Rogers's character, the idiosyncrasy of his intellect, and the poignant grandiosity of his life's work.

It is with *Out There*'s last two writers, Vincent Carter and Caryl Phillips, that Pinckney offers a closer examination of place and home as it affects black artists—especially those who have broken away and become exiles or migrants—and in so doing he begins a conversation with Phillips himself, whose new collection of essays, *A New World Order,* is largely concerned with these themes. Pinckney's discovery of Vincent Carter, who lived in Switzerland for most of the fifties, came about, he says, when he received Carter's *The Bern Book* as a present from Susan Sontag and Robert and Peg Boyers. Part novel, part autobiography, "*The Anatomy of Melancholy* for this century," it consists of such *Tristram Shandy*–style chapter titles as "A Little Sham History of Switzerland, Which Is Very Much to the Point, and Which the Incredulous or the Pedantic May Verify by Reading a Formal History of Switzerland, Which I Have Certainly Never Done, and Will Probably Never Do." Though he desired the "romance of Europe in the era of the GI Bill Negro," he perversely settled not in France, as Richard Wright and James Baldwin did, but in Bern, Switzerland, Pinckney surmises, paraphrasing Baldwin, because he did not want to spoil "another black man's hustle in a room of white people."

In this, his only published book, Carter—who later became a physical fitness fanatic—seems bemused if not stunned by his own choices. He is called Wince by the locals, and even though he is the first black man they have ever met, the Swiss regale and irritate him with their racial presumptions and faux expertise on all things Negro, especially jazz. Despite Carter's unwillingness to let paying work get in the way of his writing, which gathers dozens of rejection slips, he humbly— "with much mock heroism," Pinckney suggests—gives English lessons. Carter refers to himself as "a hypersensitive nigger" who sends himself out into the streets for experiments in "lacerating subjective sociology": in *The Bern Book,* Carter's helpless wit has extended even to the pun of his title.

Pinckney writes with sorrowful, almost exasperated eloquence of Carter's experience in Bern:

> *The Bern Book* isn't a work of memory. It is a work about ambivalence, escape, evasion, and the expatriate's creed of noble procrastination, noble withdrawal. Carter is that familiar, defensive figure in the café, the man who refuses to be practical, the artist with impossibly high standards, the stranger who is difficult to help, the black man who attacks the white friends who have just fed him or from whom he has just borrowed money.

The social type to which Pinckney is referring is not a racial one, and so it seems at first disconcerting to see the words *black* and *white* toward the end of his description. But Pinckney wants to find out what happens to the defensive expatriate when race is involved, and he is simultaneously sympathetic, skeptical, and analytical.

These qualities are engaged, too, in Pinckney's view of the British writer Caryl Phillips, who was born on Saint Kitts in 1958, raised in Leeds, and who has published his own essay collection, *A New World Order,* which deals with many of the same issues explored by Pinckney—issues of place and home for the artist of color. Pinckney and Phillips are roughly contemporaries, their first names are near rhymes, and their books are often shelved side by side alphabetically in bookstores. One can imagine—and not only fancifully—that the books of these two men have been in conversation with one another for some time.

"He does not go to Du Bois's grave in Ghana," writes Pinckney in a moment of judgment on the journey to Africa that Phillips writes about in *The Atlantic Sound.* "He refuses to make his trip a pilgrimage. He has a right to stand outside of that feeling, but it is as though he cannot afford to be moved." In Phillips's new book he visits the grave, but he is still not explicitly moved: "It is over a decade now since I followed the austerely dressed young Ghanaian man around the W. E. B. Du Bois Centre in Accra. He showed me Du Bois's study, his books, his living area and then of course Du Bois's final resting place in the grounds of the centre."

The novelist in Pinckney admires Phillips's art but seems at times to suspect him of coolness, coyness, impersonality—"By temperament," writes Pinckney, "it would seem, Phillips is opposed to what in his prologue he must do as a first-person narrator, especially a black one: explain, identify himself. Who am I? I am none of your business; but you, they, it are my business. Perhaps this tone is his way of saying that nothing is more personal than an individual's ideas."

One of Phillips's ideas is the predicament of the African-American artist in his home country, and the first section of *A New World Order,* entitled "The United States," is in many ways his best (the others are called "Africa," "The Caribbean," and "Britain"). In this first section he includes pieces on Richard Wright, James Baldwin, and the singer Marvin Gaye—all of whom exiled themselves to Europe—and on John Edgar Wideman, who, perhaps more boldly, Phillips suggests, did not. The American oppression of the black man—both subtle and overt—is hardly lost on Wideman, however, and Phillips quotes a searing passage from Wideman's *Fatheralong* that sums up the cost of staying and the privilege (however spurious), unavailable to most, of not:

> And we ain't talking here about middle-class angst cause no taxis stop for your black ass in Rockefeller Center. Nor existential maundering when you ride the commuter train in from

Scarsdale and the only seat white people ain't occupying is the one next to your brown ass. All that's part of the problem, but the bedrock issue raised by the paradigm of race . . . is whether you can be someone other than a white person in this society and stay healthy, stay alive.

As a black man who saw bananas thrown at the nonwhite soccer players of 1960s and '70s England and who witnessed the violence in London's Notting Hill during race riots two decades apart (the neighborhood now resides in the American mind as a Hugh Grant film), and as the grandson of a Portuguese Jew, Phillips has no illusions about racism in Europe. (He is equally unromantic about Africa as a diasporan homeland, implying, as many African-Americans have, that cultural attachment to it may be a sentimental folly.) But the innocent optimism with which black artists (Gaye, Baldwin, Wright) have fled to Europe suggests to him that the psychological, sociological, and artistic burdens on the African-American artist are somehow more intense and restrictive in the United States and that Europe poses a greater (even if illusory) freedom from artistic expectation (race as a part-time job, race as glorious/tedious obligation, race as coauthor of one's work). Baldwin's second novel, *Giovanni's Room,* written in France, had no black people in it at all. Marvin Gaye often wanted nothing more than to sing "Fly Me to the Moon" and "Me and My Shadow," yet in the States was asked to keep up a certain kind of black image for the Motown label. And if one looks at Wideman's editorial selection in the *Best American Short Stories of 1996,* one sees he has chosen love story after love story— all strong and haunting, but scarcely a one concerning race.

To unburden oneself aesthetically from race is, of course, impossible even if it were advisable. The artist necessarily creates not just from who but also from what he is. But it is Phillips's point, of course, that a person is always many things, and that a society that does not recognize that will prove parochial and stifling for an artist. The saddest tale he has to tell here is of Marvin Gaye, who in his escape from the pressures of the African-American recording industry fled to Belgium to pursue his art in obscurity and effacement—an annihilation of sorts. Although "like American artists before him, he was able to enjoy the freedom of not feeling any responsibility to comment on European society, including its racism," the price he paid was profound loneliness. Phillips cites a scene from a documentary film made about Gaye:

> Marvin enters a working-class bar which is full of Belgian workers enjoying a beer at the end of the day. They look quizzically at this American black man, and ask him if he's from Paraguay. Marvin confesses to being a singer from Los Angeles and they laugh at him. Then Marvin attempts to play darts. He is not very good and again they laugh at him. . . . Here, in Belgium, Marvin is neither a star nor is he an American. He has no viable role to play, not even the role of black American sex symbol which he considers so demeaning. The creases of worry on his forehead suggest that he knows what he is in Belgium. He is simply a black man.

At the time of his death at forty-four—he was shot by his cross-dressing Pentecostal minister father in a family squabble—Gaye was attempting to use comedy to send up his professional quandaries, and his final, satirical songs include one entitled "Dem Niggers Are Savage in the Sack." For a man who, as his father did before him, liked to dress in women's wigs and lingerie in private, such songwriting was a reaction to ideas of African-American manhood and the "burdensome public role of 'Sex God'" he felt the record business had foisted upon him. And here Phillips's usually sturdy phrasing grows soggy as it does sometimes, oddly, when he's passionate. "The days when he could write and perform socially committed, yet heart-wrenchingly sensitive work seemed to have receded into the distant past."

Phillips's essay on V. S. Naipaul may be the strongest in his section "The Caribbean." Here—despite the melancholy spin he has previously given American expatriation—he speaks of the "gift of displacement," a sometimes advantageous and energetic creative condition he feels is complained of unfairly by Naipaul, as if it were unique and bitter medicine, a price Naipaul alone paid for art. (That there are inconsistencies in Phillips's own thinking on these matters, depending on whom he is writing about, makes this book seem no less rich or deeply considered. Surprisingly it is just the opposite.) Naipaul's sense of his own rootlessness, to Phillips's mind, is accompanied by a contempt for third-world culture and people: "Already comfortable with his prejudices, sure of his judgement and determined to write, there is something alarming about young Naipaul's lack of self-knowledge." But Phillips writes approvingly of Naipaul's 1994 novel *A Way in the World,* calling its great accomplishment "making art out of displacement and despair." He sees Naipaul as "beginning to make peace with his homeland of Trinidad" only to return later to generally dyspeptic antipathies, beginning with *Among the Believers,* his book about his travels in the Islamic world.

Naipaul's family lost their status as Brahmins with their migration to Trinidad, and one might suspect this condition (in addition to Naipaul's own temperament) may be partly responsible for what Phillips sees as Naipaul's misanthropy, his intolerance, and the "wall of self-regard between himself and the people who produced him." But Phillips's last criticism, the one that says Naipaul has sacrificed in his art "any real expression of affection for his homeland or its people," seems intellectually spurious, since here Naipaul is being held to standards to which no serious literary critic would consider holding Sinclair Lewis or Flannery O'Connor, for instance. Nor does Phillips himself always hold it against others, including J. M. Coetzee, about whom Phillips writes well here, never, however, emphasizing what might be thought of as Coetzee's own misanthropy. That one must withhold contempt for one's homeland is not a literary idea at all. That one cannot make "outlandish, racist, unscholarly, inaccurate statements in books and in interviews, and still be taken seriously"—Phillips's charge against Naipaul—of course is. But Phillips has conflated these two things in his arguments about Naipaul. And when he gives way to strong feelings, Phillips can sound maudlin and fond of fondness for its own sake. He insists that Naipaul has turned away from his earlier work and his true subject matter: "Caribbean life—the people, the music, the heat, the flora, the fauna, the sunrise, the sunset, the history." The sunrise? The sunset? Phillips is partial to horizons and sometimes seems to be listening to music when he writes of them ("for as they stood on the deck of the ship and stared out at the white cliffs of Dover, they carried within their hearts a dream," he writes of the early Caribbean immigrants to England).

Naipaul's father's own failed literary career, and what Phillips takes to be Naipaul's quiet sneering at it, is at the heart of the issue, Phillips thinks, though he also demonstrates that he may have underestimated the son's real love and admiration for this Trinidadian journalist-father who encouraged his newly British son in every way, but also encouraged him to write sympathetically about his homeland (which Phillips himself, of course, wishes Naipaul had done). At his father's death (of "a broken heart," Phillips suggests in another treacly moment) Naipaul sent his family a mournful telegram that read in part, "He was the best man I knew." Surely, then, there was some part of Naipaul that was listening. His response to Elizabeth Hardwick that the red dot in the middle of an Indian woman's forehead means "my head is empty" doesn't seem necessarily a cultural slur but may be more complicated in its ironies; perhaps it serves as a commentary on the oppressive aspects of Hindu marriage, though Phillips will give it credit for being nothing but "idiotic."

A New World Order is a largely brilliant and persuasive book with which one will quibble occasionally. But then Phillips quibbles with himself. He closes the introduction to his section on the United States with a statement to which the remainder of his book too often gives the lie. "Race matters," he writes (as if paging Cornel West). "Sure it does, but not that much."

Not that much? Well, it's an idea.

(2002)

Margaret Atwood's *Oryx and Crake*

The novelist Margaret Atwood has wandered off from us before: once, in 1986, to the mid-twenty-first century, for a feminist dystopia, *The Handmaid's Tale,* in which women are enslaved according to their reproductive usefulness; another time, in 1996, to the nineteenth century, to make thrifty use of her graduate work at Radcliffe in the faux-Victorian novel *Alias Grace.* These were forays and raids. In her chronicling of contemporary sexual manners and politics, Atwood has always been interested in pilfering popular forms—comic books, gothic tales, detective novels, science fiction—in order to make them do her more literary bidding. Her previous novel, *The Blind Assassin,* is the best example of the kind of narrative pastiche at which she excels.

In her towering and intrepid new novel, *Oryx and Crake,* Atwood, who is the daughter of a biologist, vividly imagines a late-twenty-first-century world ravaged by innovations in biological science. Like most literary imaginings of the future, her vision is mournful, bleak, and infernal, and is punctuated, in Atwood style, with the occasional macabre joke—perhaps not unlike Dante's own literary vision. Atwood's pilgrim in Hell is Snowman, who, following a genetically engineered viral cataclysm, is, as far as he knows, the only human being who has survived. Snowman (formerly Jimmy) has become arboreal, living in trees and in shelters of junk, roaming the beaches and picnic grounds of a former park—where fungi sprout from rotting picnic tables and barbecues are festooned with bindweed—scavenging for food. His only companions are a dozen or so humanoids, the Crakers—gentle, naked, beautiful creations of Jimmy's old, half-mad scientist friend Crake. Freed from their experimental lab, the Crakers also live near the beach. They eat nothing but grass, leaves, and roots; their sexual rituals have been elegantly and efficiently programmed to minimize both sexual reproduction and unrequited lust. To them, the man they call Snowman is a demigod or a prophet. Unable to tolerate sunlight, Jimmy wears a ghostly bedsheet. For the Crakers, the real gods are Crake, whom they have never seen, and his girlfriend, Oryx, whom they have. The Crakers await the gods' return and listen to stories that Snowman tells them about Crake and Oryx. A holy, yarny scripture is already emerging.

Parallel with this vision of a blighted future is the novel's dramatic story of how the global apocalypse came to pass, told in flashback. Jimmy and Crake grow up as friends in gated communities, safe from the environmental degradation that has already overtaken the outside world. They are the privileged children of scientists who work for top-secret agribusiness and biotech companies with names like Helth Wyzer and OrganicInc Farms. The latter, for medical-transplant purposes, makes pigs that are genetically altered with human DNA; after the apocalypse, these extraclever "pigoons" go hunting for Snowman like hounds after a fox. There are other mistakes, too—creatures called wolvogs, which are exactly what you would expect. Later, Crake's classmates work on developing, for a fast-food venture, headless, legless chickens—"Sort of like a chicken hookworm," Crake says. Such genetic ambitions will not sound outlandish to anyone who has kept abreast of current poultry-farming practices or knows that scientists have experimented with splicing fish genes into tomatoes to prevent freezing.

Although the boys' daily lives are full of swimming pools, bullet trains, completely self-contained shopping malls, and games like Kwiktime Osama, they maintain a curiosity about the world outside in "the pleeblands," of which they have little experience. They have lost parents in the madness of this sinister and isolated lifestyle. Crake's father, burdened with the knowledge of pharmaceutical conspiracies, "jumped" from an overpass; Jimmy's mother, critical of her husband's work, grew depressed, then disappeared. While quite young, both boys come to suspect that their parents have been executed.

In their college years, Crake and Jimmy part ways, Crake being the more scientifically brilliant and ambitious, Jimmy the more verbal and skeptical. Crake goes to the prestigious Watson-Crick Institute (also known as Asperger's U), where the cafeteria serves shrimp (in contrast to the genetically processed fare available to the general populace), and prostitutes of one's choosing are available through Student Services: "Once a student there and your future was assured. It was like going to Harvard had been, back before it got drowned." From then on, Crake is destined to be a prized geneticist. As a student he is able to reap half the profits of anything he creates; thereafter he can name his price. Jimmy, on the other hand, is sent to the crumbling, neglected Martha Graham Academy:

> The Martha Graham Academy was named after some gory old dance goddess of the twentieth century who'd apparently mowed quite a swath in her day. There was a gruesome statue of her in front of the administration building, in her role— said the bronze plaque—as Judith, cutting off the head of a guy in a historical robe outfit called Holofernes. Retro feminist shit, was the general student opinion. Every once in a while the statue got its tits decorated or steel wool glued onto its pubic region—Jimmy himself had done some of this glueing—and so comatose was the management that the ornaments often stayed up there for months before they were noticed.

Tonally, *Oryx and Crake* is a roller-coaster ride. The book proceeds from terrifying grimness through lonely mournfulness, until, midway, a morbid giddiness begins sporadically to assert itself, like someone, exhausted by bad news, hysterically succumbing to giggles at a funeral. Atwood begins to smirk and deadpan: "There was a lot of dismay out there, and not nearly enough ambulances." She invents an assisted-suicide site called nitee-nite.com. Of Crake's experimental BlyssPluss Pill, she writes, "They hadn't got it to work seamlessly yet. . . . A couple of the test subjects had literally fucked themselves to death, several had assaulted old ladies and household pets, and there had been a few unfortunate cases of priapism and split dicks." Here she is on the scientifically designed mating rituals of the Crakers:

> Courtship begins at the first whiff, the first faint blush of azure, with the males presenting flowers to the females—just as male penguins present round stones. . . . At the same time they indulge in musical outbursts, like songbirds. Their penises turn bright blue to match the blue abdomens of the females, and they do a sort of blue-dick dance number, erect members waving to and fro in unison, in time to the foot movements and the singing: a feature suggested to Crake by the sexual semaphoring of crabs. From amongst the floral tributes the female chooses four flowers, and the sexual ardour of the unsuccessful candidates dissipates immediately, with no hard feelings left. Then, when the blue of her abdomen has reached its deepest shade, the female and her quartet find a secluded spot and go at it until the woman becomes pregnant and her blue colouring fades. And that is that.
>
> No more No means yes, anyway, thinks Snowman.

In the world of *Oryx and Crake*—a future rendered precivilized by catastrophe—one can feel the influences of Denis Johnson's *Fiskadoro,* or Walter M. Miller, Jr.'s *A Canticle for Leibowitz.* In the novel's whimsical fantasies of biological evolution and technology, one can discern the dark left hand of Ursula K. Le Guin, and in its shrugging, eschatological amusement it channels the spirit of Kurt Vonnegut. In fact, the sick joke and the botched experiment are offered up as rough equivalents and become, through the technical alchemy of the novel, a kind of trope for life itself.

Seventeen years ago Mary McCarthy, reviewing *The Handmaid's Tale,* found it unconvincing as a jeremiad: "Surely the essential element of a cautionary tale is recognition. . . . It is an effect, for me, almost strikingly missing." She complained, too, about the weak characterizations, and suggested that the novel's lack of a new language for its future, such as Orwell had created in *1984,* left its world less than fully imagined. But a dystopian novel is not intended as a literal forecast, or even necessarily as a logical extension of our current world. It is simply, and not so simply, a bad dream of our present time, an exquisitely designed horror show in which things are changed from what we do know to a dream version of what we don't. Atwood does this well. To ask a novel to do more is to misunderstand its nature. Besides, given what is known about fish-gene-enhanced tomatoes—or those genetically modified goats that produce spider silk—the biologically reengineered world of *Oryx and Crake* ceases to seem very far-fetched. As for the characters here, McCarthy would be more pleased. They are mostly male, Atwood being rare among feminist writers in apparently liking her men—if not their institutions—better than her women. (Not since Edith Wharton has a female writer filled her oeuvre with so many unpleasant female characters.) Jimmy is not only complex, sympathetic, and anchoring; he is also the observer of the new language that abounds in this new world, and the curator and lexicographer of the old words that no one uses anymore—"Knell. Kern. Alack." Atwood does Orwell, and McCarthy, one better. She even devises a kind of exuberant elegy for the word *toast*.

With such a portrait of devastation, it may be important for the reader both to know and to feel what it is that Atwood values. (It is, arguably, immoral of an author not to share.) Given all that has been destroyed, and what has survived, has she discovered anything of worth from the old world that is ours? What is enduring and significant? What can be remembered and held dear? Clearly, she tells us, language. Also lovemaking, a jazz horn solo, the attractiveness of an imperfect body, and twelve thousand years of man-canine devotion. But there is a more pervasive and recurrent idea, one that would be sentimental if it were not for its inherent animal truth, and that is the power of maternal love. Jimmy scans the world—news footage, postcards sent in code—for his lost mother. Oryx, too, reflects, "She herself would rather have had her mother's love—the love she still continued to believe in, the love that had followed her through the jungle in the form of a bird so she would not be too frightened or lonely." In this we have a theme reminiscent of Margaret Wise Brown's *The Runaway Bunny*, that children's parable of maternal devotion which is also a gender Rorschach test—the masculine perspective finding the ubiquitous and undeterrable love of the mother suffocating, the feminine finding it beautiful. Atwood takes the feminine view; here mother love is the great sustainer, the protean protector, the tender magician, and its loss the great loss.

The ur-mother in *Oryx and Crake* is, of course, Mother Nature herself—captured, tortured, and mocked, in classic gothic fashion, but elusive and indestructible, in her way. As a curious aside in this year's fiftieth-anniversary celebration of the discovery of DNA by Watson and Crick, it was reported recently that Crick's wife, a professional illustrator, did only two scientific drawings in the course of her career. One was of her husband's famous double helix. The other was of a woman running.

(2003)

John Updike's *The Early Stories*

Embedded (oh, that word) in John Updike's openhearted foreword to his collection *The Early Stories, 1953–1975* is his book's missing dedication. "Perhaps I could have made a go of the literary business without my first wife's faith, forbearance, sensitivity, and good sense, but I cannot imagine how." Indeed, the figure of the first wife recurs throughout Updike's narrative work, and throughout this book, especially in its closing stories, where, in whatever incarnation Updike fashions her, she is both vivid and benign—a sister, a conscience, an aspect of self, a fellow witness, a pal. Thus one might conclude that this huge compilation of "early" stories, which Updike wrote over a twenty-two-year period for money as well as art (selling them to *The New Yorker* was his "principal means of support, for a family that by 1960 included four children under six"), is largely about the getting, having, and leaving of the first wife, the straight American man's grab, and grab again, at happiness.

One would not be entirely wrong. Updike's protagonists in the short fiction early in his career are largely solitudinous sons and husbands, somewhat isolated from other men. His metaphors, too, are marital and filial, sometimes both simultaneously. "The world is our bride," he writes in "Packed Dirt, Churchgoing, a Dying Cat, a Traded Car," one of the best stories in the volume, "given to us to love, and the terror and joy of the marriage is that we bring to it a nature not our bride's." In "Museums and Women," he writes, "Often my mother . . . was the only other person in the room. Who she was was a mystery so deep it never formed into a question." Though both emotionally and materially frugal, men in Updike's fictional world are drawn to, dependent on, and passive before women. There is both uneasiness and comfort in this sexual land, without much profound mutual knowledge, though such knowledge is struggled toward by almost all the characters. The elegant and penetrating descriptions, however, composed from the chasm's edge—both the wisdom and the wise unknowingness—are among the main reasons one reads Updike. "Her gesture as she tips the dregs of white wine into a potted geranium seems infinite, like one of Vermeer's moments frozen in an eternal light from the left." His eye and his prose never falter, even when the world fails to send its more socially complicated revelations directly his story's way.

Updike's primary subject here is the American village, from Greenwich Village to Tarbox. ("Tar," Elizabeth Hardwick once wrote, "an odorous viscous liquid, and box—well, guess.") History, or the doings of the outside world and their intrusions upon his villagers, he has by and large reserved for his capacious novels. His immense achievement there, the now-canonized Rabbit tetralogy, is a national portrait registering four consecutive American decades, its third-person, present-tense narrative a kind of democratic flypaper (in the children's alphabet book Updike wrote with his son, the letter *V* is not for the usual *violin* but for *vacuum cleaner*), capturing everything from the latest songs on the radio to the headlines in the papers to the food in the fridge. A narrative farrago. The way we live now and now and now—in the trapped yet ongoing animation the present tense suggests. The novel's protagonist, Rabbit Angstrom, is a low-wattage Everyman in whose appetites we are asked to see our postwar American selves. When a nation has never had a medieval epoch, Updike has written, when it is founded from the beginning on rationalism and "nineteenth-century laws of material exchange," what remains "is a bald consumer . . . whose genetically determined life-events scarcely warrant the glamorization of fiction." Yet his Rabbit novels have perhaps provided this glamorization, or surmounted the obstacle.

In much of the rest of his work, one might argue, Updike explores the range of his characters' "medieval" side, lives shaped by their theological negotiations. Updike came of age, he has written, at a time that "saw the Middle Ages still in favor, as a kind of golden era of cultural unity and alleviated anxiety." He has even borrowed from medieval dramatis personae, as in his Tristan and Iseult stories (retold as well in the novel *Brazil*) or his novel *Gertrude and Claudius*. Fellow Lutheran and English major Garrison Keillor recently wrote, satirizing academic prose, "Updike's verticalization of moral peril parallels the medieval cosmology of mystical painting." But, well, it is quite conceivably so.

Philip Larkin once said that novels are about others; poems are about oneself. One can imagine a short story falling somewhere in between. Updike's stories are focused, local meditations, suffused with Updike's brand of Protestant mysticism, a Christianity not of guilt and sin but of sorrow and beauty. Each story positions itself before a moment of personal wonder and trust, then worries it. Or a story springs from an erotic wound, worries that, then spins an elegant cocoon around as a bandage. His artistic gift is equal to his intellect and, happily partnered, neither needs nor seeks to use a story to prove itself. And yet both are proven—inevitably, gracefully, repeatedly. It is quite possible that by dint of both quality and quantity he is American literature's greatest short-story writer, and arguably our greatest writer without a single great novel. Thus the significance of this new collection.

The Early Stories is arranged not chronologically by date of composition (though an index of titles provides something of a chronology) but sequentially by subject, like a novel, perhaps a great novel, in sections that could be chapters, and in which we see a masculine sensibility grow and drift and cry out through the disparately aching stages of life from boyhood to early middle age. Each labeled section of this improvised bildungsroman includes a famous story: "Pigeon Feathers" in the section titled "Olinger Stories"; "The Christian Roommates" in "Out in the World"; "Should Wizard Hit Mommy?" in "Married Life"; "The Music School" in "Family Life"; "Museums and Women" in "The Two Iseults"; "A&P" in "Tarbox Tales"; "Under the Microscope" in "Far Out"; "Separating" in "The Single Life." In each section Updike has placed other related stories—related in theme and strategy though not always in time of composition. These grouped stories constitute an inexact family. They are sometimes expansions of the more well-known story; sometimes distant relatives. Alternative points of view on the same idea are often offered. From these groupings we can see that like most writers Updike has returned to particular topics, most of which involve the large and small attempts at spiritual breakaway and reconstitution—*flight* in both meanings of the word—by white American boys and men.

"Pigeon Feathers" (in the "Olinger Stories" section) originally sat smack in the center of Updike's collection by the same name. "Pigeon Feathers" is Updike's supreme story of boyhood, one of several poignant comedies of excruciation, seemingly conjured from memory, in what has been until now, to my mind, his strongest book. The boy David Kern, after reading H. G. Wells, is struck with fear and horror by Wells's atheism. Wells's, David thinks, is "a brain black with the denial of Christ's divinity."

> And in the momentum of [the boy's] terror, hideous possibilities—the dilation of the sun, the triumph of the insects, the crabs on the shore in *The Time Machine*—wheeled out of the vacuum of make-believe and added their weight to his impending oblivion.

His own physical self protests against the eternal, demolishing universe. "His protesting nerves swarmed." The loud intimations of mortality that descend upon him in Sunday school, in the family outhouse, or as he leafs through a dictionary weigh heavily on his heart. There is, too, a backdrop of parental discontent and discord, as well as a dying grandmother. When David is asked by his mother and grandmother to kill the pigeons in the barn, his simmering adolescent and ontological rage now has a target, and what emerges is both an artist's and an assassin's sense of purpose:

> Out of the shadowy ragged infinity of the vast barn roof these impudent things dared to thrust their heads, presumed to dirty its starred silence with their filthy timorous life, and he cut them off, tucked them back neatly into the silence. He felt like

a creator; these little smudges and flickers that he was clever to see and even cleverer to hit in the dim recesses of the rafters—out of each of them he was making a full bird. A tiny peek, probe, dab of life, when he hit it blossomed into a dead enemy, falling with good, final weight.

But it is the beauty of the birds—"banded in slate shades of blue . . . mottled all over in rhythms of lilac and gray"—that restores David's sense of God and, more comically and heartbreakingly, his own grandiose corollary to that faith: personal immortality. "The God who had lavished such craft upon these worthless birds would not destroy His whole Creation by refusing to let David live forever."

Even the gorgeous writing offered in snippets here cannot hint at the literary accomplishment that is the sensitive, searching, bookish character of David Kern (it is Updike, lavishing such craft upon his descriptions of the birds, that has allowed David to live forever; art here outperforms faith), and Updike returns to Kern in other stories, including "Packed Dirt, Churchgoing, a Dying Cat, a Traded Car." In this essayistic tale Kern is a grown man—Updike makes him a writer (in "The Christian Roommates" he becomes an adman)—contemplating the restaging of missed ceremonies that is the artist's true life. He loves the worn paths of small towns. Churchgoing captures his imagination. "I tried not to go, but it was not in me not to go," Kern says within this assemblage of sweet and bitter valentines that lay out the Updikean creed. "We in America," he writes, in words that become a kind of refrain (*refrain* as both vocal noun and thematic verb in this roaming, meditative story),

> have from the beginning been cleaving and baring the earth, attacking, reforming the immensity of nature we were given. We have explored, on behalf of all mankind, this paradox: the more matter is outwardly mastered, the more it overwhelms us in our hearts. . . . There was a time when I wondered why more people did not go to church.

A bloody-minded sort of nostalgia inspires and courses through Updike's work: nostalgia without sentimentality, for no feeling seems forced or faked or secondhand. Updike's delicate, almost unspoken renunciations of time and change are shown to be spare and tepid balkings, clear-eyed allergies—and his Proustian retrievals of childhood capture much anguish and irritation recalled in grateful tranquillity. He performs the temperamentally athletic feat of nostalgia that never really turns its back on the present. In "Packed Dirt . . . ," David Kern notes the persistent sepia quality to Christianity, even in the churches of Greenwich Village: "In Manhattan, Christianity is so feeble its future seems before it. One walks to church past clattering cafeterias and glowering news vendors in winter weather that is always a shade of Lent, on pavements spangled with last night's vomit."

As his professional doppelgänger, Updike's fictional novelist Henry Bech (the eponymous hero of *Bech Is Back,* who appears in the early stories only briefly), suggests of himself, Updike shows "characters whose actions are all determined, at the deepest level, by nostalgia, by a desire to get back, to dive, each, into the springs of their private imagery." A stunned muteness sometimes befalls these men. The rituals of life derail more than those of death. David Kern, who, while his wife is in labor in an English maternity ward, quietly leaves the place and comes upon a fatally injured cat, laying it, both ceremoniously and unceremoniously, beneath a bush to die. "A life demands a life," says Kern, whose first child is being born back at the hospital. Years later, upon news of his father's failing heart, Kern feels "death had been advancing under cover and now it had struck, declared its position." Yet he cannot find the proper, consoling words for his dying father and cannot convincingly answer a hitchhiking sailor who asks what the point of Kern's writing is. But fiction is often created from the spirit of the staircase, as the French say, the words one comes up with only later, and derives from a desire—nostalgia, again—for "a ceremony of farewell." "We in America need ceremonies, is I suppose, sailor, the point of what I have written," this deeply moving story concludes.

The ceremonies of farewell that take place in Updike's second section, "Out in the World," are by and large those of a young man leaving home. How few contemporary short stories there are about college life—despite all the writing programs on American campuses—but

Updike has several. In "The Christian Roommates," we see David Kern again, this time at Harvard, but now he is a minor character, his appearance here a virtual cameo. The main character is a South Dakota freshman named Orson, who is more like the brooding boy David Kern was than the collegiate Kern, who now is confident, witty, generous, and quick. Orson is not those things. He has been nicknamed "the Parson," and among his fellow dormmates he feels he has "been sized up as someone easy to startle." Updike here shows how he is a master of the quiet plot, capturing the emotional, social, and intellectual skirmishes of student life among a handful of diversely gifted young men on a single dormitory corridor.

The story centers on the theological crises of Orson and his roommate, Henry. Henry is a self-invented "Anglican Christian Platonist strongly influenced by Gandhi." He does yoga, eats no meat, and spins using a spinning wheel and the big toe of one foot. He throws himself daily across the bed in flamboyant prayer, his face in the blanket, his arms spread out. "That's marvellous," says Dawson, another hallmate, admiringly. "It's medieval. It's more than medieval. It's Counter-Reformation." But Orson has begun to hate Henry—his appearance, his manner, his pretensions—"with an avidity of detail he had never known in love." (There is no writer more poetically articulate about irritation than Updike.) Orson's first year at Harvard, the very thing that was intended to bring him out of his closed-minded provinciality, turns out to leave a lasting mark of intolerance on him. It is "a kind of scar he carries without pain and without any clear memory of the amputation." For all his faith, he never again prays.

The other life passages that are represented in "Out in the World" include international travel, romantically available women, and New York City. One of the most stirring stories is "The Lucid Eye in Silver Town," which describes a young son's frustration with his father's lack of sophistication on a trip the two of them take to Manhattan. Both culturally peckish in their small Pennsylvania town, father and son see the city's opportunities differently—the son wants to glimpse the possibility of a future for himself there; the father wants only to admire the city's otherness, which his brother, who now lives there, represents.

Overcome with self-consciousness and loathing, the son rages hopelessly at his father, upon whom he is still so dependent. The son wants to find a book on Vermeer, but is stymied by the kinds of obstacles that typically befall out-of-towners in comic tales of travel. The boy's lucid eye (physically injured only by an eyelash, though a visit to a doctor is made), especially for the dainty, absurd details that can figure in social class disparities, is characteristically Updikean. "When my ice cream came it was a golf ball in a flat silver dish; it kept spinning away as I dug at it with my spoon." They run out of both money and time to get the Vermeer book. On the train home the son's "tantrum ended; it had been a kind of ritual, for both of us."

"The Lucid Eye in Silver Town" is this collection's first literary glimpse of New York, a city Updike himself had always hoped to live in but, once settled there, sought refuge from in search of the ordinary life he needed for material and peace. This he found not in the small-town Pennsylvania of his boyhood but in suburban Massachusetts. New York was too "full of other writers and of cultural hassle, and the word game [was] overrun with agents and wisenheimers," he writes in his foreword. "Agents and wisenheimers," mused a literary friend of mine mischievously. "Is that Shillington, Pennsylvania, for 'Hymietown'?" No, I decided, just the headlong candor of the foreword, and a defensiveness regarding provincial shelter. Also, Updike writes, he wanted "free parking for my car, and public education for my children, a beach to tan my skin on, a church to attend without seeming too strange."

Such would have been the necessary camouflage and freedom for the kind of stories Updike has collected here, with their felt kernel of felt life. A Latvian man recently spoke to me of how meaningful Updike's work was to him when he initially discovered it. "For the first time," he said, "I believed I was reading something by a fiction writer who wasn't making things up." This assumption that his fiction is autobiographical may be wearying and philistine to someone such as Updike, though also familiar and anticipated; it is one of the hazards of realism and looked at the right way is a compliment of the profoundest sort.

The section "Married Life" involves the restive state of that institution, or at least of its inmates—a subject Updike has returned to throughout the decades of these stories. Adultery, the conquered citizen's silent revolt, is already having its secret meetings in Updike's living rooms and cars, though he leaves the tales of actual divorce for the latter part of *The Early Stories*. Updike's husbands are here beginning their condition of bruised pre-exile within their marriages. The Jack of both "Walter Briggs" and "Should Wizard Hit Mommy?," two stories in which the father's storytelling to his child figures prominently in the carpet ("Tomorrow," says the little girl, "I want you to tell me the story that that wizard took that magic wand and hit that mommy"), sees the woodwork of his house as "a cage of moldings and rails and baseboards all around them." In "Unstuck," the young husband, wanting to share his Christian faith with his wife, finds himself wincing at her cavalier remarks, "feeling himself to blame. If he had given her a climax, she wouldn't be so irreligious," he imagines. Later, on his way out, "he noticed a steaming cup of coffee she had poured for him, like one of those little caches one explorer leaves behind for another. To appease her, he took two scalding swallows before heading out into the wilderness of his brilliant back yard."

It is Richard and Joan Maple, Updike's famously falling-apart couple, who most explicitly and with chilling authenticity express domestic antagonism at its most distilled, and the best stories about them are included here. Their conversations—sparring, ruthless, accusing—"had the final effect of knitting them ever tighter together in a painful, helpless, degrading intimacy." Updike's dialogue possesses, often, the feeling of transcripts, full of the dangerous currents of marital strife, and one imagines one feels the life-jolts that prompted them. "Let's not talk," says Joan Maple to her husband in "Giving Blood." But his criticism—of her smugness, of her unsexiness, of her stupidity—continues. "I asked you not to talk," Joan said. "Now you've said things that I'll never forget."

But the marriage is sustained by their forgiving lovemaking. "When their tongues at last fell silent, their bodies collapsed together as two mute armies might gratefully mingle, released from the absurd hostilities decreed by two mad kings." In "Twin Beds in Rome," the Colosseum itself is "shaped like a shattered wedding cake." In Rome, Richard Maple manages his deep irritation with "simultaneous doses of honey and gall." "You're such a nice woman," Richard tells his wife. "I can't understand why I'm so miserable with you." In this "city of steps" they finally separate, not physically or legally, but in every other way. The marriage lets go "like an overgrown vine whose half-hidden stem has been slashed in the dawn by an ancient gardener." ("The stripped and shapely / Maple grieves / The loss of her departed leaves," wrote Updike in the November poem of his *A Child's Calendar*.) Back in Boston, Joan Maple becomes involved with the civil rights movement ("Marching Through Boston"). Her self-sufficiency seems to her husband to mock as well as to reengage him, and he finds he can neither let go of her nor love her.

Although he joins her in a political march, out of sheer marital perversity—irritation again—he mimics the "Negroes" shockingly. (It is both stubborn and correct that Updike has decided not to update his terminology for this collection. Some of the locutions, however true to their period, are so interestingly antique now that their meanings are not always instantly clear. When, for instance, one of his characters walks into a roomful of "fairies," this reader, for a moment seeing wings and wands, had no idea where we were.)

"Family Life" continues, including two additional Maple stories, "Sublimating" and "Eros Rampant," with thematizing titles. One more comically squabbling one, "Your Lover Just Called," is placed in "Tarbox Tales." In its climactic outburst, we see a whole segment of the Tarbox community as well as a moment of American social history helplessly summed up:

> "Go to her!" Joan suddenly cried, with a burst of the same defiant energy that made her, on other hungover mornings, rush through a mountain of housework. "Go to her like a man and stop trying to maneuver me into something I don't understand! I have no lover! I let Mack kiss me because he's lonely and drunk! Stop trying to make me more interesting than I am! All I am is a beat-up housewife who wants to go play tennis with some other exhausted ladies!"

The tales of Tarbox—a town founded "by men fearful of attack"— follow an unanchored interlude of stories about loneliness and romantic paralysis ("The Two Iseults"), and precede the group of stories labeled "Far Out," which, proving Cole Porter right (birds *do* do it), includes the sexual romps of prehistoric animals ("During the Jurassic")—"Next came the allosaurus, a carnivorous bachelor whose dangerous aura and needled grin excited the female herbivores"—and various protozoa ("Under the Microscope"), though without Updike's original illustrations as they first appeared in *The Transatlantic Review*. These satirical stories (Updike once worked on *The Harvard Lampoon*) are narrated as the supposed cocktail parties of the doomed and are hilarious, inspired, and frothily bleak:

> The party was thinning. . . . Out of mercy as much as appetite, he ate her. She felt prickly inside him. Hurriedly—the rooms were almost depleted, it was late—he sought his hostess. She was by the doorway, her antennae frazzled from waving goodbye, but still magnificent. . . . "Don't go," she commanded, expanding. "I have a *minuscule* favor to ask. Now that my children, all thirteen million of them, thank God, are off at school, I've taken a part-time editing job, and my first real break is this manuscript I'd be *so* grateful to have you read and comment on."

The ultimate section, "The Single Life," contains the most famous Maple stories and the book's climax, the sorrowing "Separating" and "Gesturing." (The Maples are largely in a gerund state.) These stories are powerful with or without their predecessors. In them the Maples separate, openly take lovers, tell the children, divorce. And here, too, is the most affecting and trenchant toast to the first wife:

> He saw through her words to what she was saying—that these lovers, however we love them, are not us, are not sacred as reality is sacred. We are reality. We have made children. We gave each other our young bodies. We promised to grow old together.

Everything and everyone else is just shadow play, gesturing, an echo, unreal.

"Isn't it amazing," Joan says at the end, in what is one of the most unexpectedly haunting and improbably perfect lines of the book, "how a full bottle of wine isn't enough for two people any more?"

Updike's storied and nuanced sense of the friendship between husbands and wives is a generous and complex one, and rewards each return visit he makes. Ordinary friendship (a subject ironically central to the work of the deeply Updike-influenced Ann Beattie) is largely missing in his fictional world; a dearth of this subject might be considered to constrict the otherwise wide and encompassing lens of this collection. But then these are just the early stories. There are the beautiful "middle stories" presumably to come—"A Sandstone Farmhouse," "The Cats," to name only two, in which the mother's abiding and muse-like friendship persists beyond the grave. As for the "late stories"? Let no living writer this distinguished be thought to have written them yet. May David Kern's lavishing God and the second wife assist.

(2003)

Nicholson Baker's *Checkpoint*

Whatever serious subject the novelist Nicholson Baker explores, we must never forget that he is also being at least a little funny. Fond of the brisk, improvisatory miniature and heir to the cerebral comedy of Donald Barthelme, he still can seem a little misunderstood by those who would read any of his fiction as a grinding ax. Baker is not, as Leon Wieseltier suggested recently in a review of Baker's new novel, *Checkpoint*, in *The New York Times Book Review*, an attention seeker, participating in "the politics of the sewer." (Much of Baker's work is quiet to the point of prayer: his last novel, *A Box of Matches*, about a middle-aged man getting up every day before sunrise, reads like a prose poem to fire and dawn.) And although Baker is often interested in talk, and even wild talk, as Wieseltier correctly notes (Baker's most famous novel, *Vox*, is about phone sex), he has this in common with most of the writers who ever lived.

Baker's novels are largely obsessions with action versus paralysis, of both the political and the personal sort, and in his unusual explorations of this psychological mezzanine and classical theme (in *The Fermata*, the protagonist can in fact freeze others and stop time; in *Room Temperature*, an entire novel occurs while the protagonist rocks his baby to sleep; in his first novel, actually titled *The Mezzanine*, a torrential *esprit d'escalier* engenders a roaming book-length tracking of one man's mind), he is something of an original, though one might be tempted to place him alongside the English novelist Geoff Dyer: both are the same age, both have published amusing, inward-looking tributes to another admired writer (Dyer's *Out of Sheer Rage* on D. H. Lawrence, Baker's *U and I* on John Updike), and both use restless, unpredictable narratives to register the neurasthenic perils and pleasures of their own isolating hyperself-consciousness—and do so without any masculine vanity whatsoever. This, I daresay, makes them disarming and endearing literary mavericks in the heterosexual world. Perhaps one of their differences is that Baker seems seldom to leave the house (in *A Box of Matches,* a character airing a rug on the front porch railing is performing a gregarious public act) while the peripatetic Dyer—observing all-night raves in France (*Paris Trance*) or his own tears in his smeared fried eggs in Detroit (*Yoga for People Who Can't Be Bothered to Do It*)—seems never to stay home.

Baker's wit and literary context must be borne in mind when considering his most recent novel, *Checkpoint,* a dialogue between two men discussing the pluses and minuses of assassinating the president. One of the men, Jay, ostensibly has a plan to do so, but his mutating renditions of it are so laughably harebrained—one includes a final greeting to Condoleezza Rice ("Stick to the piano, baby!")—that most readers will come to realize Jay is less villainous than he is a composite of the various ways people give theatrical voice to moral indignation. His assassination fantasy is a mirror of the one the White House had first of Saddam Hussein and then of Osama bin Laden—a "decapitation" that even if realized would not have the political consequences he claims for it—just as it is perhaps mirrored in turn by Wieseltier's own attempt to, well, assassinate Baker's book ("This scummy little book" is Wieseltier's own attention-grabbing opening).

Where does wild talk end, and something else more dangerous begin? Baker is only exploring this fictionally; Wieseltier, while committing his own wild talk in a nonfictional realm, may not actually understand this. He says of Baker's creation of the would-be assassin, Jay, that strictly speaking Baker is not "inciting a crime," though at novel's end "it may be the president is really in danger," seemingly forgetting that these are fictional characters and that in a novel even someone called "President Bush" remains a fictional character. When Wieseltier lectures his readers that "neither John Kerry nor John Edwards appears to live in the universe in which *Checkpoint* was set or in the universe in which *Checkpoint* was written," an embarrassing misunderstanding of the nature of fiction is revealed. Wild talk indeed.

So one must remember that Baker is funny, that he writes about paralysis inflamed by inaction, that he is interested in wild, even crazy, mock-heroic talk, and that he, as an American writer, is living in some of the most devastating years of American political history. What does a novelist like this—witnessing the world and taking note of his own as well as others' perceptions—write? Why a novel that takes the form of a two-person radio play in which a "demented bum" named Jay argues his suicidal-homicidal political mission—"This is the one thing I have to contribute"—to a friend named Ben, who may or may not actually believe him, but argues back nonetheless, even to the point of desperately quoting Dr. Seuss ("a person's a person no matter how small"):

> JAY: And you've taken up photography.
> BEN: Yes.
> JAY: It's helpful to have a hobby. I have a hobby, too.
> BEN: Jay, assassinating the president isn't a hobby.
> JAY: I'm sure not getting paid for it. It's pro bono all the way. . . .
>   And what are you going to do with these tree pictures?

Checkpoint's Jay is furious about the Bush administration's invasion of Iraq, that "patchwork country," and this foreign policy's dishonoring of a people: "I want to say, 'Wolfowitz, you fuckhead! You're killing people! You're not humble enough before the mystery of a foreign country!'" and the triggering image for Jay's fury is something he's seen on the news, a fleeing Iraqi family, killed by American soldiers at a military checkpoint. What then takes over him is a citizen's outrage intent on (or trying to seem intent on) shedding its powerlessness. First, using Ben and his tape recorder as a sounding board, he must wend his way through his many criticisms of the White House, from Rumsfeld's fortune from NutraSweet, to the bankrupt American economy, to Lynne Cheney's denigration of Eminem:

> JAY: Lynne Cheney, this merchant of multinational MISERY,
>   man. It's staggering when you take time to think about it

for more than twelve seconds. And here she's all in a flus-
terment about the nasty lyrics of Eminem.

BEN: Eminem is no favorite of mine.

JAY: Well, no, he's not Zappa. But that woman, I'm sorry to say,
is the real obscenity.

BEN: Oh, Lynne Cheney did some good things when she was at
the NEH. You've got to lighten up a little. She's not a viper.
She was just on the board of directors.

JAY: How could she be on the board of that company and look
at herself in the mirror? How can she look at her husband
in the mirror? Halliburton and Enron and all that. Enron
wangling to profit from the pipeline across Afghanistan. It's
a sickening spectacle.

BEN: Do you think they look at each other in the mirror?

Although Jay may never "lighten up," as Ben suggests, it is Baker's
sensibility to allow his book to do so, letting it go wherever it's tempted;
the narrative clowns around at intermittent intervals, bringing its own
light to the dark, or the Cheneys to a mirror—the gallows humor that
so often marbles grief and despair. "If what I do causes an upheaval,"
says Jay, "okeydoke."

Since now more than ever we live in a world of bomber-assassins
who take their own lives along with the lives of others, their minds, from
the outside, looking cracked with the determined, fantastical pageantry
of misbegotten valor, Baker's brief take on the workings of one such
ostensible soul is as timely as fiction gets. It does not perhaps take us
convincingly inside the suicidal part of such a person's head, however—
this part still feels dismissible as madness—but with the homicidal part
he is much closer, and Jay is sometimes logical, even calm, in his arguments. "If you say, Go, men, launch the planes, start the bombing,
shock and awe the living crap out of that ancient city—you are going
to create assassins like me." People want to make their lives meaningful
in wicked times, just as writers want to make their novels meaningful,
and Ben's recommended alternatives—gentleness, love, photography,
a puppy, copying out great books word for word into a notebook—
however movingly simple or deeply believed or sweetly therapeutic,
may not do the trick for everyone.

Political argument, of course, is easier than political literature. And one can wonder how Baker's quick, stripped, cry of a book can succeed as the latter. But literature occurs when one feels life on the page. And one feels life most often when one hears more than one voice in conversation there. Does the reader of *Checkpoint* hear more than one voice?

Oh, yes. I think one doesn't have to listen too hard to hear a roar.

(2004)

Alice Munro's *Runaway*

In the myth-inflected world of Alice Munro's recent fiction, when a daughter disappears, the mother's crops are not left to wither as she searches. Instead the mother is more likely to stay put and now, with more time on her hands, actually begin a garden at long last, the plants taking hold rather nicely, though they be, to a large extent, forget-me-nots, bittersweet, or rue. Great literature of the past two centuries has sentimentalized politics, crime, nature, and madness, but seldom the family, and the wrenching incompatibility of a woman's professional or artistic expression with her familial commitments has made its way into the most undidactic of literary minds. It has appeared, to powerful and unexpected effect, in much of Munro's work, especially her most recent collection, *Runaway*. In "Silence," a mother who has come late to her vocation (in one of several apparent stand-ins for literary work, she is a local talk-show host with renowned powers of sympathy), and whose daughter has fled to some kind of alternative spiritual retreat, punishing her mother with discontinued contact, begins a life of solitude and herb growing. That same mother's parents, in a kind of backstory titled "Soon," happily take up berry and vegetable farming after their daughter has left home. Ambivalent parenting abounds. In "Trespasses," a discontented mother's psychological preoccupation contributes to the accidental death of her young daughter. In "Passion," a young wife with "pouches of boredom" at her mouth and a "bitter tinkle of a laugh" explains to her in-laws, "I don't have any appetite anyway, what with the heat and the joys of motherhood," and then promptly lights up a cigarette. "Families were like a poison in your blood," a character in the collection's title story thinks.

There are no happy endings here, but neither are these tales trage-dies. They are constructions of calm perplexity, coolly observed human mysteries. One can feel the suspense, poolside, as well as any reader of *The Da Vinci Code;* one can cast a quick eye toward one's nine-year-old on the high dive and get back to the exact sentence where one left off. The thrilling unexpectedness of real life, which Munro rightly insists on, will in her hands keep a reader glued—even if that reader is torn by the very conflicts (work to do, kid on the high dive) dramatized therein. "This is the kind of fond but exasperated mother-talk she finds it easy to slip into," Munro writes in "Silence." Though they may close with the sleepy loose ends of secrets and dreams, these stories, like life as it is recalled more than as it is lived, move forward with speed and excite-ment: there are train, boat, and car wrecks; weddings and affairs; the ever-present whiff of suicide. They are determinedly full of the marks of change—cultural and emotional—upon individuals who are as star-tled by them as any reader. A historian-friend of mine recently said, "I like Alice Munro's work because she captures so well those surprising moments of life that you never knew were possible, like suddenly find-ing yourself in a cornfield with your pants around your ankles."

Munro's interest in life's incongruous phases and fragments has given her stories their distinctive shape. Decades collide, intersect, are placed side by side in a charged and vibrating conversation. (Munro has said she sees stories architecturally, as a house whose various rooms one can roam in and out of, forgoing any prescribed order; this surely accounts for the nonlinear aspect of so many of her narratives. That memory and passion reorder a life and cause events to fall meaning-fully out of sequence in the mind often seems to be Munro's point.) Four of the stories here are essentially two novellas composed of linked parts, carrying their characters from youth to late middle age. (There is less back-and-forth between time periods in these novellas than there usually is in Munro.) This is a successful length for Munro, because it allows her, by means of tableaux, to use time deeply and extendedly as both tool and subject.

The story for the ages here, however, is surely the title one, with its multiple runaways, its ghostly gothic moments, and its exploration of erotic love—all narrative ingredients Munro has made her own. Carla, with the help of a friend, runs away from her increasingly disturbed and hostile husband. She previously ran away *with* him, leaving her family—"their photo albums, their vacations, their Cuisinart, their *powder room,* their walk-in closets, their underground lawn-sprinkling system"—for a more "authentic" life. So much for the comforts of authenticity. Halfway to her new destination of Toronto, however, "the strange and terrible thing coming clear to her" is that she cannot imagine life without her husband. As Carla flees, he persistently "[keeps] his place in her life . . . what would she put in his place?" She is drawn helplessly (that is, erotically) back, compromised by grief and uncertainty, willing to pay whatever violent price is required to keep her marriage—and in Munro it is always a little violent. The loss of her pet goat—Carla imagines, which is to say *understands* (there is no difference for Munro's female characters), that her husband has punished her by killing it—is an echo of the many violent visions that Munro's wives have of the men they've chosen, and of men in general. In "Open Secrets" (1994), a man spraying schoolgirls with a hose (Munro's work is interested in men with menacing water, especially hoses; one or two of them appear in the current collection) is envisioned by the story to be a murderer. His is a crime his wife has had to accept—though, like the goat's death in "Runaway," there is a "brief and barbaric and necessary act" reconsecrating the marriage. In this new collection the story "Powers" concludes with the incarceration of a woman by her husband, after her psychic powers dwindle and can no longer satisfactorily pay the bills. The psychic wife knows what the husband is up to—or so the story, with its own clairvoyance, imagines. But she remains passive before her fate.

In Munro's world wives glimpse the cold wickedness of their men but must devise the psychological ceremony that allows them to set that glimpse aside. It is too late in their lives for them to do otherwise. Only the very young have the emotional luxury of successfully fleeing. For a young person, a pristine heart untainted by the more damaging forms of forgiveness is still in charge. In "Baptizing," from *Lives of Girls and Women* (1971), Munro wrote eloquently of two young lovers, one of whom has almost drowned the other (men and water again: in Ovid water fuses a couple's sexuality; in Munro it distinguishes and separates).

> If we had been older we would certainly have hung on, haggled over the price of reconciliation, explained and justified and perhaps forgiven, and carried this into the future with us, but as it was we were close enough to childhood to believe in the absolute seriousness and finality of some fights, unforgivability of some blows. We had seen in each other what we could not bear, and we had no idea that people do see that, and go on, and hate and fight and try to kill each other, various ways, then love some more.

Therein lies part of the contradiction of feeling coursing through so much of Munro's work, which she expresses best three paragraphs later in that same early story.

> Unconnected to the life of love, uncolored by love, the world resumes its own, its natural and callous importance. This is first a blow, then an odd consolation. And already I felt my old self—my old devious, ironic, isolated self—beginning to breathe again and stretch and settle, though all around it my body clung cracked and bewildered, in the stupid pain of loss.

The artistic self—devious, ironic, isolated—resides at odds with the tender lover self in the same finely riven person. Munro is hardly the first writer to worry this incompatibility; Henry James, in his very different way, devoted a lifetime to it and, like Munro, was often interested in placing that theme in ghost stories of both the natural and the supernatural kind. But she is one of the most explicit in noting its obscenity, its terribleness as well as its almost comedic unsolvability. Perhaps owing partly to this, her writing never loses its juice, never goes brittle; it also never equivocates or blinks, but simply lets observations speak for themselves. In fiction real turmoil is made artificial turmoil, only to seem real again; this is literary realism's wish, and one of Munro's compelling accomplishments.

"Seduction may be baneful," Elizabeth Hardwick wrote in *Seduction and Betrayal,* "even tragic, but the seducer at his work is essentially comic." Munro's romantically game women seem to understand this even as girls, and it may be the thing that gives them, especially in this collection, their fearlessness and dignity and resilience, as well as their outwardly sleepwalking, straight-man quality. How else to explain the sexual situations they so easily wander into? Juliet, in "Chance," quickly takes up with an older, married man she meets on a train, pursuing him to Whale Bay, on the British Columbian coast, although she has learned almost nothing about him and he doesn't even know her last name. In "Passion," Grace, cued by little except a notion that romance should involve impulsiveness, abandons her fiancé to take up for an afternoon with his alcoholic older brother, whom she has just met. All the women here are attempted runaways of some sort, and they seem to feel that the situation they run toward harbors more truth and hope than the difficult daily world they run from, though the story itself will not judge. Munro's women are unforensic in their knowledge—perceptive guessers, quiet visionaries, fortuitous survivors. And the stories are uninsistent in their stance. It has been said that erotic love, like certain religions, seems to contain the meaning of life without actually disclosing it, and Munro's narratives of this—though they may, in a paragraph here or there, advocate for mystery—in general back off from faith or argument of any kind. Munro's world, with its small violent corners, is a revelation of a specific element of human experience: the impossibility of life without tedium, surprise, or paradox. There seems nothing missing in this yet again brilliant collection. If the book's last words, regarding powers beginning "to crumble and darken tenderly into something like soot and soft ash," betray any authorial worry, the beauty of the line gives the lie to it. Someone writing at this level well into her seventies, outliving the female friends to whose memory the book is dedicated and who must have been part of its inspiration, is a literary inspiration herself.

But if there *is* anything missing, it may be "Hired Girl" and "Fathers"—two haunting stories that were published in *The New Yorker* some time ago but have yet to appear in a collection. Maybe even more stories are lying in wait. Such first-rate abundance is an astonishment in any lifetime, let alone that of a middle-class mother, and is—to rework Faulkner's quip regarding Keats—worth any number of young daughters. Though, of course, for the writer it is always more complicated than that. For the reader, however, it is a lovely and simple matter of greed and joy.

(2004)

Joan Silber

When the National Book Award nominations were announced this past autumn, they were greeted with a great amount of grumbling—grumbling that I began to feel was fueled in part by the malaise presidential politics had caused to befall every conversation in the country. But grumbling nonetheless. The nominated books were criticized for having been written by relatively unknown women who all lived in New York City—though such a demographic fact might equally have been reason for celebration. (The choice of Elfriede Jelinek for this past fall's Nobel Prize in Literature was faulted, too, not for her uninflected pessimism or the threads of caustic misanthropy that weave through her work, and which in fact group her with many other recent winners, but for her insufficient fame outside Vienna, which does not.)

"The revenge of the midgets," one writer said to me of the National Book Award nominations.

"They should change the name to the 'Gotham Municipal Book Awards,'" said another.

"How are we supposed to sell books," cried various publishers, "if the book awards do this to us?"—giving it away that a book's future has already been pretty much designed in advance by a company's sales force, who look to an award neither as due respect nor as cultural candy (with all of candy's meaningless and slightly sickening fun) but as further marketing assistance on an already commercially blessed book. Even boasting a book award, a novel less well funded right from the start can have a hard time shaking off its publisher's preconceptions, turning around, and having some other life. That is, if the award comes as a surprise. But, of course, if the award is not a surprise, there will be a different sort of grumbling—as no doubt we will soon witness with the initiation of the Quill Awards, a new people's choice–style prize, set up just this year by Reed Business Information and various local NBC-affiliated television stations, apparently in response to all that autumnal muttering.

Literary muttering attended to at all, sad to say, can seem an amusing and heartening thing.

The response to the National Book Awards that left the biggest impression on me was this one, by a former nominee. He said, "Well, all I know is that if Joan Silber's *Ideas of Heaven* is on the list, it means the judges are actually reading the books."

Ideas of Heaven, short-listed for the Story Prize as well as the National Book Award (it won neither), is a beautiful and peculiar collection of interlinked stories—"a ring of stories" as the author herself describes it, since the stories form a kind of circle, the last story cycling back to give new meaning to the first, and all the stories having small, sometimes arbitrary, sometimes dramatic links among them. Its author has written four previous works of fiction, including the novel *Lucky Us,* an unintimidated update of *La Bohème* (AIDS substituted for consumption, Brooklyn lofts for Parisian garrets, Verdi's Violetta for Puccini's Mimi), and *In My Other Life,* more stories of scrappy metropolitan young people in "blithe downward mobility" making a go of it in restaurants, bars, video stores, and the drug trade. Even when Silber's characters survive to middle-class, middle-aged adulthood, shadows follow: "'They have a penned-in area for the kids,' Nathan said. 'And then the rest of the park is for the dope dealers. Don't think it doesn't confuse me to be in there with the swings.'"

Joan Silber may be one of those writers, such as Meg Wolitzer, who fast out of the gate—Wolitzer's first novel was written when she was an undergraduate; Silber's first book, the eerily mature and accomplished 1980 novel *Household Words,* won the PEN/Hemingway Award (those preening midgets!)—have miraculously become even better in middle age. *Lucky Us,* Silber's last book, a haunting bicameral portrait of two doomed lovers, is still not adequate preparation for the emotional and narrative intricacies of *Ideas of Heaven.* Both are written in the first person—from the point of view of different people who oddly share the same voice. It is one of Silber's limitations turned brazen, wise refusal that she has not bothered to create different voices for her characters. Everyone speaks in the same lively, funny, intelligent voice: the voice of the book. This comes to seem Silber's point: that what is alike about us trumps what is distinct. And in *Ideas of Heaven,* especially, even more than in *Lucky Us,* this is a necessary aspect of the conception: the book could not exist without the continuous sound and family of these like-voiced minds. The sameness of the narrative voices in completely disparate circumstances is what in part creates "the ring" and ensures both the strange comedy and the spiritual underpinning of a collection that, largely owing to the vehicle of its singular and uniform voice, has all the satisfactions of a novel.

Arguably part narrative acrostic, part musical round, *Ideas of Heaven* is divided, formally, into six sections. It begins with the story "My Shape," whose wise, breezy, declarative mezzo belongs here to Alice, a would-be actress and dancer whose buxom body keeps her from the ballet she loves. That she tells us straightaway that she "liked the arabesques and the leaping and even the strictness of Miss Allaben drilling us in the six positions" may at first seem an editorial oversight, as there are only five positions in ballet. But as the number six is key to the structure of the book, one is inclined to allow for the error's intentionality and can then imagine that the sixth position for Alice may be the one she finds herself in after she has busily renounced ballet and her young French husband. ("I went a little crazy. . . . I walked around in a heavy, dressy cape and told the children I had a gun underneath it.") In longing to be in a Broadway musical, Alice begins taking lessons from a cruel and jaded dance teacher named Duncan Fischbach—"the tools of his trade were mockery and command." In Fischbach's ultimate lesson he orders her to lick his shoe. Ah, there it is: the sixth position. "I had my own ideas about a higher purpose," says Alice, "but not enough ideas. I could have used more." She winds up back in France, with a second French husband, Giles (a Buddhist and widower), and a new life as a yoga instructor.

The next story, "The High Road," belongs to the sadistic Duncan Fischbach, who speaks in the same animated rhythms as Alice, though Alice is nothing to him; vocal echo aside, she is not in this story at all except as one of the nameless students Duncan is eventually forced to take in when his own theatrical career collapses. What Duncan's real story is—along with all the others in this book—is a love story involving unequal affections. Abjectness, that sixth position, presents itself here in the form of the bitterly unconsummated crush. As Duncan himself says, "Infatuation, when it happened, could be visionary, a lust from another zone. From the true zone, the molten center of the earth. I was in my twenties, listening to a lot of jazz, and I thought in phrases like that."

"The High Road" recounts Duncan's story as a two-time loser in love. First he falls for Andre, an African-American trumpeter, elegantly dressed courtesy of a day job in a men's clothing store in midtown. After sabotaging that relationship, Duncan falls for a grieving young tenor who has just lost his boyfriend to AIDS. "Love has made me live in ceaseless fire," sings the tenor, with a sorrowful yearning appealing to Duncan.

The tenor's favorite drink is Campari, his favorite poet Gaspara Stampa, whose sonnets are "a 1500s version of the blues." Hopeless passion, notes Duncan, "was still in high style in certain corners of the gay world." His infatuation with this tenor involves rituals of cooking, whimpering restraint, and reveries spiked with scheming. "I had underestimated the depth of the enterprise, the large and moving drama involved." He cannot win the tenor's love—he imagines that to the young tenor he must seem like "some evil old elf," untempting even for a minute. The "high road" becomes in this piece celibacy itself, a Buddhist-style renunciation of passion until it becomes not gone but at least reduced to "a hum," though a "hum that was always in my ears."

. . .

Thus begin the two angles on romantic desire worked simultaneously in *Ideas of Heaven:* romance as a condition of unsatisfied yearning that must be transformed to a tantric discipline versus romance as an ennobling comedy of sexual humiliation, here and there rewarding with love. Oh, the drama of small semantic differences.

The third story (they must be read in sequence), narrated in the now-familiar voice of Alice-Duncan, is told by none other than the sixteenth-century poet Gaspara Stampa (author of the tenor's pining lyrics); that her very American-sounding voice will not remind you at all of a sixteenth-century Venetian deters the intrepid Joan Silber not a whit. Gaspara begins her artistic life "full of yearning for an unknown agony." She soon finds the ostensible objective correlative for this craving in a tall, handsome blond named Collaltino di Collalto. "Plenty of first sons were given this kind of repeating name," she informs us defensively.

Gaspara becomes, as Silber would need her to, "sick with attraction," hoping to slake a "sacred thirst." Like Duncan, she is not afraid to suffer openly, and although her premodern times won't allow her to resort to heavy breathing into a telephone during anonymous late-night calls (surely she would if she could—as does Duncan), she suffers the piercing, binding, pressing of the heart that honors her model, Petrarch, in his eternally unrealized love for Laura. What Gaspara sings in public is "what any lover knows: you'll be sorry later, I hope you feel one thousandth of the pain I feel, why are you so cruel . . ."

She notes, "People liked best the most mournful and complaining of my songs." When her lover at long last returns from war, "I asked how everything had gone in France, and then he began to tell me at length, which was not what I wanted."

The openly American diction and vernacular rhythms restaged in sixteenth-century Venice may seem an old gag, reminiscent of loopy send-ups of Shakespeare, but in this context, which is also earnest and of a piece with the book's synoptic look at desire's mischief and heat, it forms comedic moments that are a delight against the backdrop of the premature death we know is coming in a story titled "Gaspara Stampa (1523–54)."

He got up very early the next day to hunt for boar, and he had me get up with him, to breakfast downstairs before it was fully light. Why a man would come home from war to chase a wild animal with a spear was not something I could understand.

When, of course, things end badly, "we were all smiling, as if love's wreckage were a shared joke, which I suppose it was."

Many of Silber's fictional couples have screaming fights in public places, and Peggy and Tom in "Ashes of Love," the book's fourth story, are among them. They are connected to Gaspara Stampa, too, through Rilke, whose poetry Tom continues to read on and off throughout his life, Rilke invoking Stampa herself as a figure to admire, as she exhausted herself so intriguingly in "objectless love." "I was interested," says Tom, in what is, again, the book's sole narrative voice, "in what Rilke said about *lovers* (he was always citing them as a distinct class of people), because I was one half of a fiercely attached couple."

Tom's life with Peggy initially involves a lot of travel—Yugoslavia, Turkey, and finally Thailand, where Silber's motif of Buddhism first presents itself to Tom. After he has returned to the States, has a son with Peggy, and is then abandoned by her for another man, he begins where he left off in Thailand, pursuing serenity in a Buddhist meditation group. "Ashes of Love" follows Tom straight through another marriage up to the faraway death of Peggy. He has never been able to love anyone the way he did her, and his new wife, Mattina, feels Tom's psychic distances, accusing him of using Buddhism (his own noise- and passion-management system) to learn not to feel what he isn't feeling anyway.

All this yuppie Buddhism might be easy for a reader to deride, but the sweet stubbornness with which it is continually inserted in Silber's book wins over even a recalcitrant skeptic. Perhaps religion has always been a kind of hospital. And in this story, too, as in the final one, we feel it as perhaps one of the few decent refuges for the lover whose one great love in life has already occurred. The comings and goings of love, as they are often dramatized by Silber, are a complex exchange of one kind of loneliness for another.

.   .   .

The fifth and title story is in some ways the most anomalous and fascinating, if risky and not entirely successful. Narrated in the Alice-Duncan-Gaspara-Tom voice by a Christian missionary's wife in China during the Boxer Rebellion, the story has the narrator killed at the end—a narrative device that sets up an impossible point from which to tell the story, a point seldom seen outside Faulkner or the film *Sunset Boulevard,* although Susanna Moore relied on it in her novel *In the Cut,* and others have tried. "Ideas of Heaven" is connected to "Ashes of Love" through the presence of an heirloom Chinese comb sent home to a relative and handed down through generations to Tom's new wife, Mattina. It also has in common with the book's other stories the project of fitting an entire life into a short space and shares with them, too, despite its Victorian time period, a narrator whose loving enjoyment of sex is articulated with elegance and happiness. "He was as much a novice to the act as I was," the missionary's wife says of her new husband, "and we rowed through these new waters together. . . . I saw why a man and wife must never leave one another, having been to these places in each other's company."

"Ideas of Heaven" is connected to the final story, "The Same Ground," through this story's narrator, a Parisian named, interestingly enough, Giles, whose great-great-uncle was a Benedictine priest and survivor of the siege of Peking.

It is in this sixth and concluding story, "The Same Ground," that all the book's themes, and all of Silber's skills, come together most orchestrally and touchingly. "The Same Ground" even serves as a kind of curtain call of missing persons from earlier in the book: Andre the trumpet player makes a brief appearance as a now-successful musician in Paris; Peggy makes an appearance as an angry American whom Giles once picked up hitchhiking; Alice, from the inaugural story, "My Shape," turns up in a yoga class to become Giles's second wife. Marco Polo, September 11, and race relations all have a poeticized presence here in this already thrice-told tale of grievous romantic loss—loss that haunts and frees and enlarges and scars the now newly spiritualized loser. In another link to China, Giles is married to the North African historian Sylvie, who in seeking permission for research in China is killed in a terrorist bombing on the steps of the Chinese embassy in Paris. Says Sylvie's mourning mother, "The whole world's going to blow up. That's what they want. It's going to be nothing." Says Giles after the shocking mortal consumption of his wife,

> I was doing my best not to think about anything beyond what to make for supper. . . . I didn't want to hear about someone else's bloody outrage over some murderous stupidity in the past. . . . This was an odd state of mind for someone who taught history for a living and went forth every day to explain to sixteen-year-olds why they should care about the Hundred Years War.

Once, when the class is discussing the Baader-Meinhof Gang, one of the students says, "I admire the beauty of their convictions and to blow people up is not the worst evil," and then there is a sudden silence. Giles is "the only person in the room who was free of wretched embarrassment."

The loss of Giles's wife is sandwiched between two love affairs. The first, while Giles is still married to Sylvie, is with a goatherdess named Edmée—again, Silber knows no fear. The depictions of Giles as adulterer are gentle and searching. "I was becoming wily and hollow from pretense," he admits to himself. "And no one said anything, so perhaps I was good at it." He feels even years later that perhaps he "could not be at close quarters with a woman I loved without staining myself with lies." When he finally leaves his mistress,

> it was a terrible, sentimental conversation. Both of our voices broke the whole time. I praised her loveliness and her fineness, and everything I said sounded false, though it was true. We had to stop talking so that words could mean something again in our mouths.

He returns to his wife, with desire and devotion, but when she dies, Paris becomes "enraging to walk in."

Giles's second love affair is as a widower, with the aforementioned Alice, who welds this ring of stories by returning at the end as an expatriate yogin, a kind of cheerful—that is, American—Brigitte Bardot, but with "something smudged and sad about her." And yet the dead Sylvie remains forever like an inner skin within Giles. That one life contains many; that these lives overlap and end without being complete; that the soul's quest often runs parallel with the heart's, not meeting; that for better or worse, in sickness and in health, the story of love-addled Romeo and his sexually purposeful Juliet remains one of humanity's truest narratives, imprinted over and over again in our actions and fates; that we are more alike than different in our desires and voices and connected in the largest and smallest and most astonishingly random of ways are a few of the points and opinions that converge by the close of this book and help release its emotion unexpectedly but profoundly.

Everything ends in tears, says this book—as does this book—to the extent that it ends at all, for like life the narrative curls back around and starts over again. Or sort of. Silber's ending is emotionally shattering, despite its tender wisdom and resignation. It is difficult to discern how it manages this powerful effect, except that emotion has been building throughout then carefully set aside for subsequent, artful triggering—an effect I've experienced at the end of only a few other novels, Alison Lurie's *Foreign Affairs,* say, or J. M. Coetzee's *Disgrace.*

A novel-in-stories, Silber's book proves, is not a cheat: done right it is a kind of double major, accomplishing two difficult things simultaneously—singing an aria while building a house. Human existence is not tragic—both these activities proclaim—but it is fragmented, improvisational, dangerous, accidental, maddening, and funny. Despite the tears, it is a Road Runner and Wile E. Coyote cartoon of desire and its object. It is a Buddhist comedy of the self attempting to remove the self. The core of life, as Silber demonstrates throughout her work and states explicitly in her very first book, is "tyrannically physical." The mind has a few nifty tricks for forgetting pain, as does the body, while it simultaneously attempts to learn from history, its own and others'—if this is at all possible. Is it? Silber swims through and past all of these heavenly ideas, a graceful swimmer on a leisurely swim, though her brisk, radiant prose chops the water like a sprite.

(2005)

Eudora Welty

Sixteen years ago I was in Jackson, Mississippi, and the owner of the bed-and-breakfast at which I was staying gave me Eudora Welty's address at 1119 Pinehurst Street, across from Bellhaven College. Miss Welty loves visitors, I was told, and I should feel free and welcome to go knock on her door. I was surprised that Welty was being openly offered up this way as a public site to a casual tourist fresh from Faulkner's Rowan Oak. For a minute I saw Welty as perhaps a kind of political prisoner, held hostage by southern graciousness—perhaps even the Jackson Chamber of Commerce—for I knew that no writer in her writer's heart welcomes impromptu visits from people she doesn't know. But a writer's heart is often dressed up in the local protective coloring of her address. And no writer is entirely a writer—she is also many other things. But the writer part—the accident of mind that prompts the private secreting away of phrases and ideas—is never understood the way a neighborhood might imagine, because it is never really glimpsed, though this is seldom acknowledged.

I was once also in Baltimore the year Anne Tyler won the Pulitzer Prize. Tyler was a Welty devotee and the first to interview her at length in *The New York Times*. Two journalists recounted that they had knocked on Tyler's front door to get her response to winning the prize and that, unlike Welty, she had sent them away with a brusque "I'm sorry. I'm working right now." I expressed amazement that Tyler had opened her door at all: surely that was the southern part of her, hospitably opening it. But the midwestern part—the Midwest, erroneously known for its friendliness, is natively skeptical of open arms and excellent manners—had declined a visit. Personally, living in the Midwest, if I saw strangers approaching my door, I would probably phone 911. Despite two southern grandfathers and a childhood during which I was told I was "half-southern," it is quite possible I do not have a southern bone in my body.

Nonetheless, sixteen years ago, clutching directions, I did scout out Welty's house, and though I would never have been so lowdown as to have gotten out of the car, like the most craven sort of paparazzi I stopped long enough to lean out the window and take a picture of the house—a spacious faux Tudor, set back from the curb, on a long, cared-for lawn—and then I rolled away, wondering if I'd seen the front curtains move. When I returned from my trip, I pasted the photo in a scrapbook.

That Welty had charismatic friendliness in abundance—her combination of shyness and gregariousness won over everyone—was never in her lifetime in doubt. She was a natural storyteller, a wit, and a clown. "If this sofa could talk," she said once to Reynolds Price, looking at the bedraggled plastic furnishings of the only rental room Price could find for them in Tuscaloosa, "we would have to *burn* it." All of Welty's endearing qualities are underscored by Suzanne Marrs's recent biography of her, the only one ever authorized by Welty. An unauthorized one appeared in 1998, *Eudora: A Writer's Life,* by Ann Waldron (who without Welty's approval began to feel shunned by Welty's fiercely protective friends and a bit sorry for herself, perceiving that she was rather literally disapproved of, the perennially "uninvited guest"). Welty at the time of Waldron's completed book was eighty-nine and unable to read for long spells. (Thank goodness, suggests Jacksonian Marrs, the anointed biographer.) Still, despite the biblical saying, a prophet is not often without honor in her own country: Welty was a goddess in Jackson. What a prophet is often without is privacy, peace, and any real depth of comprehension among her fellow citizens. And although this is not the task or accomplishment of literary biography, that Suzanne Marrs has waited until after Welty's death to publish *Eudora Welty* is certainly a beginning to all three.

It is also a work of love, as biographies often have to be just to get written. But of course, unlike with a work of disinterested investigation, there can be problems: a work of love may suddenly turn, in exhaustion, upon its subject; it may never look hard in certain corners out of fear of risking itself; it can grow defensive or caressing. Still, literary biography has its practitioners and even more so its readers—some looking for instruction, some looking for secrets, some simply curious to discover how a life can be lived one way on the outside and yet another way on the inside without derailing and tumbling into madness; some wanting to see if that contradiction is, as Flaubert, another writer who lived with his mother, famously suggested, the very thing that keeps sanity in place. Or if the safe living that ensures the daring art is also what keeps the grown-up a child, or a community pet, or unhappy, or drunk.

The element that is most often looked for by both biographer and reader, however, is how the life is revealed in the work, and so the work is read backward—as a source for the life—and the misstep of biographical overreading begins to mar, so to speak, the discussion of the work. I'm afraid this is sometimes done so blithely in Suzanne Marrs's book that, leaving no room for the beautiful deformities of invention, she actually refers to one character—Courtney in an early story of Welty's—as "aka Eudora," as if a fictional character were an alias, or someone the author is doing business as. Oh, well: it is a hazard of literary biography that few have avoided. Still, the phrase "aka Eudora," it seems to me, sets a new rhetorical standard for refusal even to try.

This aside, Marrs's biography, with its access to documents, friends, and the subject herself, inevitably proves an interesting and engaging addition to our understanding of Welty and to a lesser extent Welty's great ear for the voices and stories of southern life, whether it be a poor black woman shooing animals from her path at Christmastime or a white murderer mired in folksy hate. It is also an explicit and sharp retort to Waldron's earlier biography and to the criticisms leveled by Claudia Roth Pierpont in a 1999 New Yorker article. The former work, though sympathetic and vividly written, is scattered with gossipy quotes, several about Welty's supposed physical unattractiveness. The latter took Welty to task for politely turning her back on the subject of race in Mississippi, allegedly to ingratiate herself socially with Jackson insiders. Marrs's book takes on a defensive tone as she attempts to offer correctives. To counter the latter, she leans heavily on a quote by Toni Morrison that Welty wrote "about black people in a way that few white men have ever been able to write. It's not patronizing, not romanticizing—it's the way they should be written about," and offers up Welty's few friendships with African-Americans, most of whom were her caretakers in her old age. To counter the former, Marrs offers descriptions of Welty's large and luminous eyes.

It is interesting that Marrs's best potential counterarguments to each lie in photography. Welty was hardly unattractive: she was tall, thin, and in photo after photo bears a striking resemblance to the musician Joni Mitchell. Welty's occasional relationship with black people, as glimpsed in her stunning collection of Depression-era photographs, *One Time, One Place* (1971), was warm and interested, the gazes of her subjects often meeting her halfway, in the middle distance between the camera and the photograph, as if to say they understand this strange white lady with her camera, that she is not just benign but perhaps in her open curiosity good-humored and good-hearted as well. There is mutual trust, no mutual fear.

For many of her subjects this was the first picture ever taken of them. "Whatever you might think of those lives as symbols of a bad time," wrote Welty, "the human beings who were living them thought a good deal more of them than that." These photographs part a curtain of indifference "to each other's presence, each other's wonder, each other's human plight," she wrote in 1971, just eight years after she had declined to be interviewed on television by Ralph Ellison for fear of the trouble and hostility an interview by a black man might stir up for her and her mother. "In the massive correspondence available for research," writes Marrs, "Eudora used the word *nigger* four times as a descriptor." Four? Such an unrousing defense counters Pierpont's hypothesis far less well than a simple look at what Welty did with an inexpensive camera that her father had bequeathed her.

Welty was born in 1909, the oldest of three children, and the only daughter of a strong-willed Appalachian woman and an insurance man from Ohio, recently moved to the burgeoning town of Jackson to take a position with the Lamar Life Insurance Company. (Welty's parents had met when her father had a summer job in a logging camp near her mother's West Virginia home.) Welty had her father's affable face and his interest in photography; from her mother she inherited a passion for reading (though she rebelliously rejected her mother's beloved Dickens and also failed to read *Middlemarch* until she was sixty-five). She loved Woolf, Austen, and S. J. Perelman. To Woolf she once wrote a rather nervy fan letter in which she declared that Bernard in *The Waves* was an "unworthy medium" for Woolf's genius; of *To the Lighthouse,* which she loved, she wrote to Woolf:

> It dissolved all the sediment of loneliness of my dull days into a perfect amorphous stream of motion and intensity that flows clear and penetrative over the mosaic of my imagination, or perhaps yours. It was light under a door I shall never open.

Of Austen, Welty wrote, as if of her own work, "How could it be possible for these novels to seem remote? For one thing, the noise! What a commotion comes out of their pages!" As a published writer, she also wrote to Perelman, whom she had revered and imitated when younger, and he wrote her back:

> I hope you won't think I'm being unduly familiar when I ask for permission to kiss the hem of your expensive garment, but I'm an obscure member of the Welty Fan Club, whose other name, I understand, is Legion. Another paid-up member, he asks me to inform you, is Ogden Nash. None of this will pay your grocer's bill, I admit, but it may stave off boredom.

As a schoolgirl she was a popular if sheltered child, close with her brothers—funny, theatrical, she was voted "Best All Round Girl" by her high school senior class. That she graduated from high school the same year Richard Wright graduated valedictorian from the black high school in segregated Jackson seems astonishing, as does the fact that Wright and Welty even later never once met.

She went off to college to become an artist of some sort, first to the Mississippi State College for Women, where to a friend she said of the daily prayer meetings, "The way it makes me feel is what I call hell," then to Randolph-Macon, which she left (when they wouldn't take all her transfer credits) for the University of Wisconsin in Madison. A friend from Jackson wrote her at the time:

> You have become quite a will-o-the-wisp. I read in the paper where you are off for Randolph Macon, Ward Belmont, or some such place and then comes a post from Wisconsin in gleeful vein narrating how you are an art student in the beer-drinking country.

The displaced Welty found Wisconsinites cold and "flinty," but she fell under the spell of a young eighteenth-century-literature professor, Ricardo Quintana (who exists now in the corridors of the Wisconsin English Department as a small reading room and a named professorship), and in between experiments with bathtub gin and "needle beer," a corked nonalcoholic beer into which raw alcohol was inserted with a syringe—this was Prohibition in beer country—she became his most brilliant student (whether he knew this or not). After graduating from Wisconsin, she enrolled in an advertising/secretarial program at Columbia, and there began her long, complicated love affair with New York City.

It is both amusing and heartbreaking to read the spirited and desperately humorous letters of application that Welty sent out—to *The New Yorker,* to Scribner's, to *National Geographic*—begging for any sort of job. "I am a Southerner, from Mississippi, the nation's most backward state," she wrote in one. "How I would like to work for you!" She longed to stay in New York, though her mother was calling her home (her father was dying) and her attempts to find desirable work—even after her father died and she went back to the city again to pound the pavement—all failed. (Later in life she would spend summers in New York writing book reviews for the *Times* under a pseudonym.) Back home, though her writing progressed—she began to write short stories and they began to be published, first in *Manuscript* magazine, then later in *The Atlantic Monthly* and *Harper's*—she was often sick of Jackson, and her young adulthood seems to have alternated between productive spells of home life and flurries of ineffectual attempts to get out. "I feel like burning the *Clarion Ledger* every morning," she wrote in one letter.

> Well, I just won't go into it. And the Legislature a disgrace every day, and altogether Mississippi seems to get more hopeless all the time. Jeeze! The other day a bill was proposed wherebody [whereby anybody] who didn't like Mississippi could get a free ticket out of it, the state to provide the RR fare and a ten dollar bill to spend when you've got out. Hooray! I'll be the first one—I'll go somewhere nice and be a twenty-minute queen.

By this time, however, she was more than a little in love with a Jacksonian, John Robinson. He was also a writer (with Welty's help he had a story published in *The New Yorker* before she ever did), though more uncertain in his talent and ambition, and she had known him for years and corresponded with him throughout his military service in Africa and Italy during the war. She retained lifelong contact with him, and for long stretches they were close; Welty's 1946 novel *Delta Wedding* is dedicated to him and uses historical material about his local ancestors, which he provided. Robinson's homosexuality, however, would eventually make her see that intimate romance was impossible.

She had a gift for friendship but was not lucky in love. Another romantic infatuation came later in life—one with the married Ken Millar, a detective novelist who wrote famously and successfully under the name Ross Macdonald. She was probably seduced by Elizabeth Bowen on a trip she took to Ireland in 1950 (one particular Welty letter strongly suggests it), and she remained good friends with Bowen until Bowen's death, but Marrs takes great pains to dispel any idea that Welty was a lesbian. If the lady doth protest too much, it seems that this is part of the task of the authorized biography: rumor dismissal, perhaps even counterintelligence. But it does seem clear that although she had many gay friends, male and female, Welty, like so many other women writers, had a predilection for the handsome, literary, unavailable man, though Elizabeth Bowen, it will be noted, was often said to resemble just that.

Elsewhere, Marrs's biography becomes pretty much a rat-a-tat-tat of Welty's many publications, trips, parties, and dinners. Welty seemed to love any populated room that did not have Carson McCullers in it. (McCullers was notoriously disliked by many.) In trying to combat the image of Welty as a reclusive spinster, Marrs may have erred in the other direction, making "Eudora," as both she and Waldron call her, seem tirelessly social, a rollicking Holly Go-Welty, dining with the David Rockefellers, sailing off to Europe. Marrs's book can seem a reaction formation to such comments as this, from the president of Dartmouth, who said rather humiliatingly of Welty, while bestowing on her an honor:

> Eudora Welty has taught us that we have worlds to learn from a woman who has never married, who has rarely traveled, and who still lives in the home in which she spent her childhood.

In response, Marrs recounts high-spirited sojourns in Mexico and New Orleans, mining them for every vaguely wild moment or slight adventure they contain. Details from party games are included as if their fun could possibly be discerned from this vantage point. Once Welty's career is well under way, a peripatetic existence takes hold and a typical Marrs passage reads:

> From New York, Eudora went first to the University of Tennessee, then to Kenyon College for her twenty-third honorary degree and a reunion with old friend Robert Daniel. After a brief stop at home, she headed to Memphis for her twenty-fourth honorary degree, this one from Southwestern College, and then to Washington . . .

Who is Robert Daniel again? We have forgotten.

Marrs presents Welty—probably inadvertently—as a girl who could not say no (to any social obligation, speaking invitation, or tedious award). Welty once even gave a reading at the Citadel; "I'm considering giving my reading in Confederate dress with sword gestures," she joked. She even spoke at the California high school graduation of the daughter of a former Miss Mississippi. Because she was asked. This generosity became well known and perhaps exploited. Even Marrs requested that

Welty come speak to her undergraduates at Millsaps. Welty had little peace, though also often didn't seem expressly to desire any. Having as a young writer befriended two literary grande dames (Katherine Anne Porter and Bowen), she gamely stepped forward when her turn came. And there was a bit of the actress in her (she had won accolades in high school plays), which she could summon and which would often get her through. Naturally modest, however, she often felt "honoraried" to death. Only her friends William Maxwell and Reynolds Price are on the record as being concerned for her on this matter. At times it seems she was using prizes and readings the way Melville used whaling ships, as a way to see the world. But it was not successful. She was pestered and her writing languished.

The more awards (which included thirty-nine honorary doctorates) she received, with little new writing coming forth, the more ridiculous and depressed she sometimes felt. Once when she was away a thief broke into her Jackson home and made off with her typewriter, instruction manual, seat cushion, and gold membership pin from the American Academy and Institute of Arts and Letters. "He's sitting at my typewriter now, on my cushion, writing, and wearing my pin," Welty joked. She suffered two substantial bouts of writer's block, though this condition may have been indistinguishable from fatigue at nursing her ill mother, the upsetting early deaths of her brothers and father, painful arthritis in her hands, the death of her longtime agent, Diarmuid Russell, and the general loss of good friends, almost all of whom she outlived.

In addition to her photography, which surely will endure, Welty will be remembered for a handful of writings—which is really all any writer, even a great one, can hope for. The less ambitious of the novels—the exquisitely grief-stricken *The Optimist's Daughter,* which movingly dramatizes the loneliness of a young woman who has outlived everyone she loves ("Surviving is perhaps the strangest fantasy of them all," she thinks), and possibly even *The Ponder Heart*—may also be her most successful, and with their delicate melancholy and quick, dark hilarity they seem of a piece with her most accomplished short stories.

Each of these slender novels possesses the structure and theatricality of a play, and *The Ponder Heart* did in fact become a Broadway hit; with its tart and lively voices—"He loved happiness like I love tea"— it seems a natural outgrowth of the earlier "Why I Live at the P.O.," Welty's comic masterpiece, which in its spritzing monologue about sibling rivalry cleverly updates and transforms the parable of the Prodigal Son. "She's always had anything in the world she wanted and then she'd throw it away," fumes the jealous sister and narrator of "Why I Live at the P.O.," who has cleared out of her house in righteous indignation to live at the post office where she works. "Papa-Daddy gave her this gorgeous Add-a-Pearl necklace when she was eight years old and she threw it away playing baseball when she was nine, with only two pearls." (This biblical fracturing and reconstruction is an aspect of the story neither of her biographers mentions, though what is mentioned is that the email software system Eudora was named after Welty because its inventor felt that while developing it *he* was living at the P.O.)

In another, very different story, "No Place for You, My Love," in which two dislocated strangers in New Orleans take up with each other for a mysterious afternoon, we can not only experience another end of Welty's interesting range (which roams from vernacular shtick to Chekhovian Zen) but, in its comic-tragic vision of the fateful and moody visitations of love, feel an influence cast forward to the stories of Alice Munro and Richard Ford, both of whose work explores the sudden crossings of erotic lines by characters who proceed without much explanation but with private clarity and spiritual adventure. This story, along with "Why I Live at the P.O." and perhaps "A Worn Path" and "The Petrified Man" as well, seems likely for the long haul as it is determined by the canon-making mechanisms of story anthologies; another currently anthologized one, "Powerhouse," may not. Despite its intentions—to honor Fats Waller—it is so off-puttingly laced with racial clichés that it may have difficulty being understood as Welty or Marrs would have it be: as an *hommage* deliberately constructed from the white prejudice all black musicians faced. "And his mouth is going every minute: like a monkey's when it looks for something. . . . Big, arched eyebrows that never stop traveling, like a Jew's—wandering Jew eyebrows." Reading "Powerhouse" today is uncomfortable and baffling.

Welty's own brief autobiography, the lovely *One Writer's Beginnings*, was her best-selling book, and may continue to be. Money she made from it she offered repeatedly to friends who were sick. In its pages she speaks of finding the nickels that were laid upon the eyes of a baby sister who had died before Welty was born, nickels Welty was forbidden to take. These nickels, containing both life and death, are like Welty's stories themselves: treasure lifted from the pockets of the living and the faces of the dead, unspendable objects of both lightness and density, invested with largeness while remaining unsweetly small. In trying to get her work published in New York, the young Welty boarded many a train with high hopes and a hundred dollars, which she could make last two days, theater included. Editors might heap her with praise and still say no. "All this," she wrote, "would go on the train with me, up there and back. It was part of my flying landscape."

Marrs's biography piques our interest in the contemporary writers Welty herself so valued: V. S. Pritchett, whose stories she esteemed above any other living writer's; her mentor, Katherine Anne Porter, whose beautiful prose style and difficult personality prompted Welty to worry that Porter's perfectionist tinkering was life-robbing, risking the creation of a lovely casket of a book, and (as some have said) of a person; Reynolds Price, who was like an adored son to her and who seems in Marrs's pages adorable; and Welty muse and inamorato Ken Millar, whose detective novels one is inclined now more than ever to investigate. *The Eye of the Story* is dedicated to him.

If there are minor faults in Marrs's biography, how not in a book so teeming with detail? Nonetheless, even a trivial misrepresentation can rattle a reader's faith. One example here might be Marrs's characterization of the Hôtel des Saints-Pères, where Welty stayed in Paris, as "shabby"; this seems Marrs once again combating Welty's image as a perfect lady and straining to present her as a bohemian, slumming on the Left Bank, when in fact Welty continually stayed at very nice places when she traveled, and the Hôtel des Saints-Pères (last I looked) is one, just as it was when Edna Millay lived there in the 1920s. Another may be the delayed mention of Welty's height, which comes so late in the biography that it is startling: Welty was five feet ten, though osteoporosis eventually shrank her to five-three.

If there are larger problems in the book, one might be Marrs's very gingerly handling of Welty's relationship with her mother, Chestina, which was assumed by many to be stormy. (After a stroke the first thing Chestina said to her daughter when she was able to speak, in a tiny voice, was that the doctor was a moron.) Chestina in fact emerges more clearly in Waldron's unauthorized biography than in Marrs's authorized one. As the mother-daughter correspondence cannot be made available for another fifteen years (someone is waiting for the grandchildren to die?), Welty's mother remains an elusive figure—controlling, snobbish, perhaps racist in the few glimpses we get of her—and Welty would necessarily have been at odds with her when young and more forgiving later on. As Welty wrote in *The Optimist's Daughter*, "Is there any sleeping person you can be entirely sure you have not misjudged?" Henry Green, another writer Welty greatly admired, once wrote to her in warning, "Don't forget about aged parents—they are FIENDS."

Welty would not have been thrilled with any biography—and even for an authorized biographer her desire to "retain an inner self that is a 'deep black hiding place'" makes her a difficult subject. She was not brave politically—she was suspicious of groupthink of any sort, whether it contained southern benightedness or northern sanctimoniousness—and in the essay "Must the Writer Crusade?" the exasperated title speaks for itself. She dismissed feminism as "noisiness," and once, when asked whether she'd been brought up to believe a woman's place was in the home, she replied, "I don't think I was ever told where it was." She felt she was already writing about injustice of various kinds; she voted Democratic: that should be enough. Any whiff of Yankee bias irked her, and she was rightly suspicious of the literary term *regionalism,* though her friend V. S. Pritchett in a review of *The Ponder Heart* defended the traditions of regional writing, saying, "They are a protest by old communities, enriched by wounds, against the success of mass, or polyglot culture." Even in her own work, moreover, Welty wrote, "How did it leave us—the old, safe, slow way people used to know of learning how one another feels?" This from the point of view of a northern character having lunch at Galatoire's. (In the very same story, southernness is seen as the less naïve stance: a look, a mask of "life-is-a-dream irony, which could turn to pure challenge at the drop of a hat.")

In letters Welty wrote, especially toward the end of her life, she said she often dreamed in galley proofs, and the struggle of the dream consisted of trying to make corrections on the type. She wrote at a desk with her back to the window, the quiet cruise and trespass of tourists insufficiently obscured outside. If her life had fallen into a trap or two, well, the world is full of traps of all sorts and one can find some writer or other in each and every one of them. Literary biography is like detective fiction for those who don't need suspense.

(2006)

Alice Munro's *The Moons of Jupiter*

Jupiter was the first planet studied by Galileo, in whose telescope were discovered Jupiter's four largest moons as well. Now there are over sixty known moons whose presences have revealed themselves (like Alice Munro's work, shyly opening up over the years), but these first four moons are referred to as the Galilean ones, and they are named after mortals favored by the great god Jupiter—Io, Europa, Ganymede, and Callisto—whose lives are forever altered by the god's love. The mortals are all feminine in their charms, if not entirely female, and in terms of whether love is fortunate for them or not (or even merely benign), they are batting close to .500, a figure that is beyond excellent in baseball but dicier in other realms. Io, the victim of both love and jealousy, is turned into a starving, wandering heifer stung mad by a gadfly sent by Jupiter's jealous wife. Europa is abducted to Crete (by Jupiter in the guise of a bull), and without too much extraordinary suffering she bears his royal children. Ganymede, a handsome young prince who catches Jupiter's fancy, is delivered to Olympus by an eagle in order to become a sort of sommelier to the gods. Callisto, another victim of sexual jealousy, is turned into a bear then mercifully placed among the stars to avoid being shot by her own son.

In so many tales told of romantic love, beauty casts spells that are often greeted or countered by other spells. In myth Jupiter's moons have lives of deformity and transplant, and in science the moons themselves are known for their erratic orbits. How like the characters of Alice Munro. Though her protagonists are not explicitly turned into animals or cupbearers or loved by any actual omnipotent, tempestuous god, the wanderings, transformations, mischief, and anguish of possessive love—the kind of love everyone really values, "the one nobody wants to have missed out on," according to the narrator of "Hard-Luck Stories"—are her most abiding subjects. Like the ancient Greeks, Alice Munro has always known this is where the stories are. Fate, power (gender and class), human nature (mortal strength and divine frailty) all show up there to be negotiated and expressed.

"Life would be grand if it weren't for the people," says a Munro character in "Labor Day Dinner," who also offers up the line perhaps most often quoted from this collection, that "love is not kind or honest and does not contribute to happiness in any reliable way." It is an acerbic balance to the alkaline lilt of 1 Corinthians 13:4, also quoted in this story, which informs us that "Love suffereth long, and is kind." That both ideas can be held simultaneously within the same narrative universe is part of the reason Munro's work endures—its wholeness of vision, its complexity of feeling, its tolerance of mind. For the storyteller, the failure of love is irresistible in its drama, as is its brief, happy madness, its comforts and vain griefs. And no one has brought greater depth of concentration and notice to the subject than Munro. No one has saturated her work with such startling physical observation and psychological insight. "He knew he had an advantage," she writes in "Connection," the book's inaugural story, "and we had reached the point in our marriage where no advantage was given up easily." And in the final story: "You touch a man that way to remind him that you are grateful. . . . It made me feel older than grandchildren would to see my daughter touch a man—a boy—this way. I felt her sad jitters, could predict her supple attentions."

The style in which people circle one another, their mix of lunacy and hard intelligence, the manner in which our various pasts revolve simultaneously around the present, the way that children are always in a parent's gravitational pull, even when out of sight, the fact that filial love has an infinitude of stories: all these are signaled by the book's title and in the title story. "I found my father in the heart wing," it begins, and the very many things it can mean to be a daughter are echoed through three generations gathered in that wing. Munro brings both a warm eye and a cool eye to the project of loss: "I saw how the forms of love might be maintained with a condemned person but with the love in fact measured and disciplined, because you have to survive."

Survival is often the hilarious miracle of Munro's world. The harsh and mythic Canadian frontier has changed; it has found some retaliatory energy, encroached upon the home and riven it—in changing social times making a frontier of family life. And yet Munro is often joyous and funny, and this book is full not just of darkly jokey accident but of the voices of women often quite literally singing: "White Christmas" in the vivid and gritty "The Turkey Season"; "Row, Row, Row Your Boat" in the haunted "Connection"; "In the Garden" in "Accident." Women stand on their heads, make love in supply closets, gut turkeys with their bare hands. They are amused and amazed by their own journeys and landing places. A weave of surprise and inevitability in the destination more often favors surprise. "Aren't we home?" are the last words of "Labor Day Dinner." "She has a way to go yet" concludes "Accident." Munro's women may brood over their choices—which loneliness might have better suited them, which alliance might have best preserved the self: "I think of being an old maid, in another generation," begins "Bardon Bus." "There were plenty of old maids in my family. I come of straitened people, madly secretive, tenacious, economical. Like them, I could make a little go a long way." But in the end there are powers beyond them that trump even the fierce will of the willful. The transits and upheaved settings of Munro's stories make the formation of a character's life a bit "catch-as-catch-can"— a term it's possible to imagine is neither a fishing phrase nor a wrestling stance but, as a friend of mine likes to insist, the very name of a place in Canada.

In *The Moons of Jupiter*, first published in 1982, Munro began a transition to a kind of story that was less linear, more layered with the pentimento of memory, a narrative able to head through and into time, forward or backward, pulling in somewhere as a car might do simply to turn around. These are the haphazard migrations of life and love, she seems to say, and the theme of accident—happy or unhappy or both or neither—is something she revisits in story after story. In "Accident," the protagonist and her lover have their affair exposed when his son is killed sledding behind an automobile. That this is the man she eventually marries seems simultaneously cheaply arbitrary and fatefully expensive—it has transformed her life, and others', and yet not: "She's had her love, her scandal, her man, her children. But inside she's ticking away, all by herself, the same Frances who was there before any of it." The girl written forever within the woman, the childish script of adult romantic love, the incomplete life transitions trapped fast in psychic amber—these are part of Munro's presentation of the human palimpsest, and these layerings help begin the more structurally daring stories for which she has, starting with this thrilling, magnificent collection, become renowned.

(2006)

Shakespeare: The Modern Elizabethan

An academic colleague of mine once asked me who had made me into a writer. "And I don't mean one of those creative writing professors," he said to me, a creative writing professor.

"Well, who do you mean?" I asked, probably ungrammatically, a thing creative writing professors get to do.

"I mean, who was your Shakespeare professor?" he asked; he was of course a Shakespeare professor himself.

I understood what he meant: Shakespeare was elemental, formative, fateful. Unlike the work of any writer before or since, Shakespeare's plays and poetry, while taking advantage of an audience's church-acquired tolerance for long speeches, celebrated the relatively new language of English and explored the strangeness within the ordinary and the familiar within the strange—the task of every artist. He returned again and again to the pathologies of love, marriage, and family—interest in which is a prerequisite for embarkation on an American literary life.

My own Shakespeare professor, now a fellow at the Folger Library, was a brilliant, handsome, manic young man fairly fresh from Duke, who on the first day of class sang an entire verse of "Afternoon Delight," clutching the lectern with bitter energy, to demonstrate to the students the all-pervasive and maddening junk he, as a Shakespearean, had been up against all summer.

He once diagrammed *Hamlet* as a sort of Pollock painting, with color-coded chalk for the characters. He directed us in a homemade film of *Romeo and Juliet,* the Capulets in red pinnies. But in general, he simply, convincingly communicated his love of the work and helped the plays come alive. When asked by prospective students how a major in English prepared one for the real world, he did not mouth platitudes about languages or learning to think critically. He headed straight for *Antony and Cleopatra:* "When you are surrounded by enemy armies and your generals tell you one thing and your girlfriend tells you something else, listen to your generals. English literature teaches you that." When I recently met him again in Washington, he said, with unsuppressed glee: "How long are you in town for? The Queen's Folio is here!"

Though many people have tried to insist that Shakespeare must have been a secret guild of theatricals, or the Earl of Oxford, or Sir Walter Raleigh, or some other person of education and rank ("How about the theory that Shakespeare is really Cliff Robertson?" joked a friend of mine), there is no doubt the man existed. Those who are still skeptical may be the same people who, generally pessimistic about human ability, insist that the pyramids were built by space aliens, or that Joyce Carol Oates is really a committee of middle-aged men. Or else they are the same elitists who think things like the roots of rock 'n' roll are actually white.

It seems clear—or at least we can say with a certain ad hoc confidence—that Shakespeare was born in Stratford-upon-Avon 442 years ago today, the son of a Catholic mother and glove-maker father (Christopher Marlowe, his contemporary, was the son of a shoemaker—anyone got a problem with that?). He had one sister who lived into adulthood, and who may or may not have been the thwarted genius of Virginia Woolf's imagining: "What would have happened had Shakespeare had a wonderfully gifted sister, called Judith?" she wrote. What we do know, however, is that his sister was named not Judith but Joan. He also had three younger brothers, all of whom preceded him in death.

Shakespeare's eighth-grade education was enough to give him a good grasp of Latin, to help him land work perhaps as a legal assistant (the plays are full of knowledge of the law as well as of gloves), a tutor, a horse holder, and an actor. How many writers have had jobs like these? A lot.

According to Stephen Greenblatt's impressive biography, *Will in the World,* Shakespeare's father's success then failure in the glove busi-ness may have prevented Shakespeare from going on to Oxford or Cambridge as many of his classmates (and Christopher Marlowe) did, but this is not the same as an insistence that he was too uneducated to have written the plays.

In Elizabethan England, apprentices abounded, as did pages and tutors, and Shakespeare would have easily made his way in that world. Actors had to know how to speak as gentlemen or bums, and carried around their own costumes and swords. The art and value of disguise, impersonation, and adaptation are usually learned young. The father's mercantile life would have given the young son an early, indelible glimpse of all segments of society—rich and poor, rural and urban, successful and failed—and arguably gave Will, in part, the great comic character Falstaff: the drunken father figure whom the successful young man outgrows, outpaces, and renounces, though not without a chilling soupçon of hate.

Shakespeare married early and, for practical reasons, someone older and richer (where there's a will, Anne Hathaway, the old quip goes) and then left her behind to pursue revolutionary work in the world, only to return and take up companionship with her at the end. In this—and in his stalwart determination, knack for real estate, and penchant for petty lawsuits—he is reminiscent (to me) of George Washington, whose mar-riage was made similarly coolly and which for a good part of his life sat at that same convenient and pleasing distance (until retirement), while he annoyed the other Army officers in New Jersey by dancing with their wives.

That Shakespeare's most passionate loves were at first youthful and then adulterous is suggested by his plays, which scarcely have a happy marriage in them, let alone a happy family. Though one shouldn't look to fictional work as autobiography, a writer will always write from what is on his mind, and somewhat from what he knows, and so the intensity and buffoonery of youthful erotic love and the low, miserable hum of marital discontent—famous as literary muses—were probably Shake-speare's muses as well. Just as they were Charles Dickens's (another actor-turned-writer). And Edith Wharton's. And (remain) Alice Munro's.

The limberness of Shakespeare's gift is arguably best demonstrated not by the greatest plays—*Hamlet, King Lear, Macbeth*—but by two that are considered more minor, one a tragedy, one a comedy, and both written the same year, more likely the tragedy first, as the comedy is something of a satire on the tragedy. These are *Romeo and Juliet* and *A Midsummer Night's Dream.* (That they might have been accruing simultaneously on his writing table is one of those events writers and critics alike are fond of imagining.) Comedy equals tragedy plus time.

Though they each have their various textual sources—Shakespeare, like Puccini, was a notorious artistic poacher, so much so that tales of Shakespeare's actual poaching of game have attached themselves to his legend—they are distinctly Shakespearean in their look at love.

In *Romeo and Juliet,* however inconvenient Cupid's choice, the energy of youthful love hurdles obstacles: "With love's light wings did I o'erperch these walls," says Romeo to Juliet, adding, "And what love can do, that dares love attempt." Though at play's end he is dead from his own hand, as is Juliet, victims in their own plot to outsmart the rather vicious society around them. Impetuosity never had a greater poet or a greater dramatist. Or a greater comedian.

In *A Midsummer Night's Dream,* a kind of buddy tale of mind and body on a fated forest trudge, erotic love is quite literally a drug, defying all solemnity and even intelligence, washing the brain in potions, something modern scientists have at long last proven to be an accurate occurrence. The most beautiful creature of the forest is made to fall in love with a blustery bumpkin by the sad name of Bottom, who through fairy mischief is now sporting the head of, well, an ass. A donkey's head: this is grotesquerie worthy of a Tim Burton movie. And it is all in service of Shakespeare's compassionate skepticism about love.

Each of these plays contains the other: *A Midsummer Night's Dream* contains *Romeo and Juliet* in its enactment of the tragical tale of Pyramus and Thisbe but played for laughs:

> *These yellow cowslip cheeks*
> *Are gone, are gone!*
> *Lovers make moan;*
> *His eyes were green as leeks.*

And *Romeo and Juliet* contains a window onto *A Midsummer Night's Dream* in the comic relief of Romeo's friend Mercutio, who throws barbs at the mere idea of romantic love to the comic approval of his entourage: "Prick love for pricking, and you beat love down."

The structure of both these plays is intricate and geometrical. *A Midsummer Night's Dream* moves easily in a single day among four different worlds and among the various romances giddily proceeding within them (some with more elegance than others). At the end of *Romeo and Juliet* the body count perfectly, symmetrically comprises two Montagues, two Capulets, and two relatives of the Prince. Death, not love, has the final blocking, though of course there is always the curtain call, and everyone is back up and alive again, as if to keep trying. Oh, why not.

Shakespeare's London was one of the great cities of Europe, though smaller than Madison, Wisconsin, is today. It was also rife with the religious bloodshed of modern Belfast or Baghdad. When Shakespeare arrived in London as a young man, he would have passed, impaled on the famous bridge into town, the skull of a distant cousin, killed for being a Catholic. How could this fail to leave an impression?

He filled his early plays, written in his new home, with violent young men and angry mobs. When he left, rich and successful, it was to die (at fifty-two) of what doctors today have speculated was a rare cancer of the tear duct—an illness as cruelly ironic as Puccini's cancer of the throat. His beloved Globe Theatre had burned down. He could not have been happy.

But he did not know that his work would survive forever not just onstage but in book, screen, and musical form—no one at that time could have. Or that his words would inspire their own honoring thefts: Joni Mitchell took a glittering simile of his for "That Song About the Midway"; *West Side Story* and *She's the Man* borrowed his plots.

Washington, Dickens, Puccini, and Tim Burton somehow merged into one: there's your genius. Or the bare bard bones of him.

Add a dash—of Ogden Nash.

(2006)

One Hot Summer, or a
Brief History of Time

A bride on her summer honeymoon—what could be more beguiling?

Well, a younger bride, to begin with. One less destined to wear an off-white suit at the ceremony. (And what's with that, anyway? The advertising of a lady's past, the beige and ivory taint of autobiography dyed like a scarlet *A* into the very threads of her dress. Why not say it another way and wear yellow, black, or green? Why not horizontal stripes? Chinese brides wore red, as did Jane Austen's mother, who later cut up her attire for outfits for the kids. Who wouldn't want something actually bright and cuttable?)

I had always had a little trouble with anything called an institution. I was thirty-four, and had been seeing the same man for four consecutive years and living with him for two—not a record for anyone (except for him). We spent the spring fretting: Should we get married? He felt we should, in this moving-through-life way. It was what came next. (Which would in turn, of course, quickly introduce the idea of divorce; we all are fiends for narrative, plot, rising action.) I wondered whether our marrying should really be this notch in the belt of time. Shouldn't it be, rather, an emotional and spiritual referendum on us? If we needed an event, we could, say, break up. Get married or break up: that's pretty much what it came down to. Love? Love went without saying, so we didn't say it. Perhaps we were a little bored. Something, we both seemed to agree, should probably *occur*. Though, looking back, I'm not sure why. It was just motion. Momentum.

But with the tulips up, the air warming, and then suddenly the tulips down, petal-less, buglike, and leaning, still we remained undecided. We both understood I would not change my name to his, but privately I felt this might not augur well for the success of our union. I suspected, quite correctly I think now, that those women who changed their names to match their husbands' understood something about marriage that I was in the dark about.

My boyfriend was of the school of thought that marriage—like a house or a car—was a necessary accoutrement of adulthood. I was resistant to that school of thought, and wasn't really in any school of thought at all—not a certified one, not in a matriculated way. To quote Daniel Handler's *Adverbs,* I was letting my thoughts "run around the yard rather than reporting inside." Or to quote from Richard Yates's "The Best of Everything," "a familiar little panic gripped her: she couldn't marry him—she hardly even knew him. Sometimes it occurred to her differently, that she couldn't marry him because she knew him too well, and either way it left her badly shaken."

Summer was approaching, so all right, we would at least begin the process. Otherwise, I hardly needed reminding, I was risking the possibility of a life where in the "In Case of Emergency Contact" space, I would repeatedly be writing "Me." One noon hour after lunch in a nearby fish place, we strolled over to the county courthouse; there we filled out the application for a marriage license. This license was simply a permission slip, like a hunting license. It gave us forty-five days to do the deed. In that time period one could "dear-hunt," using the language of this state, although, also in the language of this state, what most hunters looked for, frankly, was a nice "rack," which may have accounted for my new fiancé's sudden clutching. Of his stomach. The clerk behind her desk raised her eyebrows.

"I'm feeling some horrible pain," said the masculine owner of this new license, looking faintly green.

"Seen it before," said the clerk, "but not usually this fast."

"This was all his idea," I said. "Or, mostly."

"I think it was the fish," moaned you-know-who, whose name, we'll say, was Mike.

"I ate the same fish," I said. "I feel fine."

"You see?" said the clerk.

Mike was bent over in his chair, clutching his stomach. But he did not excuse himself to go anywhere else. And so this is what makes marriage possible: no one actually getting up and running away.

Although a few unmarried weeks followed in which some discussion ensued, I don't really recall any of it. The next thing I do recall is getting up and dressing in an I'll-be-damned cream-colored suit. We were on our way to the county courthouse to get married that morning, with one friend and one clerk as witnesses, and then we would be getting on a plane, flying to Seattle, and renting a car so we could drive down the small Pacific coast highway to Los Angeles. This would be our honeymoon.

Outside in the judge's office, where we were to be married, a camera crew had assembled, all sitting wearily on the corridor floor with their equipment. They were from *60 Minutes* and were apparently waiting for us. "I didn't know your short stories were that well known," exclaimed Mike, looking proud and amazed.

"Yes . . . well . . . ," I said, not wanting to disappoint him so soon. What could these people want?

"We were here earlier in the week to do a story on the governor's Wedfare program," they announced. "But we left without getting footage of an actual welfare couple getting married. We just need some footage, so we had to fly back last night; we heard a marriage was scheduled for this morning."

"Us?" I asked. "But we're not on welfare."

"That part doesn't matter. No one will know that. We just have to film two people getting married in this building."

This particular parsing of reality troubled me. If they were going to pretend any couple was a welfare couple, marrying to increase state benefits to themselves, as per the governor's murky thinking on the matter (thinking that, briefly, went national), why not also save on airfare and pretend any building was this building? It was a generic municipal building. For ten seconds of footage, they didn't need this one. If something was already half a lie, then it was really a whole lie. So make it a whole one.

The crew looked bleary, as if having just concluded a blistering gig with *National Geographic*. My new soon-to-be-husband's face brightened: "We'd get to be on TV," he said to me, clearly game for this. That he was capable of being game for most anything, I realized, was the reason we were getting married—and the reason we would be divorced ten years later. But it could not be a reason for our being on *60 Minutes* as an ersatz welfare couple.

"God no," I said. The crew looked devastated.

The judge's clerk shrugged. And my husband-to-be then tried this angle: "It would be funny!"

"It could be," said the head of the crew, hopefully.

Although Mike would have donned a big rubber suit to play a betrothing walrus on *Wild Kingdom*—because it would be funny— I could not participate. "It would be bad luck," I said. "No."

"Really?"

"Really."

"She says no," said Mike.

"She says no," said the clerk to the camera crew who sat there, grumbling and tired.

"The bride says no," said the judge himself, standing in the doorway. And that is how my marriage began.

The signing of papers and saying of vows was very officey and took place under bright lights with no big city. A sweet little orchid was placed into my hand by someone. A picture I still have shows me with my hair clipped up, a way I almost never wore it unless cleaning something. Soon we were on a plane, where we were very quiet, not knowing what precisely we had done. We stared out different windows and took our respective naps, awaking to the same new fact of our lives. I thought of the James Taylor song "There We Are." ("Here we are like children forever, taking care of one another." I had just gotten married with no music at all.) I then thought of the Dorothy Parker story "Here We Are."

"So how does it feel to be an old married lady?" says the brand-new husband in that story.

"Oh, it's too soon to ask me that," says his new bride. "Well, I mean, goodness, we've only been married about three hours, haven't we?"

And here the husband studies his wristwatch "as if he were just acquiring the knack of reading time."

"We have been married . . . exactly two hours and twenty-six minutes," he announces.

"My," she says. "It seems like longer."

When we landed at the Seattle airport, the first thing I noticed were the signs and public address system announcements in Japanese— which seemed to me another clue that marriage might involve a language I didn't actually speak. I sort of noticed my new husband looking around at all the blondes (Wisconsin had once been very blonde but was less so now, and perhaps Seattle seemed a blast from the Scandinavian-American past—and his own), but that hankering outward was perhaps a necessary gesture, a final wave farewell to all the others. Why else do so many honeymooners head for beaches? We rented a car, stayed at a nice hotel, ate soft-shell crab, and phoned our parents.

"You eloped!" exclaimed my mother, as if she were impressed. I guess we *had* eloped—though I didn't really understand that then. There'd been no ladder up to the window, no dashing off into the night. I hadn't really thought deeply from the parental angle about our getting married this way, and now I regretted not having given it a longer, harder contemplation. I told my father about the *60 Minutes* thing, thinking he would find it amusing.

"You should have gone on TV! Then at least I could have seen you," he said. "Since I didn't get a chance to give you away." He didn't sound angry, or even all that sad, just sort of practical.

"But we would have been posing as a welfare couple," I said. I thought I'd been saving him money not having a real wedding.

"It might have helped the sales of your books," he said, a situation he always inquired about worriedly.

"We'll have a fancy party of some sort when we get back and invite everyone," I said. (Which we did, during which my husband never put on shoes, just wandered around in his socks, drinking beer.)

The next morning we had breakfast, took some sarcastic photos of the bed (unmade and strewn with the morning's *Post-Intelligencer*, a newspaper whose very name seemed hopelessly indicative of the occasion), and when we checked out we bought the bathrobes as souvenirs. (Good for giving away to Goodwill a decade later.) We rode some ferries, on which I grew woozy, drove around the rain forest, which was a mossy, magical land containing every possible hue of green. Although it was a National Forest, Japanese companies were already logging in it. We would hike and drive and stumble upon denuded patches full of sunlight and machinery and noise.

Then we headed south, keeping the ocean (which we never got to see in Wisconsin) in sight on our right, visiting otters and seals and dune buggy gatherings along the Oregon beaches. We stayed at bed-and-breakfasts that were once churches (this to compensate for having married at the county courthouse?) and in general tried not to quarrel. It was a road trip, and we had brought two tapes: Stephen Hawking's *A Brief History of Time* and another one called *Jazz Wolf*, which featured an actual howling wolf accompanied by some alternately plaintive and jaunty jazz. We'd drive along, wordlessly, listening to the howling of that lonely wolf—its own brief history of time. The Stephen Hawking we could only understand for about five-minute stretches, and then we'd have to rewind to listen to it over again. At this rate, the history of time would not only be far from brief, it would be a never-ending driving hazard. But I didn't want to proceed through the tape uncomprehendingly, so there was much rewinding and then ultimately the frustrated substitution of *Jazz Wolf.* "Oh, let's just put on *Jazz Wolf*" became a kind of refrain for our stupidity—something we carried into the future with us. Every marriage needs a refrain.

We drove down the winding Highway 1, which vertiginously hugged the California coast, producing more wooziness in me, despite the great beauty of everything. Beauty, after a while, you just don't see anymore—if you're immersed in it constantly. The worry of car sickness replaced it, and I didn't know whether we should be driving slower, or faster to get it all over with. Marriage!

Following our guidebook, we drove through that giant redwood tree you can drive through, and in other parts of the woods we got out. Our photo album shows me hugging the trees and my husband urinating near them. Which should tell you something, but I'm not sure what. In Mendocino, we stopped and had lunch and bought souvenirs, though the whole place seemed preserved in time in an artificial way, the charming potheads still roamed the village streets, while the actual makers of the gift shop ceramics remained hidden to avoid possible detection and derision—crockery mockery. Still, I thought I saw a whale. Which is the kind of thing you hope for your first summer as a married woman.

Eventually, after a cool, breezy day and night in San Francisco—the original shining city on a hill—where we lit a gas stove in our room and spoke incessantly of earthquakes (failing to leave our hearts or wear flowers in our hair), we turned inland and drove across the desert, which was eerily lunar day or night. Beneath the pitch-black sky, covering us like an iron skillet lid punctured by BBs, I swore I saw UFOs (perhaps near one of the several military sites sitting spookily out there in the sand). In the daytime, litter blew apocalyptically among the cactuses. My husband wanted to go to Las Vegas—and I kept making hooker jokes, which weren't really very funny. We passed signs for Death Valley, signs for the Funeral Mountains, signs for a town called Needles, and one sign that read "ZZYX RD," which I think led to Needles, and we stopped so I could take a picture of that.

Once we were in Las Vegas, in an absurdly cheap room (the city was not yet the opulent place it has become), I remained upstairs reading while the mister went downstairs to gamble in the casino. No more hooker jokes. "Let's get out of here," I said in the morning, and we drove the next day to Los Angeles and ate Italian-Greek fusion dishes with artichokes and goat cheese in them in a hip, bright place—it seemed the beginning of a kind of food I'd not experienced before, cooking that was over-the-top and unnecessarily delicious. We roamed the streets of West Hollywood and tanned our arms in the sun.

And then we flew back home, to the Midwest, to our little blue house, where we'd lived for years, and would live for a few more, and where our cat was waiting and happy to see us.

The honeymoon was over.

But that was okay.

(2006)

Stephen Sondheim's *Sweeney Todd*

Stephen Sondheim's great musical *Sweeney Todd* is an American *Rigoletto*. Both share a tone that ascends to frolic and then falls back to deepest dirge without ever losing a fine, bleak creepiness. Musical themes attach to particular characters and are replayed in both works in rousing, climactic quartets. For plot, each turns on a desire for revenge upon the powerful, which backfires and costs the title characters—wronged fathers both—the deaths of loved ones. These deaths are murders for which these once innocent baritones, in their careless vengeance, are responsible, and when their shocked, remorseful tears are shed at the end, the eyes of the audience may stay dry and unsurprised: what is mourned is lamentable inevitability more than an actual person. In both Verdi and Sondheim the human devil triumphs. The cruelty of men is indeed as "wondrous as Peru." In both tales virtuous women are inconvenienced by their own attractiveness and seized by men of means (a duke, a judge, each with his sinister revelers and toadies) from men of no means (a jester, a barber). The corruption, power, and greed that produce self-defeating madness in their victims are shown in both stories to be institutional, societal, political. Garden-variety cleverness is no match and is transformed by the end into the romping vanity of fools.

How interesting, then, that despite all its operatic affinity and Grand Guignol predilections, *Sweeney Todd* played on Broadway this past year as a stripped-down chamber concert. In this rendition, gone are the looming sets of the 1979 Harold Prince production, which sent large wooden and mechanical platforms and beams out past the proscenium of the stage—this to suggest the industrial upheaval of nineteenth-century London. Gone is Bryn Terfel of the 2002 Chicago Lyric production—one does not need the world's greatest living baritone for this role—as well as the thrilling if deafening chorus (how chorus-driven a score Sondheim has written is best discerned by a chorus of this magnitude and beauty; no humming hoofers they). And gone is the expert San Francisco Symphony, whose recent contribution staged the cast ingeniously around the orchestra and created a concert version far more theatrical than the one this year at the Eugene O'Neill Theatre.

Theatrical, that is, because characters interacted with one another. In director John Doyle's production they by and large do not. This is for two reasons. One is that they are busy playing instruments—cellos, violin, accordion, guitar, triangle, clarinet, trumpet, flute, and even tuba. This makes it difficult for one character to look another in the eye, even if that character is pleading to be kissed. As a result, the ardent if fearful young lovers are played as real buffoons as well as real cellists, surely a first. But such a dramatic sacrifice, once the whiff of stunt evaporates, is a convenience to the second reason, the Brechtian staging—stylized alienation—that emerges at first as if by default, then later by insistence. The performers are detached in their stances, in their deliveries, and in their charmless stares out over the ticket holders' heads. They mean to cast a spell over no one, and if this Brechtian idea fails to communicate itself completely, the costumes—pulled from some Weimar cabaret trunk (much leather and fishnet) and a businessman's suitcase (white shirts and ties)—indeed do help. Yet the characters' instruments sometimes succeed in plaintiveness or the suggestion of a momentarily tender heart. And to hear this Demon Barber of Fleet Street (fiercely performed by indie rock star Michael Cerveris), who slits the throats of his despised customers but nonetheless strums hauntingly on an acoustic guitar, is to witness a previously elusive side of Sweeney Todd, the man and the show, which is like a secret (brief and contradictory amid the standoffishness): tenderness contiguous with ferocity. Just as the exquisitely flatted note in the tenor aria "Johanna"—"even now I'm at your *win*dow"—takes the victory out of "win," the performance of the music has its own language, stealing past the acrobatic words.

This is the genius not just of the composer but of the simplified arrangements by the British orchestrator Sarah Travis. It is astonishing how little feels left out in this grand reduction to only nine instruments, how much is accomplished in her adaptations, how much intimacy is gained, even if one glimpses the microphones on the cellos. The singing and playing are of a piece—organic, economical, clear. The same cannot be said of the arbitrary thrift of the abstracted stage design, which substitutes a ladder, a coffin, an apothecary's shelving for the original barber's chair and bakehouse chute. A simple red light screams on overhead while downstage something resembling cabernet sauvignon is poured portentously from one bucket into another. The victim stands up and walks away (something done also in the San Francisco version). This particular staging may have more narrative meaning for those who know the story already. The evening I saw it, women in line for the ladies' room at intermission were shaking their heads and exclaiming, "I don't know what's going on—I can't follow it! Can you?" The self-explanatory lyrics, which assist a more literal set, are witty and crisp, but quick as mice, and some will escape an unfamiliar ear. "He shaved the faces of gentlemen / Who never thereafter were heard from again" is written to be sung like a brisk tumble down the stairs. Doyle's bold expressionism is probably best appreciated by someone with one other production under her belt (a forthcoming film version by Tim Burton will helpfully star Johnny Depp). Nonetheless, for those lucky enough to have seen it here or in London, Doyle's is as inspired and audacious a presentation of one of the twentieth century's great works of art as one is likely to encounter. Its tricky casting ("Can you act, sing beautifully, and play two instruments every night for weeks on end?") will make it difficult to reproduce.

But Doyle's production should not be praised exclusively for its originality and daring. As it was presented in New York there were smaller, more conventional decisions to admire as well. The direction of Patti LuPone away from her more flibberty, Angela Lansbury–style interpretation with the San Francisco Symphony better suits the hard, belting quality of LuPone's voice (LuPone's wavy stringray of a mouth is an expressive, brassy creature all its own). Here is a Mrs. Lovett whose affections for Mr. Todd are perfunctory at best. She is in business with him for the new and untorn stockings she will get to wear in the second act. When she sings to him, "Always had a fondness for you. I did," LuPone is dead in the eyes, as directed; her mind is chewing gum. Unlike in San Francisco and elsewhere, where Mrs. Lovett's emotional, not just her economic, desperation is felt, her union with Todd reveals how sentimental plans, however hollow and shameless, once articulated can temporarily build a rickety alliance, a kind of honor among thieves. In "By the Sea," LuPone not only hilariously mimics the scary sound of a seagull (as if dispelling the breathless squawk of Lansbury, which haunts any production of this show) but sings in her beat-up satin voice of a romantic idyll with Todd (she always refers to him as "Mr. Todd," in the same way the Dustin Hoffman character in *The Graduate* always refers to "Mrs. Robinson": formality politely conveying tarnish and impossibility). In Mrs. Lovett's fantasy cottage by the sea they'll "Have a nice sunny suite / For the guest to rest in." Once in a while Todd can "do the guest in." They'll be "married nice and proper." But Todd should bring his "chopper." Here Mrs. Lovett is more completely the Cockney Lady Macbeth she is only partially in other productions. The comedy of her best bits, however, is never lost. When we first see LuPone on her own, in "The Worst Pies in London," she is flicking invisible flies from invisible pies. She lures Todd in with her own tales of woe:

> *Mrs. Mooney has a pie shop.*
> *Does a business but I notice something weird—*
> *Lately all her neighbors' cats have disappeared.*
> *Have to hand it to her—*
> *Wot I calls*
> *Enterprise*
> *Popping pussies into pies.*
> *Wouldn't do in my shop—*
> *Just the thought of it's enough to make you sick.*

And here the old pro's deliberate slowing as she continues: "And I'm telling you them pussy cats is quick."

When she hints at her plan for human meat pies, LuPone's Mrs. Lovett is less coyly cajoling with Todd. Her voice is deadened with pragmatism.

With the price of meat what it is
when you get it
If you get it—
. . . Good you got it.

Todd joins in with controlled but visibly demented glee. "The history of the world, my sweet, / is who gets eaten and who gets to eat." This, the operetta's signature song, "A Little Priest," is a rollicking waltz that satirizes all of society and honors not just Verdi (and his favorite meter), or Ravel's *La valse*, which grows similarly minor and ominous as it proceeds (as if into the twentieth century), or the oom-pah-pah of LuPone's own ballyhooed though minimal tuba playing elsewhere in the show, but self-references the immortal lyricist himself ("The trouble with poet is how do you know it's deceased?"), as Mrs. Lovett tries to outwit Sweeney, offering various imaginary pies. "Tinker?" He'd like something "Pinker." "Tailor?" He'd prefer "Paler." "Butler?" He replies "Subtler." "Potter?" He says "Hotter." Finally, in cool triumph, she suggests, "Locksmith?" And he is, of course, stumped. It's a poet's joke, and places the songwriter right in the song, but the characters take it up with energy and relish.

LuPone may be gradually taking ownership of this role from its originator, Dame Angela. It is possible that the rouged and pigtailed Lansbury's eccentric, sharp-pitched twittering will someday seem a peculiar preference in light of LuPone's cool and sultry alto. A Broadway sacrilege to say, but that is the power of this, LuPone's most iconoclastic rendition. It may lose its iconoclasm (LuPone is laying late claim to another Sondheim role, too—Mama Rose in *Gypsy*, which she sang this past summer with the Chicago Symphony Orchestra, although she was perhaps cast too true to type—"the role she was born to play," boasted the advertising—and her performance there contained few surprises).

Other moments of Doyle's direction constituted intriguing improvements. Judge Turpin is complicatedly less grotesque, played by the handsome Mark Jacoby in a business suit, instead of the usual white wig and judicial robes. Moreover, Jacoby's voice complements the rich sureness of Cerveris's in the gorgeously ironic death knell "Pretty Women." The duet, not overpowered by any orchestra and aided by Travis's sensitive arrangement, particularly her plangent use of the ordinarily harsh and recalcitrant accordion, is a wonder, fascinating, combing out *its* hair—one of the best on record. And although it is hard to improve upon that singing chameleon Victoria Clark and her San Francisco rendition of the deranged beggar woman, Lucy (Clark has been mesmerizing Lincoln Center audiences as a rich southern matron in *The Light in the Piazza*), a delicately prolonged moment, when Doyle's Lucy as played by Diana Di Marzio lays her cheek lingeringly on Todd's arm, still not looking at him, while singing her recurrent "Don't I know you?" is startlingly good. Director Doyle holds the moment for several extra beats—he knows what he has. A piece of physical memory is registered there more movingly than I've seen in almost any Sondheim musical. Such freeze framing assists the story well, for it is part of the ghostly marital memory of a self-described "naïve" man—an odd adjective, uttered slowly, even uncertainly, in Todd's own autobiographical ballad—which finally if belatedly breaks the barber down.

The night I saw *Sweeney Todd*, Broadway's lights were dimmed in memory of Wendy Wasserstein, who had just died. Much farther south President George W. Bush was giving his State of the Union address. At the show's close the entire cast of ten was standing in choral epilogue, the killed had risen, as in Elizabethan drama, and the set seemed like a cross between *Assassins* and *Spoon River Anthology*. The ensemble, their throats repaired, nimbly sang,

> *Sweeney wishes the world away*
> *Sweeney's weeping for yesterday,*
> *Hugging the blade, waiting the years,*
> *Hearing the music that nobody hears.*

Only then did I fully feel a frisson of political statement roll over the stage—a frisson that didn't die (the trouble with poet is how do you know it's deceased?). Somewhere President Bush was reading, "Our differences cannot be allowed to harden into anger." Hell, no (we won't go). But, Sweeney Todd seemed to say, let them harden into rhyme. At least (try the priest).

(2007)

Peter Cameron

Peter Cameron is an urban novelist with an interest in the angle and viscosity of sunlight. He is an observer of greenery—"it was impossible to walk along that gravel path by the sea and not think *palm frond shadow*"—and the strength and direction of a current in a river or a stream:

> The sun was low in the sky and refracted in the window. He could see his own reflection, and through that, flickering in the glass, the reflection of what was ahead . . . coming back to the city is always nicer, in a way, because you travel in the same direction as the river.

His remarking of the natural world, as it intersects with the man-made, is not just a seeking of ironies and metaphors, though often it is also that. An observation such as "the reflection of what was ahead" is lovely in its linguistic play. But more often Cameron's recitation of the physical world seems like a reminder of earthly sparkle and grit he forces upon himself. Human habitation of the planet, and its great pleasantnesses, is something he is interested in being grateful for without writing a novel that would express, wholeheartedly, that gratitude. There is then the strange generosity of his at least trying—of here and there defying the melancholy and ontological quibbling (his own) that impedes the enterprise. "She felt like she wanted to pray but it went no further than that." The contemporary loss of a spiritual language is the haunting subtext of almost all that he has written.

In fact, Cameron writes with a sort of perfection of restraint that can sometimes make a first-time reader afraid the narrative may be too superficial or too precious or too English for ostensibly robust American reading tastes—according to interviews, the writers he most admires are the British novelists Barbara Pym, Penelope Mortimer, and Rose Macaulay, whose work has made brief appearances in his own. His main characters tend to be people who are in some fashion running away, so that the settings of his novels are often not where the protagonist ordinarily lives at all but a place he is observing, tentatively, for the first time.

As a result, although Cameron's writerly predilection, as with many novelists of manners, is for long scenes of tart conversation, the narrative often proceeds with a gingerly sort of emphasis on material objects. A pitcher of amber beer, rather than any of the people in the room, is what is most likely to seem "blessedly lit from within." "Luxury hotels are the real houses of God," says a character in Cameron's 1997 novel, *Andorra*. A mood of exile and foreignness is thus underscored (and later, climactically, dramatized). It is the civilized world Cameron ends up honoring, even in all its disarray (though his pen is repeatedly drawn to tidy still lifes of every sort). The natural world carefully steps back, like a sensitive suitor who knows he's been toyed with. "You would get nowhere," thinks one Cameron character, "if you were never led on."

Peter Cameron began as a short-story writer. Throughout the 1980s his stories appeared with some regularity in *The New Yorker*, where they were exemplary of a certain spare and elegant minimalism then associated with that magazine. Soon he was writing a serial novel for the short-lived periodical *7 Days* (these chapters were later published as *Leap Year*, 1990), and after that, despite two story collections, he became primarily a novelist, his most admired books being *The Weekend* (1994) and *Andorra*. The latter, set in the tiny principality of that name tucked in the Pyrenees between Spain and France (and given a seacoast and a marina the real Andorra does not have), is something of a murder mystery, and proceeds with a Mr. Ripley–style narrator less talented than Patricia Highsmith's but more interestingly contemplative, even if we recognize his debts and in advance suspect his charms.

The Weekend, with its elegiac pun on *weakened*, touches on the subject of illness and grief in the gay community but is simultaneously a kind of romantic frolic over a single long night, a *Midsummer Night's Dream* in upstate New York. In the book's title Cameron slyly puts forward what turns out to be that novel's most haunting metaphor: What idea better sums up life's brief strain at happiness (jammed between two eternities) than the idea of *the weekend*? Cameron has fashioned a living trope that sustains the entire book: life is a weekend, a hinge that joins the long nothing before and the longer nothing that follows. Between the bookending emptinesses sits existence, which in Cameron's world consists of loving, dying, and visiting. There is also usually some alfresco dining, a dabbling painter or two, and, alas, croquet.

If Cameron's focus seems a bit too trained on privileged travel, grand houses, slight and decorative employment, artistic wannabes, and effortlessly eccentric socialites, as if every society he examines were an indolent one of nineteenth-century dilettantes—"back when the world had a certain elegant order," says one character, oblivious to whole portions of history—or if his fictional world resembles perhaps a twentieth-century artists' colony, well, all of his books were written in part at Yaddo or MacDowell. A large house filled to the rafters with lonely creative types seems to be a kind of muse for him. Sometimes his characters quite literally live and work in turrets and attics. His novels have thus far featured—to name only a few—a rich murderer writing his memoirs; a closeted gay man at work on an opera based on Gide's *The Immoralist;* and several visual artists, the most recent being one who decoupages garbage cans with pages of the Bible, the Koran, and the Talmud. (Cameron arranges to have this last reviewed in *Artforum* under the title "When Is Garbage Just Garbage? When It Stinks.") "I'm going to write a book about a perfect country where it's always the nineteenth century" says a character in *The Weekend*. And although his main characters are full of doubt and yearning and intelligent observation, they also may be surrounded by fatuous Lillet drinkers who make such speeches as this:

Poor them! I'm afraid Ibiza is ruined. Although I haven't been there in years. Perhaps it's been unruined. That can happen to places, but it takes a while. You see, a place is found, then it's lovely for a while, and then it's ruined, and then if you're lucky it's forgotten, and if it hasn't become too, too ruined, it can start again—unruin itself. It's what's going to happen to the planet eventually, I'm sure. It's only natural and we shouldn't resist it. We'll ruin it with concrete and garbage and hairspray and blow ourselves up, and it will all lie fallow for a millennium or two, and then it will start all over again, the fish crawling out of the sea and eventually painting the Sistine Chapel. Mark my words.

It is all bleakly amusing, and Cameron has a light hand: he lets his characters satirize themselves. In his last novel, *The City of Your Final Destination* (2002), travel to a half-real country, psychic claustrophobia, large, old-world houses, and dubious creative and intellectual projects persist—though this time the story includes the world of literary scholarship and mines it for its spinning moral compasses and thwarted and futile figures. A University of Kansas graduate student named Omar travels to Uruguay to seek authorization for a biography of a dead writer, and spends the rest of the novel among the dead author's literary executors. He is not in Kansas anymore. But the ivory tower looks like harsh reality—dusty Kansas indeed—compared to the lives lived by this reclusive expatriated group. They—not unlike many of Cameron's characters—speak if not like actual Munchkins, then like fey, childlike residents of some wonderland or other:

"Iran, Canada, Kansas—where is your home?" asked Caroline.

"I don't really know," said Omar. "Kansas now, I suppose."

"You will stay in Kansas?" asked Caroline.

"It's difficult to get a job teaching college," said Omar. "If they offer me one, I suppose I will stay there. Or go wherever I can find a job."

"That seems a bit strange to me: to allow a job to decide where one lives. Surely you are not so cowed by reality as that?"

"I'm afraid I am very cowed by reality," said Omar.

"Oh," said Caroline. "Why is that?"

.   .   .

But in Cameron's newest novel, deliciously vital right from the start, and as inviting as if less cozy than his previous ones, no one speaks like a mesmerizing airhead from another era. Though the characters are for the most part younger than in his other novels, they seem not just smarter and less desiccated but wiser and more worldly. And the genial hum of his previous narratives has been replaced by an articulate if paralyzed cry, which is occasionally ratcheted up to a scream. *Someday This Pain Will Be Useful to You* features the ways and current crises of a Manhattan family (dismantled and demented in recognizable fashion by divorce). The first sentence alone tells you how succinctly Cameron can get to the maddened heart of the matter, the voice, the milieu: "The day my sister, Gillian, decided to pronounce her name with a hard G was, coincidentally, the same day my mother returned, early and alone, from her honeymoon." *Someday This Pain Will Be Useful to You* is a piece of vocal virtuosity and possibly Cameron's best book: it retains the lucid and unlabored prose of his previous ones but wastes less time; it may be his most successful novel on its own terms—terms that are not as modest as they may initially seem.

That in many ways this novel contains the least childlike characters he has ever created makes it especially unfortunate that the publisher has already been labeling it a young adult novel. The narrator is a smart-talking eighteen-year-old named James Sveck, who shares a bit of Holden Caulfield's snarky dismay. But he also has in common with the narrator of *Andorra* a love of smooth Roman stone and a prickly, pedantic relationship to human utterance. What Peter Cameron has done is written a sophisticated and adult book, although with fewer trellises and champagne flutes and tablecloths than in his previous books and less notice of architectural features such as newels and cornices. People speak less formally to one another, and more confrontationally, and use contractions. No one is likely to say they've slept "marvelously" the night before. They are more likely not to have slept at all:

"I can't believe you didn't notice I was missing," I said.
"Get a life, James," said Gillian. . . .

"I just thought someone might notice that I never came home."

"Oh, we would, eventually," said my mother. "You just have to stay away a bit longer next time."

In addition to bracingly comic dialogue, the novel possesses too much emotional complexity and artfulness of construction to exclude adult readers—for instance, the desire of a young man simply to be seen, let alone seen for what he is, is given several plot strands: two different instances of running away, and one elaborate instance of posing as someone else (in a computer chat room), all to win notice.

Similar assessments, of course, can be made of *Great Expectations*, as well as the most famous of American boy narrators, Huckleberry Finn. And then there is *The Catcher in the Rye* itself, and although one would hesitate to place Cameron's novel in all this immortal company, *Someday This Pain Will Be Useful to You* will very likely elicit comparisons both to those great books and to more recent ones by, say, Jonathan Safran Foer or Benjamin Kunkel.

James's best friend is not a fellow teenager but his grandmother in New Jersey, who refers to herself as "the poor man's Kitty Carlisle Hart." His father works in a high-security midtown skyscraper, has a Diebenkorn in his sun-filled office, and is about to have some cosmetic surgery on his eyes. As a kind of preemptive strike or out of idle and insensitive curiosity, he asks James if he is gay. James's mother, a thrice-married art dealer whose latest husband has absconded with her credit cards, and whose assistant is gay, also asks James if he is gay. James's sister, dating a language theory professor named Rainer Maria Schultz, is the only one in the family who doesn't ask. She is described by the flap copy as "his mordant older sister," but this is not her story. James's longest discussions are with his mother and his therapist, whom the flap copy refers to as "Teutonic." Cameron's prose, however, takes us out of labels and types of every kind:

"Well, you don't think it's weird?" Gillian asked Rainer Maria. "An eighteen-year-old boy who visits his grandmother?"

"No," said Rainer Maria. "You Americans have so little family feeling. In Germany . . . we love our grandparents."

"I'm not saying you shouldn't love them," said Gillian. "I just think visiting them is weird. It will be so good for you to go away to school, James. . . ."

"I've decided I'm not going to college," I said.

"What? Since when?"

"Today. . . . I'm thinking about moving to the Midwest."

"The Midwest? The Midwest of what?"

"The United States," I said. "The prairie states."

"The *prairie* states? I think you've read *My Ántonia* one too many times."

"Hush, Gillian. I think this is a very good plan for you, James," said Rainer Maria. "The college experience in the United States is a farce."

"Hello!" said Gillian. "You teach in a college."

"My dear Gillian, if everyone had to believe in the work he did, not much would get done in the world," said Rainer Maria.

James quite candidly does not care for people his own age, or so he says, or perhaps this is a convenience, as Cameron has always been more interested in the grown-up world, especially young adults and very old ones, even if they are childlike in their conduct. The social canvas and range of dramatic action here may seem deceptively narrow: a high school senior who lives with his mother and sister; visits his father, grandmother, and therapist; recalls a brief misadventure at an academic teen conference in Washington, D.C., called "The American Classroom"; makes a mess of a crush he has on his mother's assistant. But this apparent quietness is not atypical for Cameron, nor is a narrative strategy in which we are privy to the subdued wit of even the angriest and most unhappy people:

For a moment I could tell my mother didn't get what I meant, and then she got it. She looked at me with a sort of hurt, amazed expression. "You think I'm a tyrant?"

"I think you have tendencies toward tyranny," I said.

. . .

Neither young adult literature nor even really a coming-of-age story, *Someday This Pain Will Be Useful to You* is most surprisingly of all the subtlest September 11 novel yet written (if one can speak of the September 11 novel as a genre, and I think, with respect, that one can). So accomplished is its subtlety that one is not even aware of this novel's true subject until three-quarters of the way through, and then its mention—"You know we've never talked about September 11"—a remark made rather late in the day by James's therapist, rises up out of the story's barely submerged anxiety (it is perhaps initially, casually planted there by James's ominous visit to his father's high-in-the-clouds office) and casts on the book a sudden, brilliant light. James has been wanting to skip college and use his tuition money to buy a house in the Midwest—now we see why: two years before, he had been in tenth grade, at Stuyvesant High School, within close view of the World Trade Center when it was attacked. "I'm thinking about the woman who died on September 11 who no one knew was missing," James says to his therapist and then continues to himself:

> . . . To die like that, to disappear without a trace, to sink without disturbing the surface of the water, not even a telltale bubble rising to the surface, like sneaking out of a party so no one notices you're gone.

Disappearance of every sort has become James's fearful fascination. A child's sense of safety in the world has been catastrophically undermined, and although this is a novel full of precise, skeptical observations about everything from art galleries to divorce to looking for love in New York City, its real subject is what happens to children when they witness terrible violence. How is such an event moved on from? Who do these children become when they are grown, and what faith is no longer possible for them as they continue to live in an anarchic world that still somehow brims with pleasure, beauty, and love? James's response lies in a kind of repudiation of death. Memories will be stored in things. Perhaps, he imagines, "love could naturally result in clairvoyance." The possessions of a beloved might lend their holy voodoo.

When his grandmother leaves him her "ghostly remnants"—all her possessions—his parents want him to sell them to an estate liquidator:

> That's the word they use: *liquidate*. But I refused. With some of the money my grandmother left me, I'm paying to have everything stored in a climate-controlled warehouse in Long Island City.

As in all of Cameron's work the past is both longed for and swept away. James's climate-controlled warehouse is his own sort of church with its own congregation, a shakily stubborn protest against time, change, and disappearance. It is a bravura performance, and *Someday This Pain Will Be Useful to You* is a stunning little book, a demonstration that adolescence, like a weekend, or the countries of Andorra or Uruguay, may seem an awkward, otherworldly way station suspended between two more prominent and fixed points (France and Spain, Brazil and Argentina, the long, numb workaday weeks that may appear to represent an absence from living). Yet it remains a fundamental place in the human psyche from which no one ever really moves on:

> I was beginning to realize that the adult world was as nonsensically brutal and socially perilous as the kingdom of childhood.

Poised between childhood and adulthood, adolescence stands there for a short, vivid time howling like a dog. Eventually, it is simply buried. But buried alive.

(2007)

Donald Barthelme

When, within a year's time, both Raymond Carver and Donald Barthelme succumbed in their fifties to cancer (Carver in August 1988; Barthelme that next July), it was as if the reigning president and vice president of the American Short Story had suddenly died. Both were beloved by peers and acolytes, though they struggled for readers, and each, in separate decades, had revitalized a genre that since the invention of television has been continually pronounced both moribund and in a condition of renaissance (recovering from moribund).

Both writers were inimitable even as they were widely imitated. Carver, younger, less productive, a practitioner of a spare, gritty realism often called minimalism, was the junior executive. Donald Barthelme—sparkling fabulist and idiosyncratic reinventor of the genre, practitioner of swift verbal collages, also sometimes dubbed minimalism—was commander in chief. Barthelme's particular brilliance was so original, so sui generis, despite its tutelage at the feet of pages by Joyce, Beckett, and Stein, that even his own brothers Frederick and Steven, also fiction writers of intelligence and style, wrote more like Carver.

Carver and Barthelme were hard-drinking westerners, men's men, and alcohol and cigarettes eased their isolation (regional and existential) in a literary life amid East Coast institutions, bohemian and otherwise, though in the end both died prematurely as a result. The cultural sea changes of their adult decades were enormous, and one is reminded of all the Prohibition-era addictions that were acquired by Jazz Agers in the 1920s, young people navigating similar renegotiations of social mores. Perhaps artists of any time tend to possess introverted dispositions that need bracing and enlivening to exude even the cool, feigned indifference preferred in Barthelme's later 1950s jazz age. "Edward worried about his drinking," Barthelme wrote in an early story. "Would there be enough gin? Enough ice?"

There is no indication in Tracy Daugherty's thorough new biography of Barthelme, *Hiding Man,* that these two late, great masters of the short story ever actually met, though Daugherty's title could be used to caption the life of either of them, as it might be the appropriate title for any number of literary biographies, since presumably a writer has lived his life more on the page than off, and in such a distorted, imaginary, and playful fashion that he or she steps away from his desk and walks out into that other world half-formed, half-spent, half there—those particular fractions being optimistic.

Donald Barthelme was born in 1931, the namesake and eldest son of Donald Barthelme, Sr., a Houston architect of distinction and renown and of formidability to his children, all of whom were gifted and successful and desired to please him. Frederick and Steven became professors and novelists; the only girl, Joan, became the first woman vice president of Pennzoil. A third brother, Peter, became a successful advertising executive and wrote mystery novels. Helen Bechtold, their adored mother, was a beauty and a wit. Donald Junior's second wife and lifelong friend, Helen Moore Barthelme, in an admiring memoir she wrote even after being dumped for a younger woman, compared them all to the James family (Henry, not Jesse, though perhaps, it being the West, there was a touch of both) in stature and accomplishment.

The family home, as a material structure and as a venue for intellectual conversation, stood out in Houston. The house was designed by their father and was part of his modernist crusade. The furniture "was architect furniture, a lot of swoopy Scandinavian stuff," according to the baby of the brood, Steven. Moreover, the master bedroom had no door, which seems almost unimaginable for that era. Both Donalds revered as biblical Marcel Raymond's *From Baudelaire to Surrealism,* a book presented to the son by his dad.

In view of all this, that Donald Barthelme the writer would marry a woman with the same name as his mother, then later travel to Scandinavia and marry a Dane, read the writings of Freud, become famous for his own aesthetic crusade, and pen a novel Oedipally titled *The Dead Father* might seem something of a foregone conclusion and a biographer's delight—or perhaps, in the way of foregone conclusions, a biographer's headache.

Moreover, the first part of Tracy Daugherty's book has to negotiate many ambiguous antecedents and much referential confusion about which Donald Barthelme it is discussing, *père* or *fils* (later in life the father's entry in *Who's Who* was still "much longer" than the son's, which gave the junior Barthelme a good guffaw). Mr. Barthelme the architect was also given to cleverness and mischief similar to his son's: when he designed Texas's Hall of State, he had carved into the frieze of the building the names of fifty-nine legendary Texans. According to Daugherty:

> The first letters of the first eight names, reading left to right— Burleson, Archer, Rusk, Travis, Higg, Ellis, Lamar, and Milam— spell the architect's name, minus only the final *e.* A playful touch, a buried secret: These would become hallmarks of his eldest son's art, as well.

The son's life was full of fits and starts. There was Catholic school and a desire to be part of the arts—but which one? There was college interrupted and gone uncompleted. There were (eventually) four marriages. There were early stabs at newspaper work, music (he was briefly the drummer in a touring band), museum directing, journal editing. What he most needed took him a surprisingly long time to do: leave Houston and move to New York. A stint as a soldier in Korea, two Texan marriages, and four dead babies with his second wife—infants whose bodies were given to medical research, so there were no graves and no old-fashioned-style mourning—perhaps took the wind out of his sails (his first wife said she left him because she wanted to see the world and Don didn't). But his restlessness and unhappiness in Houston had to be diagnosed by a psychotherapist as his simply needing to get out of town. He then began to believe it.

Donald Barthelme didn't set foot in New York until he was already in his thirties—unusual for an American writer. At a Staten Island literary conference, where Robert Lowell, Saul Bellow, and Edward Albee were the faculty, Barthelme arrived as a customer. It was July 1961 and he wanted to get the great Mr. Bellow's opinion of his short stories, which was, it turned out, not a happy one. Barthelme's narrative collages, his "serious toys" infused with American music and French theory, seemed to Bellow to lack an inner life; Bellow was cranky already at having to do this conference in order to make his alimony payments.

In a way, Barthelme's work was all inner life, partially concealed, partially displayed. His stories are a registration of a certain kind of churning mind, cerebral fragments stitched together in the bricolage fashion of beatnik poetry. The muzzled cool, the giddy play, the tossed salad of high and low: everything from cartoon characters to opera gets referenced in a graffiti-like chain of sentences. Conventional narrative ideas of motivation and characterization generally are dispensed with. Language is seen as having its own random and self-generating vital life, a subject he takes on explicitly in the story "Sentence," which is one long never-ending sentence, full of self-interruptions and searching detours and not quite dead ends (like human DNA itself, with its inert, junk viruses), concluding with the words "a structure to be treasured for its weakness as opposed to the strength of stones."

The story "For I'm the Boy Whose Only Joy Is Loving You"— whose lilting title refers not to the Irish ballad "Bold O'Donahue," as Daugherty insists, but to an old Bing Crosby song called "Remember Me"—ends with a character's memory of Tuesday Weld turning from the screen to tell him that he was a good man. "He had immediately gotten up and walked out of the theater, gratification singing in his heart." When he is then physically assaulted, salt emerges from his eyes and "black blood from his ears, and from his mouth, all sorts of words." A belief in language and culture persists indomitably in Barthelme's sad, hip world and makes life worthwhile and deserving of what Thomas Pynchon has called "the radiant quality" of Barthelme's attention.

The ultramodern architecture of Barthelme's childhood no doubt lent him confidence and comfort with the ultracontemporary literary object. Poetry could be collected intact from the world, then stripped and compressed; a story could be a mosaic torqued to mirror human anxiety. One early story, "The Piano Player," from his first collection, *Come Back, Dr. Caligari,* begins this way:

> Outside his window five-year-old Priscilla Hess, square and squat as a mailbox (red sweater, blue lumpy corduroy pants), looked around poignantly for someone to wipe her overflowing nose. There was a butterfly locked inside that mailbox, surely; would it ever escape? Or was the quality of mailboxness stuck to her forever, like her parents, like her name? The sky was sunny and blue. A filet of green Silly Putty disappeared into fat Priscilla Hess and he turned to greet his wife who was crawling through the door on her hands and knees.
>
> "Yes?" he said. "What now?"
>
> "I'm ugly," she said, sitting back on her haunches. "Our children are ugly."
>
> "Nonsense," Brian said sharply. "They're wonderful children. Wonderful and beautiful. Other people's children are ugly, not our children. Now get up and go back out to the smokeroom. You're supposed to be curing a ham."
>
> "The ham died," she said. "I couldn't cure it. I tried everything. You don't love me any more. The penicillin was stale. I'm ugly and so are the children. It said to tell you goodbye."
>
> "*It?*"
>
> "The ham," she said. "Is one of our children named Ambrose? . . ." She made a *moue* and ran a hand through her artichoke hair. "The house is rusting away. Why did you want a steel house? Why did I think I wanted to live in Connecticut? I don't know."
>
> "Get up," he said softly, "get up, dearly beloved. Stand up and sing. Sing *Parsifal.*"
>
> "I want a Triumph," she said from the floor.

The placement of unexpected things side by side is not only the spirit of surrealism but also the beating heart of both comedy and nightmare, and Barthelme's work, despite its seemingly offhand oddness and its flouting of conventional storytelling, is capable of suddenly cohering in the marvelous way of Kafka. In the blackly humorous "The School," death pervades all the group projects of an elementary school class, as the children themselves both decry and embrace it. In "Me and Miss Mandible," a grown man awakes to find himself back in the fourth grade. These two stories, along with "Shower of Gold," whose setting is a television game show, are perhaps Barthelme's most widely anthologized stories, more conservatively structured, and "screamingly funny" although, apart from the undercurrent of horror, they are not especially typical.

Most of Barthelme's stories are, in the way of "The Piano Player," or "For I'm the Boy," "sites of linguistic clustering," cobbled verbal scraps collected jazzily in Joycean fashion from the buzzing urban culture to which he was so alert. He was a rainbow coalition ventriloquist, and his denser stories perhaps gasp for air. That his first three decades were spent in Houston, a sprawling city without zoning ordinances and resplendent with surreal juxtapositions (billboards next to churches next to barbecue shacks), must have been a deep and abiding influence—though his early reading of Mallarmé is usually given the credit. Although at times his stories seem similar to a political sketch by, say, Mort Sahl or Lenny Bruce (though Barthelme admired S. J. Perelman, Perelman did not return the love and actually went as far as to complain to *The New Yorker* about Barthelme's work when it began regularly appearing there), at other times, in their experimentalism and absurdist poetic chat (girded with a plangent cry), they can resemble a cross between Gregory Corso's "Marriage" and the Guy Marks song "Your Red Scarf Matches Your Eyes."

Barthelme indeed loved songs but worked hard to avoid any explicit sentimentality. Yet one can see how pure avoidance of sentimentality is impossible for him, and he often leaves it lying about in small shards for the (optional) taking. One reviewer called Barthelme's literary terrain "the cratered landscape of the broken heart." His short story "How I Write My Songs" is sturdy satire but beneath it is the voice of someone who is broke and clinging to the stilted truisms and timbers of a wrecked commercial ship. "The main thing is to persevere and to believe in yourself, no matter what the attitude of others may be or appears to be." Bellow's criticism to Barthelme's face—"Do you really believe it's that hard for people to talk to each other?"—shows that an avant-garde literary mind emerging from an emotionally laconic Texan male society to direct an art museum and read books translated from German and French (a collage in human form, a *bricoleur* in cowboy boots) was bound to be at least occasionally misunderstood. Geniuses can be the first to recognize one another and just as often the last.

In Tracy Daugherty's extensive discussion of Barthelme's work, he has a literary scholar's predilection for locating, as if they were truffles, "lifts" and "echoes" and "resonant touchstones" (from Eliot, from Perelman, from Woolf). This sort of detective work, as if it were mapping the genome of a narrative, may seem to some the downside of graduate literary education (Daugherty was once in fact a graduate student of Barthelme's): to paraphrase our current poet laureate, Kay Ryan, why become a doctor of something that can't be fixed? Daugherty's determined textual sleuthing—the kind of thing an average reader can now do on Google—means to be respectful and interesting, but it strains and sweats and risks the inadvertently hostile result of seeming to want to undermine the originality of the writer, one whom Daugherty himself claims as radical and original and at one point "the nation's finest prose stylist."

Daugherty's comparisons are labor-intensive and sometimes unconvincing—"the sentences echo Dostoevski's *Notes from Underground,*" he says even of an early newspaper article—and this gumshoe's persistence in tracking influences and mimicries, serendipitous or intentional, sometimes bogs the biographer down:

> *Time* ran an article on *Black Orpheus* and the French New Wave. . . . Whether or not Don was thinking of this article, he clearly had in mind Walker Percy's *The Moviegoer* as he began reworking "The Hiding Man." . . . Like Ralph Ellison's protagonist in *Invisible Man,* Burlingame has freed himself from the received ideas of society and church.

Even describing Barthelme's early adult life in Houston, Daugherty can get startlingly sidetracked:

In the first seven months of his marriage, Don, in his capacity as an arts reviewer, could offer his wife a wide array of cultural excitement (whenever he could get her out)—from an evening of Mozart piano sonatas performed by Paur Badura-Skoda, fresh from the Viennese Conservatory, to the Latin singing of Joaquin Garay, best known as the voice of Panchito in Disney's *The Three Caballeros* ("Disney's horniest animated feature," according to one reviewer).

The inner core of the biographical subject is invariably elusive, the golden needle in the biographer's haystack of research. So what do we really want from a literary biography? Photographs, an index, a little gossip? Daugherty is cooperative on all these fronts. Among the many images collected in the book's glossy inserts there are all four wives and both daughters; there are pictures of the young Barthelme with the impish look of a game-show host, replete with ironic smirk and a pair of thick-framed glasses. (Later, bearded and brooding wanly, his boyish sparkle fading, he was said by Pynchon to resemble Solzhenitsyn.) There are the beautiful Greenwich Village digs and more than one cigarette thrusting toward the camera lens. The index is admirable in the hypnotic way of indexes. And for gossip Daugherty lets us in on a brief affair Barthelme had with Grace Paley (all that short-story heat!). Paley lived across the street from him on West Eleventh Street, and Barthelme dedicated his sixth collection of stories, *Amateurs,* to her. There is also the tragedy of his third wife, who committed suicide by leaping off a roof in Copenhagen.

But in reading about a writer's life, what are we finally asking for? A mystery to be solved? To desire a coherent creature to emerge from scholarly clutter may be too wishful. A literary subject, trapped within the awkward amber of someone else's prose voice, is offered up to the world in the stylistic rhythms and commonplaces of biographical storytelling ("Whereas Downtown writing seemed content with polemics, Don had always yearned for transcendence"). This situation, unless twisted into satire, would only be anathema to most subjects, especially one whose ear was as attuned to the exquisite sentence as Barthelme's was.

A biography of a writer whose life is being given its enduring contours by the pen of a former student (Daugherty begins his book with a wonderfully memorable anecdote of an assignment and late-night call from Professor Barthelme) sets itself up to be a fraught endeavor. Moreover, scholarly baggage and enthusiasm can produce a quality of overstuffedness, making one long for the brisk, incisive stroll of a non-academic biographer like Daniel Mark Epstein, Calvin Tompkins, or Diane Middlebrook. What can be hoped for here, even if vainly?

Suspense. Which is an unlikely effect in the life story of a famous contemporary writer—especially one whose life was essentially an ordinary bourgeois one—and yet Tracy Daugherty manages to bring about this improbable thing. His book is a page-turner. One reads eagerly, chapter to chapter, marriage to marriage, waiting to see what happens next. That Daugherty has ferreted out this element and put it to use is an amazing and rare accomplishment.

(2009)

Clarice Lispector

Before beginning this review, I took a quick, unscientific survey: Who had read the work of the Brazilian writer Clarice Lispector? When I consulted with Latin American scholars (well, only four of them), they grew breathless in their praise. She was a goddess; she was Brazilian literature's greatest writer. Further inquiry revealed some misunderstandings about her life, a life that clearly had reached mythic proportions, with a myth's errors and idiosyncratic details. Still, Lispector was held in reverent esteem by all four, though one believed she had died tragically in a fire (not so, although in her forties Lispector was burned on one side of her body, including her right hand, by a fire she accidentally started by smoking a cigarette in bed). Others were under the impression that she was a lifelong lesbian (also not so).

On the other hand, when I asked American and British writers (nine) whether they had read Lispector's work, I could find very few who had even heard of her. Some had heard of her—they thought—but knew nothing about her and had not read her. Some had read her novels and recalled them as "intense." Others had read a short story or two in some anthology or other. (I myself have spent most of my life in this last, somewhat dishonorable category.) I then went to Amazon.com—is there a more coarsely ironic place to assess the public reception of a Brazilian woman writer?—where the customer reviews from Brasília and São Paulo were glowing. But the American responses were often tepid, including one that suggested giving Lispector's novel *The Hour of the Star* as an April Fools' gift to a person you don't like very much, telling that person it's the best book you've ever read.

Even a devoted Lispector scholar named Nadia Battella Gotlib has titled an essay "Readers of Clarice, Who Are You?" (in the collection *Closer to the Wild Heart: Essays on Clarice Lispector*), and has compared Lispector's simultaneously resistant and ingenuous texts to the sweetened plaster that is used to kill cockroaches, a substance that lures the creature then hardens it from within, killing from the inside out. (This image is Lispector's own.) To be a Lispector reader, Gotlib implies, one must necessarily be caught off guard and then taken up, as if in a beam of light, toward a place that is not death exactly but a kind of not-life. It is an "enchanted sacrifice"—though understandably perhaps not to everyone's taste.

From the start Clarice Lispector, despite the South American sun, lived in the clouds and in cloudiness. She was to the public a charismatic obscurity, a witch, a recluse, a mystery: the "Brazilian Sphinx." Her odd name made people think she was a man or working under a nom de plume (which she sometimes did, but Lispector was her actual name). She was a kind of feminist, but as someone who also at times wrote beauty advice columns and had a closet full of designer dresses, she was not a feminist's feminist. When later in life her work was called hermetic and she herself a "sacred monster," it was to her own great dismay. Elizabeth Bishop, who lived for decades in Brazil, thought Lispector was a gifted primitive, essentially self-taught and suffering from what Bishop thought of as Brazilian lassitude and unreliability. Though Bishop believed that Lispector's novels were bad and that Lispector had read nothing (except Hesse, Spinoza, Flaubert, and Agatha Christie), Bishop admired Lispector's short stories and translated several of them.

There was a whiff of the diva about Lispector: restless in a marriage that had no place for a sorceress's eye (hard on the nannies), she was just as restless in an art form that didn't really traffic in divas. She was a stern and prickly beauty: Slavic-boned and almond-eyed, a watchful expression of sex and hauteur residing simultaneously, as in the face of a cat. "Her eyes had the dull dazzle of the mystic," wrote a friend.

At the end of her life several portraits of her hung over the sofa in her Rio apartment, including one by de Chirico, painted in war-torn Italy when de Chirico needed money and Lispector was still a young diplomat's wife. (Neither painter nor writer seems to have known who the other was.) Midlife she abandoned niceties. A demanding friend, she phoned people at all hours, including the middle of the night. She exhausted her psychoanalyst after six years of analysis and befriended his young daughter instead. She cultivated an unnerving stare. When she confronted a Brazilian publisher over unpaid royalties, right in his office, after waiting for him to return from lunch, she was handed cash of such a small amount that she left the building in a fury and gave all the money to a beggar.

She was mildly interested in the poor and wrote of them—ventriloquizing in their direction—as existential symbols. She spoke in an unconventional Portuguese that included a lisp, the correction of which she attempted but then shed, returning to the lisp. Her writing did not sound like the Portuguese anyone else was writing. "The foreignness of her prose is one of the most overwhelming facts of our literary history, and even of the history of our language," wrote her friend the poet Lêdo Ivo. She was a fragmentist in a "shipwreck of introspection," though her subjects were nothing less than the nature of time, the nature of the self, and the nature of language communicating these natures. In France she was viewed as a philosopher—and at times it does seem that calling her a novelist is a little like calling Plato a playwright—but when she attended a literary conference where her work was discussed in theoretical terms (she was a darling of deconstructionists; the renowned critic Hélène Cixous remains a Lispector devotee and, like many, refers to her as simply Clarice), Lispector left the panel early, saying later that not understanding a word that was being said about her own work made her so hungry she had to go home and eat an entire chicken.

She was a quiet torment to her translators, insisting that in her virtually untranslatable prose every comma be preserved. Ronald Sousa prefaces his translation of her 1964 novel *The Passion According to G.H.* by throwing up his hands. Lispector violated traditional expectations, he wrote, and "such violation has robbed me of useful ways of structuring my presentation. . . . This result may or may not be called 'translation,' but then that undecidability is only fitting in regard to a work that may or may not be called a 'novel.'"

First-time readers might be advised to start with the Giovanni Pontiero translations, which have been enthusiastically praised and do seem successfully to capture a real voice on the page. Oddly, Lispector's own translations—of Agatha Christie, of Anne Rice—were widely considered careless and second-rate and done for the rather little money they paid.

Much of this is set forth in the impressively researched new biography of Lispector *Why This World* by Benjamin Moser, a cultural journalist who for one intense period of his life forsook his day jobs (at Random House and *Harper's*) and made Lispector his raison d'être, traveling the world to every place she had been, and creating an international history of the years 1920, when Lispector was born, to 1977, when she died. Moser's is a well-written and remarkable book, and almost everything I can now say about Lispector's life derives from it.

Lispector, the youngest of three beautiful and brilliant girls, came to Recife in the northeastern part of Brazil when she was five, a self-described "Russian immigrant" (actually Ukrainian) with her syphilitic mother and would-be mathematician father. They were escaping the Jewish pogroms that in the 1910s persisted in the villages and woods of the countryside of her birth. Her mother's disease was contracted when she was raped by a gang of Russian soldiers. Only at the end of Lispector's life did she discover that her mother, who died when Clarice was nine, wrote, too, keeping private journals. Lispector's older sisters were writers as well. Nonetheless, she began as a law student and then a journalist, and remained a journalist throughout her life and in some ways remained a lawyer as well, in that much of her fiction involves seeking the precise words for crimes and interrogating the moral intricacies of facts.

She married a career diplomat who was stationed in northeastern Brazil (which was a strategic Allied base in World War II) and then later in Naples, Bern, southern England, and Washington, D.C. Though the life of a diplomat's wife might seem the perfect one for a writer—did it not work for Mary McCarthy?—with its travels and staff, its only burdens being residence away from home and having to be polite all the time, she chafed both as a dutiful diplomatic wife and, later, as an intellectual among intellectuals. She learned to say "Isn't that nice" as the former and "I don't know" as the latter. And although she was initially good at polite appearances, after two decades it all proved a kind of soul-death (freedom versus duty is an early theme in her work). Her private life as a writer was not entirely taken seriously by her husband, and so she left him and with their two sons went back to Brazil, the only country that knew her work, and where her first book, *Near to the Wild Heart* (drawn largely from her own childhood), had been a critical sensation just before she left.

In many ways, she did not return soon enough for happiness. She arrived in Rio as a divorced, middle-aged woman with two sons, one of whom was schizophrenic. Solitude, social awkwardness, and concern for her son all infected her well-being. She became obsessed with an almost childlike desire "to belong," and friends were driven away. Brazilian culture in the 1960s was heating up, and everything from bossa nova to political activism made Rio an exciting place to be. But fiction writers could not make a living there. Nonetheless, Lispector resided in a fashionable part of Rio at one end of Ipanema Beach, with a live-in maid. She collected a generous amount of alimony, wrote journalism, ghostwrote a starlet's glamour column. Also under a pseudonym she became a paid agent of Pond's, using a beauty advice column to extol the virtues of the company's skin cream. (There: I've buried the lead.)

Lispector's uncategorizable work causes the reader to mimic her own processes: that is, her sentences are often in search of themselves and are constructed from the very casting about that a reader may undergo in having to find a term that is suitable to describe them. Zadie Smith has proposed "constructive deconstruction" (as opposed to a tradition of "lyrical realism"). I would suggest "epiphanic collage." (Or on less receptive days, "expressionist journaling.") The Jewish mysticism that is sometimes attributed to Lispector has much to do with the feeling in her work of chasing after a fleeing God, though her most compelling deity was language in service of the mind's self—from which language, too, for Lispector, had stepped away and required summoning back. Language, for her, was the self's light. (Moser never once uses the word *narcissism.*) She worried it with self-consciousness, like a cat with a slippery mouse:

> The great, neutral reality of what I was experiencing outstripped me in its extreme objectivity. I felt unable to be as real as the reality that was reaching me—could I be starting in contortions to be as nakedly real as what I was seeing?
>
> —*The Passion According to G.H.*

Even in her first book, published when she was nineteen, she was fond of the exquisite abstraction:

> The dark, murky night was cut in half, separated into two sombre blocks of sleep. Where was she? Between the two halves, seeing them—the half she had already slept and the half she still had to sleep—isolated in the timeless and in the spaceless, in an empty gap. That interval would be discounted from the years of life.
>
> —*Near to the Wild Heart*

Furthermore, her relationship to animals grew increasingly spiritual, taking Spinoza's pantheism into the heart of both her life (dogs were often her closest friends) and her work. In some of her narratives animals seem a stay against the abyss; other times they reflect that abyss in their eyes, in a manner resembling a destroying lover. She sometimes pits an animal and a person in a dialectic of mutual assassination. She is interested in the complexity of a creature: the eyes of a cockroach; the mute, humid hippopotamus; cats mistaken for suckling pigs. Theirs is a world that sees "no danger in being nude." One of her finest stories, "The Buffalo," from her collection *Family Ties,* takes place in a zoo (its closing notes of love-maddened self-mutilation are reminiscent of the brutal ending in Elfriede Jelinek's *The Piano Teacher*). "Careful, Nature thinks" is one of her oft-quoted lines. As is "Do not mourn the dead: they know what they are doing."

Lispector reads as a lively intelligence sometimes veering toward hysteria then falling back, as if in a faint, and flattening to aphorism and pronouncement. Psychology and setting by and large remain vague; such modernisms are dispensed with in favor of starkness, tragicomic paralysis, and crying out. She is a postmodernist of some sort, but Moser, perhaps wisely, does not attempt any label at all. He discusses her work in great detail, book after book, with sympathy and insight, and admirably eschews jargon though he underemphasizes her wit. Lispector was terrifically funny, but it seems this is not made much of by anyone writing of her, though it is essential to the vitality of much of her prose. *Near to the Wild Heart* begins its second paragraph:

> Resting her head against the cold, shiny windowpane, she looked into the neighbor's yard, at the great world of the chickens-that-did-not-know-they-were-about-to-die.

In *The Hour of the Star,* the narrator announces:

> The action of this story will result in my transfiguration into someone else and in my ultimate materialization into an object. Perhaps I might even acquire the sweet tones of the flute and become entwined in a creeper vine.

In *The Apple in the Dark,* written in Chevy Chase, Maryland, just before she left her marriage, a black humor, conveyed through decrescendo and juxtaposition, is the offsetting fruit:

> Ah, she said with simplicity, it's like this: let's say someone is screaming and then someone else puts a pillow in their mouth so they don't have to hear the scream. Because when I take a pill, I don't hear my scream, I know I'm screaming but I don't hear it, that's how it is, she said adjusting her skirt.

Even her letters are witty. Of a negative review, she wrote that that particular critic "acts like the man who beats his wife every day because she must have done *something.*" From Bern, the land of cuckoo clocks and snow, she wrote her sister, "This Switzerland is a cemetery of sensations."

.   .   .

If there are other weaknesses in Moser's biography, they are largely organizational: there are repetitions, as well as subjects that once begun are
then dropped. The character and nature of her marriage seem almost
completely missing for twenty-two chapters; as is, to a lesser degree,
her relationship to her sons. Although we do see her observing her boys
and writing down their cute remarks in notebooks, her relationship to
mothering veers from being primary to less than secondary and then
back again in a flash. Her love life seems to go almost completely out
after the fire in her forties, and her lifelong attachment to the handsome gay poet Lucio Cardoso has unexplained hiatuses. Also the smitten translator Gregory Rabassa's much-reprinted line, that Lispector
was "that rare person who looked like Marlene Dietrich and wrote like
Virginia Woolf," is never questioned for its sexism—i.e., is beauty a
contraindication of an intellectual life? Would anyone say this of Haw-
thorne, Fitzgerald, or Camus? The remark irritated Lispector mostly
because she had never read any Woolf.

Moser is impressive, however, in his interest in and take on Brazilian politics. Providing authoritative historical backdrop is his forte.
And though Lispector wasn't especially political, after the military coup
of the 1960s she joined in protest with other artists and with young
people, with whom she felt like-minded on everything. She clung to
young people. The strongly anti-Communist Elizabeth Bishop, on the
other hand, seemed to distrust the young and supported the military
coup—which may come as a surprise to her admirers.

Moser would like us to see Lispector's death at fifty-seven of ovarian cancer as a literary symbol—he places it in a metaphorical system
of eggs that runs through Lispector's work. "The chicken exists so that
the egg may traverse the ages," she wrote in "The Egg and the Chicken
(I)." "This is what a mother is for." But her illness seems less significant
as figuration than it does as a disease that disproportionately afflicts
Ashkenazi Jewish women. In other words, despite everything, a Jewish
death. As was her own mother's, which Lispector never stopped mourning, and this, according to her latest biographer, more than anything
else, informed the long, artful wail of her work.

(2009)

Barack Obama

In 2008 Barack Obama's new book was *Change We Can Believe In,* but for most of the reading public all of his books were new, and his early memoir, reissued, had begun to be read widely that same year. Unlike *Change We Can Believe In* and *The Audacity of Hope, Dreams from My Father* was not a book about policy. It was written before the politician who wrote the others had even been hatched (*hatched* as a plan rather than as a creature). *Dreams from My Father* contains Obama's most spellbinding writing and was the book most Americans were talking about in 2008. It offers a vulnerable portrait of the boy who became the man even as it underscores that boy's toughness and makes resilience its theme. First published in 1993, when Obama was thirty-one and selling very few copies (before the bulk of its first printing was then pulped), a signed first edition now sells for five figures or sometimes six. When thinking of *Dreams from My Father,* it is sometimes hard to banish thoughts of the missed investment opportunity this sixteen-year-late reading involves. For those of you who missed out on this deal, get in line and we will pool our dimes to hire a cheap hypnotist who will rid this from our minds so that we can concentrate on what is more important—or at least more literary.

Dreams from My Father is surely (ironically, via its partially tele-scoped pacing and its storytelling license generally) one of the truest glimpses into Obama the young man and the young boy. Written when

Obama wanted to be a writer (rather than commander in chief) and when he was thinking of readers rather than voters, it offers a candor and vividness one will not see in a more straight-ahead political memoir. There are sex and drugs, but they are completely unsensational. He is matter-of-fact and unself-pitying even if self-pity might be considered a thematic corollary to his subject of identity.

Unlike his later books, which are agendas of hope and reform, *Dreams from My Father* is less about idealism than about boulders in the road: Does one smash them, climb over them, go around them? Napping or retreating aren't options. What Obama offers is an intriguing portrait of family restlessness, which afflicted both his parents and his grandfathers as well as Obama himself—a restlessness that caused him not to shy from challenges but to use boredom and frustration and good intentions to step up and over them. In *Dreams from My Father,* family yarns are unspooled and analyzed, as if they were indeed dreams, with a dream's strange fleeings and chasings and believable changes. One of the most memorable is of his four-year-old Kenyan father running away with his sister, who was running away to find their mother, who had also run away; it is a heart-stopping tale of African village life. Equally stunning is the stoical story of the Indonesian stepfather, who attempted to toughen the young Barack by boxing him in the face. If one is wondering who this new leader of the Western world really is, *Dreams from My Father* is the book to read.

(2009)

The Wire

Set in post–September 11 Baltimore, the HBO series *The Wire*—whose sixty episodes were originally broadcast between June 2002 and March 2008 and are now available on DVD—has many things on its rich and roaming mind, but one of those things is Baltimore itself, home of Edgar Allan Poe, H. L. Mencken, Babe Ruth, and Billie Holiday. Baltimore is not just a stand-in for Western civilization or globalized urban rot or the American inner city now given the cold federal shoulder in the folly-filled war on terror, though it is certainly all these things. Baltimore is also just plain itself, with a very specific cast of characters, dead and alive. Eminences are pointedly referenced in the course of the series: the camera passes over a sign to Babe Ruth's birthplace, tightens on a Mencken quote sculpted into the office wall of *The Baltimore Sun;* "Poe" is not just street pronunciation for poor (to the delight of one of *The Wire*'s screenwriters) but implicitly printed onto one horror-story element of the script; a phrase of Lady Day wafts in as ambient recorded music in a narrative that is scoreless except when the credits are rolling or in the occasional end-of-season montage.

But there are less famous Baltimoreans throughout (local filmmaker John Waters is given an ambiguous shout-out in the final season, and he shouts ambiguously back in the DVD's bonus features), and all are part of the texture and mythology that *The Wire*'s producers are putting on display both with anger and with love. The dartboard in a union boss's office in the series's second season features a photo of the former owner of the Baltimore Colts, who moved the team to Indianapolis in 1984; scenes shot in Baltimore churches use the actual congregations; real-life hot-dog joints (Pollock Johnny's!) now reside in *The Wire's* televised amber; actual purple-walled soup kitchens and cemeteries and neighborhood corners have acquired mythic status.

More than one former reporter from *The Baltimore Sun* has written for the show. Baltimore heroin kingpins have cameo appearances, and one, Melvin Williams, who was arrested by producer Ed Burns when Burns was "a police" (as it's said in Baltimore), is given the role of the Deacon, which he performs arrestingly with lines such as "A good churchman is always up in everybody's shit. That's how we do." The list goes on. Baltimoreans name their pets after the show's characters. Some former members of the cast still roam the streets, now as celebrities. Young people use characters' pictures from the show for their own profile photos on Facebook. British tourists come to Baltimore for *Wire* bus tours. This array of consuming response—domesticating ownership, emotional identification, and devoted pilgrimage—is only part of the very many personal reactions to the show.

The use of Baltimore as a millennial tapestry, in fact, might be seen as a quiet rebuke to its own great living novelists, Anne Tyler and John Barth, both of whose exquisitely styled prose could be accused of having turned its back on the deep inner workings of the city that executive producer David Simon, a former Baltimore reporter, and producer Ed Burns, a former Baltimore schoolteacher and cop, have excavated with such daring and success. ("Where in Leave-It-to-Beaver-Land are you taking me?" asks *The Wire's* homeless police informant Bubbles, when driven out to a leafy, upscale neighborhood; the words are novelist and screenwriter Richard Price's and never mind that this aging cultural reference is unlikely to have actually spilled forth from this character; the remark does nicely.)

So confident are Simon and Burns in their enterprise that they have with much justification called the program "not television" but a "novel." Certainly the series's creators know what novelists know: that it takes time to transform a social type into a human being, demography into dramaturgy, whether time comes in the form of pages or hours. With time as a medium rather than a constraint one can show a profound and unexpected aspect of a character, and discover what that character might decide to do because of it. With time one can show the surprising interconnections within a chaotic, patchworked metropolis.

It is sometimes difficult to sing the praises of this premier example of a new art form, not just because enthusiastic viewers and cultural studies graduate students have gotten there first—"Heroism, Institutions, and the Police Procedural" or "Stringer Bell's Lament: Violence and Legitimacy in Contemporary Capitalism" (chapters in *The Wire: Urban Decay and American Television*)—but also because David Simon himself, not trusting an audience, and not waiting for posterity, in his own often stirring remarks about the show in print interviews, in public appearances, and in audio commentary on the DVD version, has not just explicated the text to near muteness but jacked the critical rhetoric up very high. He is the show's most garrulous promoter. In comment after comment, even the word *novel* is not always enough, and Simon and his colleagues have compared his five-season series to a Greek tragedy (Aeschylus, Sophocles, Euripedes are all named), Homer's *Iliad,* a Shakespearean drama, a serialized narrative by Dickens, an historical document that will be read in fifty years, a book by Tolstoy, and Melville's *Moby-Dick*. This leaves only journalist Joe Klein to raise the ante further: "*The Wire* never won an Emmy?" Klein is shown exclaiming in the DVD features on the final episode. "*The Wire* should win the Nobel Prize for Literature!"

"It could have—if we'd done everything wrong—been a cop show," Simon has said. And in its admirable and unblinking look at a cursed people—America's largely black and brown urban underclass—it is arguably biblical, Dantesque, and (*Masterpiece Theatre* be damned) more downstairs than upstairs. Despite Simon's assertions, however, the series has some origins in legal and police shows such as *L.A. Law* and *Hill Street Blues*—not to mention Burns and Simon's own Emmy-winning *The Corner* (2000), a rather shapeless precursor (a faux documentary about poverty and drugs in the mostly black neighborhood of West Baltimore, filmed with a handheld camera and a blues soundtrack), as well as *Homicide,* based on Simon's own book about the Baltimore Police Department, which ran from 1993 to 1999. *The Wire* is the polished, mature version of efforts begun before; it is not entirely sui generis but it is beautifully evolved. Nor is the force of the conventional medium entirely absent. Although there are no breaks for commercials, one feels the pressure and shape of an hour imposing itself on each episode, even if the plot of each remains unresolved and the pacing broodingly languorous despite sharp-edged cutting.

The Sopranos helped prepare the way for this format as well, though the nature and mood of *The Sopranos* is essentially comedic, a family drama laced with amusing and operatic artifice, as is the current AMC series *Mad Men*. Recognizable authenticity, new and trenchant social commentary, and tragic class warfare have not really been high on the agenda of any other cable series, and it is a source of some bitterness for *The Wire*'s creators that it never had the wide audience that these other series have had.

Simon uses an analogy of white flight to explain it: white people will tolerate up to 8 percent of the neighborhood being black before they begin to leave, turning the neighborhood into a black one. *The Wire*'s cast is over 60 percent black, and the white viewer flight was almost immediate. A teenage actor who plays one of the middle-schoolers of the show's fourth season and who was not privy at the time to Simon's analysis remarks of the show's lost viewers, "The messed-up thing is they can't handle the truth."

The Wire, of course, is a deliberately far cry from *Adam-12* and *Dragnet*, the cop shows of Simon's childhood. Its newness as a narrative art form is underscored most convincingly by its power on DVD, where it can be watched all at once, over sixty hours: this particular manner of viewing makes the literary accolades and the comparisons to a novel more justified and true. On the other hand, so engrossing, heart-tugging, and uncertain are the various story arcs that watching in this manner one becomes filled with a kind of mesmerized dread. In this new motion-picture format the standard, consoling boundaries and storytelling rhythms are dispensed with—mostly. One is allowed a wider, deeper portrait, a panorama, of entrepreneurial crime, government corruption, a harassed underclass, and faulty institutions of every sort—sprawling portraiture that aims at inclusivity.

Even though its city hall has been mum, Baltimore's Police Department has given *The Wire* its endorsement, as have the kids of East and West Baltimore. Moreover, the show's themes can seem reiterated everywhere in the world, from out-of-work shrimpers and autoworkers, to the meth cookers of the Ozarks, to the poppy growers of war-torn Afghanistan (oddly, Hamid Karzai has two brothers who live in the Baltimore area). It is sometimes hard to think about the world's troubles without thinking: This is just like *The Wire*.

In exposing the nerves, fallout, and sealed fates caused by a remorse-less breed of capitalism and its writing-off of whole swaths of the populace, and by insisting on its universality as a subject, *The Wire* has much in common with great political drama everywhere; the plays of George Bernard Shaw (in which rich and poor are both given language) come to mind. The newly elected mayor of Reykjavík will not allow anyone in his political party unless they have watched all five seasons. The mayor of Newark is also a fan. So is Barack Obama, whose favorite character is the gay, drug dealer–robbing gunslinger Omar Little—a new hero in queer studies, one of the few characters in the show who honors "a code," and the only one whose ongoing motivation is love for another person.

In the intricate network of *The Wire* the story lines derive from the worlds of street-corner drug dealers and big-time traffickers, the police of homicide and drug enforcement and "special crimes," the in-office brass, the dockworkers who knowingly and unknowingly unload the drug shipments, the union leaders, the foreign suppliers, the public schools, the newspaper, the mayor's office, the city council, the lawyers and judges of the criminal justice system, the prisons, the soup kitchens, the rehab facilities, and the group homes with their revolving doors. This is the metaphorical "wire" that connects all the various institutions and habitats of the city. It also refers to the high-wire act of brave policing and honest work—difficult and rare.

More literally, the title signifies the wiretap that narcotics detectives are constantly trying to get judicial consent for and then set up before the dealers—drug lords, "hoppers" (the lowest-level drug dealers), lieutenants, and other "soldiers"—get wind of it and switch to a different system. At one point, with their cell phone codes cracked, and with the detectives successfully up on the wire, the players in "the game," as the drug business is called, are either not using phones at all or else tossing them away after every use. Not only does the wire demonstrate the ingenuity of dealers and detectives as they elude each other, but surveillance itself becomes the show's metaphor for what drama does in listening in on the world. It also embraces the Wildean sense of art's cleverness as well as its uselessness. Utility versus futility is everywhere at the center of David Simon's own view of the show. The great waste of human spirit and endeavor is dramatized, ironically, with great human spirit and endeavor.

Season 1 introduces us to the Barksdale drug operation headed up by Avon Barksdale, his sister Brianna, and his right-hand man, the wannabe businessman Stringer Bell. The syndicate is operated out of a nightclub and then a funeral parlor, and when Avon is incarcerated, Bell attempts to hold meetings using *Robert's Rules of Order.* (The result is a kind of skit.) The business has as its primary territory housing project towers that are exploded in Season 3, an image deliberately designed to recall September 11. (Baltimore early on got rid of its old housing projects; other American cities followed.) This detonation is mostly viewed through the eyes of kids who are watching everything they've known reduced to rubble—and not unceremoniously.

Stringer Bell, played by the African-British actor Idris Elba, is the enigmatic Gatsby figure, yearning for legitimacy, sporting wire-rimmed glasses, and attending economics classes at the local community college. He aims to become a legitimate businessman, a fate that is finally handed over to Marlo Stanfield at series end, though Marlo (played with eerie but prideful injuriousness by Jamie Hector) doesn't want it. Brianna Barksdale is one of several mother characters who give the lie to lip service paid to family values in a drug war–torn family by forcing their reluctant kids onto the streets to sell dope. In a white male–written show with few women, and, yes, a stripper or two with the requisite heart of gold, these "Dragon Ladies," as one of the kids calls them, are part of a *Wire* subset of women marred if not mutilated by ambition.

Still, these portrayals seem complex: emotionally ugly and specific enough to be convincing. They are eye-popping to watch, especially Michael Hyatt as Brianna, who demands of her son that he do hard prison time for the organization, and Sandi McCree as De'Londa, who exclaims loudly that her son should be put in "baby booking," where he might learn to be a man. These women, not drug-addled themselves, eat up the screen, even when they are quiet and must merely flash a look. Women who pimp their children are breathtaking in their monstrousness—absent from *The Wire* are any wise, reassuring matriarchs—and these bleak characters succeed in taking the viewer's breath away. Simon is not interested in viewer comfort; the conventions of prescriptive political fiction do not capture his imagination very deeply; he is far more interested in the unholy bargains everyone makes in the maelstrom of societal injustices. For a feminist heroine the show has only the quite imperfect Detective Kima Greggs, and, only because in her strength, humor, passion for work, and apparently secure hold on her biracial identity and lesbianism, she is slightly better than almost anyone else.

Each season explores an institution that has gone hollow with gamesmanship. Most of Season 2 focuses on Baltimore's dockworkers, particularly Frank Sobotka (played with a smolder and a fat suit by baby-faced Chris Bauer), a union head who stares out at Baltimore's abandoned mills and grain piers and notes that they are now condos. His torment and lament—that this country once made things—is the nation's own. His particular fate is a tragic one, Shakespearean in its emotional mix of small onstage relatives and large offstage forces, and his relationship with his nephew is one of several uncle-nephew relationships in *The Wire* (Avon and D'Angelo; Proposition Joe and Cheese) that wordlessly announce the gaping holes left in families hit by law enforcement and hard economic times. Season 3 introduces the politicians and Season 4 the school system and the children it fails. Season 5 concentrates on the diminished and compromised role of journalists.

The most intriguing phrase Simon has used regarding *The Wire* is to say that it is about "the death of work." By this he means not just the loss of jobs, though there certainly is that, but the loss of integrity within our systems of work, the "juking of stats," the speaking of truth to power having been replaced with speaking what is most self-serving and pleasing to the higher-ups. In a poker game with the mayor, one folds on a flush to allow the mayor to win. (As opposed to the freelance stickup man Omar, who, beholden to no one, shows up at a kingpin's poker night with two pistols and the Dennis Lehane line "I believe these four 5s beat your full house.") Police departments manipulate their stats for the politicians; schools do the same; newspapers fake stories with their eyes on prizes and stockholders. Moreover, in the world of *The Wire* almost everyone who tries to buck the system and do right is punished, often severely and grotesquely and heartbreakingly. Accommodation is survival at the most basic level, although it is also lethal to the soul.

Ideas are no good without stories. Stories are no good without characters. In drama, characters are no good without actors. If the integrity of *The Wire* derives from the intentions of its creators, its power lies, in an old-fashioned way, in the brilliant acting of a varied and charismatic cast. Not to diminish the quality of the writing or the careful cinematography, but little of Simon's agenda would convince without the series's acting: this is how the humanity of various people is given its indelible life. *The Wire*'s producers claim it contains the most diverse cast ever on television, and it is hard to doubt that.

What depth of acting talent we have in our contemporary world, even if so much of it is not in Hollywood. Some of *The Wire*'s standout performances are from British or Irish actors who mimic American accents so impressively that their real voices in the commentaries are startling. Of course the Baltimore gloss is less convincing and sometimes even absent, but the rest of America is fooled: Dominic West, as the "true police" Jimmy McNulty, is from Britain; Idris Elba as Stringer Bell, also British, is of Ghanaian and Sierra Leonean parentage; Aiden Gillen, who plays Tommy Carcetti, the calculating politician who on occasion gets passionately if momentarily swept up in his own rhetoric, is from Ireland.

Some of the actors in *The Wire* are amateurs and some are pros educated at Juilliard and Yale. Gbenga Akinnagbe and Felicia Pearson, who play Chris and Snoop of the Marlo Stanfield gang, are prime examples. Akinnagbe is a professional actor and Bucknell graduate, and Pearson is a Baltimore rapper and quite literally an ex-con, having done time at the Maryland Correctional Institution for Women for a homicide committed when she was fourteen. She had never acted on-screen before but was brought to the set by Michael Williams (Omar), himself a former dancer, then placed prominently and without a name change in Seasons 4 and 5: her real-life nickname is Snoop.

Together, Snoop and Chris form a duo that according to Stephen

King are two of the scariest assassins ever put on the screen. Snoop bears a pretty mime's pale impassivity; Chris's starburst hair gives him a clown's silhouette though his face remains stonily dour. Together, dour clown and mime, they are assassins in an escapee circus act, caught in a zombie script that would terrify not just Baltimore's finest but Baltimore's finest horror writer. At the beginning of Season 4 they buy a nail gun that Snoop suggests they use as a weapon—the screenwriter's nod, perhaps, to Cormac McCarthy's cattle bolt. Snoop and Chris fill up abandoned row houses with the bodies of young black men (number one males, in police terminology) who have in some way disrespected their boss, Marlo, creating a charnel house straight out of Poe.

No one is really looking for these victims—oh, for a missing blond cheerleader, think the cops, whose budgets have been slashed (reduced wages, no witness protection funds, flat tires on their cars, DNA samples going bad in broken refrigerators)—and by the time the bodies are found there are well over a dozen. "My number in the office pool is twenty-three," says Detective Bunk, cigar in mouth, so convincingly played by Wendell Pierce.

In the Barksdale gang, the hopper, the lieutenant, and the deputy kingpin who are killed for going their own way (Wallace, D'Angelo, Stringer Bell) are portrayed by actors possessed of especially beautiful and sensitive faces. Their deaths play viscerally and haunt the show; Seasons 1 and 3 are largely built around them. (Almost everyone a viewer might quixotically root for is eventually killed; even if the killing is not lingered over, the show pulls no punches.) Avon Barksdale initially seems green and weak next to the handsome and charismatic Stringer, but the several layers of Avon's manipulations are put forth with fluid skill by Wood Harris, and when we see him again in Season 5 his performance has solidified into a nuanced affability made sinister by power. One of the series's most telling scenes is in Season 3, when Harris and Elba stand on a terrace overlooking the city, anxiously disguising their characters' mutual betrayals with sentimental memories of a shared boyhood. Here Avon's extra layer of artifice, his hardened street-soldier smarts, triumph over the man who would like drugs to be a business rather than a war.

There is not a feeble performance in the entire show. While David Simon is achieving remarkable verisimilitude, supplying the scripts with a glossary, and making sure the writing is both on message and real (*bitch* is used mostly to describe men; only black actors use the N-word, and often affectionately), the actors sometimes improvise imaginatively (often with the prop and costume people), reaching for the curious displacements of art. Lance Reddick plays Lieutenant Daniels as a princely African-American Spock aboard the starship *Baltimore*. Robert Chew plays the drug lord Proposition Joe, whose wistfulness for the old days is expressed in his tender repairing of broken clocks. One defiant and suspended policeman, Herc—played by Domenick Lombardozzi, whose Bronx accent is already a conspicuous and pleasingly unexplained dislocation (try not to think of Tony Curtis in *Spartacus*)—defiantly opens his front door wearing a Wisconsin T-shirt with the logo SMELL THE DAIRY AIR. Omar sports a long, waxed duster to accompany his shotgun and bulletproof vest, making him seem very much an urban Jesse James, and the lighting, editing, and quite self-conscious cinematography in various showdowns assist in this motif. (In the one episode where Omar is on a Caribbean isle, he seems so out of place the story line quickly summons him back to cowboy land.)

J. D. Williams as terminal corner boy Bodie emerges as a tremendous actor with or without his white do-rag, filched from a production of *The Crucible*. And the middle school quartet in Season 4—Michael, Namond, Randy, and Dukie—are a gut-wrenching ensemble, but Julito McCullum's performance as Namond, replete with ponytail and earrings, seems singular in its range. His character is given more to do, but as an actor he is there for every moment of it. His tears before his mother, his fury at the universe, his jokes with his pals—"Yo, you must be one of those at-risk kids!" he says self-satirically to Dukie when his friend orders the turkey grease at a Chinese restaurant—all this makes Namond's successful if narrow escape from the neighborhood one of the few bearable outcomes in *The Wire*'s many stories. (And one of the only times when reaching out to a cop doesn't result in catastrophe.)

It is a small statistic, as with the ex-con Cutty's successful boxing club, but one of human escape amid hopelessness. As the ill-fated Dukie says, "How do you get from here to the rest of the world?" Tolstoy was wrong about happy families—it is more likely hell, or hellishness, that is of a predictable sameness. Heaven will take one by surprise, as surprise is perhaps essential to it. "Sometimes life just gives you a moment," says Lester Freamon, played by the deep-voiced, bowlegged Clarke Peters, the gifted actor who has accompanied David Simon on his journey through *The Corner, The Wire,* and *Treme.* But with this much already under Simon's (and Peters's) belt, beyond, as they might say shruggingly in Baltimore, ain't no thing. The series's final words are "Let's go home," not unlike the last words spoken by the last man on the moon.

(2010)

Memoirs

It is hard not to be impressed with Fran Lebowitz's comedically acerbic dismissal of memoirs: when asked in the Martin Scorsese documentary *Public Speaking* whether she would ever pen one, she quickly replied that if your life were all that interesting, someone else would write a book about it.

Despite having some sympathy with this idea, or with caustic wit, or with avoiding writing, one can nonetheless assume that there are good reasons to embark on a memoir: the world and the self collide in a particular way that only you, or mostly you, can narrate; you would like a preemptive grab at controlling the discourse. For instance: Are you Winston Churchill? Are you Nixon in China? Are you *Pat* Nixon in China? Did you compose *Nixon in China*? (Its composer, John Adams, has in fact written an engaging memoir.) Are you connected to a fascinating and underexplored chapter in history in any manner whatever? Are you a professional storyteller with a beautiful prose style and some autobiography begging for reportage? Are you a trenchant thinker with incisive analytical powers? Do you have a social cause for which you would like to advocate strenuously? And if none of the above, are you Raquel Welch?

If not, wherefore the memoir? Are you helpless before your own life, and unsure of how to write the autobiographical novel that might exploit or explore or redream it into art? Do you have a case of what the literary critic Michael Wood has called "catastrophe envy"? Have you drunk the *Reality Hunger* Kool-Aid of David Shields's current pro-poetic essay campaign and "anti-novel jihad" and joined him (as has the brilliant Rachel Cusk) in what sometimes sounds like chiding the limp dog of fiction as if it were an unfortunate habit of lying, an omnivorous pornography of the real, instead of the struggling but majestic thing that it is? Are you coming into the house of narrative through the back door because the back door is where the money is? Are you prone to what a recent article by Neil Genzlinger in *The New York Times Book Review* suggested might be the "oversharing" of inconsequential you? "Unremarkable lives" should go "unremarked upon, the way God intended," Genzlinger wrote, in what reads like a reversal of the final lines of *Middlemarch*—George Eliot on a drink-addled day.

That many young people are already writing their memoirs is no longer a funny thing to say but an actual cultural condition. Book buy-ers have nudged publishers in this direction: we love to read memoirs. Why shouldn't we? At a dinner party is not the fiction, which consists predominantly and unfortunately of abbreviated film plots, protracted jokes, and urban myths, less mesmerizing than the real-life tales? It would be heartless not to be interested in memoirs. People are telling us their personal stories and speaking to us of their private lives, and even if the structure is rickety and the prose has, to borrow Dick Cavett's phrase, "all the sparkle of a second mortgage," we are going to hang in there because it is *true*. That the facts and details of these jumbled con-fessions are occasionally fudged and embellished, however, seems inevi-table, given the limits of memory and the demands of writing. (There are many things a storyteller must add and subtract to tell a good story.)

Dick Cavett, himself a first-rate memoirist, became the prompt for Lillian Hellman's James Frey moment when in 1980 Mary McCar-thy said on Cavett's show that every word in Hellman's memoirs was a lie. (A lengthy lawsuit ensued.) In 2006 James Frey had to account to Oprah for the fabrications in his memoir *A Million Little Pieces*, after which he began writing fiction, as if in penance. It is interesting for fiction writers who always alter and reimagine the facts of their lives to watch memoirists get in trouble for doing exactly that. That fiction prompted by the autobiographical is not the same as a memoir seems an idea that is either professionally or commercially inconvenient or just lazily and confusedly lost on many—though seldom on a novelist.

Nonetheless, excellent memoirs by novelists abound. Vladimir Nabokov's *Speak, Memory* may be the paragon (or Isak Dinesen's *Out of Africa,* or Ernest Hemingway's *A Moveable Feast*), but there are powerful ones by contemporary fiction writers as varied as Philip Roth, Tobias Wolff, Joan Didion, Mary Gordon, Edmund White, Elizabeth McCracken, and Joyce Carol Oates. Then there are people who despite doing other things have made the memoir their brilliant forte: Jill Ker Conway, Mary Karr, Ruth Reichl, to name a few.

This spring, memoirs of bereavement from two young poets who also happen to work in New York publishing have appeared. Festooned with blurbs, these prose works will find their readers and duly move them, for they are candid, questing, and tear-jerking if necessarily imperfect. Jill Bialosky's slightly mistitled *History of a Suicide: My Sister's Unfinished Life* is a bumpy but stirring attempt to get to the bottom of the suicide at twenty-one of her younger half sister, who after having been broken up with by a longtime beau, asphyxiated herself in the family garage, with her medicated mother sleeping well into the afternoon upstairs. Kim is discovered by someone else. The book is ostensibly a meditation and investigation—like most memoirists Bialosky eschews the word *catharsis,* since, as she has said when interviewed, *catharsis* implies a finishing that is nowhere to be found in these pages; it may also be one of the weakest excuses for storytelling. (Who wants to read someone else's catharsis?)

Bialosky's book includes much professional and literary handholding in looking slant let alone straight on at what will always seem an enigmatic event—the suicide of someone young and beloved. Terms are googled, experts are written and visited, Shakespeare is quoted, and the book she puts together—part commonplace book, part souvenir album, part emotional laundry list—does not succeed in solving its own puzzles, although it assists the reader in coming away with his or her own ideas.

Kim's suicide sits in the lives of Bialosky, her sisters, and her mother like a murder mystery, and the culprit the book increasingly gravitates toward is not the dozing mom or the dumping boyfriend (who, bizarrely, and with insufficient subsequent exploration by Bialosky—her invocation of *Romeo and Juliet* feels wide of the mark—committed suicide himself a few years later). Nor does she pay much attention to the blighted rust-belt landscape, with its depressing culture of erotic and narcotic highs in lieu of meaningful work. As the book spirals about its various suspects, like the circling of a helix that is the movement of depression itself, the villain who increasingly emerges—or is fashioned—is Bialosky's stepfather, Kim's birth dad, who abandoned the family when Kim was very little and who once told her she would never amount to anything. Bialosky's own Jewish father died young and left her mother a widow with three young kids; Mrs. Bialosky quickly remarried an Irish-American charmer and bounder. Characterizations here are not detached by Bialosky from ethnicity. With a checked-out mother upstairs, and gray, struggling Cleveland outside, not every reader will wholeheartedly agree.

Bialosky wants to "recognize the forces that weakened Kim's strength and attempt to re-create her inner world through my writing," but this is exactly what it is impossible for the book to do since it instead illustrates Bialosky's great distance from her younger sister. It is as if she has a refrigerator full of food, but through no fault of her own lacks the stove to cook it on. Bialosky has her own life in New York, full of a survivor's guilty happinesses but also her own personal tragedies (she is pregnant when Kim dies and a subsequent loss of the baby takes up much of the book, as it naturally would in real life).

Kim's turmoil cannot be explored, and her inner landscape—despite diary and letter excerpts—remains uncreated. When Bialosky looks in her dead sister's closet, she lists, without explication, fourteen items of clothing, almost all of which are sexy and black. The exceptions include a Cleveland Browns jacket and the Laura Ashley rose-print dress Kim wore as a bridesmaid in the author's wedding. That bridesmaid dress stops the reader: Is it harsh to ask what girl with a black leather miniskirt would want to wear this dress, would feel remotely seen or understood in it, and to wonder what bride would insist on it? Well, too many brides perhaps. One imagines Kim keeping it in order to sell it on eBay.

Elsewhere the bridal bouquet is also discovered among Kim's belongings and we see the possible rebuke that flying token might have accidentally bestowed upon her, given all that her older sisters' lives contained that excluded her: she surely felt loved by her siblings but discloses in her own writing feelings of inferiority. Although she was certainly young enough to turn her life around, contagious depression pulled her under—as did impulsiveness and drugs. Kim haunts the book like a sweet ghost—one that is perhaps begging to rest at last in a novel, where such inner lives can indeed be re-created or at least imagined with specificity: ironically, the genre of the novel, with its subtle characterizations and rich and continuous dreamscape, remains a kind of gold standard for a genre that may be usurping it.

Meghan O'Rourke's book about her own personal bereavement following the death of her mother is titled *The Long Goodbye,* and she is not kidding. Hers is a *tour de force et tristesse,* especially in its first half, which has all the virtues of a theatrical narrative—emotional crises, paralysis before the oncoming locomotive of time, a family that is its own ensemble (an ensemble that includes the smart, highly strung eldest daughter, two endearing brothers, the attractive teacher-mom and teacher-dad). After its dramatic midpoint, and with no intermission, the narrative of *The Long Goodbye* drifts and casts about, just as O'Rourke herself did in the aftermath of her mother's death as she struggled in the anguish of separation to find the proper and effective rituals of mourning and farewell.

A completely acceptable disorganization swirls about the writing, as if in imitation of O'Rourke's restless state—her mother dies and is brought back to life several times; at one point it seems that one of the dogs dies twice. The pages proceed intuitively and in a zigzag through the decades. There is once more the googling of grief—literal and metaphorical—emotional processing of every stripe, again the citing of Shakespeare (O'Rourke aptly prefers *Hamlet* though oddly never mentions anything uttered by grief-engulfed Ophelia), the revisiting of childhood memories that are now holier than they need to be, anger at others who are less comprehending ("The bereaved cannot communicate with the unbereaved" is her epigraph from Iris Murdoch), and much setting out for long, brisk runs to expel excess tension and get some fresh air.

Lecturing and historical exposition sometimes beset the book. ("The British anthropologist Geoffrey Gorer . . . argues that, at least in Britain, the First World War played a huge role in changing the way people mourned.") Its stop-and-start quality can be summed up not just by the epigraph from Murdoch but also by O'Rourke's quoting of La Rochefoucauld: "Death and the sun are not to be looked at steadily." Even the scattering of her mother's ashes, for various reasons, is done in stages and takes over a year to be completed. "The body that I had loved lay in a sandwich bag."

O'Rourke's mother, Barbara, a beautiful (she is thought to resemble Ali MacGraw) and companionable woman of "calm vibrancy" beloved by her entire family, is diagnosed with colorectal cancer when she is in her early fifties. (Her backstory includes having been her husband's high school student—she was married to him at seventeen—but the book chooses only to mention this in passing.) When Barbara gets the news of her cancer's metastasis to her brain, it is from someone named Dr. Popper, who before he leaves the examination room says, "Yeah. Two over on the left side. . . . Very unusual. So I'll get Dr. Chi."

And then it is the patient's turn to speak.

"Well, THAT was awfully casual of him!" exclaims O'Rourke's mother, who soon is in last-ditch experimental treatment with some-one named Dr. Nougat. The doctors' names alone cause dread to engulf the reader. Barbara dies at fifty-five—the halfway point of the book. Meghan O'Rourke has up until now proceeded with the vitality of a first-rate dramatist, and her mother is a character well suited to it, equipped with an irrepressible spirit and a Christmas Day death, on a bed in the middle of the living room (so that death will be less "bureau-cratic and fluorescent"), breaking the heart of everyone.

"I knew that a Christmas carol would make me cry this season," O'Rourke says later, during the anniversary of her mother's death.

> I just didn't know it would be "Frosty the Snowman," that least dignified of all carols. . . . I was driving to Trader Joe's on a rainy Sunday to buy poinsettias and eggnog. . . . As I distract-edly pressed the radio buttons, I heard the familiar bumptious

chorus, and my stomach turned with nostalgia: "Thumpety thump thump, thumpety thump thump, look at Frosty go." But it was when Frosty, knowing of his imminent demise, tells the kids, "Let's run, and we'll have some fun now, before I melt away," that tears leaked down my face.

This is the kind of thing O'Rourke does well—situating her grief amid the absurdities of everyday life. Moreover, she seems to know her mother much better than Bialosky was able to know her sister, and so her mother emerges less as a rough sketch and more as a completed portrait, a lively and memorable person, placed as if on a pedestal that is also on a stage:

> Our mother was a fierce driver. A leased BMW was her one luxury. . . . The summer before she died, Jim came up to Connecticut with me for dinner; he'd just bought a used Audi. "Barbara," he said, "I have to show you something." My mother had just begun her final round of chemotherapy, but she disentangled the chemo purse from her chair and walked haltingly out to the driveway. When she saw the car, she cried out in glee, looked at Jim, and said, "We should race!"

If like Bialosky's book O'Rourke's fails to pose some of the larger impersonal and unphilosophical questions—O'Rourke's mother and her mother's sister, who both grew up in New Jersey, came down with the same disease and New Jersey's alarming cancer rate is not given a mention—it may seem a missed opportunity. Though epidemiology and public policy might disrupt the poetry of bereavement, a reader can long to see eloquent tears made useful. Memoirs often exist precisely for this reason—and their improvised form allows for accommodations of this kind without intruding on any narrative magic. Certainly Bialosky's sister and O'Rourke's mother remain engaging subjects deserving of the deep imagining, revealing design, and solid construction of heroines in good prose fiction, but real life is messy and sometimes gracelessly crowds out an enduring story, something no memoir reader necessarily expects. Advocacy of a certain kind can be a memoirst's muse and companion and in any case is not a guest that will ruin the party. Even Nabokov's canonical *Speak, Memory* does not give us the brilliantly vivid and coherent dreams of his novels—because it simply can't.

A third memoir came my way while I was reading these other two. Entitled *Dear Marcus,* it would seem at first glance to be a fuller demonstration of the democratization of memoir that Neil Genzlinger so derides. *Dear Marcus* is a self-published first book by someone with no connection to New York publishing. At the age of twelve its author, Jerry McGill, was shot in the back in Manhattan's East Village on New Year's Day by someone he never saw. He has spent the rest of his life in a wheelchair. (As with O'Rourke the anniversary of his tragedy is a holiday and unlike O'Rourke he gives himself a treat every year—a fancy meal at a restaurant, a trip to London.) His book is subtitled *Speaking to the Man Who Shot Me,* and since this man was never found McGill gives him a made-up name and then cries out to him about his life.

There is sorrow and fury, but this is not the Book of Job. McGill clearly possessed the charm, attractiveness, and spirit to avail himself of the help and care that came his way—both within therapeutic settings and outside—and he managed to have girlfriends, graduate from Fordham University, write screenplays, make films, and subsequently become a teacher and advocate for the rights of the disabled.

> I, personally, feel like I am up for this challenge of being a person with a disability and I have had many a wonderful experience in this role, but it is hard, damned hard. . . . It is not for everyone. I have had tons of disabled friends over the years and the misconception that we are all strong, inspirational beacons of hope is an immense fallacy perpetrated by and subsisting on images in the media.

Nonetheless, although he can list the difficulties he has had with bathrooms, housing, and employment—"the powers that be in Hollywood don't think there is a huge market for stories about people with disabilities despite all of the Oscar-winning portrayals that have come from actors playing disabled characters"—he also lists, to astonish his invisible assailant, the "marvelous globetrotting pleasures" he has experienced: from sipping coffee in a Costa Rican rain forest to performing at a vintage theater in England with a troupe of disabled actors. His book is short, sweet, homespun, and inspiring in the very way that he is skeptical of. He shares with Bialosky and O'Rourke a desire for alternative outcomes: all three books wonder in many directions, posing what-ifs, and their authors toughly poke their own wounds and search the sky. One never doubts the psychic injury, but objective criticism in the face of it is like quarreling with a fish. Yet of the three authors, McGill—the African-American man with the bullet lodged in his spine—is by far the most cheerful. As he writes himself, "You can't make this stuff up."

(2011)

Friday Night Lights

On my way to a Manhattan book party recently my mind was wandering to cultural guilty pleasures: sprightly but inane movies, or half-baked television programs no sophisticated person would admit to watching, as well as other aesthetic uncoolnesses, such as, say, Josh Groban, whose precariously belted tenor, crossover repertoire, and passable Italian have made him a secret darling of vulgarians like me. When he sings "The Prayer" with Céline Dion, is the listener not in the private ocular mists of kitsch heaven? Is not one of those pearly gates real pearl? And might one pay for admission to this slum-paradise with a parterre ticket stub from *Wozzeck*?

So it was, then, with great and satisfying surprise that almost immediately upon arriving at the party, I found myself locked in enthusiastic conversation in a corner with two other writers, all three of us, we discovered, solitary, isolated viewers of the NBC series *Friday Night Lights*. We spewed forth excitedly, like addicts—this was no longer a secret habit but a legitimately brilliant drama. Though the title might make the uninitiated think of Shabbat candles, the show is actually about football in Texas, a state that I felt just then had not been this far east since the Bush administration.

"Rooting is in our blood," Janet Malcolm has written, and when traveling around this country one would be hard-pressed not to notice that sports stadiums have become to the United States what opera houses are to Germany. Every community has one, even ones without much money. *Friday Night Lights,* whose final season has just come to a close, is a weekly, hour-long dramatic series (forty-three minutes without commercials) whose focus is a high school football team and its place in a particular Texas town by the fictional name of Dillon—inspired by the real-life town of Odessa.

In West Texas, largely because of the heat, high school football is often played on weekend nights under klieg lights to crowds of up to twenty thousand people. These lit matches are just that: they light the fuse and transform these young players into local celebrities, turning these high school games into the only show in what would otherwise be a no-show town. In rough terrain blighted further by the dusty winds of economic collapse—droughted ranches, oil rigs mute and still as scarecrows—these games are the week's high point for these boys and for the adults (parents, uncles, unemployed older brothers, boosters) who try to live vicariously through them. The town wants to win at something. The high school coach signs a two-year contract and often has to look for another job immediately following. If the team loses, the town will remind him by pounding For Sale signs into his front lawn or accosting him over ice cream at the local Alamo Freeze. In *Friday Night Lights,* when the coach's wife takes a job as a guidance counselor to help out, she is told that the last guidance counselor killed herself.

Friday Night Lights is held together by a cast of disconcertingly attractive young people with pink, wavy mouths (a few seem straight out of a Beverly Hills casting agency, marring slightly the verisimilitude). They play kids named Tim Riggins, Tyra Collette, Jason Street, Lyla Garrity, and Matt Saracen, whose names envelop and suit them better than any others could, including the actors' own. Equally attractive is the only high-functioning family in Dillon: that of Coach Eric Taylor and his wife, Tami, who are played with deep and beautiful concentration and chemistry by Kyle Chandler and Connie Britton. The Taylors often speak politely over each other, simultaneously, as if in an Altman film, and when they genuinely lose their tempers, which is seldom, it is transfixing, even when the sparring sounds mild. When Tami is made high school principal and begins to respond to her husband's work issues with platitudes of fatigue, he says, "You know who I miss? I miss the coach's wife." And she replies, recognizably, "You know who I can't wait to meet? The principal's husband." The portrait of their relationship has been described by Daniel Mendelsohn as "the finest representation of middle-class marriage in popular culture." And it is a far cry from the marriages one has seen on *The Sopranos* or *Mad Men,* as well as other marriages in Dillon, Texas.

The series wants Dillon to function as a microcosm of larger working- and middle-class America: it takes its fifty or so hours and opens a window on American family, education, community race relations, athletics, social class, and its various brokennesses. But lest you go away, it keeps you involved with the drama of high school—its romantic student soap operas, its tense and dire administrative politics, plus the multigenerational home life that has dads in prison, dads in Iraq, dads gambling and drinking and roaming around the country while Grandma sits in the front room. This is where the role of the coach as holy father (not for nothing does he lead the team in prayer before each game) is underscored: these boys are the coach's congregation. He is their shepherd and they are his flock. And despite its unflinching glance at some really tough lives and an unforgiving landscape, this is a television show and will not submit easily to despair.

The same cannot be said of the grim movie off which the series is spun. Both its people and its setting are hard-bitten and haggard. Billy Bob Thornton as the real-life Coach Gaines appears pale and grisly, with vampiric, beet-hued lips and stark, hollowing cheekbones. And although Connie Britton here also plays the coach's wife, with her permed 1980s hair and constantly startled expression, she and Thornton look like characters who have wandered off the set of an inexpensive horror film. The panorama of sad houses with For Sale signs reads like a chorus crying for long-withheld help, and the desert landscape seems to hunger for a night sky that will cool and be-glitter it.

The camera work is grainy, quick, and cold, as if the lens could bear neither to blink nor to stare, and the feel and the look of the film are sociological and anthropological—an outsider going by with a crew in a truck. If some residents of Odessa, Texas, were not pleased by either the movie or the book on which it was based (its author, the journalist H. G. Bissinger, says he received death threats), it's because no one likes to be told their home is depressing; everyone likes to think their lives are a little better-looking than that.

But at the time this movie is set, in the late 1980s, *Money* magazine ranked Odessa as the country's fifth-worst city to live in. Its racism was legendary. Molly Ivins called it an "armpit," and Larry McMurtry's *Texasville* refers to it as "the worst place on earth." Odessa was founded in the late 1800s by huckster land surveyors from Zanesville, Ohio: it never lost the taint of betrayal. Even the high school boys, who are based on real-life people and in the film use those people's real-life names (as opposed to their more innocent fictional counterparts on TV), appear as toughened and worn as the adults are tired and dazed. "We gotta lighten up," says one of the film's football players to his friends. "We're only seventeen."

"I don't feel seventeen, do you feel seventeen?" replies another of the boys, as with deadened eyes they skeet-shoot into the Texas sky. In fact, they look leathered and thirty, as if all the childhood had been knocked out of them long ago. Set in 1988, when the United States was not involved in any war in the Mideast, the film version of *Friday Night Lights* was made in 2004, when two such wars were occurring. It is reminiscent of a war movie (the football impact scenes are brutal and the sound editors have the volume on high for each wince-inducing hit, underscoring the disposability of the boys—"You have to worry about the safety of these kids," one sports announcer says after some bone-cracking tackles).

But the subtext, unspoken even in the DVD commentary, is that this is our warrior class: this is where our soldiers come from. The film was made, at any rate, to look that way. It never enters a classroom or has a female character say much of anything. "I don't understand women and I don't feel comfortable presenting them," says the film's director, Peter Berg, in the bonus commentary. The climax of the film, which is the Texas state championship game against Dallas's Carter High School, is shot and cut along the same lines as the climax of Spielberg's *Saving Private Ryan*. So says Peter Berg.

Although Berg also directed the television pilot, establishing the pace and look of the series, the television show is warmer and greener; it had to be to keep viewers watching for five years. There is better music, for instance, "needle drops" by Ryan Adams and by Iron and

Wine, as well as many singer-songwriters from the local Austin scene, which gives the feeling of high school life back to the kids. (As it was in the film, the Midland, Texas, band Explosions in the Sky is also used.) In the series, though the homoerotic ties of boys and team sports can be noted and felt, they are not as aggressively put forward. In the film there is a father-son pair that is the major romance—"You got one stinking year to make yourself some memories" are the father's words of love—and the original edition of Bissinger's book starts off with locker room photographs of hugging teammates and shirtless players blow-drying their hair.

The series is more interested than the film in how these boys relate to girls, and although sometimes clueless about the girls themselves—cheerleaders, pageant contestants, and rally girls who often appear doe-eyed, manipulative, attention-starved, and shrill (the rising action written for them requires rising voices as well)—gender-wise the series is a substantial expansion on the movie and book. In fact, by comparison, it is a veritable encyclopedia of the female psyche. The mayor of Dillon is a woman, a committed football booster and lesbian who "before she began to play for the other team," as it's said in Dillon, once had an affair with Lyla Garrity's father, Buddy. And although the first season handed the viewer a world of housewives, cheerleaders, and strippers, their experiences are put forward with sympathy and wit.

The TV series, set almost twenty years after the time of the film, also repeatedly dramatizes how the relationship of grown-ups to children in this town—is it Dillon? is it Odessa? is it all of America?—is more often than not flipped: that is, the kids take care of the hapless grown-ups who have stayed on in the down-and-out setting of their own upbringing. It is a sad reversal—there is not one father of a son on the show who is not meddlesome, obstructive, or damaging, and many of the mothers aren't much better—but it's a burden that on television often enlarges rather than diminishes the kids. The series is also shot closer to Austin than to West Texas so that the look of the land is less desolately lunar than in the film. One feels that the TV show is less about weariness than about the struggle for moral rectitude. The essential goodness of the boys is never in doubt (though the wobbly first season foolishly makes a villain out of a young Katrina refugee).

Yet everything about these kids is going to be challenged (if often incoherently) by the various scriptwriters. In real life teenagers are often challenged to the point of destruction, and even in Berg's film the boys are, in effect, partly denatured—roughened and distressed to match the parched turf—but less so here in TV-land. In this particular prime-time representation, small-town Texas culture is less about hardened exteriors and shredded dreams than about preserving, finding, and acquiring integrity and decency: family duty, Christian kindness, and charity are its hallmarks. For decoration there is also a lot of cleavage.

Unlike *The Wire,* which works as a visual novel, *Friday Night Lights* does not possess confident and overarching story lines, and there are so many loose ends and dead stops and panicked plot moves that it might have been written by writers who thought the series was about to be canceled the next day. (In fact, there were indeed dire network discussions regarding the program's low ratings.) Scripts often seem frantically assembled with no memory of what came before. Story elements are shuffled, parachuted in, forgotten about. People are added and subtracted, and only sometimes is there an imprisonment or a marriage or a baby shower to explain. Often characters just disappear. It is one of the show's troubling ad hoc aspects, exacerbated perhaps by one of its virtues: the cast had a hand in the dialogue and often improvised scenes and rewrote lines. Kyle Chandler, script in hand, is said to have once phoned the director to insist, "I don't need to make this speech. I can do it with a look."

Chandler can do just about anything with a look. The expressive restraint of his smoldering gaze and his squinted grin of chagrin is one of the most intriguing aspects of *Friday Night Lights,* even if it is overrelied on. When called on to say lines such as "I'm offering you everything I got. This is not just about football. I beg of you: think about what I just said," he makes the words pierce and soar. When he says to his team, "Listen up, gentlemen," it doesn't much matter what he actually says afterward: everyone is drawn to attention. And when at a coaches' poker game he gets up to leave early, saying, "I've been cheating all night, looking at his cards, and I still can't beat him," the line reading is such that we know he is actually a bit tipsy and missing his wife.

So that is the way the series's chief architect, executive producer Jason Katims, proceeds: a little willy-nilly. The camera work—three cameras filming simultaneously—is excellent and done in a "run-and-gun" filmmaking style, all of which allows the cast additional set pieces, scenes, or ad libs. But using that many cameras leaves the really hard work of the storytelling to the editors. And having to bring each episode in at forty-three minutes clearly resulted in some unhelpful excisions, as well as some dubious inclusions. There is perhaps too much of Tim Riggins's blustery older brother Billy, and too much of the Garrity clan, though Buddy Garrity gets some of the funniest lines in the show (as when, desperate and gasping, he confides to Eric Taylor that "the Boosters"—a coven of unelected village elders—"may have my phone tapped").

To a one, the actors who play the young football players perform with nuance and openheartedness. Seldom have teenage boys been this emotionally articulate. The distinctive qualities of each one offset the idea of their warrior fungibility as enacted on the team. All are riveting, and their adolescent Texan mumbles, even when explaining the difference between a skinny post and an out-and-up, do not require subtitles, though the thought of subtitles crosses the mind. All the characters say *yes sir, no ma'am, please,* and *thank you*—sometimes as in "Becky. Shut up. Please?"

The show's handling of race becomes more sure-footed in the later seasons, once Michael B. Jordan, the actor who played Wallace in Season 1 of *The Wire,* joins the cast as the new black quarterback of the East Dillon Lions. (Midseries, even after winning the state championship, Coach Taylor, as punishment by the politburo of self-interested Boosters, is removed as coach of the West Dillon Panthers and sent to the poor side of town to make a team there from scratch.) Whereas desegregation for its own sake proceeded with great difficulty in Texas, the gerrymandering of school districts for purposes of football is accomplished in a hurry. And if the redistricting doesn't work, there are always ghost mailboxes that can be set up by the Boosters, and illegal recruits in the guise of charity. "Feel his hair," says the younger sibling of an African-American girl, touching her sister's white boyfriend's head. "It's like grass." In fact, two characters on *The Wire* are murdered in David Simon's Baltimore just in time for the excellent actors who play them to join *Friday Night Lights,* where boys are not killed, only maimed (one waits for the Army to scoop one up, but it doesn't happen until the finale montage).

The action happens mostly on the football field. And the dramatized football plays, studied on video and in printed diagrams in ring binders by the characters—both male and female (the East Dillon quarterback's girlfriend wants to be a coach, not a rally girl)—are more engaging than one might expect. One looks forward to the games, as does every denizen of Dillon, which is what the viewer becomes. Periodically, to end an episode or a season, a wedding or a rodeo is arranged so we get to see the whole cast gathered up and milling around, as if in a curtain call, to remind us of the community we've come to know.

Over the five years of the show there is time for the kids to change, and change they do. By the end they can all look people in the eyes while speaking. The alcoholic Tim Riggins, brimming with sweet sex and soft rage, reminiscent of a brawny Jim Morrison, begins the show saying of his aggressive tackles, "That dude could be Santa Claus and I'd still hate him. . . . I just like to hurt people," and ends it by turning Panther decency into saintly martyrdom. The good Texan grandson Matt Saracen, who begins so dutifully and diffidently, becomes an urban Chicago hipster. And when last we see the endearing albino nerd Landry Clark, before he goes off to Rice University, he is getting an "epic" lap dance at the local strip joint and in self-parodic tones says happily to the dancer, "I want to know absolutely everything there is to know about you."

It would not be entirely accurate to say the entire show was discussed in our mad corner at that Manhattan party. The people I was speaking with mostly wanted to discuss the character Tim Riggins, played by Taylor Kitsch. Kitsch heaven! Lyla Garrity was a dismissible minx. Tyra Collette, who runs for class president by saying, "Nobody here is getting laid if you let Ginny here have the prom in the gym," had distracting hairdo instability. The girls in general held less interest, and the coach's new baby, Graciebelle, held the least of all. (According to Jason Katims in the DVD commentary, Graciebelle is portrayed by a toddler who is one of "three twin sisters," a remark that certainly gives one pause.) Even Landry Clark and Matt Saracen and stormy, stalwart, black-Irish Eric Taylor—the characters who possess the most forceful gazes, mesmerizing scenes, and unexpected psychological moves in the show—received short shrift. It was the brooding, beautiful, and slightly doomed Tim Riggins, handsome as a statue and bleakly craving good-ness, about whom no one could stop talking. Tim Riggins: through the wonders of long-form and instantly shareable narrative, he was the realest person in the room.

(2011)

9/11/11

Like many people, I watched 9/11 on television from a thousand miles away. Also like many people, I found myself asking, among the dozens of terrified questions that crossed my mind, Do I know anyone who works in the World Trade Center? I was pretty sure that I didn't. And I was about to relax ever so slightly and guiltily, when I suddenly remembered—wait a minute—that my brother worked there. Or had. He'd been there during the first bombing, in 1993, and I wasn't certain whether the state administrative office he worked for was still situated there.

It turned out that his office had moved just across the street. My brother was in the WTC subway station when the first tower was hit, and, after the second one was hit and the adjacent buildings were evacuated, my brother, covered in ash, and unreachable by anyone, walked eight hours home to Queens. The next day? He returned to work and sat there at his desk for two hours, waiting for others to show up—until at last it became clear that not a single other person was going to. And so he left. The cough he already possessed became permanently worse.

When I think about his returning to his empty office and just sitting there, I like to imagine that it was not out of some heartbreakingly robotic sense of duty that might run in our family but, instead, due to the universal human desire to return to the fictional normal; the normal and the everyday are often amazingly unstoppable, and what is unimaginable is the cessation of them. The world is resilient, and, no matter what interruptions occur, people so badly want to return to their lives and get on with them. A veneer of civilization descends quickly, like a shining rain. Dust is settled.

In the past ten years, we have done that only sort of. The absurd, brutal cycle of revenge that 9/11 was part of, that all war is part of, has continued. (Terrorism is guerrilla war waged by stateless and under-funded communities—or at least the gullible, restless young men within them.) Opportunists who wait for acts of war in order to take material advantage of the chaos will quickly set up their schemes and profiteering. They showed up for work—perhaps not the very next day but soon enough, and the invasion of Iraq ensued, the anniversary of which is less likely to be remarked upon or even precisely remembered. (Politics, as David Rieff has written, is the ghost at the banquet of any national commemoration.) Instead? This year, the death of Osama bin Laden was cheered by many members of a generation reared on the good-versus-evil wizardry of J. K. Rowling. I recently taught a class of quite brilliant university students, most of whom, when asked to name their desert-island book, said Harry Potter and then good-naturedly debated among themselves which volume was best. (They noted, too, that they were the same age as Harry Potter, having begun middle school exactly when he began Hogwarts. I remarked that I was the same age as Osama bin Laden and received some startled looks.)

I have continued to teach brilliant university students whose desert-island discs are hip and arcane but whose desert-island novels are always Harry Potter. A magical, Manichaean, neobiblical view of the world might be less possible for those belonging to an older generation, whose desert-island book might be, for example, Graham Greene's *The Power and the Glory*, and so the death of bin Laden was, in general, treated more soberly by the middle-aged. The new boss, as Pete Town-shend once said, may be the same as the old boss. And one whiskey priest can be replaced by another.

The fierce idealism of younger generations continues in every part of the world. And yet who would want to rid the young of their ideal-ism? It leaves us without even the gruesomely cheering Harry Potter readers, celebrating bin Laden's assassination. It would leave us with people even more mysterious and unnerving. Who may or may not optimistically show up for work the next day. Whose commitment to the resumption of the everyday may be as shaky as terrorism's proponents would like it to be.

Ten years ago in the pages of *The New Yorker*, writers grappled eloquently with the bombing of the Twin Towers, meticulously describing the billowing smoke, the blue sky, the recurrent dreams of flying low through a city. The word *cowardly* was semantically parsed. Bravery was praised. Middle-of-the-night calls were confessed to, and an intelligent attempt was made to contextualize the event in a longer global history of political tragedy and war conducted in urban streets. Yet what has transpired in the ten years since 9/11, both here and in the Middle East, was not anticipated by any of these writers, all of whom are paid for their finely tuned imaginations. J. K. Rowling, showing up at her desk in the aftermath, feeling a generation's bolt-of-lightning scar, and imagining a long battle laced with fantasy, may have outwritten everyone.

(2011)

GOP Primary Debate

Already in a condition of satire, the opening of the Tea Party–hosted GOP debate on Monday night in Tampa presented the eight Republican presidential candidates as good-looking characters—the Diplomat, the Newcomer, the Firebrand—who would have to battle one another off the electoral island. Music, brassy and tense, and a baritone voice-over let you know that this reality show was part of the ongoing Apocalypse Lite that has infused our television programming and made the networks almost unwatchable. There was little even Jon Stewart on his show the next evening could do to make fun of what was often comedically predigested—except to say that the red, white, and blue stage looked like the inside of Betsy Ross's, well, sewing room. I'm paraphrasing.

There is always something if not a lot to learn by watching a circus—one is both amazed by and sorry for the animals. The clowns are clearly just pretending. The self-pity one arrives with enlarges to become societal. In a certain way all the candidates on Monday struggled admirably. The Mormons (Jon Huntsman, Mitt Romney) as well as the Catholic Rick Santorum actually knew the words to the national anthem and were the only ones to sing along. They seemed like Mama's sweet choirboys. The others, with more husky snark and testosterone, and I do include Michele Bachmann, did not sing, and nothing in the eyes gave a look of knowing what song it might be or what verse anyone was on. But everyone's hands were on their chests or in anatomically approximate places. (Romney may have been clutching his side—his performance next to high-testosterone men has not always been good. In 2008 he withered next to John McCain and sometimes looked as if he might burst into tears; he is somewhat more confident now but similarly dweeb-spirited next to Rick Perry, whose voice is gruffer and lower—perhaps too gruff and low to sing.)

In the Tea Party audience on the Florida State Fairgrounds, even fewer seemed to know Francis Scott Key's words.

It is indeed the audiences who are getting scary. The MSNBC crowd last Thursday applauded the state of Texas's record-breaking death-row executions. On Monday in Tampa at least one person cheered the prospect of (in a question posed to Ron Paul) an uninsured man in a coma being left to die. Monday's audience also booed Perry's defense of public education for children of illegal immigrants, as well as Paul's skeptical remarks about American exceptionalism ("We're under great threat because we occupy so many countries. We have nine hundred bases around the world"). This kind of hoo-ha heartlessness is recession road rage at its worst, and that this is the electorate these candidates are trying to court often seems to startle even them, though this is reflected less in the policies they endorse than in their faces, which can veer to and from their lecterns in disorientation and fog.

Each of the candidates did have something genuinely interesting to offer: Paul is strongly antiwar. Perry would like to give the children of illegal immigrants the right to go to university. Bachmann seemed to have the goods on Perry (a genuine scandal involving the pharmaceutical company Merck, a former staffer who was a lobbyist for Merck, and Texas's executive mandate for a controversial vaccine made by Merck). Herman Cain would like a simplified tax system with no loopholes and a rule that says no congressional bill can be longer than three pages. Huntsman has a more progressive though also flattened tax system (you can see him, with nervous dismay, counting his island days). He is also trying to keep science in the platform and religion out and would (like Perry) work to wind things down in Afghanistan. Newt Gingrich is honing his wittiness, something of which he's always been proud (Bachmann brings her loud, rough laugh to it all, so he may be flirting with her). Romney is tall. Romney also arranges his face warmly when others are speaking—unlike Perry, who often looks concussed, though Perry's beauty, a cross between Burt Reynolds and Hilary Swank, springs to life when the suggestion that he can be bought for only five thousand dollars comes up. He has a price, he seems to suggest, but it's much higher than that. And—as reports roll in—so it is.

The garish red theatrical set of last Thursday's MSNBC debate, which caused most of the candidates to show up in popping blue ties (and Bachmann in a high-collar blouse, an attractive style she is ruining for Democratic women), had on CNN's Monday debate become mostly blue, making it a red-jacket (Bachmann) and red-tie affair, although a few (Gingrich, Paul, Santorum) seemed not to have gotten the memo. Romney and Perry were once again put center stage, and this time Perry's suit was slightly lighter and browner, suggesting that perhaps he will be the running mate in what is shaping up to be the likely GOP ticket—in imitation of that other cowboy and nebbish team of former Democrats, Reagan and Bush.

Throughout the many subsequent debates that's what we are going to be watching: Mitt and Rick getting to know each other. It's up to everyone else to go after them. That this will be going on while the tired but dignified Barack Obama tries to get his jobs bill passed and has to endure the wrongheaded wave of Clinton nostalgia that has swept over his party is our democratic system at its circus-saddest. But Obama's situation is a reminder that, despite the seeming meaninglessness of the debates, until election reform really takes hold (a key reason to explore space for other inhabitable planets or at least for other supreme courts), the primary matters. It can create divisions that haunt for years. The voters that now complain the most about Obama are the skeptical ones he never had in the primary to begin with. In a system of government designed for gridlock by eighteenth-century visionaries in a hurry and a huff, one can long for a parliament with a prime minister, something we almost had with LBJ. Who then got out, exhausted. But with a legacy.

(2011)

Werner Herzog's *Into the Abyss*

A documentary film is often part stunt, part lab experiment, and the way a documentary filmmaker pursues his or her story will always involve a bit of amateur sleuthing, as well as improv. That such scriptless adventures have attracted a great director like Werner Herzog is curious but not alarming. Good documentary films can be made cheaply, and we seem to be living in an abundantly golden—or at least copper (pennywise)—era of them. Herzog's latest film, *Into the Abyss*, much like his 2005 documentary, *Grizzly Man*, uses the camera as a Geiger counter to locate some of the more toxic elements of the American cultural psyche as seen through the questing mind of a pseudosqueamish European. Here the setting is small-town Texas's well-traveled road to death row. Once again, in his soft, Teutonic off-camera voice, Herzog insinuatingly and gently coaxes his interviewees while his camera registers a more ambiguous, startled fixation on people and places, plus a willingness to stare bluntly. Director and camera are like good cop, bad cop.

While given the banal subtitle *A Tale of Death, A Tale of Life*, Herzog's documentary doesn't have its hands on entire tales as much as the shiny pieces of many. The project seems to have initially aimed to tell the story of Mike Perry, a Texan inmate who had been on death row for ten years, since the age of eighteen, and who, when Herzog meets him, is scheduled for execution in eight days. Although the boyish, bucktoothed Perry eagerly speaks to Herzog and breaks the viewer's heart (almost all who are interviewed speak movingly and with great ostensible openness; how confessional reality television has prepped their personalities one can only guess), Perry's family refused to appear in the film—a very large hole. So Herzog is forced to roam around the whole Texas scene of small-town dysfunction and capital punishment protocol.

The actual crime—the shooting by Perry and his friend Jason Burkett of three people in order to steal a red Camaro in a gated community—is so senseless and stupidly conceived it is really just a worst-case portrait of teenage boy drunkenness, impulsivity, poverty-addled sociopathy, and a country so awash in weapons that it has arrived (perhaps once more) at a point in history where every high schooler knows how and where to get a gun. (This aspect is missing from Herzog's social critique, which focuses on capital punishment.) The coveted red Camaro, a kind of CSI MacGuffin, now sits in a police crime lot with a tree growing through its floor.

The first person interviewed is not Perry but the Death House reverend, who will speak to Perry of God (everyone in this picture, except Herzog, speaks of God) and who, as a gesture of kindness, will hold Perry's ankle during the execution on the gurney. The reverend is against the death penalty, but in thinking about it before the camera he veers off into an anecdote about a golf trip and his relief at not hitting a squirrel and killing one of God's creatures, and we can see how, when pressed to illuminate its own contradictions, the human mind can go on the fritz. This may really be Herzog's theme. His later interview of Fred Allan, the former captain of the Huntsville staff that straps the prisoners to the gurney, is a stirring example of someone who cracks under the pressure of paying work that involves killing up to two people a week. After the execution of Karla Faye Tucker, to whom Allan had begun to feel close, he had something of a breakdown and eventually quit his job, forswearing capital punishment as well as his pension. Although he has nothing to do with Mike Perry's story, he is an important part of Herzog's film.

Perhaps the most moving soliloquy belongs to Delbert Burkett, the jailed father of Mike Perry's partner in crime, Jason Burkett. Jason— who appears in the film looking simultaneously soldierly and apprehensive—is given life imprisonment, rather than the death penalty, thanks to his father's testimony during the sentencing hearing, which so moved and mercifully softened the jury that he reiterates his eloquently self-blaming remarks for Herzog. Although his son Jason was living in a trailer park at the time of the murders, Delbert at that same age had won a football scholarship to the University of Texas at Austin, only to drop out his senior year and, demoralized, eventually become a drug addict and thief and abandon his family. He and his son, both incarcerated, recently spent a holiday dinner together, handcuffed, a low point in the father's life that he describes with a kind of naked shame. His memories of Jason as a sickly child with several neuroblastomas (a deadly cancer) that required painful bone marrow treatment are heartrending and give a further glimpse into the injury and difficulties that can beset an already wobbling family and send it off the rails.

Herzog is interested in American violence reflected even in the names of Texas towns—Cut and Shoot is one—as well as the way that death and mayhem lying literally next door are moved on from, whereas superstitions—rainbows and departed spirits—are not. Crater Lake, a spot where bodies were infamously disposed of, and which in the Perry-Burkett crime was also used for that purpose, is a stone's throw from the gated community in Conroe that harbored the beloved Camaro. A new house near the crime scene is shown with a long, winding driveway that paves over the spot in the woods where one of the bodies was found. Herzog's camera takes an unflinchingly quiet look.

Dedicated to the victims and their families, the film gives perfect expression to the fear of a phone ringing: one of Herzog's bereaved interviewees has had the phone removed from her house.

In seeking the bizarre, Herzog has one thing after another just fall into his lap. Perhaps nothing seems stranger than the marriage of inmate Jason Burkett to a young Kansas woman who takes an interest in his case and begins writing to him. She is well groomed and plainspoken, filmed against the backdrop of a cozily domestic living room. Their courtship, which she recounts to Herzog, is a perversely mythic one that echoes the Wild West's sending east for schoolteachers and wives. After their marriage she manages to become pregnant with Jason's child—he wants fifty children, he says—and although she is at first reluctant to reveal the illegal details of this, Herzog's Viennese therapist's voice, not completely unlike that of Hannibal Lecter talking to Clarice, entices it out of her. She then, holding up her smartphone, shows us the ultrasound of the fetus, a ghostly image that Herzog's camera does not succeed in turning away from. "Scott Peterson gets a hundred letters a day," says Melyssa Thompson-Burkett, in an attempt to distinguish herself from other women who have fallen for handsome death-row inmates. Like so many other people in this riveting film, she does not on the surface appear to be crazy.

(2011)

Suzzy Roche's *Wayward Saints*

Suzzy Roche is mostly known as the youngest member of the three-sister band the Roches. The heyday of their somewhat cult following (*cult* in this case meaning "passionate, but shy of glamorous commercial levels") began in the late seventies and crested in the mid-eighties. The Roches themselves hung on professionally in various combinations and incarnations into the 1990s and beyond; Suzzy has recorded both alone and with her sister Maggie. Many a fan has stared at their album covers, contemplating Suzzy's long dark hair, her playful stances, her scrawny baby-of-the-family girlishness while trying to figure out which voice is hers in the tight, intricate harmonies that fill the Roches' recordings. What might be less well known is that Suzzy Roche—who is now in her mid-fifties—is part of a larger musical clan: with the folksinger Loudon Wainwright she has a daughter, Lucy, who is also a singer-songwriter and whose half siblings are Rufus and Martha Wainwright, the children of Kate McGarrigle of the much-loved McGarrigle Sisters.

The Roche-Wainwright-McGarrigle intertwinings comprise a musical family the sprawling brilliance of which has not been experienced perhaps since—well, we won't say the Lizst-Wagners—but at least the Carter-Cashes. The extended family oeuvre, though varied, often has a conversational, smart-kids-at-summer-camp quality that is both folky and jokey. The Roches' own wistful, clever songs are written with a sweet street spontaneity and prosody, and their clear, pure voices are like a barbershop trio of sassy angels. Sometimes they are overdubbed, to enlarge the sound, and the effect is close to celestial. But most often they sound like plucky girls riding home on a school bus, making things up as they go along. Their lyrics have unexpected line breaks and enjambment. In "The Train," from the Roches' first album, Suzzy writes,

> *I sit down on the train*
> *with my big pocketbook*
> *the guitar and a sugar-free drink*
> *I wipe the sweat off of my brow*
> *with the side of my arm*
> *and take off all that I can*
>
> *I am trying not to have a bad day*
> *everybody knows the way that is.*

In the later song "My, My Broken Heart," she pines,

> *I would be as good as maybe grandma*
> *but I must get a grip on*
> *my, my broken heart.*

In "My Winter Coat," the Roches sing (à la Lorenz Hart in "Everything I've Got Belongs to You"), "The cuffs are purple which perfectly suits / a pair I already had of boots."(One is reminded of the Yoda-like syntax of Hart's "There's a trick with a knife I'm learning to do.")

The Wainwrights, each performing before their individual audiences (in 2006 Rufus—a crooning balladeer who, like his father, has a bleak comic streak—devoted an entire Carnegie Hall concert to the songs of Judy Garland), write and sing with a similarly loose, improvisatory aspect. The 1970s novelty song "Dead Skunk in the Middle of the Road" by Loudon Wainwright has been the biggest family hit and atypical for all. The McGarrigles were renowned Canadian musicians; their most famous and beautiful song, "Heart Like a Wheel," was covered by Linda Ronstadt. But despite—or maybe in keeping with—their penchant for the whimsical and ad hoc, the Roche sisters have been the most adventurous and original act in the family and have even recorded amusing yet exquisite a cappella versions of compositions by Handel and by Cole Porter.

If Suzzy Roche were to sit down and write a novel that was not about music and family, what a disappointment that would be. But not to worry: her charming and agile literary debut, *Wayward Saints,* has as its protagonist a famous musician named Mary Saint, who is finally going home to Swallow, New York, the small town where she grew up, in order to give a concert there. She will as well reunite with her mother and dedicate to her the (fictional) rock hit "Sewer Flower," whose Rochean lyrics include "she grew out of cow dung and a dirty little song was sung" (Roche herself has written a song to go along with the novel—"It's what you are / not what you ain't / you're a wayward saint"). Whether Mary deigns to lay eyes on her father, who terrorized her childhood and is now sitting quietly in a nursing home, remains to be seen.

Despite the broken family that forms the emotional backdrop of her tale, Roche's descriptions are emphatically familial: not only are friends a family, glimpsed deer are a family, and trees are a family. "Far into the woods, back behind the camp, stood a circle of evergreen trees and most days I wound up there. Now I know that those trees were actually a family, and I'll tell you how I know that, too. I must have sensed it because I liked to sit right in the middle of their circle and sing." Sisterly beams of light shine down in slanted columns: the stage is set and lit by nature. In this transcendental setting Roche's heroine, Mary Saint, also experiences a vision of the "Other Mary": "She told me that all the slanted beams of light belonged to her, and not to God, and she also let me in on the secret about the trees being a family."

A mystic Catholicism haunts the book's pages, as do more pagan gods. The narrative's guiding of her heroine home for her concert is gingerly and mythic, as if Mary Saint, with her dark celebrity, were a kind of Eurydice, who has been kidnapped into some unknowable world ruled by devil fame, and who might not complete the journey out if the anxious loved ones turn expectantly and look with too much eagerness. It is ironic that the mother who awaits, gazes and gazes without ever properly seeing. She looks at her daughter with the same flummoxed perplexity that any mother of a rock star might. "The two women sat looking up at the moon and stars. Mary pointed out the different constellations to her mother, and although Jean couldn't really see the shapes, she told Mary that she could." Those lines are this warmly matter-of-fact book's nimble benediction: a mother's incomprehension, a daughter's mystery, the heavens looking on. Can we get an Amen.

(2012)

Lena Dunham

Is it the partially handheld camera or the partially handheld life that makes one woozy when watching the bold and talented Lena Dunham, whose much-anticipated show, *Girls,* will air on April 15? In *Tiny Furniture,* her award-winning house-of-mirrors film, Dunham wrote a script starring her family and friends, most of them playing the people they somewhat are in real life, but with different names. And despite the privilege of these Manhattan lives, the mood of the film, especially as it attempts to portray young quasi adults in postcollege purgatory, is sometimes so depressing—often the way a clown (e.g., Charlie Chaplin, Joan Rivers, Stephen Colbert) can be depressing, and I do think Dunham has clown aspirations—that one does not know always where to look.

The youthful sex of educated, family-funded drifters that Dunham puts on the screen is mostly heartless and degrading, and not remotely exuberant, which is her point. One imagines that Dunham is hoping you'll also find it funny, but in middle-aged viewers a protective, parental feeling toward these young people might make this impossible. The writer Rebecca Mead has referred to the sex scenes in *Tiny Furniture* as "dispiriting," which seems to be only the tip of Dunham's psychosexual iceberg. It looks like careless cruelty between nudists. Which may be what life in one's early twenties often is, and if we have forgotten, Dunham means to remind us. But, in compensatory fashion, there is cute homoerotic flirtation among Dunham and her female friends to warm and console.

Dunham's mother, the artist Laurie Simmons, known for her work with miniature décor, plays the mother, Siri, in *Tiny Furniture*. Dunham plays the daughter Aura, and Dunham's real-life sister, Grace, plays Aura's teenage sister. In their two-tubbed bathroom in a giant Tribeca loft (their actual home) the two women artists, mother and daughter, are sometimes seen soaking simultaneously across from each other, as if they were reflections. Aura has discovered Siri's diaries from when she was Aura's age, and they mirror many of Aura's own preoccupations with love, her identity as an artist, and soothing her general worry about her destiny. (These are Laurie Simmons's real-life journals.) "Did you ever have a job that wasn't taking pictures of stupid tiny crap?" the employment-challenged Aura yells at Siri. As artist-mother (and artist's mother) Siri seems less "preoccupied," as some reviewers have written, than deeply tired. Her grown daughters are beyond-their-years starved for her attention and approval, competing with each other to sleep in her bed—where Mom is mostly, well, trying to get some sleep.

The title *Tiny Furniture* refers explicitly to the artwork that Siri makes at home, as well as to the ways in which—as the film follows Aura to jobs, trysts, and parties in the months immediately following her graduation from college into an unwelcoming economy—replication is utilized in art, and reality is reduced to plaything. It also seems to refer to the film's *Alice in Wonderland* quality. Almost every character seems a study in some kind of mental illness, and, as when Alice devours the Eat Me cake, the furniture can grow suddenly tiny around Aura—who looms large in her own mind, though, to her credit, she seems always game and rarely defeated, despite all. She almost never says no.

Lena Dunham, as she has said herself, despite her self-involvement, knows no vanity. (While at Oberlin, she made an unflattering video of herself in a bikini and posted it on YouTube, where it received over 5 million hits and many scathing comments.) She is boundaryless in a way that is a little TMI in life but has its dangerous thrills in narrative art; if some of it includes pointless invasions of privacy (people in the bathroom), mostly we don't notice or care. Are Lena Dunham and her world as preciously interesting as she hopes? Strangely, yes.

Thus Judd Apatow joined her in making an HBO series, which

became *Girls*. The show seems very much an extension of her film, utilizing some of the same cast members, although here Lena is named Hannah and lives in Brooklyn, and her parents are neither artists nor New Yorkers, but professors who live out of town and would like to pull the plug on the cash flow that has been supporting their daughter for two years. In one of the tense family scenes at which Dunham excels, Hannah's mother declares, "We can't keep bankrolling your groovy lifestyle."

"I am busy trying to become who I am," Hannah argues, requesting $1,100 a month to live on. She is working on a memoir. She believes she may be the voice of her generation. Or rather, "*a* voice of *a* generation."

"I've worked very hard," counters her mother, thinking of her own retirement. "I want to sit by a fucking lake."

"I could be a drug addict. Do you realize how lucky you are?" says Hannah—words I have heard in my very own house.

"You're being played by a major fucking player," her mother warns her father.

There is a history of television comedies about young women triumphantly taking on the big city. *That Girl*, starring Marlo Thomas, seems out of memory-reach for the world of Dunham's show, but both *The Mary Tyler Moore Show* and *Sex and the City* are explicitly referenced in the script—and explicitly subverted. These older shows were laughably fake in their depictions of city girls: they were designed to buck up women viewers, to give them pretty bachelorettes who were stumbling but still smiling. Marlo Thomas's effervescent Ann Marie twirls a parasol at Lincoln Center and flies a kite in Central Park and generally postpones indefinitely marriage to her loyal boyfriend, Donald. Mary Tyler Moore, with no beau at all, tosses her hat in the air with unrepressed chipperness (in the opening credits of *That Girl*, Marlo Thomas appears to be weathering stronger breezes and hangs on to hers). These programs from the sixties and seventies were far more conventionally feminist than *Sex and the City*, paying closer attention to a young woman's professional efforts than to her shopping and dating. But they did not dare present real unhappiness, or real anything at all.

In the opening montage of *That Girl*, Marlo Thomas sees a twinned version of herself in a store window, and the mannequin looks down and gives her a you-go-girl wink. There is a bit of this narcissistic wink in Dunham's work, without which it might be unwatchable. And I mean unwatchable in the very best way. "You couldn't pay me enough to be twenty-four again," says Hannah's doctor, examining her patient for an STD. Dunham has teleported herself into the future in order to see herself as a survivor—a presurvivor, not yet quite survived—of a terrible time. It's what true comedic artists do.

(2012)

Wisconsin Recall

The attempt to recall Wisconsin's Governor Scott Walker (and several state legislators), which culminates in Tuesday's recall election, began two emotionally bitter winters ago. A piece of Walker-sponsored legislation known as Act 10 was put forward without much public warning: it was a proposal that, among other things, increased state employees' contribution to health care (a substantial cut in their take-home pay) and removed public workers' collective bargaining rights (an exception being made for police and firemen, who had supported Walker's campaign). Shoved forward during a February thaw, Act 10 was thought to be shrewdly if mischievously timed—a Friday!—but it backfired. The weather was sunny and warm for winter and rally organization began that weekend: Madisonians, a huge portion of whom work in some way for the public sector—not only teachers but sanitation workers, prison guards, and hospital staff—took to the street and marched on the capitol, occupying it for months, while joined by people from all over the state, as well as by Susan Sarandon and Jesse Jackson.

At that time, the protests were full of surprising unity, even between protesters and police, who would high-five one another in a friendly manner despite the cops being on duty. All was nonviolent. Farmers drove their tractors around Capitol Square, parents brought their children to show them what civil disobedience looked like, taking photos of the kids holding Recall signs. Teachable moments as family outings were everywhere. Microphones were set up, speeches were given, music was played, chants were chanted, pizza was delivered, drums were drummed. For weeks people clapped, shouted, and danced. By St. Patrick's Day the feeling of angry campout and festival was still in the air, though there were more leprechaun costumes and some of the chants had been hijacked by teenage interlopers: *Hear it loud, hear it clear, we want union rights and beer.* Nonetheless, it became a source of local civic pride that the protests seemed a direct prompt to the subsequent Occupy Wall Street Movement. Some Madisonians would claim the Arab Spring as well. Scott Walker took to wearing a bulletproof vest.

Despite the assertion by journalist David Brooks (and others) that Americans live in more like-minded communities than ever before and are therefore cut off from values and opinions at variance with their own, more than a year later Wisconsin's recall of its governor and several legislators is now said to have pitted neighbor against neighbor. It is being called "a civil war," and as in our American Civil War some family members are not talking to other family members. Despite a history of bipartisanship, people have chosen sides (as midwesterners tend to do in divorce; not for them the pseudosophisticated friends-with-all approach). Tales of confrontation abound: a driver with a RECALL WALKER bumper sticker might be tailed on the highway then passed in the adjacent lane by someone holding up a FUCK THE RECALL sign.

There have been calls for civility and healing as well as for further debate. Days before Mother's Day, on the eve of the Democratic primary to choose Walker's opponent in the recall, Kathleen Falk, the former Dane County Executive who had been one of the first candidates out there, garnering union and environmentalists' endorsements but mysteriously considered "unelectable" even by her admirers, said the state was crying out for "a mother's touch." It was not her finest moment. But when she said "a budget is a moral document" she was back on track.

The widely considered "more electable" Milwaukee mayor, Tom Barrett, who defeated Falk in the primary, has been defeated by Walker before, in the 2010 gubernatorial election, so what constitutes electability for the Democrats is a little fuzzy. Barrett was said to have run a lackluster campaign in 2010, but luster is still not his strong suit: he remains stolid and mild and intelligent, perhaps temperamentally unsuited for campaign life, though he can do fieriness if absolutely necessary. Everyone is slightly in drag: Barrett, the people's mayor of Milwaukee, is chiseled, handsome, and dignified in an almost regal way; in a rally with Bill Clinton, even while costumed in a Milwaukee Brewers jacket, the very tall, polite Barrett made the crowd-pleasing Clinton look like a raspy, wispy tough guy.

Meanwhile, Scott Walker, in public debates, looks sleepy, even a bit cross-eyed. To study his notes in a televised debate he bows his head so low that viewers see his bald spot in back. The pose looks almost like shame. But when he lifts his head up again he becomes magically fast-talking. Since Walker never graduated from college, in public settings he plays his Eagle Scout card in a way that impressed even me, though I know the Eagle Scouts boast a bunch of unlikely suspects (among them, the film director David Lynch). With Barrett and Walker facing each other down, the recall election has the look of a rematch, although Democrats have consistently said it is not. With Barrett behind in the polls, the recall also has the sad-making whiff of futility.

In phrasing handed to him by someone on his campaign, Barrett has declared himself "rock solid" while Walker is the "rock star" of the national right wing. (Walker blames the left for "starting it"— "it" being the state's affairs going national—with activist movie stars, union support, and continual media coverage last winter.) In addition to his right-wing, right-to-work policies, Walker's out-of-state speaking engagements are an issue, as is his quest for a national profile, especially since it has involved the unprecedented accrual of out-of-state cash. At another moment in time this might be a genuine sticking point in the traditional midwestern who-do-you-think-you-are? psyche, but voters may care less about Walker being a "rock star" than Barrett's campaign managers are hoping. It is not the most stirring theme to run on.

There can be a begrudging provincial respect for someone in the national eye, even if it's the eye of a storm, and of the Tea Party, and of the out-of-state billionaires who have helped fill Walker's campaign coffers, which are now up to $31 million—an unprecedented amount in Wisconsin political history. Walker, who last year fell prey to a taped prank phone call from a blogger pretending to be one of the Koch brothers, is now using Koch cash to run Willie Horton–style ads, the most recent featuring a photograph of a dead Milwaukee toddler (somehow blaming Barrett's law enforcement team).

Barrett, partly because of recall rules that limit a challenger's resources, has no such national money. But to insistently call Walker a "rock star" may exalt Walker more than is understood by the Barrett campaign, which is hoping for the mythic Wisconsin wholesomeness to prevail at the polls. Certainly corruption seems to surround Walker and he has a criminal defense fund already in place—the first time a sitting governor has ever had one. Rumors of indictments are in the air, regarding both Walker's time as Milwaukee County executive and his current use of state moneys. But many people in self-contradictory Wisconsin, the home of both the Progressive Party and Joe McCarthy, may not care very deeply about the charges against Walker.

As the state struggles financially, and Walker and his Republican henchmen in the legislature attempt to bestow both tax and environmental breaks on "job-creating" open-pit mining companies, while rejecting $810 million of Obama stimulus money for a high-speed train, the town-gown-style split that has always existed along various fault lines across the state has reemerged, this time cutting through small-town neighborhoods, Indian tribal land, and even academic departments. Wisconsin has long been considered a collective of liberal college communities connected by interstates crisscrossing the farmland. But especially with the rise of suburban sprawl, it has become much more unpredictable than that.

If Walker wins, the sorrow of so much grass-roots political effort coming to naught will be profound. From "Obama Nation to Abomination" quipped local radio-show host Michael Feldman, though the extent to which the recall election is also a referendum on the Obama presidency is unclear. A June election, its timing determined by recall rules, is not a November one. Over 100,000 students have dispersed for the academic year—many are out of state for the summer; some entering freshmen have yet to turn eighteen. Wisconsin has a long history as a swing state: in 2000 Al Gore won it by only 6,000 votes, and if Florida had been successfully contested, Bush was going to demand a Wisconsin recount; in 2004 John Kerry took Wisconsin by only 16,000.

Despite this, and despite the Republican legislature's newly stringent voter ID laws, Wisconsin could still be Obama's. But it won't be the comfortable margin of 2008. Well, the whole world is watching— sort of. If only the whole state were voting.

(2012)

Richard Ford's *Canada*

Richard Ford is a writer of jangling personal fascination to many in the literary world. Charming and charmed, he is an embodiment of interesting and intimidating contradictions: a southern childhood, a midwestern education, a restless adulthood occurring not just in New York and New Jersey but in seemingly every state whose name begins with *M* (or *L*). Brief stints in law school and the Marines (and an application to the CIA). Wanderlust and a knack for real estate. The Irish-American southerner's gift of gab. The belligerent responses to book reviews, the poor spelling, the beautiful French, the mercurial temperament, the indelible child characters from someone with no children at all. He cuts a transfixing figure for even an ordinary reader's curiosity: the book-jacket photographs with their silvery bronze patina suggesting a pale-eyed cattle rustler, his laser-blue gaze smudged simultaneously with apprehension and derring-do, a Tin Woodman tint evoking a man of metal and mettle, in sorrowful quest of his forgotten heart.

When, in 2008, Ford left his publisher, Knopf (which was the original publisher of four of his books, although not even the first four), for HarperCollins, news of his departure was reported on the front page of the *Times*'s Arts section. Such is the swirl around the man, even as the work itself, at its best, is pure vocal grace, quiet humor, precise and calm observation. And so, in a time when the novels of even his most brilliant contemporaries are often fleet and attenuated, the telltale sign of waning energies or multibook publishing contracts, a hearty meal of a novel from Richard Ford, even if it *is* titled *Canada,* represents a warm moment in American letters.

Opening in Montana in 1960, *Canada* is a story told by Dell Parsons, the son of a retired Air Force pilot and a schoolteacher—parents who have turned hapless bank robbers, and who are quickly apprehended and sent to jail. Dell also has a twin sister, named Berner. "Berner and I were fraternal twins—she was six minutes older—and looked nothing alike." (Twins who are not the same sex are always fraternal, not identical: that a narrator would stop to explain this is unfortunate and a mistake, perhaps of the proofreading variety, which it would be good no longer to see in a novel.) The narrative proceeds in the perfectly melded voice of the adult Dell, who is now a retired English teacher, and the fifteen-year-old Dell, who has witnessed his family break apart forever. It is a prairie America of box elders and elms not yet done in by beetles. The deer and the antelope play, or sort of. Families are presumed to be solid, although they are put together in a hurry.

The narrative moves leisurely, as Dell ponders why his parents embarked on their foolhardy robbery: his father had gotten into an illegal business deal with local Cree Indians; he then needed money and feared for his children's lives. The narrator's mind churns and circles, like a buzzard over a corpse. Young Dell is a budding chess player, and he has learned patience in contemplating the moves of others: "Each one was sacrificing something—a strength—to achieve an advance toward a goal." The family has lived a peripatetic existence, moving from airbase to airbase. Dell has learned from his mother, who is Jewish, and who fears and disparages these communities, to keep his distance, to absorb profound breaks in his life, and to understand that everything one loves can be taken away, and that one must register and contemplate facts and meanings later, in a spirit of acceptance. As indeed both mother and son do in a literary fashion by the story's heartbreaking close. "Things happen when people are not where they belong," Dell also learns.

If one is looking for a powerful through line of suspense and drama, one will not find it in this book; instead, one must take a more scenic and meditative trip. There are novels that are contraptions, configured like cages, traps, or flypaper, to catch things and hold them. *Canada* is more contrary: searching and spliced open and self-interrupted by its short, slicing chapters, then carried along again by a stream of brooding from a son and brother with a hundred questions and only a few answers. Looking back, Dell references Ruskin—"Composition is the arrangement of unequal things"—and the idea is given large significance at the novel's beginning and at its end.

Dell's measuring of facts and reconsidering of criminal events may remind one of William Maxwell's novella "So Long, See You Tomorrow," but Dell Parsons is also reminiscent of the sixteen-year-old Joe Brinson of Ford's 1990 novel *Wildlife;* those two teenage boys have 1960 Great Falls, Montana, in common, as well as a desire to explore one's own culpability in family life gone bad and to examine the foibles and cracked wisdom of vain and damaging older men. Ford's Canada, where Dell is smuggled from Montana by a family friend after his parents are arrested and his sister runs away (not to be seen again by Dell for fifty years), is a swatch of Saskatchewan whose frontier-saturated qualities have elements in common with the improvised set of Robert Altman's *McCabe & Mrs. Miller,* where the nineteenth century rushes headlong and ramshackle into the twentieth, and people's hobbies and outfits and demeanors seem to derive from every decade imaginable, like a modern-day opera.

The place is a sanctuary for exactly the sorts of desperadoes who recur in Ford's fiction. These men, including the more upstanding ones in his Frank Bascombe trilogy (*The Sportswriter, Independence Day, The Lay of the Land*), often seem on the lam from things that require clarification and pondering. Ford has long made dissection of a certain unsavoriness part of his skill as a writer—he can parse spoiled masculinity like the finest of feminists—most famously in the widely anthologized short stories "Rock Springs" and "Communist." A boy's experience of adult carelessness has often been his subject. As Dell says of his parents, "They were always running from the past, and didn't look back at much if they could help it, and whose whole life always lay somewhere in the offing." That simultaneously acute and blunt anatomy, as in "Communist" and *Wildlife,* performed by a young man observing his elders, often involves the witnessing of gratuitous cruelty: "We saw three magpies pecking a snake as it hurried to get across the pavement.

Our father swerved and ran over it, which made two thump-bumps under the tires and the magpies fly up."

When Dell is put to work with a wild-goose gutter in the Saskatchewan hunting trade, under the care of a character with traces of makeup on his face and the terrific name of Charley Quarters, he is given more such men to contemplate. Quarters is perhaps the most vivid:

"So did you hear all about me?" Charley Quarters said. We were rattling along through the dark in his old International Harvester. . . . His truck stank of beer and gasoline and the same strong sour-sweet stinging odor I didn't recognize. . . .

Charley was even stranger in the daylight—his knobby head larger, his shoulders unnaturally narrow, his legs bandied out at the knees where his boots stopped, his black hair still clutched back with his rhinestone barrette.

One of Dell's few breaks from this life of goose butchering is an interlude where, in a poignant longing to go to school, he rides his bike out of town to one he has heard about, finding himself at what turns out to be a Catholic home for wayward girls. This allows Ford to set up a sharp, memorable scene straight out of the world of Alice Munro:

"What do you think you're here to do?" the tall, older-looking girl said in a hard, unfriendly way, as if she wanted me to leave. Her long body loosened up when she spoke. She cocked her hip, as if she expected me to say something smart back, like Berner would've done.

"I just came out to see the school," I said. . . .

"You're not allowed in here," the nice girl with the skinny arm said. She smiled at me again, though I could tell it wasn't friendly. It was sarcastic. One of her side-front teeth was gone and a space was dark inside her mouth, which ruined her nice smile. Both girls had bitten-down fingernails and scratches on their arms and measly bumps around their mouths, and hair on their legs, like mine. . . .

"What's your name?" the smaller girl with the skinny arm said.

I gripped the handlebar and set my foot on the pedal, ready to push off. "Dell," I said. . . .

"Dell's a monkey's name where I come from. Shaunavon, Saskatchewan," the older girl said, unbothered by the nun who was quickly approaching. The girl suddenly reached her long arm farther through the gap in the bars and fastened a terrible grip on my wrist, which I tried to get away from but couldn't. She began pulling me, while the other girl laughed. I was tipping sideways, my right leg and just my shoe heel holding me up, but beginning to fall.

"Don't touch them," the nun was shouting. I wasn't touching anybody.

"He's afraid of us," the smaller girl said and started walking away, leaving the older girl imprisoning me through the bars. . . . "I want to make a man out of you," she said. "Or make a mess."

The novel contains two or three thrillingly written set pieces, and this is one of them. They are part of several lessons Dell learns about acceptance—something that his mother once tried to teach him— though what he really learns is passive resilience with a chess player's field awareness, something that his mother, who kills herself in jail, turns out not to have as much of as her twin children.

There is a story about John Cheever that was once told at Yaddo by a painter in residency there. She was sitting next to Cheever discussing upstate New York, and told him, "Last year, I went to Cohoes to buy shoes with Hortense." "Oh, what a wonderful sentence!" he exclaimed. *I went to Cohoes to buy shoes with Hortense!* At which point the painter thanked her lucky stars that she wasn't a writer, since she had no idea what was remotely lovely about that sentence.

Richard Ford's *Canada* may be a similar experience, though his focus is on a different America from Cheever's, and his lyricism is the reverse of, say, Nabokov's tight, pebble-hearted poetry. Ford's language is of the cracked, open spaces and their corresponding places within. A certain musicality and alertness is required of the reader; one has to hear it instinctively and rhythmically.

> In the night when I got up to use the toilet, I found my father alone at the card table with his Niagara Falls puzzle spread out like a meal in front of him.

> Ripe wheat stood to the road verges, yellow and thick and rocking in the hot dry breeze that funneled dust through our car windows and left my lips coated.

> After that we saw a big coyote in the road with a rabbit in its mouth.

> His complexion looked orangish and roughed up with acne whelps and he had a band-aid on his neck.

The beauty of these sentences may have to do precisely with Dell's referencing of Ruskin: "Composition is the arrangement of unequal things." "Card table" and "Niagara Falls." "Road" and "lips." "Coyote" and "rabbit." "Roughed up" and "band-aid." Arranging variety is also what the young chess player learns as he proceeds; not every component has the same powers, but they are offered up in combination with purpose, bluff, and patience. "Loneliness, I've read, is like being in a long line," Dell notes, "waiting to reach the front where it's promised something good will happen." The world of Ford's *Canada* is full of impulsivity, self-hypnotics, and gambits that do not pay off. But some do. The "ACTUAL BONNIE & CLYDE DEATH CAR—WILL PAY $10,000 IF YOU PROVE IT'S NOT," an attraction that the young Dell sees with his father, in Biloxi, Mississippi, and contemplates again at the novel's end, may be as eloquent as Ruskin or chess in its bleakly sly statement about the arrangement of things. Ford himself has placed it there.

(2012)

Ethan Canin's "The Palace Thief"

There is a kind of long, fate-obsessed story of which Ethan Canin has become an American master. His accomplished handling of time—sometimes seeming to take a life in its entirety, exploding then knitting it together slightly out of sequence to better reveal the true meaning of an experience—results in fictions of tremendous depth, wisdom, and architectural complexity.

In "The Palace Thief," narrative time is woven whole by the slightly mournful voice of a man looking back at the debilitating confines of his life. He is like a monk in a moral hair shirt, sitting on the edge of an extremely narrow (Procrustean?) bed. Images of cells, prisons, slavery show up in the story to underscore the service to the rich and powerful that has constituted not just this man's livelihood but his entire spiritual existence. His lack of self-pity is a kind of blind spot—and the sly coincidence of his expertise in Ancient Rome is not lost on the reader. Canin does not sentimentalize his protagonist and make him more respected, admired, or powerful than he is. The story keeps the ruling class in their golden palaces and will not allow into the story the reassuring sop that the rich do not always win—or anything that would let us imagine that. (One sometimes forgets that, in the tale of David and Goliath, David quickly becomes a figure of power and might: not here, where the smallness of one man remains so no matter what authorial fondness is draped upon him.) It is Melville of whom we may be reminded: "Bartleby, the Scrivener" or *Billy Budd* or "Benito Cereno" is perhaps the model, especially in Canin's examination of ironic or quietly inverted hierarchies within the workplace. Canin lets his narrator look behind the images and events that may prompt our awe, especially those attached to power and social class but also those attached to service, devotion, the enforcement of justice—not to leave them smashed and demolished but to reassemble them with a tempered and diminished faith. By the end the story allows us to see even more than its protagonist and narrator can.

The class divide between the rich and their educators has been remarked upon for centuries, and the unworldliness of schoolteachers, from Miss Jean Brodie to Mr. Chips, is hardly without literary precedent. But all is a trickier task in shorter form. And what it means to be an American teacher of the privileged in the twentieth century has its own particulars, angles, and puzzles. The compression of this long story summing up not just one life but several is an ingenious accomplishment. Moreover, it contains Canin's special skill at mixing public and private events—part of the national experience too often ignored by our writers. Canin's fiction is always a construction of vital surprise, what the literary critic James Wood has called "livingness," set forth in perfectly textured prose. He is interested in the moment when a person's life turns, or his destiny is defied, or his character is revealed or anatomized for the inexplicable thing it is. He makes time rush forward like Gatsby's car or Ahab's ship, while his men remain children in the bodies of the old. It is heartbreaking business and, here, in "The Palace Thief," expertly done.

(2012)

Homeland

One of the intriguing aspects of the gripping and widely praised Show-time drama *Homeland,* a story about the machinations of CIA counterterrorism analysts and their prey, is that it is fearlessly interested in every kind of madness: the many Shakespearean manifestations—cold revenge, war-induced derangement, outsize professional ambition—as well as the more naturally occurring expressions, such as bipolar disease and simple grief. *Homeland* ruthlessly pits these psychic states against one another in different permutations and settings, like contestants in *The Hunger Games,* to see which will win, which will die, which will kill or be killed, which will bond or marry or breed or starve.

Homeland's opening credits show images of the burning towers of the World Trade Center, and its initial season ends with a young woman being strapped to a medical table and fitted with a bite plate so she can undergo electroconvulsive therapy. There is your spectrum. That later in the second season this same young woman will be quizzed about this experience with hostility, curiosity, and flirtatious compassion by a torture victim is one of the many gladiatorial moments of psychological derring-do this series has to offer. Its writers go out on limb after limb and seem unfrightened not just of loose ends and blind alleys but of out-and-out nuttiness both as subject and as method. Madness is as madness does.

Homeland's star is the brave Claire Danes depicting the brave Carrie Mathison, whose bipolar disorder is a secret she is trying to keep from the CIA (which would withdraw her security clearance if it knew) and whose second-guessing and sixth sense (the hunch sense) make her a kind of drug-sniffing dog for the counterterrorism unit that employs her. (People who do their work fully, and the only way they know how, are often apprehensive about being called brave, as if their underwear were showing or life-threatening spinach were in their every smile. Danes nonetheless has put vanity aside for this performance. Compare her with the always pretty analyst played by Jessica Chastain in *Zero Dark Thirty*.) The pressured speech and flights of ideas that are symptoms of the character's disease are also useful in elaborate detective work, since really only an obsessive and insomniac can puzzle it all the way through.

The most visually arresting image of both *Homeland* seasons thus far does not involve a single gun or explosive or death of any sort but is a bulletin board whose color-coded components are created by Carrie through days of mania, and are decoded, understood, and assembled like a piece of installation art by her mentor, Saul Berenson (Mandy Patinkin), when she is yanked off her project. Seeing the camera pull back on this decorated corkboard is like watching a world come to light.

Carrie's ten-year search for the al-Qaeda terrorist Abu Nazir takes her directly toward a recently rescued Marine sergeant, a handsome redhead named Nicholas Brody (Damian Lewis), who was a prisoner of war in Afghanistan. Carrie suspects that his long stint as a prisoner means he was turned by Nazir and has come back home to wreak havoc on his own soil. Her colleagues—at least in the first season—are not buying it. Except for Saul Berenson, who is more persuadable, since he knows that Carrie is exceptional at what she does. (Patinkin's performance is superb but he does not hide his Broadway roots: a simple knock on Carrie's door has more than a little ragtime in it; each carefully pitched syllable he utters is pegged to a note, and as his voice climbs and moves emotionally he sometimes seems to be singing. When Saul says to Carrie, "You're the smartest and the dumbest fucking person I've ever known," he delivers this potentially throwaway line with such concentration, restraint, and theatricality that it becomes the most dramatic utterance thus far in the entire series.)

Also exceptional is Damian Lewis as Brody—at least in the first season. As the homecoming Marine he adroitly portrays the military veteran's vexed reentry to America, not just with trembling and vomiting but with nuanced glance and grit, even as his every move is being monitored by the CIA. In one of the show's perverse switchbacks, early on Carrie watches the surveillance footage of Brody and his wife in their bedroom, and by the second season is herself in bed with Brody and a subject of the surveillance that her colleagues observe in mortified fashion. Entering the footage she was once just monitoring is part of a motif of pornographic fantasy that haphazardly peppers the script. One of Carrie's CIA "assets," a sex worker from Sandusky, Ohio, arranges lovers for a Saudi prince; in another story thread Brody is asked to kill someone he believes he has already killed. Enactments and reenactments abound.

When Brody walks through the bright plastic aisles of an American hardware store, the viewer can share his experience of the shop's gaudy abundance. He is looking for a doormat that might work as a prayer rug. He has converted to Islam, a fact he must keep hidden from everyone he knows. He has become a public relations pawn: the military brass would like him to play the hero card and redeploy; the White House would like him to play the hero card and run for Congress; Abu Nazir would like him to play the hero card and put on a suicide vest to take revenge for the U.S. military drone program that has killed Afghan citizens.

Brody's return to his home is juxtaposed with flashbacks to the physical and psychological torture and the emotional manipulations he endured at the hands of Nazir. Here *Homeland*'s editors and camera crew do some of their best work. We see Brody forced brutally to assault his friend and fellow Marine Tom Walker, and to dig his own grave. These heartbreaking scenes are some of the most devastating in the entire show. Even upon multiple viewings, when you have new information that allows for a reinterpretation of events, the scenes retain their awful power. The intercut flashbacks also efficiently reveal Brody's life through the years as the tutor of Nazir's young son, who is then killed in a drone attack. This attack is the event out of which almost everything we watch is born, and to this extent *Homeland* can be viewed as a criticism not just of cyclical revenge in general but of the

American drone program in particular. Mandy Patinkin, who feels the show is strongly pacifist, has even been on talk shows discussing the evenhanded politics of *Homeland*'s scripts.

In *Homeland*'s second season the editors are so overloaded with plot threads and have to make such quick cuts that there are several inadvertently funny U-turns and the narrative becomes perilously head-spinning and surreal. But in Season 1's opening episodes all is well, and the series's debt to its model, the Israeli television program *Prisoners of War,* is presumably expressed, though that program is otherwise unavailable in the United States.

Watching Brody through the eyes of his daughter, Dana, brilliantly played by Morgan Saylor, can also be interesting. Despite his eight-year absence, this teenage girl is Brody's true soul mate, much more so than his bombshell of a wife, who seems always to be stuck with lines like "I don't understand. What is happening?" Dana is the person who stands next to him in the first Yellow Ribbon press photo. She is the one he puts his arm around. She is the one who first sees him praying—and understands it. Her intuitive knowledge of her dad becomes important in unraveling certain pieces of information, especially in the extremely jammed Season 2 finale, which concludes the way a giant fireworks show concludes: with everyone dazed and caught in traffic.

In this finale two American characters played so perfectly by British actors whose accents never slip—Damian Lewis as Brody and David Harewood as David Estes, the CIA counterterrorism director—are zapped from the narrative, one to a mysterious freighter in international waters, and one to the afterlife, as if the actors' visas had expired. The carnage is preposterous, and getting the show back on more convincing psychological territory will be the task of Season 3. This is where the daughter will have to be relied on, as she is perhaps the only person in her father's several worlds who has surmised who he is in all of them, and so she is a repository of viewer confidence. She will certainly remain one, at the very least as a kind of psychic and interpreter. It's satisfying to see her brought forward in the story lines—even if her younger brother is getting ominously left behind—and one feels a serious actress's career is in the making.

. . .

The main problem with *Homeland* is not even the writers taking Adderall or whatever they did in the second season that eliminated suspense and brought instead an unhinged intensity of movement that barely allowed space and time enough for the cast members to occupy their roles. The main problem with the show is a kind of elephant in the room. Written into several important plot points is the "love" Brody and Carrie have for each other. For this "love," she will hide him from the authorities. For this "love," he will kill the vice president (although he is also doing this somewhat for his daughter's spurned sense of justice and for the drone-killed son of Nazir; there is a convergence and confusion of motives in this terrific murder scene, which is done through distanced technology involving a pacemaker—an echo of the drone strike for which the vice president is responsible).

The problem with the Brody-Carrie "love" is that it is unconvincing, and it is unconvincing for many reasons having to do with common sense. But that is not all. Awkward and unlikely love can be trumped by genuine sparks. But viewers will sense a lack of chemistry between Lewis and Danes, two otherwise gifted performers. Perhaps the editing is too abrupt—one minute there is shouting and despair, the next there is smiling in a cozy cottage. Good on-screen chemistry can win out, but these actors project only a cold canned heat.

Is this because their characters are damaged goods, too jangled inside and too full of apprehension to create the trust and stillness that romance requires, qualities Brody's friend Mike has in spades, especially around Brody's wife? When Lewis goes to touch Danes's face, we fear he may strangle her. When Danes smiles at him it looks effortful, mere flirtation or perhaps even nervousness. When Brody says to her in their final scene, "You gave it up to me," and Carrie adds, "Completely," few viewers will agree.

Almost every character in this show has been a double agent of some sort, but especially Carrie and Brody. Yet a double agent may also have a purity of purpose that operating solo allows: you can pick and choose who is worthy of hate and who is worthy of help. A double agent can crawl out of the ideological teamwork and love the forbidden, which both Carrie and Brody have done. A double agent can determine independently who is a "bad guy"—as does Special Ops Agent Quinn, looking very IRA and defying his orders to assassinate Brody—since every belief system has some. But shared torment is not enough for love between spies. Quinn, too, seems to believe in the Carrie-Brody love, but only when viewing it through a sniper's scope. All of *Homeland*'s characters are soldiers and soldierly, but they are also players in a game where the cards are thrown down ever more quickly and no one really has your back. Friendly fire can occur at any moment. This is too tense-making for what purports to be a love story.

Moreover, is madness times two ever sexy? It is perhaps useful to compare these *Homeland* lovers with those in the current David O. Russell film, *Silver Linings Playbook,* where Jennifer Lawrence and Bradley Cooper generate quite a bit of sparkle despite both their characters being mentally ill. Of course, *Silver Linings* is a comedy and has dancing in it—a surefire cinematic express train to romantic love. Cooper and Lawrence may snarl and shout but they still seem like attractive screwballs in their own sexually charged tale, which just happens to be a screwball comedy.

Give Danes and Lewis a country cabin, a roaring fire, and a bottle of wine, and we feel only anxiety. The confessing of life secrets seems therapeutic and expository rather than intimate, and Carrie's irritated "You interrupted me" startles before the hearth. Creepy cello music in the background does nothing to assist. Perhaps their conversation has too much storytelling to do—it is almost always propelling the plot along—and the sideways moves of courtly dillydally and pillow talk can find little opportunity or conviction. One of the final dialogues between Carrie and Brody includes this exchange about Nazir:

> "He played us all from the beginning."
> "How? By letting himself get killed?"
> "Why not?"
> "Because it's insane."

Insane, indeed. In the bonus feature that follows on the box set, the producer Alex Gansa refers to them as "star-crossed lovers" in the grip of a "powerful love." But this is not true: they lack mutual trust or any palpable erotic vibe. They are not bonded and they part without any persuasive anguish—or, rather, they briefly cling then separate, their anguish only sketchily enacted. There won't be a damp eye in the house. Carrie and Brody's love is in a film noir, while they themselves are in a television series.

But Brody has been sent off to Canada so that the writers can figure out what to do next. All is in a state of disconclusion, and Season 3 awaits. Carrie will return to her true partner, her closest colleague, Saul, who, as he recites the kaddish before a roomful of corpses, has the look of new ambiguity to him: even though he cannot pass a single polygraph test, he has become the acting head of the CIA. As was said to many Americans after September 11, "You are all in Israel now." Or maybe not. Presumably the show will continue to take received ideas and transform them. It may still fall short of art, but stay tuned. It is likely to continue to shatter viewers' expectations and then glue them back together again, half-cracked.

(2013)

Jane Campion's *Top of the Lake*

Jane Campion's police procedural *Top of the Lake*—a miniseries that aired this spring on Sundance Channel and is now available on Netflix—has the look of transcendence and the theme of sexual postapocalypse. The catastrophe that is men and the different catastrophe that is women are foregrounded against the romantic sublime—breathtaking and perhaps occasionally computer-enhanced locations in New Zealand, shot unmockingly by the Australian cinematographer Adam Arkapaw (who also shot the crime drama *Animal Kingdom*). The landscape gives Campion's tragic ironies and bone-dry comedy a little something spiritual upstage, like a humming chorus. Part *Deliverance,* part *Road Warrior,* part *Winter's Bone,* part *Hobbit*—as well as part Old Testament and part New—*Top of the Lake* creates, in spite of its self-aware collaging, something quite original in this harsh, lush South Pacific. For Americans unfamiliar with this fantastical backdrop, it may in its initial minutes seem to be Japan or British Columbia, with high mountains plummeting dizzyingly to water. It is hard at first to tell *where this is.* One is reminded of Ava Gardner's (probably apocryphal) comment on arriving in Melbourne to film *On the Beach.* "I'm here to make a film about the end of the world," she is said to have told the press as she glanced around, "and this seems to be exactly the right place for it."

Although much of the patchworked story occurs in a small town where the Southern Lakes police have a station and desks and look at files and interrogate witnesses in an aggressive fashion, Campion is interested primarily in two adjacent communities—one of women and one of men—both of which have gone off the grid. These communities consist of refuseniks of the libertarian and sexual variety, staked out against modernity, supporting their lifestyles with illegal activities (in the case of the men) and divorce settlements (in the case of the women). Using a dozen or so shipping containers, a string of outdoor lights, and a generator, the women have set up a desert sanctuary—on a plot of land called (thank you, Toni Morrison) Paradise. There are massages, meditation and hairstyling sessions, support discussions, and naked Gauguin-style swimming, plus a pseudoguru named GJ, played with crisp, enigmatic derision by Holly Hunter. Under GJ's guidance, the group's consciousness is not so much raised as smacked around. She believes in biology as the primary teacher of her flock. "Just go with the body!" she goads them, letting it be known that she despises their minds. The women who have followed GJ here are recovering addicts of various kinds. They include Bunny, who pays men to have seven minutes' worth of sex with her, and Anita, from Syracuse, New York, who is getting over the grief of having had to euthanize her best friend, a violent and possessive chimpanzee. GJ is a figure of mysterious magnetism and caprice. She has picked the settlement's location totally at random, closing her eyes and putting her finger on a map. Campion does not overuse her, which makes her every appearance in the series riveting.

The men, on the other hand, are the local lugs. Sometimes seen in the dartboard-decorated pub, the younger ones occasionally communicate in animal sounds: they are largely the motherless sons of the area's de facto patriarch, a drug dealer named Matt Mitcham, who, as a major landowner, controls the area's law enforcement and seems to have sired half the town's population. (The threat of incest lies everywhere in Campion's story line.)

The mesmerizing Scottish actor Peter Mullan plays Mitcham as a bellicose aging hippie gun-nut anarchist, one with an inexplicable brogue. Like all great villains, he controls the series as he controls the community: with charisma and bullying. That he is rough-and-tumble handsome makes the viewer's response to him all the more uneasy. One may find oneself hoping that a good-looking man depicted washing a dish or two, as he is, won't turn out to be completely evil. Mitcham also regularly flogs himself with a belt, stripped to the waist and on his knees, before his mother's gravestone. He holds the series together through sheer force of personality, and the moment he appears by surprise, mid-lake, from below the deck of a large motorboat is one of the most hair-raising screen/scream moments since Jessica Walter emerged from the next room as the new apartment mate in Clint Eastwood's *Play Misty for Me*. When Mullan as Mitcham is absent, Campion's world grows safer, less full of dread, and less interesting. Even in the final episode of the series, when his ostensible cremains are placed triumphantly on a tabletop, they possess the feeling of a genie in a bottle.

Elisabeth Moss does serviceable work as the dewy-skinned detective Robin Griffin, who comes to town to visit her dying mother and escape a fiancé about whom she is ambivalent. Like the other women, she is there for a "bit of a think," as she puts it to Al, a local police sergeant, on one of their several dates—but soon she is investigating the disappearance of a pregnant twelve-year-old named Tui, who happens to be (what else?) the daughter of Matt Mitcham. When asked who the father of her baby is, Tui writes on a scrap of paper "No one." Tui's confusion as to how she became pregnant is less diffidence or ignorance or a virgin-birth allusion than a real clue to solving the case. Alas, it is continually misinterpreted. As in most police procedurals, each step forward by the detective is at a diagonal, so each hunch is at once astute, revealing, and slightly inaccurate. Because the path to answers is zigzagging and in constant need of correction, and because Campion has seven episodes to fill, there is room for detour. Sexually violent backstories are ignited (Griffin, we discover, was gang-raped at a high school prom and subsequently had a child of her own); new characters come to town and earlier ones disappear; blind alleys are run up, with or without canine assistance. A face-concealing blue hoodie becomes the most plot-pointed hoodie since the red one used to terrifying effect in Nicolas Roeg's *Don't Look Now*. Like Roeg's Venice, Campion's town is an insular maze with plenty of secrets, as well as a built-in idea that no one is really watching. Many of its residents, however, have fled. Or have tried. Or would like to. But if one has a legal conviction, like Robin's ambiguous love interest and former prom date, Johnno (also Mitch's son), one cannot even escape to Australia, which of course long ago was once solely for convicts. The sense of *nowhere to go* is accentuated by the encasement of mountains. If one cannot flee, however, there are places to hide in the surrounding bush, tents to pitch, and birdsong to learn as a summons for food and allies, as in *The Hunger Games*—another tale of corruption and exploitation in the literal and moral wilderness.

Not for nothing is short-haired, blue-eyed Elisabeth Moss made to look a lot like Kyle MacLachlan of David Lynch's anti-*Brigadoon*, *Twin Peaks*. Campion alludes to Lynch not just via Moss or the many cinematic peaks but most explicitly in a scene where Moss pulls over a vanload of women and asks where they are going.

"Book club," they lie.

"Oh, whatcha reading?" she asks.

There is silence, then someone says, *"Blue Velvet."*

Moss persists. "Didn't know it was a book. Who wrote it?"

A woman growls, "We don't care."

It is the funniest homage in the series, and because Campion herself wrote the novelization of her 1993 film, *The Piano*, the humor goes in several directions at once. The scene also may express some tossed-off cynicism about contemporary readers and the sororal dependence on language activities. For the series's societal dropouts, words are seldom useful or true; the survivalist tactics of listening closely to one's body and not talking too much are always paramount. The result is an oddly quiet production. Even GJ, the gnomic pronouncer of the body's superiority to the mind—"Disillusionment! Get that and get it good!" she advises; "Stop your helping"—grows tired of the streaming thoughts of the "crazy bitches" she has attracted, and by the end diverts herself with curt inquiries to an assistant about the best air routes to Reykjavík and the current price of gold. One is reminded of a line Hunter delivered playing a producer in *Broadcast News:* told that it must be nice to feel you're the smartest person in the room, she replies, "No, it's awful."

Those who have seen *The Piano*, another tale of New Zealand, may feel clued in to Campion's directorial coding. Tattoos suggest a nurturing man, and conventional appearances, societal authority, and middle-class righteousness are likely to obscure sadism. (The men whom Griffin and her mother love are prominently tattooed.) New Age keyboard arpeggios signify a transient meditative state. And speech—

its misuses and deformations, its futility and taint—is an object of deep suspicion. This despite Campion's wonderful film *Bright Star,* about the poet John Keats. (Although poetry, too, it might be argued, is about verbal inadequacy, the ineffable as it struggles into analogue.)

Perhaps Campion's skepticism about language is one of the reasons she has thrown in so many incongruous accents. (Holly Hunter played a mute in *The Piano;* her voice-over was in an invented accent heard only by the audience.) When Elisabeth Moss's accent wobbles, her character is said to have been living in Sydney. When GJ speaks in Holly Hunter's tight-lipped Georgian sibilants, she is said to be "a Swiss national." Though hilarious, this explanation is uttered deadpan and received matter-of-factly, as if this far corner of the earth were routinely visited by such global runaways. Matt Mitcham's Scottish trill-gargle-bray goes unremarked completely.

This eclecticism of vocal style has been used by others. In Terrence Malick's *Days of Heaven,* though Linda Manz was playing a girl from Chicago, her Brooklyn-accented voice-over never threw the viewer out of the film for a minute (that what she was saying often contradicted what was on the screen only increased the narrative richness). And no man from Wisconsin ever spoke as Daniel Day-Lewis did in Paul Thomas Anderson's *There Will Be Blood.* But Campion clearly believes that certain "mistakes," rather than remove us from the story, pull us further into its power; irrealism can add not only to the dream logic—the "movieness"—of the movie but also to its convincing magic, since such incongruities are often part of life. "The confusing signals, the impurity of the signal, gives you verisimilitude," Donald Barthelme once said.

The most haunting and heartbreaking parts of *Top of the Lake* have to do with mothers and sons; this is the relationship Campion's story most believes in. What few examples she offers of such relationships are suffused with the deep devotion, hope, and remorse that constitute love. One mother-son bond involves the drug-addicted Simone (terrifically acted by Mirrah Foulkes) and her bone-collecting semi-mute son, Jamie (played by Luke Buchanan), also a friend of Tui's. Jamie is employed by the local coffee shop, where at-risk kids are put to work as baristas. At first the clean and orderly café seems familiar and neutral; adult characters repeatedly assemble there to drink coffee and discuss

Tui's case. But slowly the shop, modeled on a Danish initiative to assist troubled teens, becomes a character, with its own unspoken lines. Its walls, lined with photos of the local children, begin to stare back at our detective, much like her own working wall of suspects' photos. It all casts a freckled light on the idea that it takes a village to raise a child, suggesting that a village may widen the possibility of things going wrong. (One hears the echo of GJ's "Stop your helping.") In seeking answers, Campion's tale finally has few places to turn. One may think back on *Wild Kingdom* if not *Animal Kingdom,* and on the suspense of animal appetites: Will the submerged crocodile eat its mate right there in the water, or graze on the tender gazelles onshore? The natural world at the top of the lake is all emerald moss and sexy fog. But humans, as they always do, add drugs and guns and money and violence.

Top of the Lake is not especially didactic, despite criticisms that Campion is programmatic and thus predictable in her take on dangerous men and wounded women. And despite the strictures of a medium that demands intermittent commercial breaks and a piled-up finale, and despite story questions that might easily be answered by DNA tests but are instead scuttled by quick cremations, *Top of the Lake* is a complex and spooky work of art. Campion uses her storytelling tools loosely but laceratingly; cold steam rises from the plot holes. She, her cast, and her crew give felt life to the world's vast variety of creature and tone, fashioning an experience no viewer could have possibly dreamed up alone. This is what television at its collaborative best is supposed to do.

(2013)

Blue Is the Warmest Color

Can a moviegoer set academic theory aside and still ask, What is the cinematic male gaze, and is it so very different from the female one? Is the camera inherently masculine, a powerful instrument of anxiety, and lust, forever casting women as objects? (The phallic pen has never once deterred a woman writer.) And when is a gaze not a gaze but some-thing else—something prurient or false or constructed as if through a rifle sight or, as one filmmaker friend of mine has said, "as something to be viewed in the safety of a dark theater"? Moreover, is "gazing," with its fraught exile and exiling, what a camera should be doing any-way? Shouldn't the camera instead be trying to get past the gazeness of its gaze—that is, its condition of exclusion—and engage with the observed, knitting together an alliance between viewer and viewed? Is looking necessarily a form of desire? Of covetousness or envy? Was not the ultimate male gazer Hans Christian Andersen's poor Little Match Girl?

These are questions inadvertently raised by Abdellatif Kechiche's recent Palme d'Or–winning film, *La Vie d'Adèle,* nuttily translated into *Blue Is the Warmest Color* for Anglophone audiences. (In partial expla-nation, the graphic novel the film is somewhat based on is called, in French, *Blue Is a Warm Color.*) The film is not blue in the emotional or pornographic sense. Nonetheless, its brilliant star, Adèle Exarchopou-los, portraying a girl also named Adèle (suggesting coauthorship of the character; also Arabic for "justice," and we do see her in one political march), plays her throughout in a fluctuating state of low-level depression. And the movie's protracted sex scenes, which feature two young, athletic actresses (Exarchopoulos and Léa Seydoux) with perfect bodies (when their characters visit an art museum to look at the nudes, it presents an opportunity to glimpse, albeit in marble and oil, some actual figure flaws), have proven a source of controversy, wherein critics have both employed the terms "pornography" and "male gaze" (*Salon* et al.) and deliberately avoided them (Manohla Dargis et al.). The film has already been banned in one Idaho theater, a fun fact that is getting a lot of press.

Largely what is wrong with Kechiche's overdirected ecstatic sex scenes is artistic; they go on too long and are emotionally uninformative, almost comedically ungainly and dull to watch, as most long sex scenes are. (Did we learn nothing from Vivien Leigh's little morning-after smile in *Gone With the Wind*? There are more elegant and succinct ways of communicating coital satiety than perspiring and exhausted flesh.) These scenes in *Blue Is the Warmest Color* constitute an almost fatal narrative mistake. Cinematic sex (unlike pillow talk, and that includes the pillow talk here, as well as that of Rock Hudson and Doris Day) is not all that fascinating because it is not all that shareable. What is being experienced by the characters is not something that can be felt by viewing. But the other problem is that despite these young women appearing expert in what they are doing in bed, the sex may be inauthentic—no youthful fumbling here.

Manohla Dargis has written in *The New York Times* that their pantomiming is obvious; others have noted that Kechiche's lesbian sex is laughably constructed with pornographic tropes; Julie Maroh, the author of the book the film is based on, has also complained of the bedroom choreography. For a filmmaker whose strength seems to be a vital naturalism, these are sticking criticisms.

From a narrative perspective the most perplexing problem with these sex scenes is that they mute and obscure the actresses, who otherwise, in many other parts of the film, offer their intelligent faces and voices to the screen in subtle and moving ways. In visual media the body is often deeply inexpressive compared to the heart's great canvas—the face. The sex between these characters, as is true of most carnality, causes the interesting parts of these women's personalities to recede. The actresses for long stretches of time become action heroes, and the portrait of them that the film has ostensibly been working on grinds, so to speak, to a halt.

One can see then that the movie is doing a lot of narrative wheel spinning at these young women's expense. The director has not arranged for a story with surprises or ideas or momentum or much structure at all, and so, well, he is stalling. He has become one of the "ball-busting directors" that an actor-character at the film's end tells Adèle is his reason for having quit the movies and gone into real estate.

The film begins with fifteen-year-old Adèle going to school, looking quite young in her knit cap. She is viewed from the top of a hill, with the attractive city of Lille spread out below, and we watch her, camera at her back, as she descends. Will the entire film suggest that the leaving behind of home and childhood is a descent? Possibly. At her high school, she loves literature. The first classroom discussion is about love at first sight in Marivaux's *The Life of Marianne*—so the movie introduces the idea of the powerful gaze right at the get-go. Another teacher discusses *Antigone*, explicating the lines between childhood and adulthood—at least for Greek girls.

Although Adèle has one great pal (a gay boy), the school yard is a slightly vicious place with much sexual gossip and social speculation, and at home Adèle has dinner (always spaghetti) with her parents, the three of them watching television while they eat. In general Adèle's soft, wide mouth hangs open throughout the film, revealing an attractive overbite too long associated with French actresses. She pulls her hair up, lets it fall again, ties it back up—continually. Between the slack mouth and the unstable hair, we see quickly that Adèle does not quite know who she is. But she is a creature of appetites, and much time is spent watching her pliable mouth chew—pasta, candy, oysters. Director Kechiche, whose 2007 portrait of female resourcefulness, *The Secret of the Grain*, revolves around a couscouserie, gives us lots of footage of eating, as if, in a gastronomic nonwitticism, he sees love, especially love between women, as one big restaurant. We also see Adèle dancing in various settings—her dancing is something of a motif—but uncertainty is written all over her face, even when her arms are raised over her head. We see youth's beauty but rarely its exuberance.

When we first meet the older, more confident Emma (Seydoux), she is in a romantic headlock with another girl but turns surreptitiously to size up Adèle. It is a purposeful, appraising leer, and although the audience will recognize it as lecherous and see Emma instantly for what she is—a player—Adèle is smitten, like a character in one of the novels she reads. (One may momentarily worry about the windy circle of hell reserved by Dante for Francesca da Rimini, reader of love books, and in fact winds do blow Adèle's hair around throughout the film.)

Adèle and Emma meet again in a bar, where Emma almost picks Adèle up, or at least discourages others from doing so. Emma recognizes Adèle as confused and underage but soon is trolling the edge of the school yard to fetch her. She courts Adèle with confidence and kindness. Though she looks quite young herself, Emma is meant to be older and more sophisticated, an ambitious artist, and the radiant Seydoux does well in communicating the psychological edge Emma has on Adèle.

The movie then travels through a few years of their love affair together, and we see that Emma, who at first seems comfortable with Adèle as her housekeeper and muse, will soon find her too mundane, not glamorous or ambitious enough for her artist friends. When Emma encourages Adèle to become a writer, it seems meretricious and self-serving on Emma's part. Adèle doesn't want to become a writer and is not much interested in the grad-school-style discourse that is supposed to pass as intellectual—*Klimt is decorative; no he's not; yes he is* (yes he is). All is meant to suggest that Adèle is running with a headier crowd than the one from her high school days, and as someone who loves her job as an elementary school teacher, she may always be an outsider in Emma's world.

There is a reason adults are requested to stay romantically away from teenagers: a minor is more easily overwhelmed, damaged, seduced, hurt. There is a power differential, which can be compounded by class differentials as well. That the film is one big illustration of this should not escape our notice. Can one talk about adult sex with minors, if it's a European film? One should hope so. And clearly the film is somewhat aware of this problem, since like Mariel Hemingway's character in Woody Allen's great but troubling *Manhattan,* during the course of the movie Adèle turns eighteen. A birthday cake is lit and candles are blown out. Whew! Everyone is internationally legal now!

But damage of some kind—even if it's the damage of love—has been done. Instead of being outgrown, Adèle's vulnerability seems to have seeped in and overtaken her permanently. Romantic love has subtracted from her life, rather than added to it, and she seems shatteringly alone. One may be reminded of the tragic Marie in *The Dreamlife of Angels* (1998), also set in Lille, or of Isabelle Huppert as Beatrice in *The Lacemaker* (1977)—two French films that take the social class differential of lovers head-on. Beatrice's imaginary Greek windmills are analogous to Adèle's eighteenth-century romances. And although Adèle is not likely to crack and break completely, she will be bent in difficult winds. The chances of her thriving do not look promising at all.

Girl meets girl. Girl loses girl. There's not much else going on here for three hours. In under three hours, Shakespeare did much better with the vagaries of adolescent love, taking them less seriously and for what they are, but foregrounding them against larger societal themes of war and peace. Does sexual orientation on its own, in the twenty-first century, make for a story? Pedophilia, sexual predation, and wounding class divisions in Kechiche's film are stumbled up against then retreated from, dodgily, glancingly—not really even gazingly. The portrait Kechiche offers of France, mostly the city of Lille, is unceasingly pretty, demographically diverse, and replete with delicious cigarette smoking. He is not seeking quarrels. He wants things to be as attractive as they can be—all things considered—and sidles up to sentimentality. But his lead actress has run away with the film in a complicated way.

Nineteen seventies film theory (Laura Mulvey, John Berger, and others) sometimes had it that the male gaze is directed at a woman, and the female gaze is directed at the male gazing at the woman (Hitchcock's *Vertigo* builds its entire plot on this dialectic between viewer and viewed). Yet from the current vantage point, in this somewhat antique model, the female gaze may consist of a composite vision and be the more complex and authoritative, by virtue of containing additional information. Then again, of course, the male gaze may be watching the female gaze as well, which adds an additional layer of power and perception, becoming a tertiary gaze, and then the female may gaze back, ad nauseam, in the nature of a hand-slapping game or the infinite regression of a Quaker Oats box or the badinage of Abbott and Costello.

Such theory, often written in a prose with the forensic caress of an appliance warranty, may not be a useful way to look at films, especially when one is dealing with the high caliber of acting—visceral, rangy, possessed—that is on display in Kechiche's film. The sex scenes notwithstanding, almost every moment contains a dramatic presence where interiority is brought forth via concentration, utterance, silences. This deserves a separate sort of notice. The close-ups of the young, still-forming face of Exarchopoulos show that the director knew precisely what he had when he cast her. The camera work shows Exarchopoulos knowing what she's doing as well. Et cetera. Ad infinitum.

An esteemed British actress was once asked why in such a small country as England there were so many great actors. "It's because we're *always* acting," she said. This past year has brought forth astonishing performances from young French-speaking actresses, not just Seydoux and Exarchopoulos, but Émilie Dequenne in the harrowing Belgian-French film *Our Children*. Have young Francophone women newly seized a form of cultural expression for themselves? Have they kept their chic, insouciantly coiled scarves but broken free from something more oppressive? Or are they simply—and not so simply—always acting?

(2013)

Bernard Malamud[*]

The auto-correct on my computer always wants to turn *Malamud* into *malamute,* which may be apt, since a malamute is strong, beautiful, carries heavy freight, and according to Wikipedia also has a plush underbelly. Something similar perhaps can be said for Malamud's stories—their seriousness and yet their gentleness—but I won't spend too much time worrying this accidental metaphor.

The brilliant stories of *The Magic Barrel* are largely about faith, love, work, and their various entanglements. The collection's characters are scholars, cobblers, egg candlers, tailors, census takers, doubt-ridden rabbis, floorwalkers at Macy's. Their occupations are identified early so we know that the story will be—somewhat—about work and its perils—especially as it intersects with love and spiritual resilience.

The narrative voices are of their time and place yet original and unprecedented in American letters: the stories are told with the sideways moves of self-interruption, of overlapping thoughts, of long, fluid, conversational syntax that suddenly dives inward for free, indirect discourse.

Malamud's narrative voice makes one grateful for the limberness of English and the history of America as a country of immigrants. The

[*] A memorial tribute delivered at the PEN/Malamud memorial reading, December 5, 2014.

inverted syntax of Yiddish meets the English language and the syntax winds into little eddies and reversals. (It is how I myself often speak—for what I should change?—even though I was raised a Baptist. This comes from the passage of time, from reading, from travel, from friends, from confusion.) It also makes one grateful for Malamud's nimble use of all this—and despite the flourishes of voice his stories are compressed and move along with great speed to surprising places. Repeatedly in *The Magic Barrel* a man is led out of his comfort zone to encounter an unexpected solace elsewhere. The reader takes these sometimes breathless journeys with him. Perhaps my favorite of these is a story titled "Angel Levine." It is a story of disbelief, dancing, and patched-together faith. "The world is full of Jews," it cries joyfully in the end, meaning that earth is flecked with unexpected kith and kin and mercy and one may not always recognize such in their various incarnations. Leaping past preconceptions leads to blessedness, or something like it. The disguises of God: this is what Malamud wrote of best.

(2014)

Miranda July

I first met Miranda July years ago at a faraway literary conference in Portland, Oregon. Along with Rick Moody and others we were on a panel that was supposed to converse authoritatively about narrative structure. When it came time for July to speak, she stood up and started singing. She was large-eyed and lithe. I don't remember what song it was—something she had written herself, I believe. I was startled. Who *was* this woman? (Her performances and short films had not appeared widely enough to have caught my notice.) I was then mortified, not for her, since she seemed completely at ease and the audience was enthralled, but mortified for narrative structure, which had clearly been given the bum's rush. (Well, fiction writers will do anything to avoid this topic: it is the one about which they are the most clueless and worried and improvisational.)

Sitting next to July was the brilliant Denis Johnson, who, inspired by his neighbor, when it was his turn (figuring out whose turn it is can be the most difficult part of a panel) also began to sing. Also something he had written himself. I may have laughed, thinking it was all supposed to be funny, realizing too late my mistake. There was a tragic aspect to one verse in the Johnson song. I believe he did not sit down because he had not stood to begin with.

Then it was clearly, or unclearly, my turn. If not the wallflower at the orgy, then I was the mute at the a cappella operetta (a condition

typical of many a July character though not of July herself): I refused to
sing. I don't remember what I said—I believe I read from some notes,
silently vowing never to be on another panel. (The next panel I was on,
in Boston, I thought went well by comparison. That is, no one burst
into random song. But when I said as much to the person sitting next
to me, the editor of a prominent literary journal, he said, "Really? This
was the worst panel I've ever participated in.") So my introduction to
July was one at which I watched her redefine boundaries and hijack
something destined to be inert and turn it into something uncomfort-
ably alive, whether you wanted her to or not. This has been my experience of her work ever since.

July's first feature-length film, the now-famous independent *Me
and You and Everyone We Know,* also upends expectations. (July writes,
directs, and stars in all her films.) In many ways, while remaining a love
story, the film is about the boundary busting that is ruleless sexuality—
stalking and sexual transgression—though here the predators and per-
petrators are gentle and female. A boy is coercively fellated by two
slightly unpleasant teenage girls devising a competition. Low-level
sexual harassment is everywhere and July sometimes plays it for laughs.
Two kids in a chat room lead someone on a wild-goose chase, writing scatological comments in the language of very young children, and
despite all this it is hilarious. A shoe salesman named Richard, who has
set his hand on fire in front of his sons, is hounded by a woman named
Christine (played by July herself), who does not know him but who is
erotically obsessed with him. She has psychically and perhaps correctly
marked him as her mate (the telepathic heart is at the center of much
of July's work).

Another character, a middle-aged woman seeking a partner online,
finds herself hooked up with a five-year-old boy in the park. Images of
flame and precariousness recur—the burning sun, the burning hand, a
bright goldfish riding in a plastic bag on a car roof. And yet all is put
forward with tenderness and humor. The desire for human love goes
unquestioned and its role in individual fate is assumed to be essential.
July's Christine, a struggling artist who works as a driver for Elder-Cab,
possesses a thin-skinned empathy for everyone, and her love for the
shoe salesman (who is played in convincingly addled fashion by John
Hawkes) is performed with both vulnerability and purity of passion.

In her two feature-length films the chemistry with her male leads is quite strong: they as well as July are like openly soulful children, attaching without reason or guile, and July is quite focused on this quality of connective vulnerability, as well as on children themselves. Her work also engages with the criterion offered up by the character of a museum curator looking at Christine's own works: "Could this have been made in any era or only now?" With July it is a little of both. She focuses on people living "courageously with grace," while also quietly arguing with a culture that asks us to do that.

July's second film, the underrated *The Future*, continues her exploration of the dissolution of lines between self and other, life and death, animal and human. When one brings up one's admiration of this film to others, one is often greeted with the dismayed and dismaying "Oh not the one with the talking cat!" It's indeed narrated by a deceased cat (voice-over by July). Even if this is initially strange—the cat speaking from its own afterlife about how one must sometimes wait forever and on into death for one's real life to begin, which is the life with love in it—at the end it is quite beautiful, as is the film, which was based on a performance piece July first did at the Kitchen in New York. Both that piece and the film feature not just the talking cat (named Paw-Paw) but a dancing shirt as well.

The Future tells the story of Sophie and Jason, a young couple in Los Angeles who are stalled in their lives and can neither move successfully forward nor out. Everyone else seems to have gotten the hang of it—marriage, responsibility, children—and Sophie (played by July) sees her friends and acquaintances in a kind of time-lapse photography, moving ahead without her, on into grandchildren. When to disrupt her inertia Sophie, a struggling dancer, leaves Jason for an inappropriate older man—someone with a job, a house, and a daughter—the longing both Sophie and Jason still have for each other, the closeness of their ties, the tender habits of their connection become a kind of telepathy, and time is literally frozen by Jason, to keep Sophie from saying the unsayable breakup words. (One of July's recent projects has involved an app she created that allows other people to say unpleasant things on your behalf, such as "I think we should see other people.")

July's love interest here is played by Hamish Linklater, who has a placid, natural vibe with his costar. They have the sleepy reticence of people who have known each other their whole lives and yet there is something tentative and sexy between them. July even filmed a graphic sex scene with Linklater that she decided not to include in the film, since she felt it got carried away. "Everyone should film a raunchy sex scene for their movie then delete it," she says in the DVD commentary. But the childlike innocence of these young people causes them to be unable to imagine any future world at all. Jason thinks that even his door-to-door canvassing for environmental causes is all for naught, all too late, that climate change has passed its tipping point and the world is already, for all intents and purposes, over and unsalvageable. The film may end with an ocean scene, a talking moon, a pontificating cat, the inevitable reunion of the lovers, but it is profoundly stirring nonetheless. Like much of July's work it is about the nature of time, which finally, sadly, is no one's friend; nor does it provide enough of itself: so terrible and cruel and its portions so small, as the old joke goes.

July's first book of literary fiction, the 2007 story collection *No One Belongs Here More Than You,* was a rare short-fiction hit. For those who bought it for its bright yellow cover and bold sans-serif font in order to face the jacket outward in the guest room bookcase or the study where it can be made into a warm and welcoming *objet,* it may come as a surprise to learn that the volume contains at least two brilliant stories, especially the longest one, "Something That Needs Nothing," which first appeared in *The New Yorker.* It is about two young women, an unnamed narrator and her friend, Pip, who begin their runaway lives by scamming and sexually servicing older women: "We were targeting wealthy women who loved women. Did such a thing exist? We would also accept a woman of average means who had saved up her money."

Boundaries are shattered. Politesse is thrown out the window. Purity of passion ensures not a thing. The narrator tries to keep Pip's interest by wearing a wig. When, overheated and delirious, she removes it, she is left utterly alone. What a woman will do for love is once again on the author's mind.

How is this "twee," "fey," "winsome"—the words that are sometimes hurled at July and her work? (Wes Anderson is occasionally labeled thus, but when one googles "Wes Anderson" and "fey" one gets a lot of pictures of him and Tina Fey.) David Sedaris on *The New Yorker* fiction podcast, interviewed about July's "Roy Spivey"—a story about the mutual psychological deformities brought about by encounters with celebrity—was asked how he felt about July's harsher critics. He confessed bafflement. "They're just jealous," he said. And one is inclined to agree.

A young art student I spoke with recently said, "Miranda July is between generations. The older generation thinks she belongs to young people. But we don't think about her much. She seems middle-aged. The things we're doing now she did first, but most of us don't appreciate that." That, too, sounds plausible.

Which brings us to her latest event, a somewhat bonkers debut novel entitled *The First Bad Man.* The narrator is a sensitive single woman named Cheryl Glickman, neither young nor old, neither here nor there; she seems quite buffeted by the random events of life, and when she allows her employer's twenty-year-old daughter, Clee, to come live with her, she is quite literally buffeted. Cheryl works for a women's self-defense nonprofit run by Clee's parents, and Clee is well schooled in body slams and other sorts of martial moves and postures.

Cheryl does her best to keep up but escapes this particular abuse by entering various psychic parallel universes she has devised. She fantasizes about a relationship with her coworker Phillip and she obsessively seeks a baby named Kubelko Bondy, whom she sees perpetually in other babies she encounters day to day. "Are you Kubelko Bondy?" she sometimes asks babies or the protruding abdomens of pregnant women, and mostly the answer is affirmative. Throughout July's work she seems to believe in these alternative psycho-spiritual spaces and matter-of-factly presents them. They are often aided by technology—cell phone photos and the like.

As Cheryl goes from being Clee's enemy, to Clee's lover, to Clee's new mother—"it would not be told as a great American love story for our time"—the book gets a little bogged down. Either despite or because of the violent roughhousing, Clee never comes into sharp focus, though late in the novel we are told she looks like Scarlett Johansson. Which gives one pause.

Still, there are amusing moments: "The Gregorian chant CD was not 'our song' but it was very similar to the one we'd heard on the radio that first morning." *The First Bad Man* is not the sexual horror story it initially seems (though many characters are in sadistic relationships) nor is it the coming-out story it seems briefly to be, but it does become a different kind of coming-out story. Once Clee becomes mysteriously pregnant (the likely birth father, revealed at the end, finds the baby, Jack, "standoffish" and so believes he is not the actual father), the novel clicks into gear.

Compare the glancing treatment of the newborn in, say, *The Portrait of a Lady* to the concentration on the newborn here—"Jack took one look at him and had a massive bowel movement that exploded his diaper; yellow cottage cheese was everywhere"—and the reader can see which is the novelist on whom nothing will be lost. "A real mother throws her heart over the fence and then climbs after it," thinks Cheryl. Also, "I felt like a statue of something virtuous." Also, "Was I like honey thinking it's a small bear, not realizing the bear is just the shape of its bottle?"

We don't always know what intimate life consists of until novels tell us.

Thus, three-quarters of the way through, *The First Bad Man* takes a hard right turn and becomes a powerful mother-son love story—it is as if July became a mother herself during the writing of the novel. (I believe she did.) Mother love is everywhere, though it often feels like "a very feverish pity." July's faux-cinematic ending reaches into the future to give this tale of an abandoned infant (Clee's) and a lonely single foster mom, Cheryl, an ending that is all wish fulfillment. When one throws an ending happily into the future, one risks sentimentality, or at least overly neat conclusions. When one concludes by throwing happiness into the past, one can end with a moment of unrealized, elegiacally positioned hope, which is often less sentimental since such promise is seen whole and is usually partially doomed and more precise than the rapturous gauze of faux cinema.

July risks the sentimentality. But somehow, because the ending reprises and builds upon a small piece of large hope placed earlier in the book—Cheryl's vision of her adult son, which becomes a premonition—it leaves one breathless. A reader may burst into tears whether it's warranted or not. The book's epilogue is moving—like an avalanche is moving. And one realizes only then that one has been waiting the whole time for this very thing.

And so one welcomes the multitalented Miranda July to the land of novel writing. She is difficult to categorize. She is between generations. She believes in psychic connection, the spiritually purifying aspects of passion, the porousness of the self. Her lines sing. She can sing. She doesn't know that much about narrative structure. No one belongs here more than she.

(2014)

True Detective

The low-key romance that grows between two people working side by side has sometimes been the subject of great literature. It constitutes the most optimistic part of Tolstoy's *Anna Karenina* and the least grue-some part of Hardy's *Far from the Madding Crowd,* which ends with an authorial lecture on camaraderie and how men and women are often denied it when confined to gender-specific work. Both novels make their arguments for fond, sensible bonding born of cooperative labor.

Television understood this (somewhat) early on, and at least by the 1960s producers began to fabricate work situations where male and female characters (well, maybe only one female character) could week after week banter and attach without having actually to date: the comedy writers' room in *The Dick Van Dyke Show;* the investigative reporters and their researchers in *The Name of the Game;* various West Coast detectives and their secretaries or assistants (*Mannix, Ironside*); *The Mary Tyler Moore Show's* Minneapolis television newsroom. No passion was truly in play in these job settings, but sibling-like intimacy and affection between the sexes was the glue that held the ensembles together week after week.

Still, as glue goes, American screen narrative has mostly preferred the bromance, the cowboy aspect of two male detectives getting to know each other on a hot or cold case (women detectives in the United Kingdom—Helen Mirren in *Prime Suspect,* Gillian Anderson in *The*

Fall—have tended to go it alone), and if the brotherly duo also expresses our nation's federalist principles, as well as its difficult class divisions, by having one educated person at the state or national level team up with a local law enforcement officer who has never left town, well then, people, we have a show. The only gender reversal I've seen of this—*The Heat,* starring Melissa McCarthy as the local cop and Sandra Bullock as the FBI agent—was set in Boston and played for laughs and was one of the funniest movies I've ever seen.

When *True Detective* aired last year on HBO, it was squarely in the familiar trope of two guys getting to know each other on the job, doing some squabbling, some drinking, and having each other's back. At the end there is a long, predictable rescue of one by the other. And yet it seemed entirely original. This is due to several elements that are all in perfect sync with one another: the Louisiana setting (its shabby gulf towns, its tent meetings of bayou Baptists, its silvery swamps), the exquisite cinematography of Adam Arkapaw, and the acting, all threaded on the same needle by the director, Carey Joji Fukunaga. These worked together to give the show the look of a great film, where characters seem a natural part of the locale: through sensitive photography the setting seems to liquefy and flow into the cast to form (not just inform) the characters' blood and spit, vowels and squints, head-shakes and struts. Their hot tears are a warm rain from the wide celluloid sky. This is assisted by first-rate actors, who possess the highest powers of concentration. The ability on a camera-laden set to inhabit a character without a twitch of distraction or preoccupation or visible hint of the internally or externally irrelevant is a scary but brilliant feat. Ordinary people cannot do it. But I have seen great actors do it even at cocktail receptions full of cell phones. In a world where major writers have announced that they cannot focus on their work without extracting or blocking the modems in their laptops, this kind of thespian concentration is worth noting. (One thinks of the writer Anne Lamott's remark on her own maturing undistractibility: "I used to not be able to work if there were dishes in the sink," she has said. "Then I had a child and now I can work if there is a corpse in the sink.")

. . .

Woody Harrelson as Louisiana cop Marty Hart with his angry under-bite, interesting blood pressure spikes, and recognizable male jazz moves gives a performance that grows more impressive on subsequent viewings, while Matthew McConaughey as the former DEA agent Rust Cohle with his extravagant enigmas and bored-to-the-gills gnomic utterances is instantly mesmerizing. He believes the world is "a giant gutter in outer space." When Hart, his CID partner of three months, asks him if he's a Christian, he says, "In philosophical terms I'm what's called a pessimist."

"What's that mean?" asks Hart.

"It means I'm bad at parties."

"Let me tell you," replies Hart. "You ain't great outside of parties either."

Rust Cohle feels the entire human species should do itself a favor and just walk off into the eternal sunset. He himself is intermittently on the wagon and doesn't have the temperament for suicide. He and Hart are a hoot and were made for the long police vehicle rides that Hart would like to turn into a silent zone and yet never does.

"Why don't you just watch that car commercial if you like McConaughey's acting so much?" a *True Detective* skeptic recently said to me. (I love that car commercial, though I've now forgotten what car it is for.) Harrelson's and McConaughey's performances are indelible and distinctive if easily parodied; one can go to YouTube and find some amusing imitations. (I recommend a video titled *True Barista*.) But as with many parodies, they honor with their mockery—no writer was ever parodied more than Hemingway—and parodies do not necessarily disparage their sources but rather sing cozy, observant ditties alongside them, as the Greek etymology of the word *parody* recommends. In any case, simultaneously embracing laughter and the object of that laughter is only irony and Keatsian intelligence, not assassination. Watching Harrelson and McConaughey together is pure joy.

There is a bit of Hemingway in *True Detective:* the terse vale-of-tears dialogue, the visitor from far away filling up with the air of a new land. Hart and Cohle (not pronounced "soul" but we feel the blackened spirit) garden and enact their forensic partnership, sharing one woman, many cigarettes, and a mild fascination with each other, while remaining their own best advocates, a psychological project that seldom lets up. Hart clings to his hard-won normalcy—wife, kids, house, job—even if it bores him.

Cohle has left all that. He lost his only child and is now completely on his own in the world, having been raised by a Vietnam vet survivalist in Idaho to whom he no longer speaks. Cohle's shoot-out with some biker drug runners is filmed and scored to resemble something from that war—so says the show's writer and creator Nic Pizzolatto—so we are made to understand that the 1960s have forever hovered in a damaging way over the children who grew up in that decade. This idea continues in Season 2, when Rachel McAdams as the daughter of a haughty spiritual leader speaks derisively of having grown up on a "hippie" commune.

Cohle, the former DEA undercover agent, has been put on a murder case with Lake Charles cop Hart because the crime seems to be of a serial nature. A visitor from another world, which may only be Texas, where his previous work records have been redacted, Cohle takes notes in a large ledger and speaks as if he were the CEO of a nihilist fortune cookie company. He is reprimanded on his existentialism by the partially spellbound Marty. "I wouldn't go around spouting that shit I was you. People around here don't think that way." Despite the region's tent-top religiosity, Cohle's oracular soliloquies will be deemed unhinged. In a gentler moment Marty says to Cohle, "For a guy who sees no point in existence you sure fret about it an awful lot." Harrelson brings a nice comedic drawl to his line readings. His Marty Hart is trying to be a good family man but remains an ordinary hothead and philanderer who has married up in society and is of several minds about it. As a result, he takes up a little torridly with a court stenographer, which gets him kicked out of the house, putting him in closer domestic proximity to his work partner, setting parts of the story in faster motion. The show's languidness, however, is part of its charm, part of its cable medium, and the imitative fallacy notwithstanding, part of its portrait of the South.

Even to say that *True Detective* has a plot—that is, a story that proceeds as a set of human actions and their consequences—is to miss what there is to admire about the series's ambling and rich narrative (not the story, which is alternately incoherent and trite). The narrative is really more an assemblage of characters and scenes. To summarize the plot would make it seem boring and absurd. In short, the detectives are trying to track down who or what is responsible for some ritualistic murders of women—either a cult or a lone sicko or both. They have to interrogate the local tough guys both in and out of jail and there is a lot of vague talk about the "Yellow King," a term used to give a screenwriter's loose idea a little mythic buttressing.

Although the writing may be the weakest link in the show (it is helped in Season 1 by T Bone Burnett's music, which is steadily mindful of ambience, mood, roots), the first-season script has things to recommend it, primarily a useful time-straddling structure in which convincingly older incarnations of Hart and Cohle are under investigation by Internal Affairs and are allowed, in response to the interrogators' questions, to offer additional if laconic interpretations of each other throughout the eight episodes.

Pizzolatto also provides sharp, amusing dialogue custom-fitted to the actors, plus a deep understanding of Louisiana, where he grew up. A scene shot in a Lake Charles strip club located directly across the street from a girls' dancing school is something a fiction writer cannot make up persuasively, despite the facts, despite the serendipitous signage, so Pizzolatto doesn't include it (but mentions it in the commentary). He knows when reality is interesting, when reality is irrelevant, and when reality is no excuse. This sense of what to leave out comes from sifting through one's profound knowledge of a locale. Intelligently exploiting a terrain largely unfamiliar to the viewer works well here and has been effective in other off-kilter police procedurals, from Joel and Ethan Coen's *Fargo* (which used the snow of the directors' boyhood Minnesota to great advantage) to *Top of the Lake*, in which Jane Campion's native New Zealand is filmed with intimacy and awe (by *True Detective*'s own Season 1 cinematographer, Arkapaw).

Thus it is disappointing to see *True Detective*'s Season 2 return to the belly of the beast of conventional cop dramas: Southern California. And a lot of what was sometimes disparaged about the first season of *True Detective*—its southern gothic noir, its amusing faux philosophy, its virility—will be missed in the much limper second season. A motif of impotence pervades all the bedrooms in Season 2; the setting is an L.A. suburb named Vinci—Latin for "overcome, spent." Teeth and teethlike objects spill out like the most Freudian of dreams. "What the fuck is Vinci?" one character asks. "A city. Supposedly" is the reply.

"We get the world we deserve," says the new season's poster. Alas: we don't even get the second seasons we deserve. Season 2 has a different crew, different cast, different directors, and most unfortunately a different cinematographer. It doesn't resemble the first season much at all. T Bone Burnett still does the score, but the music is heavy, unintegrated, full of dread: Leonard Cohen sounding gruff and demonic in the title sequence; a chanteuse in a nightclub called the Black Rose wailing "this is my least favorite life" only fifty minutes in; a baleful jazz trumpet accompanying pensive aerial shots of nighttime highways. All do little but subtract by attempting to underscore. Burnett goes for something gloomier and synthetic here—the music working largely as interior monologue for the new characters, who now have an even lesser script to live in.

The primary creative holdover from the first season is Pizzolatto, and so one may recognize the same random pacing, the nonconverging story lines, the villains in scary masks, strangers wearing angel wings, the gingerly skirting of the subject of race, the nonstop interest in sex workers, a weary sympathy for the devil, the damaged perpetrating their own damage, and the abundance of flat female characters who are "rounded out" by scenes that have them scold their men and show "agency"—as is said in craft discussions. These new detectives of Season 2—Antigone, or Ani, Bezzerides (Rachel McAdams) rocking her family anger, Ray Velcoro (Colin Farrell) rolling his desperate family love, and Paul Woodrugh (Taylor Kitsch) racing away from the mideastern desert, Tikrit, and a guy he once slept with—are all psychically burned to a crisp. The dialogue is hard-boiled and tight—when not desperately working at exposition.

"Can I ask how much you drink in an average week?" a concerned doctor noting Ray's redlining liver asks him.

"All I can," Ray replies.

As in the old TV show *The Mod Squad,* which these cops seem to be referencing in their beauty, their backstories, their leather jackets, their inscrutability and recruit potential for undercover work, this is an impressive trio of California young people, though it is sometimes hard to notice their appeal when they are so dissolute, disgusted, or just weary and hidden from the sun in windowless interiors whose ocher lighting and general color scheme are something like Edward Hopper meets Dennis Hopper. (At least one scene is a direct visual quote from *Nighthawks*.) In the shadowy, claustrophobic rooms the crew's lights sometimes hit an actor's face in the copperish air (a visual pun?) and eyes glint and glisten, catlike, often without motivation. When our true detectives first meet one another and form their accidental trio at the end of Episode 1, they have been summoned in the middle of the night: two of them are drunk, and the other has just tried to commit suicide; all of them are staring at a rest stop picnic bench on which sits the upright corpse of a missing city manager who has had his genitalia cut away and his eyes burned out.

This is our welcome to *True Detective*, Season 2. The funny sparks of life that lit things up between Hart and Cohle will be hard if not impossible to find here—bits of *Chinatown, The Big Sleep, Twin Peaks,* and other detective films will lumber in instead. Any humor will be in the hands of Vince Vaughn as a struggling casino owner named Frank and will probably be inadvertent. Vaughn, who like George Clooney radiates tidy, unsexy handsomeness—Vaughn's delicately featured profile is similar to Julianne Moore's—has difficulty melting into the fabric of this program, trouble blending with its look and tone, and so stands out as very much himself, as in, *What the heck is Vince Vaughn doing in this show?* He has his mouth full spouting nonsense like "Sometimes your worst self is your best self." Or "It's like blue balls but in the heart." Or "Never do anything out of hunger. Not even eating." As well as other lines that, as *The Atlantic* has pointed out, sometimes sound as if they'd been Google-translated from Farsi.

Vaughn's rushed delivery resembles that of the character he played in the romantic comedy *Wedding Crashers*. This same-in-every-film movie-star trait he also shares with George Clooney, though not with the utterly transformed Rachel McAdams (who was also in *Wedding Crashers*). In fact, party crashing may be the real metaphor of this season of *True Detective*; the McAdams character, Ani, does in fact crash a party ostensibly for investigative purposes; she is there to rescue and be rescued, the meat of all cop dramas, as well as to recover an ugly child-hood memory from Dad's dubious commune.

Early on may be too soon to say that Vaughn is miscast (though one wonders how the show might have been improved if Vaughn and Farrell each had the other's role). Vaughn's hypnotically askew performance grows on the viewer. Perhaps his performance will become legendary with time. (The city of Vinci is already practically named for him!) He plays Frank with inexpressive manipulativeness, a dapper low-level gangster who is also an outsider. His face has the stillness of a hit man's, but every once in a while fear darts across his empty eyes. Though the tallest in any room, Frank is in over his head, again a crasher, and at season's end Vaughn begins to own the cartoonishness of his two-bit psychopath and bully, and his Proustian death trudge in the final episode could have been funny but strangely is what it's supposed to be: a ghost story. We see him as perhaps the rivetingly rotted peg that has held the house together from the start. After all, this is the land of show business, of visions in the desert.

Still, one hears Vaughn's own tedium in lines like "Osip, we talked this through in Paris, Caspere's absence don't mean a thing," but when the Russian thugs with whom Frank is trying to do land deals speak better English than he does, it ends up eliciting some viewer pity, plus a smile, if a quick one. Frank lives literally in a glass house, and so we wait for the stones to come boomeranging. The incomprehensibility of the story line—mine pollution! toxic dumping! the demise of the family farm! high-speed rail proposals! high-end hookers! spiritualists who size up auras like net worth! mysterious suicides!—can only be alleviated by a dash of predictability. But instead of remaining in all that glass (he later carves up a treacherous henchman's face with some), Frank unexpectedly downsizes to a Glendale bungalow with wallpaper. And eventually to plane tickets to Venezuela. When the body count around him gets a little high—killing calms and tames him, as is said of hawks—he becomes a thrilling arsonist.

Meanwhile, the mod squad—Ani, Ray, and Paul—is having its private adventures. With righteous indignation Ani/Antigone, sporting a nonstop fume and seethe, plus ombré hair that is cleverly used by season's end to indicate the passage of time, takes on her bogus guru of a dad, who in his—or the writer's—sloppy neoclassicism has named his other daughter Athena after the "goddess of love." Really! Also, like her older counterparts in *The Fall* and *Prime Suspect,* as well as the French police procedural *Spiral,* Ani will have to endure reprimand and suspension for sexual misconduct with a subordinate. Women! In her required group therapy, where she is the only female participant and the scene struggles unsuccessfully toward a humorous moment or two, there is too much vacant glowering for things to lighten; there is no tension or shared secret that might produce the release of energy humor requires. Comedy has to have its finger on the pulse of irreverence, something Season 1 understood, but Season 2 is too full of its own earnest regard for Ani's contemptuousness, despite McAdams's often admirable performance. Audience anticipation cannot be comedically disrupted because the entire movement of the story is desultory, without suspense, and the characters are too often defeated by it, despite a handful of well-directed set pieces: the shoot-out at the end of Episode 4; Ray and Frank with their guns drawn under a breakfast table in Episode 6; the entirety of Episode 7, shot with close-ups and crane shots and some real emotion.

Ray—who as he says isn't good at being muscle and yet Frank hires him as such twice—on very little evidence (a bad tip) has avenged a long-ago rape of his long-ago wife. In a gaping hole in the story line the possibility that Ray is not the biological father of his son is going to be used against him in a custody battle. A legal consultant might have informed the scriptwriter that regardless of biological parentage, California, like most states, makes the man who is married to the mother at the time of a child's birth the father of that child and also provides for "marriage by estoppel." Ray is his son's legal father regardless of the child's flaming red hair. DNA tests are irrelevant in this custody contest.

That this forensic error continues into judicial hearings and right on through the finale, as if it were suspense, is unfortunate. Getting ready for his day in court (or his interview with Internal Affairs, who knows for sure?), Ray starts chewing gum and drinking water and in general cleans up nicely. He casts an alert sidelong glance at Ani—a bit of foreshadowing. Watching the gifted Colin Farrell work hard—with complicated feeling and no Dublin accent whatever —in scenes that often add up to nothing is, unfortunately, a little like watching his career itself.

"I'm enjoying this soberish you," Frank tells him, "where your head doesn't dip and fall when I talk."

All this while Paul is resisting the claims that his sexual past and his days in black ops keep making on him (one of the plot's many improbabilities is that it suggests a gay affair would be grounds for blackmail even when one is no longer in the military). It is satisfying to see Taylor Kitsch shake off his defining role as *Friday Night Lights*'s Tim Riggins. Nonetheless, Kitsch may be the only one here who is better when speaking and moving than gazing off pensively, which the directors have him do too much of, even into mirrors, and often when he is simply fixing his expression he sometimes seems lost as an actor, as if he doesn't know the camera's still rolling. (*Esquire*, in a piece called "What Is Taylor Kitsch Doing with His Face?," had some fun with the actor's dazed gaze during a sex scene.)

Midseason, at the end of an astonishing shoot-out filmed like a battle in Fallujah, an episode concludes with Ray and Ani stooped in anguish but leaves Paul unbent, surrounded by carnage and looking guiltily triumphant if also unclear about what has just happened. Paul is a "god warrior," and perhaps confusion goes with being such a deity. One wants to shout "Cut" before the camera does cut, though when the camera does, it freezes to an eloquently composed frame of dubious victory, pulled back to view a devastating scene, which makes one suddenly optimistic about the rest of this wild show's second season, as if it finally has gotten its legs beneath it.

But things grow random again. The time line lurches. The music becomes even stranger, often playing against what is on the screen: incongruous 1940s orchestral strings accompany a drugged-out orgy, for example. Just as early on we see Ray's father watching Kirk Douglas in *Detective Story*, in the finale a poster of Sam Peckinpah's *Bring Me the Head of Alfredo Garcia* is shown long enough to let you know Pizzolatto's narrative aspirations, though a PowerPoint presentation might have been more clarifying. The mod squad, despite being taken off the streets after their huge shoot-out, are all working from their new posts in evidence, insurance fraud, and gangster consultation to get back out in the field again and to locate some missing persons (a script doctor!) and to solve some not very interesting crimes (misuse of a good cast!).

Along with cadmium and uranium (and more than a nickel or two), talent has been carelessly disposed of, devaluing some good ground. "Mine runoff," party crashing, the recessive gene of the red hair of Satan, plus waste management generally are the leitmotifs of *True Detective*'s second season. Though not everything amounts to a hopeless wreck: when we lose Kitsch's Paul in a scene that is pretty much a steal from Martin Scorsese's *The Departed*, it has the same devastating effect as losing Leonardo DiCaprio. And when there is finally some eros in the room between the remaining two detectives, it, too, is emotionally convincing: they kiss like they mean it. Consequences ensue and haunt. Colin Farrell enacts the Gypsy Husband that memoirist Emma Forrest (*Your Voice in My Head*) claimed him to be. He is the Heathcliff in the house, and despite the sentimental gestures toward the innocence of children and the strength of women, which the script nods at hurriedly as it rushes headlong to its close, his true detective proves Hardy right: love of work is love indeed.

(2015)

Making a Murderer

Wisconsin is probably the most beautiful of the midwestern farm states. Its often dramatic terrain, replete with unglaciated driftless areas, borders not just the Mississippi River but two great inland seas whose opposite shores are so far away they cannot be glimpsed standing at water's edge. The world across the waves looks distant to nonexistent, and the oceanic lakes stretch and disappear into haze and sky, though one can take a ferry out of a town called Manitowoc and in four hours get to Michigan. Amid this somewhat lonely serenity, there are the mythic shipwrecks, blizzards, tornadoes, vagaries of agricultural life, industrial boom and bust, and a burgeoning prison economy; all have contributed to a local temperament of cheerful stoicism.

Nonetheless, a feeling of overlookedness and isolation can be said to persist in America's dairyland, and the idea that no one is watching can create a sense of invisibility that leads to the secrets and labors the unseen are prone to: deviance and corruption as well as utopian projects, untested idealism, daydreaming, provincial grandiosity, meekness, flight, far-fetched yard décor, and sexting. Al Capone famously hid out in Wisconsin, even as Robert La Follette's Progressive Party was getting under way. Arguably, Wisconsin can boast the three greatest American creative geniuses of the twentieth century—Frank Lloyd Wright, Orson Welles, and Georgia O'Keeffe—though all three quickly left, first for Chicago, then for warmer climes. (The state tourism board's campaign slogan *Escape to Wisconsin* has often been tampered with by bumper sticker vandals who eliminate the preposition.)

More recently, Wisconsin is starting to become known less for its ever-struggling left-wing politics or artistic figures—Thornton Wilder, Laura Ingalls Wilder—than for its ever-wilder murderers. The famous late-nineteenth-century "Wisconsin Death Trip," by which madness and mayhem established the legend that the place was a frigid frontier where inexplicably gruesome things occurred—perhaps due to mind-wrecking weather—has in recent decades seemingly spawned a cast of killers that includes Ed Gein (the inspiration for *Psycho*), the serial murderer and cannibal Jeffrey Dahmer, and the two Waukesha girls who in 2014 stabbed a friend of theirs to honor their idol, the Internet animation Slender Man.

The new documentary *Making a Murderer*, directed and written by Laura Ricciardi and Moira Demos, former film students from New York, is about the case of a Wisconsin man who served eighteen years in prison for sexual assault, after which he was exonerated with DNA evidence. He then became a poster boy for the Innocence Project, had his picture taken with the governor, had a justice commission begun in his name—only to be booked again, this time for murder.

Ricciardi and Demos's rendition of his story will not help rehabilitate Wisconsin's reputation for the weird. But it will make heroes of two impressive defense attorneys as well as the filmmakers themselves. A long-form documentary in ten parts, aired on Netflix, the ambitious series looks at social class, community consensus and conformity, the limits of trials by jury, and the agonizing stupidities of a legal system descending on more or less undefended individuals (the poor). The film is immersive and vérité—that is, it appears to unspool somewhat in real and spontaneous time, taking the viewer with the camera in unplanned fashion, discovering things as the filmmakers discover them (an illusion, of course, that editing did not muck up). It is riveting and dogged work.

The film centers on the Avery family of Manitowoc County, home to the aforementioned ferry to Michigan. Even though the lake current has eroded some of the beach, causing the sand to migrate clockwise to the Michigan dunes, and the eastern Wisconsin lakeshore has begun to fill forlornly with weeds, it is still a picturesque section of the state. The local denizens, whether lawyers or farmers, speak with the flat *a*'s, throatily hooted *o*'s, and incorrect past participles ("had went") of the region. There is a bit of Norway and Canada in the accent, which is especially strong in Wisconsin's rural areas and only sometimes changes with education.

The Avery family are the proprietors of Avery's Auto Salvage, and their property—a junkyard—on the eponymous Avery Road is vast and filled with over a thousand wrecked automobiles. It is a business not unlike farming in that in winter everything is buried in snow and unharvestable. The grandparents, two children, and some grandchildren live—or used to—on an abutting compound that consists of a small house, a trailer, a garage, a car crusher, a barn, a vegetable garden, and a fire pit.

In 1985 Steven Avery, the twenty-three-year-old son of Dolores and Allan Avery, was arrested and convicted of a sexual assault he did not commit. There was no forensic technology for DNA testing in 1985, and he had the misfortune to look much like the actual rapist—blond and young—and the traumatized victim, influenced by the county investigators, who had the whole Avery family on their radar, identified him in a lineup as her attacker. Despite having sixteen alibi witnesses, he was found guilty. The actual rapist was allowed to roam free.

After the Wisconsin Innocence Project took on his case, Avery was finally exonerated in 2003. DNA tests showed that he was not guilty and that the real attacker was now serving time for another rape. Avery then hired lawyers and sued Manitowoc County and the state of Wisconsin for wrongful imprisonment and for denying his 1995 appeal (a time during which DNA evidence might have set him free), which the state had mishandled, causing him to serve eight more years.

Days after Avery's release, Manitowoc law enforcement was feeling vulnerable about the 1995 appeal and writing memos, redocumenting the case from eight years earlier. The civil suit was making headway, and only the settlement amount remained to be determined; it was going to be large and would come out of Manitowoc County's own budget, since the insurance company had denied the county coverage on the claim.

Then, in November 2005, just as crucial depositions were both scheduled and proceeding and Avery stood to receive his money, he was suddenly and sensationally arrested for the murder of a freelance photographer named Teresa Halbach, who had come to Avery's Auto Salvage on Halloween to photograph a truck for an auto magazine, and whose SUV had been found on the Avery property, as eventually were her scattered and charred remains. Avery had two quasi alibis— his fiancée, to whom he'd spoken at length on the phone the afternoon of Halbach's disappearance, and his sixteen-year-old nephew, Brendan Dassey, who had just come home from school.

No one but Steven Avery ever came under suspicion, and county investigators circled in strategically. After getting nowhere with the fiancée, they focused on the nephew, who was gentle, learning-disabled, and in the tenth grade; they illegally interrogated him and suggested he was an accomplice. They took a defense witness and turned him into one for the prosecution.

Brendan was then charged with the same crimes as Avery: kidnapping, homicide, mutilation of a corpse. Prodded and bewildered, Brendan had made up a gruesome story about stabbing Halbach and slitting her throat in Avery's trailer (the victim's blood and DNA were never found on the premises), a fictional scenario that came, he later said, from the James Patterson novel *Kiss the Girls*. When asked why he'd said the things he said, he told his mother it was how he always got through school, by guessing what adults wanted him to say, then saying it. In an especially heartbreaking moment during the videotaped interrogation included in the documentary, and after he has given his questioners the brutal murder tale they themselves have prompted and helped tell, Brendan asks them how much longer this is going to take, since he has "a project due sixth hour."

It is a crazy story. And the film's double-edged title pays tribute to its ambiguity. Either Steven Avery was framed in a vendetta by Manitowoc County or the years of angry prison time turned him into the killer he had not been before. But the title aside, the documentary is pretty unambiguous in its siding with Avery and his appealing defense team, Jerry Buting and Dean Strang, who are hired with his settlement money as well as money his parents put up from the family business.

One cannot watch this film without thinking of the adage that law is to justice what medicine is to immortality. The path of each is a little crooked and always winds up wide of the mark. Moreover, nothing is as vain and self-regarding as the law. In Wisconsin prisoners will not get their parole unless they sign formal admissions of guilt and regret. (This kept Steven Avery from his own release when he was younger; he clung to his innocence.) These exacting corrections procedures are almost religious and certainly Orwellian in their desire to purge the last contrarian part from the human spirit. Any contempt for the law—even by a lawyer in court—will not go unpunished. And if one has the further temerity to use the law against itself—filing a lawsuit against law enforcement, for instance—one should be fearful. Especially in Manitowoc. Or so say many of the locals in front of Demos's camera.

As portrayed in *Making a Murderer,* however, the law is not so vain that it doesn't point out the low IQs of the defendants (an IQ test, it could be asserted, largely measures the *desire* for a high IQ) while omitting the fact that in Wisconsin most lawyers are practicing law without ever having taken a bar exam. (If someone has attended law school in the state, the bar exam is not required to practice there—a peculiarity of Wisconsin.)

If the film does not do a good job in positing an alternative theory of the murder—surely it does not believe the sheriff's department killed Teresa Halbach, or does it?—this is because the filmmakers are busy following the charismatic Buting and Strang in their courtroom defense and pretrial investigation. These are men of the finest skepticism. In their skilled and righteous run at the state they also seem the only ones in the film in possession of cool, deep, permanent mental health, and thus these ordinary-looking men suddenly resemble movie stars. A Twitter lovefest has sprung up around them, beginning soon after the documentary first aired, and their faces have been posted online accompanied by girlish hearts and declarations of love.

But handsome is as handsome does, and Buting and Strang are not allowed to suggest that others might have committed the crime—due to a Wisconsin law involving third-party liability. And thus everyone's hands are tied. The trial must proceed as one that is about police corruption and reasonable doubt. Nonetheless, we see any number of suspicious civilians with odd affects who may or may not have had the means, motive, and opportunity for murder.

Halbach's killing is largely presented as a motiveless crime, though her brother, her ex-boyfriend, and a couple of Avery family members are seen on camera with odd expressions and bewildering utterances. ("Odd Affect" could be the film's subtitle and would certainly describe the demeanor of many of the court-appointed attorneys as well.) Halbach's roommate did not report her missing for almost four days. Her former boyfriend is never asked for an alibi, and can't remember precisely when he last saw her. Was it morning or afternoon? He can't recall. Nonetheless, he was put in charge of the search party that was combing the area near the Avery property in the days after she was finally reported missing.

So who did this? Possibly Steven Avery. But it looks like a crime that can never be properly solved. The story Avery's defense team tells of law enforcement planting evidence is completely convincing, and such conduct is hardly unprecedented in tales of true crime. The Averys were not allowed on their own property for eight days while police roamed and rooted around, after which the scattered cremains, Avery's blood in the victim's car, and the victim's spare car key were all "discovered." Blood taken from Avery in 1995 was also found to have been tampered with in police storage.

But showing that there was police-planted evidence does not solve the crime; it only underscores its not proven status for purposes of a courtroom defense. And so the filmmakers' story—if it is a crime story, a human story—is missing parts. One may be struck by the complete absence of drugs and drug business in a neck of the woods where such activities often feature prominently. The victim's personal life is almost entirely missing and so she seems a tragic cipher.

And although she and her scarcely seen boyfriend are broken up, he still figures out how to hack into her cell phone account and attempts with anxious nonchalance to explain on camera and on the stand how he did so, though it seems to have been done with some extremely lucky guessing involving her sisters' birth dates. Messages are found deleted. This seems more damning than the three calls Avery himself made to Halbach, returning a call from her the day she disappeared. The fact of Avery's calls to Halbach was left out of the film (though it was offered as evidence in the trial), as if the filmmakers themselves were unreasonably, narratively afraid of it.

Early on, because of Avery's civil suit, Manitowoc investigators were ordered by the state to allow neighboring Calumet County to do the primary investigation into the murder: conflict of interest, due to the wrongful imprisonment civil suit, was recognized from the start. But this order was not enforced and Manitowoc sheriffs did not stay away, and the opportunities for evidence planting were myriad. The prosecutor and even the judges are seen to proceed with bias, professional self-interest, visible boredom, and lack of curiosity. At one point the special prosecutor is seen in the courtroom staring off into the middle distance, playing with a rubber band.

The story one does see clearly here is really a story of small-town malevolence. The label "white trash," not only dehumanizing but classist and racist—the term presumes trash is not ordinarily white—is never heard in this documentary. Perhaps the phrase is too southern in its origins. But it is everywhere implied. The Averys are referred to repeatedly by others in their community as "those people" and those "kind of people." "You did not choose your parents," says an interrogator, trying to pry answers out of sixteen-year-old Brendan, though his parents are irrelevant to the examination and are not being criminally accused of anything.

Yet the entire family is socially accused: outsiders, troublemakers, feisty, and a little dim. What one hears amid the chorus of accusers is the malice of the village. Village malice toward its own fringes has been dramatized powerfully in literary and film narrative—from Shirley Jackson's "The Lottery" to Arthur Miller's *The Crucible* to the Michael Haneke film *The White Ribbon* to Suzanne Collins's *The Hunger Games*. One saw it also in the Perugia of Amanda Knox's ordeal. Trimming the raggedy edges is how a village stays a village, how it remains itself. Contemporary shunning and cleansing may take new and different forms but they always retain the same heartlessness, the unacknowledged violence, the vaguely genocidal thinking. An investigator ostensibly on

Brendan's defense team speaks openly of his distaste for the Avery family tree and says, "Someone said to me we need to end the gene pool here."

The German word *Mitläufer* comes to mind: going along to get along, in a manner that does not avoid misdeeds—one of the many banalities of evil. Certainly one feels that frightened herd mentality among Manitowoc law enforcement as well as members of the jury, the majority of whom were initially reasonably doubtful but who, swayed by a persuasive minority, soon unified to a unanimous vote of guilty. Even the jury in Brendan's trial did not question the nature of the defendant's several and contradictory confessions, such was their prejudice against the boy.

It may or may not be useful to recall that early German settlers of Wisconsin, escaping the nineteenth-century military autocracy in Europe, once believed that the American Civil War would break up the Union, producing some independent states that could then come under German rule. These ordinary German citizens did not get their own state, of course, and in fact had to share it with Scandinavians, Poles, and even Bulgarian and Cornish miners, but certain stereotypical German burgher traits—from rule-boundedness to tidiness to anti-Semitism— are sometimes said to have persisted in Wisconsin life. (A shocking number of Nazi sympathizers once resided in Milwaukee.) A reputation for niceness may obscure rather than express the midwestern character.

When watching two New Yorkers construct a film about the sketchy Wisconsin legal system, one may overreach for cultural memes. (Cogent thesis-making is not this film's strong point, or its mission, and so a viewer is likely to veer off independently. Thus the Internet and media are full of armchair sleuths and amateur psychologists in the growing discussion of the film.) But conformity and silence on the job are elements in this tale, and they are timely subjects. Businesswoman and amateur social scientist Margaret Heffernan has recently been publicizing the results of her workplace survey of "willful blindness." According to Heffernan, 85 percent of people know there is something wrong at work but will not come forward to report or discuss it. When she consulted with Germans, they said, "Oh, yes. This is the German disease." But when she consulted with the Swiss, she was told, "This is a uniquely Swiss problem." In the United Kingdom: "The British are really bad at this." And so on. Willful blindness is everywhere, though touched on only glancingly in the film.

And so it comes as something of a surprise that what the documentary does linger over most single-mindedly—either deliberately or unconsciously—is the theme of mother love (perhaps not unrelated to willful blindness on the job). It is not just Brendan's mother, Barb, who is her son's impressively fierce defender. Barb is described by her son's lawyer as a bulldog, and clearly the lawyer is afraid of her. In her close protectiveness toward Brendan she quickly understands that he is ill-served by the court-appointed defense.

But the filmmakers' story is also of Steven Avery's aging and devoted mother, Dolores, who packs up boxes of photocopied letters and transcripts and sends them everywhere—from *60 Minutes* to *20/20*—hoping to get some journalists interested in her son's case. The effect of the media is a fraught one in this film—local TV news influenced many of the jurors, and the prosecution often used the press to communicate in unethical ways. *Making a Murderer* has invited parallels to the podcast *Serial,* which has recently, and intrusively, played a role in getting a convicted murderer a new hearing, though the evidence in that case was more substantial and readable: a crime of passion by a jealous and brokenhearted boy. The Teresa Halbach case is much more mystifying.

Meanwhile, short and lame and chewing on her lips, Dolores Avery visits her son in three different prisons in Wisconsin and one in Tennessee. She speaks to him on the phone regularly and optimistically. In her fruit-printed housedresses and floral shirts she faces the camera and conducts calm tirades against the legal system that has taken her son away. The filmmakers give her more screen time than anyone would ordinarily expect—and she and her husband close the documentary with a sense of domestic resilience. Their son and grandson are in prison for murder. Their business has gone under. Yet they will continue. Arm in arm! A vegetable garden of kohlrabis! A smile of faith and hope! The film is in the grip of its own sentimental awe. But there are worse things in the world.

(2016)

Helen Gurley Brown

Somewhere back in the day Helen Gurley Brown said that after a certain age the only things a woman could rely on to improve her appearance were good posture and expensive jewelry. At least that is my recollection, though I no longer recall the exact source or context. The gender specificity, the whiff of doom in the goal, the daft simplicity, the conciseness, the candor, and the plausibility caused it to stick in my head (although my most recent earrings were bought for three dollars from a street vendor). Perhaps this is because everyone who already has their ears pierced and pricked for this kind of suggestion is tired and looking for quick, pithy advice—especially, it is assumed, women, around whom a many-tentacled advice industry was fashioned long ago, with its golden age perhaps corresponding to the golden age of magazine publishing, suburban housewifery, and leisure time—again, somewhere back in the day. That men—both gay and straight—were once a considerable audience for these women's magazines, unacknowledged in the official target demographics, is another topic entirely though I will mention it here in passing.

I also recall once getting in the slowest grocery store line so I could flip through Brown's *Cosmopolitan* in order to discover what "5 Things," advertised on the cover alongside its monthly, near-taxidermic décolleté (who can recall the faces perched above?), were sure to "Drive Men Wild," but not finding them anywhere and having to put the magazine back. Well, Brown may have only been pretending to know five (her husband did the cover headlines). And although she undoubtedly knew some number of viable things, in her first book Brown advises dozens of rather dubious ones, from broccoli almondine, to joining the wealthiest chapter of AA, to letting your lacy slip show beneath your office desk. "Unlike Madame Bovary you don't chase the glittering life, you lay a trap for it," she wrote in *Sex and the Single Girl.* She believed in showing an interest in sports:

> I've found that it helps hypo your interest to have a small bet on one of the teams. Or to know somebody's brother or cousin you can root for. One football season I "adopted" Jon Arnett of the USC Trojans. I pretended I was his mother and felt how she would feel watching the game. (Actually she probably had cold compresses on her head with somebody staked out at the TV set to tell her when it was over.) Then because of some NCAA ruling . . . Jon was benched for a semester and I lost heart. Now on Rose Bowl day and during the World Series I simply chloroform myself.

As for good posture and expensive jewelry? She herself had multiple plastic surgeries and underwent breast augmentation at the late age of seventy-three.

Of course, evolving and proliferating social and domestic roles for women have been discussed from the moment discussion was born, and it is sometimes interesting to look back and see which individual women move into that evolution with a professional eye to claim a historical moment for themselves or just to make one up. There are always currents to ride and they are ridden.

Hence a look back at the social swirl of the 1950s, '60s, and '70s, with the new biographies *Not Pretty Enough: The Unlikely Triumph of Helen Gurley Brown* by Gerri Hirshey and the more innuendo-laden *Enter Helen: The Invention of Helen Gurley Brown and the Rise of the Modern Single Woman* by Brooke Hauser. Both Hirshey and Hauser believe that Brown was something of a pioneer and that her life and writings laid the groundwork for later commercial white-person fictions such as *Sex and the City* and *Mad Men,* which (somewhat) extol the virtues of work for women as if it were a new and glamorous idea. Both biographers spent a lot of time at the Helen Gurley Brown archives at Smith College and have generous things to say about the librarians there.

What does "modern single woman" even mean anymore? It is a phrase that has been with us for quite a while, and may be an improvement on "spinster," although "spinster" is being hiply refurbished and celebrated as a lifestyle and not a temporary or pseudocrippling condition. ("Single" and "modern" have ephemeral youth built into them, so the word *spinster* has been reclaimed as a preference for women of any age dismayed at having to depend on men for very much. See *Spinster: Making a Life of One's Own* by Kate Bolick.)

Helen Gurley Brown, we glean—perhaps more from her own writing than from the biographies of Hirshey and Hauser—was obsessed with the ostensibly fun culture of American offices and corporate expense accounts in a postwar boom economy. She began her own office career in the 1940s when she was still in her teens; she eventually became a successful copywriter for a Los Angeles ad agency, her first major client being Catalina swimsuits. She worked even on weekends, and stayed late when the men went home to their families. She then moved on to another agency, which doubled her salary, and there she began naming lipsticks and writing copy for Max Factor; according to Hirshey, she became "the highest paid woman in West Coast advertising."

At thirty-seven she owned a Mercedes and a stock portfolio and had never been married. Although she didn't believe in worrying about that, she had begun to worry. Marry late, she nonetheless advised:

> You can have babies until you're forty or older. And if you happen to die before *they* are forty . . . you [will] avoid those tiresome years as an unpaid baby sitter. . . . Frankly, the magazines and their marriage statistics give me a royal pain.

When baby boomers such as Lesley Stahl are currently peddling books on their own besmitten grandmotherhood (see Stahl's *Becoming Grandma*), Brown's fifty-year-old advice can still seem refreshing and iconoclastic.

Well, Brown took on many sacred cows that had already been half-throttled or at least smacked about in various marginalized counter-cultures. Somewhat amoral regarding sex (although she felt a woman should never bargain sexually for a dinette set), she lived a lot of her life as a quasi courtesan, which led to pleasure, love, heartbreak, adultery, nutritionists, psychotherapy with the author of *Sex Can Be Art!* (in group therapy when she was called a "slut" she had to go home and look up the word), and eventually marriage to the film producer David Brown, a bright, successful, devoted man. There was some subsequent adultery thrown in here and there for excitement, though the marriage was strong, allowing each to dance with others, Brown's quite literal preference at social gatherings. She and her husband worked together. They buoyed and anchored each other. They plotted together. They ate diet Jell-O together. Though the courtship had its bumps, once they were married they were thought of as inseparable.

When early in their marriage her husband happened upon some amusing—nay, sparkling!—letters his wife had written to friends, he encouraged her to write a book. (Mr. Brown liked writers and had something of a crush on the novelist Rona Jaffe.) Mrs. Brown wrote as she spoke (advice she continued to give writers). And since they both knew that sex sold, and Mr. Brown felt that Mrs. Brown had some interesting things to say about the bachelorette life—in Hirshey's phrase, "some lubricious operating instructions" for being single—Helen Brown sat down with her high-speed typing and began several different sorts of drafts.

What she ended up with was in large part a spirited rebuttal to a widely discussed 1960 *Look* magazine article, "Women Without Men," which had offended her with its depiction of a parched and barren single life. Hirshey astutely notes the social class anger in Brown's book, but also acknowledges that Brown was interested not in a revolution but in practical navigation of an unfair system that was not going to change in time for *you:*

> Her message was beamed to working single women with limited options and means, those who were still thrashing in the steno pool, who slept fitfully in a crown of bobby pins when the salon was too dear.

One person's shocking truth confided vividly and recognizably can make others feel better. That is perhaps the very heart of the modern and certainly is at the core of Brown's sense of sisterhood. It also came from every part of Brown's life: the Arkansas girlfriends, the California psychotherapy, the reading of novels, all of which consoled her.

With disapproval from her family and blurbs from Joan Crawford and Gypsy Rose Lee, Helen Gurley Brown soon became the best-selling author of *Sex and the Single Girl*. The book contained no-nonsense advice, a wised-up older-sister tone, some recipes, some beauty tips, some bawdy anecdotes, stock tips, racetrack tips (bet the favorites to show), a defense of anorexia (a word never used; the extremely thin Helen Brown simply believed in not eating), and decorating suggestions for the bachelorette pad. Imitations ensued, including *Sex and the Single Man*, over which Brown sued for title infringement.

One book that followed Brown's and imitated her get-the-heck-out-of-your-childhood philosophy was Jean Baer's *The Single Girl Goes to Town* (1968), which more or less advises the single girl to choose Los Angeles or New York only, not to bother with other cities, saying that in Malibu "every night there is a party somewhere, and if you're not invited, just walk in. Nobody cares." Lest you think this is simply the freewheeling 1960s, Baer's book also contains an "Earnings Chart" to calculate the financial worth of your targeted man, plus gift suggestions for various hostesses—whose parties you may be crashing.

Both Baer and Brown fail to warn against being arrested as a stalker, or a burglar, or being murdered by someone you don't know as you eat your picnic alone in a park (Brown's suggestion as a man-snare), but instead both do warn against the misleading if endearing charms of "homosexuals" (now that gaydar has been invented, this seems a bit antique). David Reuben's *Everything You've Always Wanted to Know About Sex* (1969) didn't come out until seven years after Brown's book, but clearly there was consumer demand for all.

Gurley, steeped in Alfred Kinsey's 1953 report on female sexuality, was ahead of other authors of how-tos in pronouncing openly on what so many already privately knew. But that it was a woman saying all this—be free! enjoy sex! have more than one partner! stay financially independent!—seemed like news, though it was not news to Brown or her Arkansas gal pals, who had always lived this way. Her book was a sensation and was even sold to the movies, or rather its title was sold to Warner Bros., at $40,000 a word, as *Life* magazine put it, which resulted in a script cowritten by Joseph Heller and an otherwise unremarkable film but for its surreal and interminable car chase (Heller's idea of the madcap single life?), its all-star cast, and a scene in which Natalie Wood, playing a fictional psychotherapist named Helen Brown, eerily falls into the ocean at night and almost drowns.

Helen Gurley grew up in Little Rock as what she called a hillbilly, though as Hauser rightly points out she was sturdily middle class (her mother was a teacher, her father a state legislator). But then she had a taste of poverty and tragedy when her father was killed in a freak elevator accident in the state capitol building, and the insurance money subsequently ran out. Her sister was disabled by polio. Their mother eventually moved them first to Tulsa and then to Los Angeles, where Brown remained and went to secretarial school; over the decades she held nineteen different office jobs there.

It was a particular moment in social and economic history. A young woman could move around at that time and not cling to a partner or any one job because female office employees were in demand (for one thing, they were underpaid) and rent was affordable. Brown had a lively prose style, compulsively wrote thank-you notes with her favorite term of endearment ("pussycat"), and believed in women not so much as sex objects but as sex subjects; men were the actual objects. She had a confessional bent. Like Joan Rivers and Nora Ephron she was not a creative genius but a disciplined workaholic with a springy cadence in her sentences; she, too, felt bad about her neck; she, too, wanted to make a lot of money. She, too, was an amusing woman attached to something larger in the culture and wished to report on it.

The sexual revolution was not feminism, though there was a blurry overlap, and both movements had their waters muddied then clarified then expanded by gay rights and gender liberation. Is it politically permissible to wear false eyelashes and high heels and protest the meaninglessness of life without romantic love, wondering out loud where you went wrong? Well, you can if you're Prince. But only if you're Prince? The disruption and dismantling of patriarchal sexual culture can occur in a lot of different ways and it has taken various kinds of people to do it. Social change involves a more or less generalized smashing but from a collection of angles and directions, sometimes from both inside and out.

After the financial debacle of the movie *Cleopatra* (1963), many attached to the studio that made it were fired. David Brown was one of them, but he landed a publishing job in New York with New American Library. The Browns then left California for good. What would the newly notorious Helen do? For the time being she wrote magazine and newspaper columns. With the help, encouragement, and connections of her husband (he was a former managing editor of the old *Cosmopolitan;* for those following the "feminist" path of Hillary Clinton out of Arkansas, pay heed to the helping hand of marriage), Helen Gurley Brown was eventually given the star vehicle she was looking for: editor in chief of *Cosmopolitan,* which was at that time a moribund but commercially minded literary magazine that the Hearst Corporation felt needed revitalizing.

Brown tarted it up. She shortened the articles. Her ethos and aesthetics were mostly her own but somewhat in step with the sexual revolution and with a general desire to eschew a female culture devoted to household chores. Brown kept the celebrity interviews but added a psychotherapy column, plus controversial articles on abortion and the birth control pill. But she did not want anything "fancy." She said that her magazine was for "girls who have never heard of Mike Nichols."

Cosmopolitan flew off the stands. Readers were also perhaps looking for those tips that David Brown cleverly advertised on the cover next to all that Francesco Scavullo photography. Although seemingly a weird new outgrowth of *Playboy, Cosmo* was also a precursor to a magazine such as *O,* with its soothing working woman's downtime-in-a-bubble-bath quality. *Cosmopolitan* stood outside any official dogma except to "keep the lonely girl company." And when she became editor in chief and made a big success of it, Brown's journey—Hirshey would say "unlikely triumph"—was complete. The scarlet woman who claimed to have slept with 178 men before she was married and who had never gone to college was now settled into something she had always wanted: an enterprise to run. She loved most people. She met Jacqueline Susann on the Park Avenue median strip in front of her apartment building and they became fast friends. She met Gloria Vanderbilt, with whom she became even closer. The Browns were said to move among their peers as plain, simple, and genuine. There was always something small-town about them that they exuded.

Helen Gurley Brown's penchant for the soft/hard sell was sometimes thought to have come from her years in the advertising business. Not much is made in either Hirshey's or Hauser's biography of Brown's southernness. Arkansas is the South, but this is underplayed though it was very much part of Brown's character and her story. Her self-proclaimed "hillbilly" roots were mostly just southern. Of course she was hardly the first steel magnolia to take Manhattan by storm (Truman Capote and his invented Holly Golightly brought many real-life imitators). But her personal niceness, "whispery half smile," coy flirtations, desire to amuse, locked-in attentiveness, and "just folks" quality came largely from a societal expectation of women in the South, perhaps the only expectation she conformed to once transplanted. I recently listened to a friend who, after having sung the praises of charming southern women, did an impression of a generic northern woman responding conversationally to a man attempting to engage her: all warmth drained from his face as he pursed his lips and said in ostensible mimicry of the Yankee female, "And what is that supposed to mean?" (I laughed my head off because why not.)

If Hauser's biography sometimes reads like a screen treatment about making a glamorous life (her epigraphs are often movie quotes, particularly from Marilyn Monroe films, and she uses "Cut to" as a transition; photos, including one of the Browns' grave in the Ozarks, are affixed), Hirshey's book—once it gets past its bitter complaint about the Hearst Corporation's virtual gag order on quoting Brown's office memoranda—is a bit more like a novel in its attention to narrative tension and pacing and smooth writing. Moreover, Hirshey cleverly transforms her final pages into something akin to an oral history, with several of Brown's good friends—from the playwright Eve Ensler to Barbara Walters—chiming in. Here is Hirshey on Joan Rivers speaking of Brown's famous frugality:

> Cheap! Don't get Rivers started. She recalled a day when she was in a cab and noticed Helen at a bus stop, trying to juggle overstuffed work satchels. Rivers rolled down her window and hollered at her: "Helen, calm down and take a cab! Your husband made *Jaws*!"

Brown was politically criticized by better (more conventionally) educated feminists, but she was close to women and believed in sorority—if that is a feminist principle. I think her biographers would say, yes, it is. Once, the young Kate Millett and her fellow Columbia students took over the *Cosmopolitan* offices and requested that Brown attend a consciousness-raising session and confess to her hang-ups. This Brown did with alacrity (she had spent all those California years in group therapy) and had only gotten to hang-up number eight when she was asked to sit down and be quiet. There was some froideur with Gloria Steinem and a complete standoff with Joan Didion. But she admired Betty Friedan and raved about *The Feminine Mystique* in print. Like Rivers and Ephron, Brown believed in "Having It All" and wrote a book by that title. "Having It All" is more a fanciful cri de coeur than a feminist idea—most men don't "have it all"—but it is true that some women do have more energy, opportunity, and fecundity than others, and if they claim to have some advice in that direction that goes beyond dumb luck and childhood zip code, let us see how useful it is.

Brown in her seventies had to be pried from her post at *Cosmopolitan*. She was given a decorative title as head of the international division (Hirshey reminds us that there are women in hijabs reading the magazine still). The Hearst Corporation also created a facsimile office for the elderly Brown, one that resembled her former one to a T, though the new one was fake—Hirshey suggests that perhaps even the fax machine was not plugged in, that perhaps nothing was plugged in. At the end, still in her Pucci dresses and fishnet stockings, Brown was wheeled into this office daily and mostly took naps there.

Her legacy, imprecisely feminist, is one of putting the pleasure principle dead center in a woman's life—painful cosmetic surgeries notwithstanding—only slightly more complicated than "Girls Just Want to Have Fun." Her biographers defend her from feminist derision and snobbery, and the reader understands this protective inclination, which is rooted largely in affection: Brown was companionable, charitable, self-deprecating—one wants to come to her aid. Hirshey and Hauser do not want her to seem an absurd figure but a unique confection of several eras, cultures, and social strata. She was not an intellectual but nonetheless a wee bit of a philosopher. Her critics might line up to say: Why should men and women have to get tricky with one another? Why all the artifice? Why must snakes be charmed, flesh be doctored? Adults should be treated and behave as adults.

Yes. But girlfriend, or, rather, *pussycat,* no matter how evolved, we all contain our basest selves, right up until the end. Get out the fishnets and cast them. Seize life—it's really there. Such are the ongoing tidings of Helen Gurley Brown.

(2016)

Ezra Edelman's *O.J.: Made in America*

Martin Luther King, Jr. and others have said that Sunday in America is the most segregated day of the week, but the O. J. Simpson verdict, acquittal on all charges, came in on a Tuesday. The jury, after having been sequestered for the better part of a year, took only three hours to deliberate. It knew enough and now wanted to go home. Leaning into the jury box, Simpson's defense attorney Johnny Cochran had closed with a rousing speech that the verdict would be not just about Simpson but a vote for racial justice generally. "Are you, members of the jury, with the Brothers or with the Man?"—as coprosecutor Christopher Darden described it ahead of time in an objection to the defense strategy. Unknown to a lot of the white world, this idea of voting for something larger than O.J. was felt in many places, not just at the lawyers' tables.

When the 1995 verdict was announced, it was a sunny October morning in L.A. Members of the LAPD had come on horseback to the front of the courthouse, in case there were riots. People at work and at home were glued to the broadcast. I myself was standing in front of my television set while my baby napped upstairs, snoozing through his last full year of racial blindness, a condition Simpson quixotically believed in and sought for much of his adult life. "I'm not black; I'm O.J.," he repeatedly said, though racial community and fellow feeling would come to his rescue in the end.

Even in the Bronco "chase"—a minimalist newsreel thriller à la Andy Warhol—those who had thought of Simpson as "white" joked bleakly that now that he had cop cars following him he had become black again. (A similar line is uttered by a neighbor over the fictional rendition of Christopher Darden's fence in the exposition-jammed dialogue of *The People v. O.J. Simpson,* the docudrama that garnered five Emmys and disconcertingly serves up the case as entertainment and courtroom soap opera.) Young people had cheered on the Bronco from highway overpasses.

On the day of the verdict, stock trading dwindled. Water usage dropped. So much work stopped that it was estimated that there was "480 million dollars in lost productivity." Such nationwide attention and suspense suggested that at least some part of the public was alert to this verdict as a species of referendum. Could an African-American man with money get the same breaks that white men with money did? Simpson was a prize to be competed for.

Black Americans erupted in jubilation at the news of Simpson's freedom. Crowds hugged in the streets, and the cheering outside the Los Angeles Superior Court startled the LAPD's horses, which reared back and then were trotted away. In the wake of so many acquittals for the killing and maiming of black Angelenos—Eulia Love, Latasha Harlins, Rodney King—here was one for the other side. In the courtroom one of the jurors thrust his fist in the air in black power solidarity. He was an upstanding citizen but also a former Black Panther—something missed by the prosecution during voir dire.

White Americans were by and large vexed and perplexed. Jeffrey Toobin, who covered the case for *The New Yorker,* exclaimed a little cluelessly about the verdict, "I actually thought I might pass out from shock." Seventy-seven percent of whites believed that Simpson was guilty; 72 percent of blacks believed him not guilty. Rather than closing the gap, the trial increased these percentages by roughly ten points from what they had been pretrial, widening the racial divide in opinion and perception. Whites and blacks had watched the same trial and seen very different things; their responses to the acquittal took place in separate worlds. "Black people too happy, white people too mad," observed the comedian Chris Rock about the reactions. "I haven't seen white people that mad since they canceled *M.A.S.H.*"

. . .

At the time I had only one white friend who believed completely in Simpson's innocence—that is, that despite a trail of blood from the crime scene to the Simpson home, he was utterly framed, from beginning to end, not just the victim of perjury and illegally enhanced evidence. This friend has also been known to argue that the Apollo moon landing was an elaborately staged hoax prompted by the Cold War, a belief held by 60 percent of Russians to this day. In a minor coincidence, O. J. Simpson was in a movie, *Capricorn One,* also about a fake space landing; in so many parts of his Los Angeles life, reality was ostensible, continually represented as something up for grabs.

Most other friends of mine, black and white, shared with me the view that despite the amount of incriminating evidence, the LAPD—primarily in the form of the bigoted police detective Mark Fuhrman—had planted and mishandled some of it and lied on the stand and that the case in the courtroom was tainted and so not necessarily proven beyond a reasonable doubt. There was, furthermore, no murder weapon with fingerprints. There was no witness. DNA expert Barry Scheck had poked holes in the forensic science he himself had helped develop. If a man with Simpson's celebrity and money could not stand up successfully against the judicial system with that system's habit of casual fudgings, then no black man could. Simpson was the most famous man to stand trial for murder, let alone the most famous black man. "White people couldn't accept that O.J. never broke down," the white father of a black son said to me. "White people were waiting for him to fall apart in that courtroom, but he never did."

But when I spoke at dinner about it with a well-known (white) film director who believed completely in Simpson's guilt, and I said offhandedly that I found the logistics puzzling—I could not understand how one person acting alone could have murdered two people like that, so quietly yet brutally, with children asleep upstairs—he looked aghast. "Really? You don't?" he said. And then he stood up next to the dinner table and enacted it with a samurai's choreography and an invisible weapon that seemed to be a double-edged sword (well, what isn't?). Watching the director move so assuredly, if somewhat indecipherably, convinced me that he was in the right line of work. But his invisible murder weapon—like the murder weapon that failed ever to make an appearance at the trial—could have used some assistance from a prop department. (The FX docudrama, which leans heavily on Jeffrey Toobin's book *The Run of His Life: The People v. O. J. Simpson,* suggests in passing that Simpson may have learned some knife techniques from a film he was rehearsing about Navy SEALs.)

The Simpson trial kept people talking for years. It was a touchstone of race, class, and gender tensions. If not the trial of the century, as it was rather dramatically called, it was certainly the trial of the nineties. And lest Americans have forgotten, or weren't born yet, or have had their young imaginations muddled by the docudrama—which is replete with the Kardashian girls, plus John Travolta and Nathan Lane doing camp versions of Robert Shapiro and F. Lee Bailey (though strong, deep performances are elicited from the actors playing Marcia Clark, Christopher Darden, and Johnny Cochran)—a new, sober, and intelligent documentary, produced and directed by Ezra Edelman, the Emmy-winning son of the activist Marian Wright Edelman, has emerged from the unlikely source ESPN to look closely at Simpson's entire life and times and to see him as the complicated construction that he is. It is titled *O.J.: Made in America.*

Many of the books, articles, and films on O. J. Simpson over the years have been aptly titled or subtitled, in Dreiserian fashion, *An American Tragedy.* When one looks at tragedies, one is not looking so much at the protagonist's pure or lusty and always unlucky victims. The story—its meaning and complexity—lies with the perpetrator: Othello, Don José, Canio's Pagliaccio in *Pagliacci;* only the doomed Carmen gets the title of the opera she is in. And Simpson's story is an opera—a heartbreaking drama that will always be titled "O.J.," not "Nicole and Ron." The tragic hero is one who is in some way exceptional but (as in the above-named tenor roles) is gripped by a fatal flaw that is often jealousy compounded by dislocation. There may be issues of authenticity or fame-induced impostor syndrome or some other variety of exile. Some fault line in society runs through him as well. His strived-for success feels hollow. He is spiritually homeless, humiliated by his lover and maybe also by his work if the fun part is over (Don José), or if he hopes to rest on his laurels (Othello), or if his job is tawdry show business of some sort (Canio/Pagliaccio). Perhaps as part of the story there are themes of race and class or a narrative of comeuppance. All these elements figure into Simpson's epic fall. After divorcing his high school sweetheart, he married the beautiful eighteen-year-old waitress whom he'd met in a restaurant, and when she turned out not to be the perfect wife for an aging, womanizing man—she retaliated with infidelities of her own—he began to terrorize and hit her.

Edelman's documentary, like the FX docudrama, shows the Rodney King beating right at the start (in the documentary it is shown at the start of each of the five episodes in an opening credit montage of public moments that figure in Simpson's fate and is explored more fully in Episode 2). In our current time, when some of the most shocking police brutality has emerged for public viewing, one might imagine that the King beating would seem familiar. Yet quite the opposite is true: the footage of it still shocks viscerally to this day. Its pointlessness and sadism resemble a lynching. At that time there were no body cams or cell phones and the LAPD had no idea they were being observed; it was at night and the amount of time given over to the violence is grotesquely leisurely and unperturbed. The black community always knew such things occurred, but when the film evidence emerged, at long last there was proof for the courtroom.

Less than two weeks later there was surveillance footage of a grocer shooting black teenager Latasha Harlins in the back of the head. At a time when a conviction for crack possession got black people decades in prison, that the grocer in the Harlins murder served no prison time and the Los Angeles cops in the King beating were acquitted of state charges led naturally to community outrage and unfortunately to fiery riots that did nothing to bandage wounds anywhere. When an unarmed black man is killed with impunity by police designated to protect and serve, setting the occasional empty car on fire may seem a natural if desperate response to years of underlying tensions. But whole black neighborhoods going up in flames in Los Angeles reduced poor Rodney King himself to saying, "Can't we all just get along?"—a question whose answer had already been uttered.

.   .   .

Daryl Gates, the head of the LAPD at the time, was famous for weaponizing his police force. He defended chokeholds. He introduced SWAT teams and snipers, a move that was imitated in some other urban police departments, often to disastrous effect (as shown in the Utah community of the 2015 Scott Christopherson–Brad Barber documentary *Peace Officer*). Edelman's documentary focuses minimally on Gates, but does manage an extended interview with Mark Fuhrman, the police detective who lied during the Simpson trial regarding his personal history of racism and racist epithets, and who eventually lawyered up and pleaded the Fifth, even to the question "Did you plant evidence?" The prosecution's loss was less about the glove found at Simpson's house (which sort of *did* fit and clearly belonged to Simpson) than about the Fifth Amendment. Also, the forensics team confessed on the stand to taking the blood of the accused from the lab back to the crime scene, admitting it was an unusual thing to do. Though maybe it wasn't. In any case, the prosecution's trail-of-blood case was no longer a slam dunk.

Given the several causes for reasonable doubt, after 267 sequestered days, hovered over by guards and given the occasional conjugal visit, the jury felt entitled to take only three hours to deliberate. Since they had already been present for the entire trial, they believed they'd had more than enough time for a decision. Nonetheless, the jurors were slandered and reviled for doing so, and continue to be even to this day.

Edelman's documentary brilliantly portrays the social backdrop to race in Los Angeles at that time, a police culture of officially sanctioned excessive force, leading to several shattering events: the Watts riots, the police killing of Eulia Love in front of her home in 1979, and eventually Rodney King in 1991. In L.A. from 1940 to 1960 the African-American population had grown by 600 percent, many people fleeing Louisiana and Texas only to face California racism as stark as that of the Jim Crow South. "We didn't ask these people to come here," says Bill Parker, who preceded Gates and was head of the LAPD during the Watts riots. Parker himself was raised in Deadwood, South Dakota, and although he cleaned up the internal corruption on the force, he also turned it into a quasi-military presence, a pernicious, occupying army in black neighborhoods. Reputedly he recruited cops from the KKK.

The Simpson family had come to California from a Louisiana farm, and Orenthal James was born and grew up in the San Francisco projects. His father became a drag queen and left the family, dying of AIDS in 1985. The documentary leaves viewers to imagine on their own how a black gay father at that time might have affected a son caught up in the stultifying hypermasculinity of sports. It surely bound Simpson to his mother, who appears in Edelman's film as a sweet, pretty, religious woman, wheeled mutely in and out of her son's long criminal trial.

Though Edelman's film is not about Nicole Brown, she is seen as the great beauty everyone upon meeting her instantly declared her to be. We see her lovely in her wedding dress, basking in the sun with her young child, playing basketball by the pool with her husband's friends, who adored her. We see her sexy modeling shots. In fact, beauty is very much a theme in this narrative: both Simpson and Brown were so good-looking that no actors could convincingly play them (in the docudrama *The People v. O.J.,* Cuba Gooding is miscast as O.J., and Brown is given no written part at all; she is seen only once as a blurry, blond corpse foregrounded at her own funeral). In a film industry full of beautiful people, the casting problem is usually the opposite—the actors are too attractive for the people they are playing. A documentary, using actual footage of all involved, does not have this problem. In Edelman's case he can also use, and does, home movies and photographs of both victims, so that an honoring trace of their presence persists. But he does not linger there; his story is not about them.

If a hero embodies the unspoken virtues and vitality of a society, the tragic hero, beneath an admirable veneer, flecked with the marks of youthful struggle overcome, also embodies a society's secret illnesses. Simpson suffered from many things having to do with American success and celebrity and rags-to-riches financial swings, including disconnect from the black community. He also suffered from rickets as a child and severe arthritis as an adult; his beauty when young fed into both insecurity about its loss and sexual entitlement, which fueled jealousy, rage, and narcissism. More contemporary pathological categories might include borderline personality disorder, mental compartmentalization, and concussive head trauma (CTE) from playing football, but speculative medicalizing diminishes the story's power.

Edelman's documentary would like implicitly to link Simpson's troubles to the culture of sports, though it also compares him unfavorably to Muhammad Ali, Kareem Abdul-Jabbar, and Jim Brown, other athletes who were aligned with the civil rights movement and were "race men," which Simpson never was nor aspired to be. He was an ambitious party boy from a party school—USC in 1967 was pretty much beyond the reach of the black community—and after his subsequent professional running back days were over, Simpson was both driven and anxious about money. As his movie career went through its vagaries, he strove to be a successful businessman. He served on corporate boards and did endorsements for rental cars and honey-baked hams, though what he really wanted, a little unrealistically, was to be head of a movie studio. According to the documentary, he was supporting his in-laws.

For many years he was wealthy, famous, and handsome in a land—Los Angeles—that prized such things even more than elsewhere. He loved Hollywood and felt, foolishly—perhaps like Michael Jackson, whom Johnny Cochran also once represented—that he had transcended race. He seemed to feel that lavish materialism would express his accomplishment, that it would signify his success as a black man, that it would speak for itself. He was counterrevolutionary.

The documentary handles the trial itself in efficient ways. Interviews with the present-day Mark Fuhrman and the now almost unrecognizable Marcia Clark are perhaps the most interesting, although throughout managing defense attorney Carl Douglas has some of the most memorable remarks. Of Robert Shapiro, he says, "He was not known as a trial dog with two *g*'s." Of Cochran: "Johnny was always that stalwart defender of justice fighting against the Bastille." Of the strong and unusual diversity of the jury: "O.J. turned and said, 'Guys, if this jury convicts me, maybe I *did* do it.'" The verdict was not inexplicable, as much as it might have seemed so to white people watching the trial from their living rooms. The prosecutors, according to Marcia Clark, felt they had lost the case by the time Fuhrman invoked the Fifth. Though Clark closed her case by emphasizing the domestic abuse, hoping to appeal to the women jurors, domestic abuse was not the crime with which Simpson was being charged.

Edelman shows Clark cursing out paparazzi in front of her home when she is called back into the courthouse for the verdict; it's clear she knows she has lost. As for the vulnerable and complex Christopher Darden, who initiated O.J.'s trying on of the glove (which prompted Cochran's triumphant rhyme, "If it does not fit, you must acquit"), he refused to be included in the film, a loss for Edelman, who also did not have Cochran or Robert Kardashian, both now deceased, nor Judge Lance Ito, who despite inviting Larry King into his chambers has since rebuffed all publicity. This past spring, however, a somewhat charming and middle-aged Chris Darden did go on *The View* and on the *Today* show (where, among other things, he defended his decision to have Simpson try on the glove and did not deny having been romantically involved with Marcia Clark during the case).

Edelman negotiates the legal turns of the trial (most involving blood evidence and its contamination) without getting too bogged down with courtroom psychodrama and the media frenzy that attached to all the participants. The falling-out of Shapiro and Cochran at the end is little more than too many bigwigs at the table but provides an interesting coda. Cochran's "playing the race card" included "playing the Nazi card," and he was not above invoking Hitler when speaking of Fuhrman's racist views. It is an example of "Godwin's Law" or "Reductio ad Hitlerum" and was an unnecessary move on Cochran's part—the first person to say "Nazi" loses the argument, my own students like to say—but Cochran did not lose, and Shapiro's peeling away and grandstanding after the verdict, holding solo press conferences in which he criticized Cochran and Bailey, were merely self-serving.

But *O.J.: Made in America* continues well past the trial. It follows Simpson as he tries to salvage his life despite having become a social pariah in Brentwood. It shows him before he finally leaves for Florida to protect his assets, after losing the civil suit brought by the Goldmans and Browns. Simpson is shown making faked footage—reluctantly packing up, pulling out of the driveway, telling the cameraman to go, waving him away—in order to sell these films to tabloids. The civil suit had assessed the damages at $33 million and he had no other way to make money.

The years in Florida are squalid and surreal. Celia Farber, an *Esquire* journalist who interviewed Simpson at the time, said she began to feel "sorry for him . . . I kept feeling he was a victim." The level and scope of negative feeling toward him, his banishment from practically everything, she felt had a component of racism in it. But knocked off all his pedestals, instead of doing good works, Simpson escaped into strip clubs and unsavory parties. Although the black church reached out to help him, and he had read the Bible and the Koran in jail, he did not get religion. He took up golfing with a new social set much lower down the ladder than those he had golfed with in Brentwood.

The documentary takes us through the final extraordinary sentencing of Simpson in 2010 for an absurdly small crime—a chapter the public may not have paid much attention to. Because Simpson had lost all his corporate contracts, he was making money through the signing of memorabilia. (This is how he paid his lawyers during the trial as well: signing footballs and T-shirts in jail.) In the strange mishandling of his personal property after the civil case against him, much personal memorabilia, such as his Heisman Trophy, never intended for sale, went missing. To retrieve some of these possessions, Simpson hatched a plan with some dicey new Florida pals. It was less like a crime and more like a caper out of a movie. They would find the shady memorabilia salesman in a Las Vegas hotel room and confront him.

Because two of his friends were carrying guns, it was called "armed robbery." Because Simpson said upon entering that nobody was to leave the room, it was called "attempted kidnapping." When Simpson pleads with the court that he didn't know he was committing a crime, one is inclined to believe him. But the Nevada judge, clearly not liking the outcome of Simpson's previous criminal trial, and making a kind of end run around the double-jeopardy clause in the Constitution, sentenced Simpson to over thirty-three years (with parole after seven). The number was thought to mirror the $33 million awarded in the civil suit, and the day of the sentencing was the anniversary of the murder charge acquittal. Ron Goldman's father, Fred, was in the Las Vegas courtroom doggedly looking for justice and solace. Fred Goldman's long, bitter vigil and enthusiasm for the Nevada court's over-the-top conviction could not possibly assuage his sorrow. One cannot judge such grief. Though one can compare it, if one dares, to the extravagantly and unsettlingly ready public forgiveness of Dylann Roof by the families of the victims of the Charleston AME church shooting in 2015. Amazing grace indeed, as Barack Obama noted.

Edelman's documentary shows O.J. now in prison looking gray and overweight while trying to put the best spin on things—his coaching of the prison teams, for instance. When the murder trial is brought up by the parole reviewers, Simpson looks crestfallen. He wants to be rehabilitated in the public mind, and the question serves as a reminder that this will never happen. How did this life go so awry? The documentary veers simultaneously toward and away from the question, probably since at the heart of most individual madness there is a kind of mystery, although the sociological threads—sports, race, criminal justice, domestic violence, celebrity, sex, hedonism—are all named and explored. The film is excellent at putting what it can in its cultural context.

What the film does especially eye-openingly is look at the much-maligned jury and interview two rather sympathetic members. (Further deliberation—something that was expected—might have left the public with a hung jury, a mistrial at best.) Even if there hadn't been perjury, mishandled evidence, and general and specific reasonable doubt, if one is a juror and perceives there is a kind of war that involves race, one may feel oneself drafted as a soldier and choose sides. War—which includes battle cries, uniforms, songs, artillery, recruits, and often dishonest, obscuring vocabulary (*engagement!*)—is the fog itself.

The documentary suggests that the jurors felt themselves invited into it, called upon to take care of one of their own, and by the end were battle-weary but not AWOL. In a place where deference to police had been built into the legal system, aggravating racial tensions for decades, this jury would fight back. Did the prison system need one more black man? Did it require this particular black man? The crucial police detective on the crime scene had pleaded the Fifth multiple times to questions regarding evidence tampering; the prosecution's case had a large wobble in it; how was a conviction possible?

The jurors, for the most part black women from downtown L.A., clearly felt closer to Rodney King than to the white model who had married an admired sports hero. Redemption for one of their own sweetened the technical correctness of the verdict. Nonetheless, with unveiled scorn, coprosecutor Bill Hodgman looks into Edelman's camera and shockingly calls the jury "unfit," "a bad lot," a product of "reverse social Darwinism."

How curious but inevitable that our artists and comedians are more fearless in their opinions (than, say, our politicians) when it comes to the matter of black lives mattering; in speaking of police culture, after this summer's tragic Dallas shooting of three cops, Bill Maher has said, "You cannot shoot unarmed people continually without someone shooting back." When two weeks later a black therapist was shot as he lay with his hands raised in a Florida street next to an autistic patient, the still-living therapist asked the cop why he had shot him, and the cop replied, "I don't know."

Because he could. Because deep down he believed he was worth more than the black man in the street. Because our country being awash in guns more than any other country in the world (Yemen is second) makes many policemen trigger-happy. Because frightened cops make for frightened citizens. Because it feels like a war. "People keep saying, 'We need to have a conversation about race,'" Toni Morrison told *The Telegraph*. "This is the conversation. I want to see a cop shoot a white unarmed teenager in the back."

On the subject of O.J., Chris Rock is even edgier. His routine on this topic mentions the $25,000-a-month alimony Simpson was paying his estranged wife when he "hadn't made a touchdown in twenty years." Violence during divorce is statistically notorious; almost everyone going through a family breakup is for a time half-crazy, and sometimes it shows up on the legal dockets, as Rock himself comprehends. Ron Goldman was Nicole's boyfriend, Rock shouts, and was known to drive around L.A. in the Ferrari that O.J. had bought for her. "I don't even own a Ferrari. But if I saw someone driving my Pinto, that shit would blow up like *The Godfather.*" Rock pauses with his comic's wicked grin. "I'm not saying he should have killed her, but I understand." Prideful rage, as Rock insists, is the story.

But the story's outcome rests on a civil right of innocence until guilt is "proven" in a trial by jury. And with Cochran leading the way, the jurors surely had the same fact pressing on them as they came to their conclusions and did their work: the stressful, repeated grinding down of the black man in America—his rights, his image, his identity, his safety, his employment, his finances, his health, his sanity, his dignity, his liberty, his spirit. When we look around at our country and its institutions—as Edelman's documentary asks us to—we can see so much that is sacrificially tainted with this particular human casualty.

As a result, in the operatic Simpson tragedy (which includes loving "not wisely" but also not too well) we can see a hinge to another love story: that of O.J. and his Angeleno jurors—people identified by number rather than name and whose subsequent condemnation and ostracization mirrored his own. Race trumped gender *and* class. As Edelman tells it, Simpson's story is intricately entwined with the jury's, like the rose and briar vines sprung from doomed lovers in old ballads. The agonist-antagonist-protagonist was saved by a Greek chorus of his peers. Saved somewhat. Saved sort of. Saved slightly.

(2016)

Thoughts on Hillary Clinton, December 2016

In 2007 and 2008 I wrote a couple of pieces on Hillary Clinton (which I have not included here). The first one began: "When most of us first saw Hillary Clinton it was on *60 Minutes* right after the 1992 Super Bowl and she was seated by her man saying she was not one of those women who would stand by him." The second piece divided her 2008 supporters into four camps: (1) the no-illusions camp ("You shouldn't vote with too much hope in your heart"); (2) the camp of wounded projection, which includes a lot of women who sacrificed for their husbands, too; (3) the "we need a woman for president in my lifetime" camp—no matter who she is; (4) conflicted macho men seeking redemption.

The pieces, which now seem a little OBE, were very much of their time and steeped in the details of the 2008 Democratic primary, during which I was canvassing (in Wisconsin and Indiana) for Barack Obama, who seemed a much more significant and useful figure—historically, sociologically, and temperamentally. Because of her marital leg up (no mischievous innuendo there—don't search!), I didn't find Clinton a deeply feminist choice. I didn't see her as representing any systemic change. I did think, on the other hand, that she was smart and quick and had more "charisma" (why this word?) than the press gave her credit for—both she and Obama could get wonky and dull on the trail when tired; nothing wrong with that—she had a big laugh and real warmth and sometimes the heat of a beautiful villainess, like the aging queen in *Snow White,* everyone's favorite character in the Disney film. She was a centrist and a hawk and sometimes dodgy; she publicly recounted dodging fictional sniper fire in a Ronald Reagan–style mind-movie set in the former Yugoslavia. She also had a hand in one of the biggest foreign policy catastrophes of our time. This, despite the fearsome Clinton Machine, doomed her in a campaign against a younger, less established online community organizer of oddly named peace-loving dwarves (our young people).

When she ran inevitably again in 2016, this time as the Democratic nominee, I at long last voted for a Clinton. Had to for the Supreme Court. She was strong on *Roe v. Wade.* She seemed strong on tightening gun laws. She was adamant about Citizens United. These things, for a change, did not seem to have a waffle in them. (One had to put aside Iraq, NAFTA, the demise of HillaryCare, the crime bill, the welfare bill, Waco, Texas, the Goldman Sachs speeches, and other dubious maneuvers with which Clinton and/or her husband were associated; one had to hope for the best.) Environmental concern was clearly not a priority of anyone's, and this seemed mind-boggling. (Clinton was going after Donald Trump's voters when wooing Jill Stein's would have won her some states.) We seemed to have two frackers as our major party candidates. Still I assumed—based on very little, apparently—a landslide for her.

But then I noticed that she was not stumping much with Tammy Baldwin in Wisconsin. There seemed to be no Clinton headquarters in Wisconsin that had an actual phone number. The mayor of Madison subsequently complained in *The New York Times* that he did not ever get a call from Hillary. In the summertime, elsewhere, she made mention of putting Bill in charge of the economy. Why? (Bill did not even know to stay off the attorney general's portion of the tarmac and as a result gave us James Comey and his variously damaging email announcements.) Hillary confidently and happily said she might reserve for herself the task of picking out the new White House china. Not only was she getting ahead of herself, she was talking about dishes, not Beijing. She pivoted overconfidently toward suburban female Republicans, alienating the young. She seemed to have trouble getting traction anywhere outside the party base. When she should have been campaigning for midwesterners, at a fund-raiser she suggested a lot of them were a basket of deplorables. Why, why, why? I returned to my wish that the Clintons had gotten out of the way and let someone such as Elizabeth Warren run, with Warren's truth-to-power stance and attachment to the working class. That so many people voted for a septuagenarian socialist proved there was hunger for an alternative. (Bernie Sanders had won the Wisconsin primary, which should have concerned the Clinton campaign but apparently didn't.) In a state full of government workers who use email, her personal server issue was paid attention to. And in a state that is not shy about third parties, third-party candidates could determine outcomes. And did.

Meanwhile, Scott Walker and Paul Ryan and Ron Johnson were out and about in Badgerland energetically derailing Russ Feingold's campaign as well as Clinton's. Johnson boasted charmingly in TV ads that he was one of the few nonlawyers in the Senate, and this had great appeal statewide, especially in a year when a businessman who had never held public office was hypnotizing not just the media but the land. Ted Cruz had won the GOP primary and Wisconsin Republicans and evangelicals knew (eventually) to get behind Trump. The draconian and quietly petulant Paul Ryan came around big-time. But the Democrats were asleep at the wheel, letting insiders pose as outsiders. Well, both parties were doing that.

There is much Monday-morning quarterbacking still going on, but Clinton's popular-vote lead of almost 3 million votes, meaning almost 3 million people were disenfranchised, is a depressing thing to contemplate. Would we not plot regime change of a country with a similar sham democracy? Well, Clinton was playing a board game and knew the byzantine rules and all the answers to the questions on the cards, but forgot to move her markers around the board.

Will she be missed? Clinton, like Trump, and better than she knows, can cast a spell. Watching her throughout 2016, I noticed how attractive and savvy she could be. I watched her every debate. She was in a man's game, and fiercely and mostly unflappably she took it on: I noticed how good-looking she was when she was having fun. It was hard to take one's eyes off her. I studied her outfits and statement necklaces. (Let's be real: The clothing of women in public life is fair game for passing commentary since it is so various, arduously assembled, and deliberately chosen—see Melania's pussy bow.) I liked what Clinton was wearing in June in Columbus speaking against Trump and (too briefly) for the economy. I loved what she wore during Benghazi-gate, even if her attitude looked callous. I admired that yellow suit jacket at her town hall in New Hampshire, a state she should have won in the primary just based on that town hall, where she was excellent, compassionate, and in charge. She looked striking in dark, forest blue-green jackets, but it was that mustard-gold one in the Milwaukee PBS debate that impressed me most, with its "backward in heels" quality. Okay, I joined thousands of other women looking for similar attire on eBay. Her jackets became an online shopping subcategory on Google and her pantsuits the theme of a fantastic, exuberant flashdance in Washington Square Park (available on YouTube). Were we not all a little obsessed with her, even as she cooperated with the national Trump fascination by reducing her campaign to a referendum on him? She and Trump sometimes seemed to be a squabbling couple: Big Loner Papa and Working Mom. Working Mom tends to lose in that game. And she lost by 107,000 even while winning by 3 million.

And so she leaves a blank spot in the landscape—or will we see her in public life doing good works, as we saw with the Carters and will surely see with the Obamas? Did she only want to be president for herself? Time will tell. Wearing those baseball caps, which only sometimes hid his "defiantly ridiculous coiffure," Trump (and his faux-guru campaign of "I'm with YOU," inverting Clinton's more point-of-view-challenged "I'm with Her") waded recklessly in and out of various coded channels of white identity politics—Disco Sucks, *All* Lives Matter, Law and Order, Make America Great Again. His convention theme song was "You Can't Always Get What You Want." Running for president seemed mostly to be one of those things on his bucket list, like being on *America's Got Talent*. Actually winning the office did not seem to be on the list and visibly stunned him. Not a politician, and less a businessman than a show-business man—part Crazy Eddie, part Henry VIII, part AWOL Andrew Jackson—like the reality-show participant he was, he seemed in it for the adventure and applause. The actual White

House may be a bit frumpy for his taste. And governing will be more complicated and tedious than he expected. He immediately went on a "thank you" victory tour to get back to those crowds. He is a barker for the American carousel—*of course it takes talent to do that well,* wrote Oscar Hammerstein with a pitying wink. In the same song Hammerstein also wrote, *But he wouldn't be President unless he wanted to be!*— and maybe Trump will walk off the job to tend to his golf courses and hotels, leaving the position to Mike Pence (whom the GOP would prefer). Trump has already dispensed with the daily intelligence briefings. Too repetitive! *Mercurial* is a word that only begins to describe him. But if he walks away, perhaps the word *beautiful* will be returned to us. It would be nice to get it back. On the other hand, he may not want to leave the set of the biggest reality show he will ever be in. One suspects his desire for a show (rather than a program) will prevail.

Meanwhile, we will see what's on Hillary's bucket list. She has admitted to having no hobbies. (What working woman has hobbies?) After she gave her gracious concession speech on November 9, she stepped away from the podium and plunged almost suicidally down into the crowd. Several alarmed secret service agents dove in after her. We'll watch how she resurfaces. First the futile recount. And then what.

(2017)

Stephen Stills

Several years ago an academic colleague and I embarked on what we called a "Stills-off": we would listen to our record collections and get the musician Stephen Stills's oeuvre down to its top five songs. Then we'd see whose list was better. I assumed our choices would overlap, and high among them would be "4 + 20," whose piercing Appalachian melancholy seems to belong more to the ages than to a moody twenty-four-year-old, as well as "Find the Cost of Freedom" with its sea-shanty sound of grief and endurance. We would both surely include his Buffalo Springfield resistance anthem "For What It's Worth," which with Stills's calm, urgent baritone and rhythmic stops holds up as well as any political song ever written; originally released to protest a Los Angeles curfew—its composition probably began earlier, when Stills was only nineteen—it has endured long past its original occasion. According to Tim Rice, it is "one of the best songs ever written with just two chords." (Rice is a lyricist; the song has more than two chords.)

But my colleague and I could not stay away from Stills's rocking guitar solos, which when revisited on various recordings mesmerized us—"Crossroads," for instance, or "Ain't It Always," pieces that got Stills labeled "Guitar God" on YouTube. Then there is "The Love Gangster" (from his first Manassas album), on which Bill Wyman of the Rolling Stones plays bass, earning him a partial writing credit. Wyman wanted at the time to leave the Stones and join Stills's band; the instruments on

Manassas are all in the hands of virtuosos. (Stills has put out recordings where, like Prince, he has played all the instruments and sung all the parts—"Do for the Others," a lovely, lonely song of resignation from his first solo album, is aptly named—but Manassas did not require that solitary effort, though the band is entirely Stills's brainchild.) "Stephen is a genius," said Neil Young in his book *Waging Heavy Peace.*

And so our lists began to burst at the seams and soon the Stills-off seemed an increasingly stupid exercise. Stills, now seventy-two, has often been named one of the top rock guitarists of all time and is the only musician to have recorded with both Jimi Hendrix and Eric Clapton on the same album—Stills's first solo LP (1971). *Rolling Stone* has listed Stills as both #48 and #27 in its periodic top 100 guitarists list, though he is famously underrated and probably better than what either of those numbers suggests. His work has sprung from every stripe of American music—blues, folk, rock, "songs with roots," as he has put it; he was *Americana* and *singer-songwriter* before those terms were used. And although as a child he began as a drummer and tap dancer, the only percussion one is likely to hear from him now might be when he knocks rhythmically against an acoustic guitar. Once, on a 2006 tour that was being filmed, he tripped over some electrical cords and fell to the stage with a certain percussive flair. "We've got more lights than we're used to," he said. "We usually don't care if they can see us because we're old."

A year following my misbegotten Stills-off, I attended a sold-out concert in Nashville by The Long Players, a tribute band that for its concerts performs one single album from start to finish. This time they had chosen *Déjà Vu* (witty!), which is the first and best (and was for a long while the only) album by Crosby, Stills, Nash & Young. (Ampersand and no Oxford comma for Young: when he needs to get out of a band, he flees quickly.) No sooner had The Long Players begun with Stills's "Carry On" than the capacity crowd was standing—this cannot always be counted on with members of the AARP—singing along at the top of their lungs, knowing every single word. Jubilant, revelatory, the evening was more than a geezer-pleaser: it was baby boomer church, late-middle-aged ecstasy, a statement of a generation that it had not just yet entirely surrendered to the next. I was starting to suspect that no American demographic has had an album—not even one by the Beatles or Bob Dylan or Joni Mitchell—so completely downloaded into their memory banks as this 1970 album had been.

The summer after that concert, on a porch in New England, I found myself among several dinner guests sitting about postprandially in the July night. Suddenly a guitar appeared, and just as suddenly we were all singing Stephen Stills's "Helplessly Hoping." Though we did not know one another that well, working from brain muscle memory we knew the song so automatically that harmony was possible. There was no Beatles or Dylan song we could have sung as successfully. I began to marvel, yet again, at how much, for a particular generation, the songs of Stephen Stills were marinated into our minds, our spines, our bones.

Now it was the following spring, March 2017, and a friend and I were waiting for Stills to step onto the stage of Nashville's legendary Ryman Auditorium with the Allmanesque Kenny Shepherd and an old hipster keyboardist Barry Goldberg, a blues-rock ensemble called The Rides. (Stills once said that Crosby, Stills, and Nash called themselves by their names not just so that they could be free to come and go but because "all the animals had been taken.") The Rides, the blues band of Stills's dreams, he says, got its name from Shepherd's and Stills's shared love of cars (though Stills also loves horses). "We're not Prius people," Stills has said. That he is still playing gigs at his age is evidence of his stubborn professionalism (from the time he was a teenager—from the early Au Go-Go Singers to Buffalo Springfield to Manassas—he was the one to organize his bands). It is also his salute to another musical generation (Shepherd and company) and demonstrates his love of the cradling lope of the blues. (Ahmet Ertegun, Stills's beloved friend who produced reunion after reunion of CSN and sometimes Y, often keeping them afloat, died in 2006.)

The Ryman audience is again primarily of the generation that came of age during the 1960s and '70s—a sea of snowy hair. Stills himself was twenty-two during the Summer of Love. Because of prodigies like him, who were enabled by the radio—especially ones in cars—in their connection to an entire country, almost every kind of music remains emotionally available to an audience this age, except perhaps hip-hop. (Hip-hop demands a young, nimble mind; most of this crowd was born too soon to wrap their heads around it and cannot sing along the way young people can.) But Stills will have everything in his tool chest that his particular crowd might desire. (He has even done some crossover with Spike Lee and Public Enemy for the film *He Got Game,* but he will have left that home.) Stills may be hobbled by arthritis—backstage he fist-bumps rather than handshakes with fans; he has carpal tunnel and residual pain from a long-ago broken hand, which affects his playing—and he may be deaf, but Beethoven, too, became deaf. Drugs and alcohol may have dented Stills somewhat, forming a kind of carapace over youthful sensitivity, as well as its sidearm, cockiness—qualities one often saw in the face of the young Stills. Some might infer by looking at the spry James Taylor or Mick Jagger that heroin is less hard on the body's infrastructure than cocaine and booze. "Stills doesn't know how to do drugs properly," Keith Richards once said. But one has to hand it to a brilliant and beloved rock veteran who still wants to get onstage and make music even when his boy's beauty and once tender baritone have dimmed. It shows allegiance to the craft, to the life, to the music. It risks a derisive sort of criticism as well as an assault on nostalgia. But it invites admiration, even awe.

It also comes on the heels of a "definitive biography" by British author David Roberts. Titled *Change Partners,* after one of Stills's own songs, the book is an act of hurried, sloppy, aggregated love, an activity that can sometimes have a fun side. Ignore the typos—mistakes such as *sewed* for *sowed* or *daubed* for *dubbed*—and don't go looking for any psychological depth. Roberts has collected most of his data from widely available interviews. A speedy checklist of girlfriends—Judy Collins, Rita Coolidge, Joan Baez, Susan St. James—plus wives and children will largely have to do for the personal side of things. Stills's "Rock & Roll Woman" is declared a valentine to Grace Slick. Roberts is far more interested in constructing a chronicle—flow charts would have been helpful—of the constantly shifting permutations and reunions that formed Stills's ongoing musical associations through the decades and that early on gave us the sublime Crosby, Stills, and Nash (and sometimes Young) cobbled from The Byrds, The Hollies, and Buffalo Springfield. They reassembled through the years like jazz musicians, performing their songs live in the improvised and unexpected manner of jazz. The songs in concert rarely sounded the same twice and never like the studio versions. The "beautiful Celtic keen of Graham's and David's cat's purr, and my cement mixer," as Stills described their voices together. To those looking on, it seemed Nash had the organizational skills; Crosby had the intuition; Stills had the musical chops and the most brilliant songs; Young—like a comet zooming in and out of orbit—had the poetry and mystique and artistic searching but did not join the choirboy harmonies at which the other three excelled. "Neil wants to be Tony Orlando and we're Dawn," joked Stills in the 2008 documentary *CSNY/Déjà Vu*. Young had organized the 2006 concert tour as a war protest and decorated the stage with yellow ribbons. Stills seemed afraid it was political kitsch, but he went along.

The Roberts book may err on the side of sportscasting in announcing the Billboard rankings for each album Stills and the others put forth, and he is constantly putting Stills and Young in competition with each other. One's eyes glaze over at sentences such as "The finer points of the release were not enough to return Stephen to the upper echelons of the charts and *Illegal Stills* stalled at Number 30 (US) and Number 54 (UK)." In interviews Stills himself has seemed indifferent to the horse race—sometimes modest, sometimes scornful, sometimes tongue-tied with or without attitude, but always shy and often wry and amusing. He is the most talented and the most politically active but the least self-promoting of this famous trio/quartet.

Though born in Texas of midwestern parents, Stills was primarily a Florida boy (Tampa, St. Petersburg), with a dash of Louisiana and Costa Rica. Stills speaks Spanish; his father was a building contractor whose peripatetic business life often followed the military. The family life mirrored that of many postwar families ("What do we do, given life? We move around," wrote Stills in a 1972 song.) Stills's father continually relocated the family, even to Central America. Stills went to five different high schools, including a military one. Skilled at several instruments, he played in high school bands, including marching ones, and he has since donated money to the University of Florida marching band. He clearly believes such bands are where many musicians get their start.

Florida has always been an interesting hub of musical styles—a farrago of Appalachian, country, gospel, blues, Latino (Caribbean and Cuban émigré), and Seminole traditions. In jazz the great bass player Jaco Pastorius is often thought to be an embodiment of the region's unique sound, guitar notes bending in tropical, otherworldly tones. Hip-hop, too, has its own South Florida subgenre. In rock there were Jim Morrison, the Allman Brothers, and Lynyrd Skynyrd, who named themselves after their Jacksonville high school gym teacher. Ray Charles made his early reputation in Florida, as did Tom Petty. Stills brought what might be but isn't called country-folk-Latin-blues-rock to his bandmates, whatever band he was in. One can hear most of the influences simultaneously as early as "Suite: Judy Blue Eyes" (1969), a folk-rock love song written about Judy Collins, but whose rousing coda has a strong Latin flavor, due to Stills's overlaid vocal track. CSN performed it at Woodstock, Stills wearing a poncho. Stills composed songs quickly, but unconventionally, often pulling together tracks he had recorded earlier in his studio, before he knew where they might land—the equivalent of a writer's notebook or a chef's pantry. He liked to cook, both literally and figuratively, for his bands. "Carry On" was written in eight hours.

Again one may circle back to wonder—skeptically, impertinently—what causes a musician to keep playing into his advanced years, even if he is bringing an entire generation along with him. Neil Young allegedly once played a new and unpopular album in its entirety before a British audience, to much grumbling from the ticket holders who wanted to hear something familiar. When he announced toward the close, "Now we're going to play something you've all heard before," the crowd cheered in relief. And then Young played again the first song he had played that evening. He has worked at some price, and eccentrically, not to become a human jukebox.

Of course, it is a paying job to tour, and Stills has incurred the expenses of a celebrity who grew up without much. Jimi Hendrix, when asked about the problem of singing the blues once one has made so much money from doing so, noted the hardship of musicians' making money (they are then harnessed by recording companies to make more). Hendrix was overworked and deeply ambivalent: "Actually, the

more money you make the more blues you can sing," he told Dick
Cavett. Stills himself wandered into fame's trappings: cars, drugs,
horses, country houses (one in England purchased from Ringo Starr),
seven children both in and out of wedlock, fine wines, ex-wives (including his first, the singer Véronique Sanson, the daughter of celebrated
French Resistance fighters; "My French never got over the hump, you
know?" he said of that divorce, and one imagines that "Marianne"
was written about her). David Crosby, on the other hand, who drifted
toward addiction and eventually solitary in a Texas penitentiary, was
"Hollywood royalty," the privileged son of Floyd Crosby, the renowned
cinematographer of *High Noon*.

Sometimes the desire to make music fuses nicely with the need
to make a living. Stills was always focused and driven, although this
attribute is usually credited to his intermittent and more sober partner,
Graham Nash (we could drink a case of Nash and still be on our feet).
Change Partners chronicles Stills's both specific and general doggedness,
his ongoingness, his formation and re-formation of bands, beginning
most successfully (after some pavement pounding in Greenwich Village) in Los Angeles, where in 1966 he assembled Buffalo Springfield
(named after a steamroller that was repaving streets), which included
Richie Furay, Bruce Palmer, and Neil Young, who had just driven down
from Canada in his legendary hearse, ostensibly to locate the actual
77 Sunset Strip. Tom Petty described Stills's guitar playing at that time
as "fluid and bluesy" and Young's as "fuzzy and angry." Stills admired
Young's playing, and Young was in awe of Stills's voice—one need only
listen to the haunting Buffalo Springfield demo of "Four Days Gone"
to hear why. (Stills's voice had just a dozen more years before it began to
lose its supple perfection.) For decades after, Crosby, Stills, Nash, and
Young kept reemerging in various configurations, though each member
was determined to do his own solo records. Hence Ahmet Ertegun's
title for their first live album, *4 Way Street*.

Backstage at the Ryman, preshow, Stills sits at a table and signs mer-
chandise. When it is my turn in line, I hand him a fan letter and he
sticks it respectfully and unopened in the inner pocket of his black

sport jacket. (That women's jackets don't have these intimate pockets is a sorrow to me, though a boon to the handbag industry.) He wears thick, clear-framed glasses, a silvering goatee, and his hair is a light caramel hue to remind one of his blond youthful beauty.

In the Roberts book women speak repeatedly of Stills's handsomeness and his shyness. People were drawn to him. Black musicians often felt he was the only one of CSNY they could connect with and attributed it to Stills's southern, country-boy roots. Hendrix wanted Stills to join his band. For a stretch Stills, a left-wing activist, was also the only one in CSNY who could vote—Crosby had felonies, Nash was English, Young was Canadian. Stills made midterm elections his political focus—and though active in presidential campaigns from JFK onward (in the fall of 2016 he wrote a protest song against Donald Trump), he has also made appearances on behalf of local congressmen across the country, urging Americans to think about our government's legislative branch. This he began doing with some success during the Nixon administration, helping to create Tip O'Neill's House of Representatives, and we should expect similar efforts in 2018. In 2000 Stills was part of the Credentials Committee from Florida during the Democratic National Convention and in previous years served as a delegate. One can see the doggedness etched in his face.

Perhaps because my friend and I are from a university, Stills now mentions he recently received an honorary degree from McGill. Because he has been a working musician since he was a teenager and never went to college, he is visibly proud of and amused by this McGill doctorate. He says he is going to do some work with the neurologist Daniel Levitin, the author of *This Is Your Brain on Music*. I don't mention the Roberts book, which makes no reference to this and is probably not a book Stills has even read, though there is a handy index for skimming. Stills signs our CDs, and we thank him and move on. There is a line forming to have one's photo taken with him, and out of a fear of carnivals and cameras my friend and I do not get in it. My head is full of Stills's songs, one of which from decades ago includes these words: "Help me . . . / My life is a miserable comedy / Of strangers / Posing as friends." Nonetheless, Stills is tolerating the backstage meet-'n'-greet/merch-perch rather well, although there is little revel in his demeanor—how could there be? He's a trouper, a player, a soldier, a generous musician with his audience and his bandmates. But he is not an award-winning actor. In interviews he tends toward droll diplomacy, restraint, a dry quip. His signature costumes onstage and on album covers have been football jerseys, military jackets, and that poncho.

Grit, then, is the theme. Stills is one of the last remaining rock-'n'-roll geniuses from a time when rock music was the soundtrack to an antiwar movement—"For What It's Worth," "Woodstock," "Ohio" (about the 1971 Kent State shootings)—back when the global counterculture was on the left rather than the right. Roberts's book makes this inexactly clear. Stills has been on the scene from the start, forming Buffalo Springfield when Jimi Hendrix was being booked as the opening act for The Monkees on tour. He has seemingly played with everyone—from Bill Withers to George Harrison. He was the first person to be inducted into the Rock and Roll Hall of Fame twice in the same night for his work in two different bands. "What a wonderfully strange and beautiful cast of characters life has handed to me," he said in his acceptance speech.

And now on the Ryman Auditorium stage he cuts loose with the young, strapping Kenny Shepherd. Stills often steps back in a paternal fashion, and the Shreveport-born Shepherd does his Delta blues thing, long blond hair flying. Spotlights move around the stage searchingly, and I consider the musicians—Leonard Cohen, Prince, Leon Russell—who have died this past year and whom spotlights will never find again. Stills lets Barry Goldberg, the seventy-five-year-old keyboardist, play his best-known song, "I've Got to Use My Imagination" (a 1974 hit for Gladys Knight and the Pips). Congenitally deaf in one ear and now partially deaf in the other, Stills is brave to attempt his own "Bluebird," with its difficult singing, and on its high notes his voice becomes a bit of a bray. "I've always sung flat," he has said smilingly into cameras, and this embrace of time's wear and tear feels spiritually strong and unselfpitying. Soon he unbegrudgingly performs what has become something of an albatross for him, his hit single "Love the One You're With." The human jukebox aspect of a rock concert is difficult to avoid. He shakes out his hands to rid them of pain. Colorful freshly tuned guitars are brought in at regular intervals. Overly warmed up, at one point he takes off his jacket and flings it across the stage. "Oh, well," I say to my friend. "There goes my letter." The band closes with Neil Young's "Rocking in the Free World." (It is a custom of Stills's concerts to include one song by Young.) Shepherd remains a gifted, impeccable, shiny part of it all. But Stills is the one we love. He's the one we're with.

(2017)

Acknowledgments

Thank you to the many eagle-eyed editors and copy editors through the years, as well as to the tiny handful of people who thought this book was a good idea and encouraged it. You know who you are. A copy is in the mail, with gratitude.

—LM

A NOTE ON THE TYPE

This book was set in Adobe Garamond. Designed for the Adobe Corporation by Robert Slimbach, the fonts are based on types first cut by Claude Garamond (ca. 1480–1561). Garamond was a pupil of Geoffroy Tory and is believed to have followed the Venetian models, although he introduced a number of important differences, and it is to him that we owe the letter we now know as "old style." He gave to his letters a certain elegance and feeling of movement that won their creator an immediate reputation and the patronage of Francis I of France.

Composed by North Market Street Graphics,
Lancaster, Pennsylvania

Printed and bound by Berryville Graphics,
Berryville, Virginia

Designed by Soonyoung Kwon